PLUTARCH

Liv

British Library Cataloguing in Publication Data

Plutarch

Lives of Aristeides and Cato.--(Classical texts, ISSN 0953-7961)

1. Greece. Politics.Aristides, ca.530-468 B.C.
2. Roman Empire. Politics. Cato, Marcus Porcius 234-149 B.C.

I. Title II. Sansone D. III. Series

938,03 0924

ISBN 0-85668-421-X
ISBN 0-85668-422-8 pbk

Printed and published in England by ARIS & PHILLIPS Ltd,
Teddington House. Warminster, Wiltshire, BA12 8PQ, England

Contents

INTRODUCTION

If the Lives of Plutarch are read at all today, it is because they represent a valuable ancient source for the more interesting periods of Greek and Roman history. English-speakers who are unable to read Plutarch's Greek are likely to encounter the works of the biographer in the form of the accurate and readable Penguin translations by Rex Warner and Ian Scott-Kilvert, conveniently grouped into chronological packages with titles like "The Age of Alexander" and "Fall of the Roman Republic." For the scholar, Plutarch's value as a historical source has been enhanced in recent years by the appearance of a number of excellent commentaries on individual Lives. Garzetti's commentary on the Life of Caesar (1954), Calabi Limentani's on the Life of Aristeides (1964), Hamilton's on the Life of Alexander (1969) and Frost's on the Life of Themistocles (1980) have done a great service for the historian. But, at the same time, they have served to reinforce the prevailing perception that Plutarch was himself a historian who chose to present his history palatably disguised as biography.

There have been times when this perception did not prevail. There have also been times when Plutarch's Lives were regarded with a degree of esteem that would surprise most readers of those works today. An advertisement, for example, in the first edition (1762) of Oliver Goldsmith's Life of Richard Nash included the following comments: "What histories can be found (says the Marquis de Montesquieu) that please and instruct like the Lives of Plutarch? He paints the Man whose Life he relates; he makes him known such as he was at the head of the armies, in the government of the people, in his own family, and in his pleasures. In short, I am of the same opinion with that author who said, that if he was constrained to fling all the books of the ancients into the sea, Plutarch should be the last drowned." Similarly, in his Reveries (1782), Rousseau says, "Among the small number of books that I occasionally reread, it is

Plutarch who most of all holds my attention and benefits me. He provided the earliest reading of my childhood; he will be the last of my old age. He is almost the only author of whom I can say that I have never read him without some profit." And Alfieri records in his autobiography (1806), "But tbe book of all others which gave me the most delight and beguiled many of the tedious hours of winter was Plutarch. I perused five or six times the lives of Timoleon, Caesar, Brutus, Pelopidas, Cato, and some others. I wept, raved, and fell into such transports that if anyone had been in the adjoining chamber they must have pronounced me out of my senses." Finally, with more enthusiasm than accuracy,[1] Emerson declared in an address entitled "Heroism" (1838), "But if we explore the literature of Heroism, we shall quickly come to Plutarch, who is its Doctor and historian. To him we owe the Brasidas, the Dion, the Epaminondas, the Scipio of old, and I must think we are more deeply indebted to him than to all the ancient writers. Each of his 'Lives' is a refutation to the despondency and cowardice of our religious and political theorists. A wild courage, a stoicism not of the schools, but of the blood, shines in every anecdote, and has given that book its immense fame." These four men of letters, from four countries, are not isolated instances; numerous additional examples could be cited to illustrate the enormous influence exercised by Plutarch and his Lives over the past few centuries.[2] Even in our century, we can find occasional evidence of a strong appreciation of Plutarch's Lives. The fictional hero of H. G. Wells' Tono-Bungay (1908), for example, is made to recollect, "And I found Langhorne's 'Plutarch' too, I remember, on those shelves. It seems queer to me now to think that I acquired pride and self-respect, the idea of a state and the germ of public spirit, in such a furtive fashion; queer, too, that it should rest with an old Greek, dead these eighteen hundred

[1] Plutarch never wrote a Life of Brasidas. His Lives of Epameinondas and Scipio have been lost since the middle ages.

[2] For the history of Plutarch's influence since antiquity, see especially R. Hirzel, *Plutarch* (1912).

years, to teach me that." And a real president of the United States credited Plutarch as his political preceptor. Harry S. Truman recalled, "My father used to read me out loud from [Plutarch's Lives]. And I've read Plutarch through many times since. I never have figured out how he knew so much. I tell you. They just don't come any better than old Plutarch. He knew more about politics than all the other writers I've read put together."

It will be seen that it is not as a historian, or even as a biographer in the modern sense of the word, that Plutarch has been so highly valued. Rather, those who regard Plutarch as among the greatest of ancient authors appreciate him principally as a moralist and as a purveyor of political wisdom. Our own age of which President Truman is clearly not representative, generally finds such authors not to its liking, unless their moralizing is decently cloaked in the fashionable garb of irony and satire. But if we are unable to share the enthusiasm for Plutarch that Rousseau and Alfieri felt, we must not do him the disservice of imagining him to have been a writer of a sort different from what he in fact was. He was not, as he himself tells us,[3] a writer of histories. Still less did he profess to be the chronicler of The Age of Alexander or the Fall of the Roman Republic. He was a writer of, among other things, biographies. But even recognizing this is no guarantee against misunderstanding his works and the intentions that necessarily lay behind them. We must try to understand what kind of biography Plutarch was writing (or thought he was writing) and, in order to do that, we must consider what the art of biography was like in Plutarch's lifetime.

Plutarch's lifetime lay within the century immediately following the death of Christ.[4] Plutarch was born some time in

---

3 See the opening chapter of the Life of Alexander.

4 The best account of the details of Plutarch's life and society is to be found in Jones, to which the following is heavily indebted. See also Ziegler, "Plutarchos."

the forties AD, during the reign of Claudius, and died during the reign of Hadrian, in about AD 120. His family belonged to the local aristocracy of the small Boeotian town of Chaeroneia, where he made his home throughout his life. He lived, therefore, in circumstances that allowed him the opportunity, of which he gladly took advantage, to pursue an education that included both philosophical and oratorical training and to travel regularly to the cultural centers of his world, namely Athens and Rome. In his youth Plutarch studied in Athens with the Academic philosopher Ammonius, who imparted to him a lifelong devotion to the works and thought of Plato. Later in life he was made an honorary Athenian citizen, and his circle of acquaintances included a number of men who were prominent in the political and cultural life of the city. During his frequent visits to Rome, Plutarch delivered lectures on philosophy and made the acquaintance of several individuals who were involved at various levels in the administration of the empire. Plutarch spent much of his time with his friends on both sides of the Adriatic engaged in discussion of literary and philosophical matters, of local and imperial politics, of items of cultic and antiquarian interest. The contents and the civilized tone of these discussions are reproduced in the large number of works that Plutarch composed in dialogue form, most notably in the collection known as Table Talk.

Plutarch will have supported himself with the income from his estate. But his wealth not only provided him with leisure, it also imposed on him an obligation to expend some of his time, energy and resources on political and civic affairs.[5] So, throughout his life Plutarch served his own city and other cities in a variety of capacities. His standing, his training and his learning suited him for the various ambassadorial posts, magistracies and priesthoods that he was called on to fill. These included service as the chief executive officer of the Amphicty-

---

5 For the nature of these obligations in Plutarch's day, see R. Lane Fox, *Pagans and Christians* (1986) 52-57.

onic council, as supervisor of the quadrennial Pythian Games and as priest of Apollo at that god's Delphic shrine. One can imagine that Plutarch's performance of these duties was characterized by enthusiasm and conscientiousness, but not ambition. For Plutarch never rose to the higher levels of administration, preferring instead the relative quiet of such remote towns as Delphi and Chaeroneia and the satisfaction of literary pursuits. The greater part of Plutarch's literary output seems to have been the product of the last quarter-century of his life,[6] during that period which, according to Gibbon, a man would without hesitation name if asked to fix the period in the history of the world during which the condition of the human race was most happy and prosperous.

The document known as the Lamprias catalogue, included in a number of the mediaeval manuscripts of Plutarch's works, gives a list of the large number of writings attributed to Plutarch that were available at some time in late antiquity.[7] Fewer than half of those works survive today. Still, the existing corpus is a large and varied collection, comprising works as diverse as political biographies, philosophical dialogues in the manner of Plato and essays on literary, ethical and antiquarian topics. The collection is nowadays regularly divided, evenly but rather arbitrarily, into Lives and Moralia, the latter being the convenient designation for those works that are not biographical in nature. But, in fact, all of Plutarch's writings, the Lives included, could well be described as moral essays.[8] For there is a humane moral purpose that pervades the works, in whatever genre, not unlike the moral purpose that character-

---

[6] See C. P. Jones, "Towards a Chronology of Plutarch's Works," *JRS* 56 (1966) 61-74.

[7] For the Lamprias catalogue, see Barrow 193-94 and F. H. Sandbach's introduction, text and translation in the Loeb edition of *Plutarch's Moralia* XV (1969) 3-29.

[8] See the fine essay on Plutarch by A. W. Gomme in *A Historical Commentary on Thucydides* I (1945) 54-84.

izes the varied writings of the essayist and biographer Samuel Johnson. But the moral quality of the Parallel Lives is often obscured by the practice of reading individual Lives in isolation, without the companion Life and without the comparison that makes Plutarch's purpose intelligible. When we read these Lives as Plutarch wished them to be read, and especially when we read them with a clear understanding of the nature of the tradition to which they belong, it will become apparent that they possess a striking originality.

The Parallel Lives were not Plutarch's first effort in the biographical genre. Before he embarked upon the project that was to ensure his literary reputation, Plutarch composed a series of Lives of the Caesars, comprising biographies of all the Roman emperors from Augustus to Vitellius. All that survives of the collection are the brief and disappointing Lives of Galba and Otho, but even if their quality is indicative of that of the series as a whole, the Lives of the Caesars represent an original and important contribution to the history of biographical writing. For Plutarch transposed to a Greek context not only Roman subject matter, but a Roman literary form. For, although biography is ultimately a Greek literary genre, Greek biography was, before Plutarch's day, concerned almost exclusively with setting forth the lives of poets, philosophers and men of letters. Biographies of political and military leaders were composed by Romans like Cornelius Nepos[9] and like M. Aemilius Scaurus and P. Rutilius Rufus, who set forth their own lives in writing. With the exception of Satyrus, the existence of whose Life of Philip II is open to doubt, the only author known to have composed a Life of a statesman in Greek before the time of Plutarch is Nicolas of Damascus, who was associated with the court of Augustus and who wrote a Life of that emperor. Thus, in composing his Lives of the Caesars, Plutarch was doing something that was, if not unique in Greek, at least quite unusual. And his project was even more unusual in that it was composed as a se-

---

9 J. Geiger, *Cornelius Nepos and Ancient Political Biography* (1985).

ries of Lives in chronological sequence. There is a precedent of sorts in Latin literature, namely Nepos' arrangement of his Lives in an apparently orderly sequence. But Plutarch's real inspiration appears to have come from those series of Lives, written in Greek, of philosophers and men of letters that were the forerunners also of Diogenes Laertius' Lives of the Philosophers.[10] Plutarch's mixture of Greek and Latin elements in his Lives of the Caesars is indicative of his innovative outlook and forecasts his striking juxtaposition of Greeks and Romans in his Parallel Lives.

In addition to the Lives of the Caesars, which perhaps exerted an influence on the Roman writers Suetonius and Tacitus,[11] Plutarch also, at some time in his career, composed the individual Lives of Aratus and Artaxerxes, which still survive, as well as a small number of Lives attested only by entries in the Lamprias catalogue. But it was the Parallel Lives that engaged Plutarch's creative energies and occupied the last twenty or twenty-five years of his life. There can be no doubt of the originality, even uniqueness, of the Parallel Lives. For no one had previously composed pairs of biographies, with the intention of comparing one life with another. (Nor do we know of any subsequent attempts in antiquity at composing Parallel Lives, with the exception of the work of a certain Amyntianus, of which we know almost nothing.) Again, there is somewhat of a precedent in Latin literature, namely the biographies of Nepos, which were composed in pairs of series: Lives of Roman and foreign generals, Lives of Roman and Greek historians, etc. Unfortunately, we possess only a fraction of Nepos' large work, so that we cannot judge the nature or the extent of his comparative method. We do, however, possess enough of Nepos' work

---

[10] For these, see J. Mejer, *Diogenes Laertius and his Hellenistic Background* (1978) 60-75, 90-93. Not all of the works, however, referred to by Mejer are strictly speaking biographies.

[11] Jones 62, 77-78, B. Baldwin, "Biography at Rome," *Collection Latomus* 164 (1979) 100-118.

to know that his interest was in events rather than in character, so he cannot have used his comparisons, as Plutarch did, for the purpose of illuminating character. The idea of comparison has a long and productive history in Greek and Roman rhetorical theory and practice, and evidence of its exploitation is at hand in the works of a host of orators, historians and practitioners of other genres.[12] We may mention, in addition to Nepos' biographies, two works closer in time to the Parallel Lives, Quintilian's comparative survey of Greek and Latin literature in the tenth book of his Institutio Oratoria and Valerius Maximus' collection consisting of series of Roman and foreign anecdotes grouped under various heads. But Plutarch's use of comparison is more extensive than Quintilian's and less superficial than Nepos' or Valerius'.

It is not only Plutarch's comparative arrangement that signals the originality of the Parallel Lives. As we have seen, the very act of composing Lives of statesmen and generals was, at least in the context of Greek literature, somewhat of a novelty. For, while Nepos had written Lives in Latin of, for instance, both Aristeides and Cato, there had never been a biography of either of these men written in Greek. Nor, for that matter, had anyone before Plutarch written a Life in Greek of Pericles or Themistocles or Alcibiades or Lysander. Thus, Plutarch's first pair of Parallel Lives, the (lost) work that consisted of Lives of Epameinondas and Scipio, was original in two respects: These were the first biographies of these two men to be written in Greek, and this was the first biographical work in any language that had as its principle of organization the comparison of two individuals, one Greek and one Roman.

This experimental procedure of Plutarch's served a variety of purposes (and it would be uncharitable to deny that these were Plutarch's own purposes). In the first place, by composing Lives of Romans in Greek Plutarch was not only familiarizing his fellow Greeks with the details of Roman history, but he

---

12 F. Focke, "Synkrisis," *Hermes* 58 (1923) 327-68.

was also making biography of the Roman type (that is, Lives of statesmen and generals) available to a Greek audience. In the second place, his Lives of Greeks served to extend the Roman type of biography to include a larger number of subjects; for, while Nepos had already composed Lives in Latin of, for example, Themistocles, Pericles and Alcibiades, Plutarch was the first author whom we know to have composed Lives of Nicias, Demetrius or Philopoemen in any language. Finally, and most importantly, by composing his Lives in pairs and setting before his reader two Lives for comparison, Plutarch allows himself and his reader to concentrate on moral and paradigmatic features. Plutarch regarded this aspect of his biographical craft as of enormous *practical* consequence (and, to judge from the effusive comments of some of Plutarch's admirers quoted above, his conviction has been shared by others). For, what Plutarch does in his Parallel Lives is to select subjects in such a manner that he can explore the ways in which similar personalities react to different circumstances and the ways in which similar circumstances are responded to by different personalities. This procedure inevitably focuses attention upon that intersection of character and environment that is the concern of the study of ethics. It should not be thought that Plutarch's analysis is particularly striking or profound. Indeed, to the modern reader, nurtured as he is on the works of Freud, Strachey and Boswell, Plutarch's treatment of character is bound to appear remarkably shallow and naive. But it must be borne in mind that Plutarch is in large measure responsible for the importation of this ethical concern into the biographical genre.

And it is this ethical concern that enables Plutarch to reconcile his abiding adherence to the philosophy of Plato with his practice of the biographer's craft. For there is a fundamental incompatibility between strict Platonism and a concern with the details of an individual's life. For this reason, Plutarch's Greek predecessors are found for the most part among the adherents of the Peripatetic school, whose members perpetuated Aristotle's passion for collecting and organizing data in every possible subject. The influence of Aristotle's school on Plutarch's biographies is unmistakable, but that influence is primarily in the area of ethical theory;[13] there is little evidence that the Peripatetic practitioners of the biographical art shared Plutarch's (or Aristotle's) commitment to the study of ethics as a guide to political life. But we can also discern faint traces of a tradition of Academic biography. This tradition is much less strong than that of Peripatetic biography, and needs to be reconstructed out of fragments of evidence. For the biographies that can with reasonable certainty be assigned to this tradition, with one important exception, either do not survive or were written after the time of Plutarch. These latter include such late and interesting works as Porphyry's Lives of Plotinus and Pythagoras, Iamblichus' Life of Pythagoras and Marinus' Life of Proclus. These are nothing at all like the biographies of the Roman type (nor are they related to Peripatetic biography). Rather they are Lives of philosophers, and they portray their subjects as holy, almost divine, men, as paradigms of intellectual attainment and moral rectitude. The authors of these works were themselves philosophers in the Platonic tradition, and it is possible to trace this Academic type of biography back to Xenocrates of Chalcedon, who was himself a student of Plato's and whose (lost) Life of Plato deserves to be regarded as the first biography.

That there is in fact a tradition of Academic biography that stretches from the time of Plato's younger contemporaries to the Neoplatonists of the third century after Christ and later is clear from the work of Philo of Alexandria, who was a philosopher in the Platonic tradition and who died at around the time of Plutarch's birth. It is one of the curiosities of the scholarship concerned with the history of Greek biography that the two most significant contributions to that scholarship make no mention whatever of Philo's role.[14] For Philo's Lives of Abra-

---

[13] A. Dihle, *Studien zur griechischen Biographie* (1956) 57-103.

[14] F. Leo, *Die griechisch-römische Biographie* (1901) and A. Momigliano, *The Development of Greek Biography* (1971). Philo is also ignored by D. R. Stuart in his *Epochs of Greek and Roman Biography* (1928). M.

ham, Joseph and Moses, especially the last, hold a uniquely significant position. For there are such striking similarities between the way in which Philo portrays Moses and the way in which the later Neoplatonists portray the subjects of their biographies that there can be no doubt that we are dealing with works belonging to the same tradition. And yet there is no evidence that any pagan biographer had any knowledge whatever of Philo's work. Furthermore, just as it is impossible to trace Philo's influence on later biography, so it is impossible to specify Philo's literary sources. (Jewish sources can be ruled out, as there is no tradition of Jewish biography in antiquity at all.) Even if Philo were wholly original and had no antecedents in the writing of this type of biography, we would still be faced with the problem of the sources of the Neoplatonic biographers. And, since Philo himself cannot have been their model, the most reasonable assumption is that there were other biographies, now lost, that influenced both Philo and the Neoplatonists, that belonged to the Academic philosophical tradition and that emphasized the moral and intellectual virtues of their subjects, whom they portrayed as nearly divine teachers. The only biography before the time of Philo that we can assign with any certainty to this tradition is Xenocrates' Life of Plato,[15] about which we unfortunately know almost nothing. If there were others, even their existence is no longer recorded.

It was Plutarch's original contribution to the development of biography to combine this Greek, Academic tradition with the Roman tradition of biography concerned with the lives of political figures. All the subjects of Plutarch's Parallel Lives are involved in political life, and half of them are themselves Ro-

---

Hadas and M. Smith (*Heroes and Gods: Spiritual Biographies in Antiquity* [1965]) do not ignore Philo, but they fail to clarify his significance within the Greek biographical tradition.

[15] See A. Swift Riginos, *Platonica: The Anecdotes Concerning the Life and Writings of Plato* (1976) for the biographical tradition concerning Plato, which included an account of Plato's Apollonian birth that began to circulate already in the time of Xenocrates.

mans. But at the same time, Plutarch likes to represent the men whose Lives he is writing, if at all possible, as philosophers, as teachers and as men whose virtue gives them an almost divine status as models of behavior. For example, Plutarch compares Dion and Brutus on the grounds of their adherence to the philosophy of Plato, and he bases his Lives of these two men on an examination of the degree to which their philosophical background influenced their political and ethical behavior. Likewise, in his Lives of Phocion and Cato the Younger, Plutarch is especially concerned to point out the Stoicism of the latter and the Academic training of the former. In the pages of Plutarch, Pericles consorts with Anaxagoras as an equal, and Alexander with his teacher Aristotle. And, in his lost Life of Epameinondas, Plutarch surely portrayed his hero as a devoted follower of the principles of Pythagoreanism. The role of his heroes as teachers is also of great importance to Plutarch. This is particularly evident in the Lives of those men who can be regarded as lawgivers, namely Theseus, Lycurgus, Solon, Romulus and Numa. But elsewhere as well we find Plutarch using the word "teacher" as the highest term of commendation. Pelopidas, for example, is hailed after his death by the Thebans as "father, savior and teacher," and Cato the Younger is constantly spoken of as instructing the soldiers under his command, his fellow citizens and even foreign kings. Even the unattractive Marcus Crassus is represented briefly both as a philosopher and as a teacher to his slaves and workers. Finally, some of Plutarch's heroes attain that level of beatification and near-divinization that is characteristic of the subjects of Neoplatonic, and perhaps Academic, biography. Theseus, of course, is worshipped as a hero after his death; Lycurgus is given a temple, and receives honors of the sort accorded to a god; the mysterious disappearance of Romulus is remarkably similar to the end that is met with by the hero of Philo's Life of Moses.

We can see traces of these features in the Lives of Aristeides and Cato as well. Neither of these men can be regarded as in any sense a philosopher, and Cato is even represented as despising philosophy as a whole.[16] But Plutarch goes out of his way to inform us (29.3-4) of the influence that the Pythagorean philosopher Nearchus and the doctrines of Plato had on the young and impressionable Cato, and he clothes Aristeides, without any evidence, in the *tribon* (25.5), the threadbare cloak that is virtually the uniform of the philosopher in Plutarch's own day. Furthermore, the figure of Socrates runs, unexpectedly, like a Leitmotif through this pair of Lives.[17] While the connections with Socrates are of the most oblique sort imaginable, and while none of this actually makes either Aristeides or Cato into a philosopher, Plutarch represents these two men in a much more "philosophical" light than the authors of either the Roman or the Peripatetic type of biography tend to portray their subjects. As far as the emphasis on the role of Aristeides and Cato as teachers is concerned, we find that, although Plutarch does recount in some detail the latter's full involvement in his son's education (47.5-9), it is primarily the less formal and more public lessons provided by these two men that Plutarch is concerned to keep before our eyes. Aristeides teaches his fellow commanders (5.2, 8.5, 20.1, 23.3) and Cato teaches the Roman people and its leaders (28.8, 53.4, 57.2). But it is by their virtuous example, for the most part, that they serve as instructors, both to their contemporaries and, through the agency of the Lives, to posterity. And it is this, as far as Plutarch is concerned, that makes it reasonable for a follower of Plato to write biographies, even biographies of men of action. For what he is supplying is, in a sense, patterns of lives not unlike those that Er witnessed being displayed to the souls that had undergone purgation in the Platonic myth.[18] But, instead of merely setting these patterns before us and advising us to act like this, or warning us against acting like that, Plutarch attempts as best

---

16 See 50.1. (For the purposes of this edition, the chapters of the two Lives have been numbered consecutively.)

17 See 1.2, 1.9, 27.3, 34.1, 47.3, 50.1, with Commentary.

18 Plato *Republic* 617d-18a.

he can, in good Platonic fashion, to *give an account* of why this behavior is admirable and that is discreditable. The comparisons, and the method of composing Lives in pairs, seem designed primarily as a method of enabling an account to be given, by helping to illuminate ethical choices and by putting them in a kind of perspective.

In particular, we see virtue, not in the abstract, but exemplified in the real world of political interaction and military engagement. And, because two examples are being held before our eyes more or less concurrently, we are constantly compelled to make judgements, not only of the sort, "Is this act admirable?" but of the sort, "Is this virtuous act more admirable than that virtuous act?" By thus setting up a kind of scale of virtuous acts, Plutarch seeks to conduct his reader toward the practice of virtue, not merely by displaying patterns of behavior that ought (or, as Plutarch provides in the case of Demetrius and Antony, ought not) to be imitated, but by an anagogic method that involves the almost continual application of judgment and reason. The aim, ultimately, is to become as much like the gods as is humanly possible, and becoming like the gods, according to Plato,[19] involves making oneself upright and pure with the help of reason. In this way it is possible to reconcile the writing of biography with adherence to Platonic principles. And it is for this reason that Plutarch stresses those elements of his subjects (in this pair, particularly Aristeides) that can be regarded as, or that come close to being, divine. Plutarch informs us (58.2) that the gods are self-sufficient, and that the closest humans can come to divine status is to become as self-sufficient as possible (Plutarch appears not to be aware of the non sequitur). While Cato is wholly admirable for his ability to be satisfied with the absolute minimum, his virtue is somewhat tainted, as far as Plutarch is concerned, by an excessive interest in commercial enterprise and by an obsession with money. For this reason Aristeides is more virtuous and more nearly divine. This divine character of Aristeides is also

[19] *Theaetetus* 176b.

apparent in Plutarch's extended discussion, in chapter 6, of the epithet "the Just," which is regularly attached to Aristeides' name. For it is justice and virtue that make men divine, and Aristeides is the model of the virtuous and just man.

SELECT BIBLIOGRAPHY

Astin, A. E., *Cato the Censor* (1978)

Barrow, R. H., *Plutarch and his Times* (1967)

Blass, F., *Plutarch's Ausgewählte Biographien* IV (1872)

Calabi Limentani, I., *Plutarchi Vita Aristidis* (1964)

Davies, J. K., *Athenian Propertied Families, 600-300 B.C.* (1971)

Flacelière, R. and E. Chambry, *Plutarque: Vies* V (1969)

Frost, F. J., *Plutarch's Themistocles: A Historical Commentary* (1980)

Gossage, A. J., "Plutarch," in T. A. Dorey (ed.), *Latin Biography* (1967) 45-77

Hillyard, B. P., *Plutarch: De Audiendo* (1981)

Jones, C. P., *Plutarch and Rome* (1971)

Jordan, H., *M. Catonis praeter librum de Re Rustica quae extant* (1860)

Kienast, D., *Cato der Zensor* (1979)

Malcovati, H., *Oratorum Romanorum Fragmenta*^{4} (1976)

Perrin, B., *Plutarch's Themistocles and Aristeides* (1901)

—, *Plutarch's Lives* II (1914)

Pritchett, W. K., *The Greek State at War* I-IV (1971-85)

Rhodes, P. J., *A Commentary on the Aristotelian Athenaion Politeia* (1981)

Russell, D. A., *Plutarch* (1973)

Scullard, H. H., *Roman Politics 220-150 B.C.* (1973)

Sintenis, C. and R. Hercher, *Plutarchs Aristides und Cato Maior* (1870)

Walbank, F. W., *A Historical Commentary on Polybius* I-III (1957-79)

Wardman, A., *Plutarch's Lives* (1974)

Wehrli, F., *Die Schule des Aristoteles*[2] I-X (1967-69)

Ziegler, K., "Plutarchos," *Paulys Real-Encyclopädie der classischen Altertumswissenschaft* XXI.1 (1951) 636-962

—, *Plutarchus: Vitae Parallelae*[4] I.1 (1969)

A NOTE ON THE TEXT

For the purposes of this edition, I have not collated the manuscripts anew, but have relied on the evidence for the text published in the recent editions of Ziegler and Flacelière. This is, however, a newly constituted text, and differs in many places (for the better, it is hoped) from the texts of earlier editors. The critical apparatus has been severely curtailed. It includes all the instances (apart from minor orthographic alterations) in which the reading adopted in the text is not found in any of the manuscripts, but is the result either of conjectural emendation or of the evidence of some other witness to the text. Variants among the existing manuscripts have been very selectively, perhaps idiosyncratically, recorded; the apparatus contains only the most important or interesting discrepancies. The reader is referred to the editions of Ziegler and Flacelière for full reporting of the manuscript evidence and for a detailed account of the manuscript tradition. The text relies upon the readings of the following three manuscripts almost exclusively:

S = Seitenstettensis 34 (11th or 12th century)

U = Vaticanus Gr. 138 (10th or 11th century)

A = Parisinus 1671 (AD 1296)

LIVES OF ARISTEIDES AND CATO

ΒΙΟΣ ΑΡΙΣΤΕΙΔΟΥ

1. Ἀριστείδης ὁ Λυσιμάχου φυλῆς μὲν ἦν Ἀντιοχίδος, τῶν δὲ δήμων
Ἀλωπεκῆθεν. περὶ δ' οὐσίας αὐτοῦ λόγοι διάφοροι γεγόνασιν, ὁ μὲν ὡς
ἐν πενίᾳ συντόνῳ καταβιώσαντος καὶ μετὰ τὴν τελευτὴν ἀπολιπόντος
θυγατέρας δύο πολὺν χρόνον ἀνεκδότους δι' ἀπορίαν γεγενημένας·
2 πρὸς δὲ τοῦτον τὸν λόγον ὑπὸ πολλῶν εἰρημένον ἀντιτασσόμενος ὁ
Φαληρεὺς Δημήτριος ἐν τῷ Σωκράτει χωρίον τε Φαληροῖ φησι γινώσκειν
Ἀριστείδου γενόμενον ἐν ᾧ τέθαπται, καὶ τεκμήρια τῆς περὶ τὸν οἶκον
εὐπορίας ἓν μὲν ἡγεῖται τὴν ἐπώνυμον ἀρχήν, ἣν ἦρξε τῷ κυάμῳ λαχὼν
ἐκ τῶν γενῶν τῶν τὰ μέγιστα τιμήματα κεκτημένων, οὓς πεντακοσιομε-
δίμνους προσηγόρευον, ἕτερον δὲ τὸν ἐξοστρακισμόν· οὐδενὶ γὰρ τῶν
πενήτων, ἀλλὰ τοῖς ἐξ οἴκων τε μεγάλων καὶ διὰ γένους ὄγκον ἐπιφθό-
3 νοις ὄστρακον ἐπιφέρεσθαι· τρίτον δὲ καὶ τελευταῖον, ὅτι νίκης ἀναθή-
ματα χορηγικοὺς τρίποδας ἐν Διονύσου καταλέλοιπεν, οἳ καὶ καθ'
ἡμᾶς ἐδείκνυντο, τοιαύτην ἐπιγραφὴν διασῴζοντες, ''Ἀντιοχὶς ἐνίκα·
4 Ἀριστείδης ἐχορήγει· Ἀρχέστρατος ἐδίδασκε.' τουτὶ μὲν οὖν καίπερ
εἶναι δοκοῦν μέγιστον, ἀσθενέστατόν ἐστι. καὶ γὰρ Ἐπαμεινώνδας, ὃν
πάντες ἄνθρωποι γιγνώσκουσιν ἐν πενίᾳ καὶ τραφέντα πολλῇ καὶ βιώ-
σαντα, καὶ Πλάτων ὁ φιλόσοφος οὐκ ἀφιλοτίμους ἀνεδέξαντο χορηγί-
ας, ὁ μὲν αὐληταῖς ἀνδράσιν, ὁ δὲ παισὶ κυκλίοις χορηγήσας, τούτῳ μὲν
Δίωνος τοῦ Συρακοσίου τὴν δαπάνην παρέχοντος, Ἐπαμεινώνδᾳ δὲ
5 τῶν περὶ Πελοπίδαν. οὐ γὰρ ἔστι τοῖς ἀγαθοῖς ἀκήρυκτος καὶ ἄσπονδος

1.1 ὁ μὲν Westermann: οἱ μὲν SUA 1.2 γενόμενον S: λεγόμενον UA| ἐπιφθόνοις Blass: ἐπιφθόνων SUA

LIFE OF ARISTEIDES

1. Aristeides, the son of Lysimachus, belonged to the
tribe Antiochis and came from the deme Alopece. Of the
varying accounts that have circulated concerning his wealth,
one has it that he spent the whole of his life in straitened circumstances and that, after his death, he left two daughters
who remained for a long time unmarried on account of their
2 lack of means. Now this is the prevailing version of the story, but Demetrius of Phalerum attempts to combat it in his
book, Socrates. There he says that he knows of an estate in
Phalerum on which Aristeides is buried and which had belonged to him during his lifetime. Furthermore, he produces
three facts which he considers evidence of the affluence of
Aristeides' family. In the first place, he had held the office of
archon eponymous, for which he was chosen by lot from
among the members of those families that belonged to the
highest income bracket, the so-called Pentacosiomedimnoi.
In the second place, he was once ostracized and, according to
Demetrius, this penalty was never inflicted on the poor, but
rather upon those who belonged to the upper class and
whose overbearing insistence upon the prerogatives of birth
3 had aroused invidiousness. Finally, he left as victory dedica-
tions in the precinct of Dionysus certain choregic tripods
which even in my day were on display, with the following inscription still upon them: "Winning tribe: Antiochis. Chore-
4 gus: Aristeides. Poet: Archestratus." Now this last item,
while it appears to be nearly decisive, is in fact of no consequence. For even Epameinondas, who was born into dire
poverty and who remained, as everyone knows, in that condition until the day he died, ventured to subsidize a public
performance on a lavish scale, as did the philosopher Plato.
The latter is recorded as choregus for a boys' dithyrambic
chorus, although the expense was actually borne by Dion of
Syracuse, and Pelopidas provided the funds that enabled the
former to serve as choregus for a chorus of men with flute
5 accompaniment. After all, men of quality do not bear impla-

πρὸς τὰς παρὰ τῶν φίλων δωρεὰς πόλεμος, ἀλλὰ τὰς εἰς ἀπόθεσιν καὶ
πλεονεξίαν ἀγεννεῖς ἡγούμενοι καὶ ταπεινάς, ὅσαι φιλοτιμίας τινὸς ἀ-
6 κερδοῦς ἔχονται καὶ λαμπρότητος οὐκ ἀπωθοῦνται. Παναίτιος μέντοι
περὶ τοῦ τρίποδος ἀποφαίνει τὸν Δημήτριον ὁμωνυμίᾳ διεψευσμένον·
ἀπὸ γὰρ τῶν Μηδικῶν εἰς τὴν τελευτὴν τοῦ Πελοποννησιακοῦ πολέμου
δύο μόνους Ἀριστείδας χορηγοὺς ἀναγράφεσθαι νικῶντας, ὧν οὐδέτε-
ρον εἶναι τῷ Λυσιμάχου τὸν αὐτόν, ἀλλὰ τὸν μὲν Ξενοφίλου πατρός,
τὸν δὲ χρόνῳ πολλῷ νεώτερον, ὡς ἐλέγχει τὰ γράμματα, τῆς μετ' Εὐ-
κλείδην ὄντα γραμματικῆς, καὶ προσγεγραμμένος ὁ Ἀρχέστρατος, ὃν
ἐν τοῖς Μηδικοῖς οὐδείς, ἐν δὲ τοῖς Πελοποννησιακοῖς συχνοὶ χορῶν
διδάσκαλον ἀναγράφουσι. τὰ μὲν οὖν τοῦ Παναιτίου βέλτιον ἐπισκε-
7 πτέον ὅπως ἔχει. τῷ δ' ὀστράκῳ πᾶς ὁ διὰ δόξαν ἢ γένος ἢ λόγου δύναμιν ὑπὲρ τοὺς πολλοὺς νομιζόμενος ὑπέπιπτεν· ὅπου καὶ Δάμων ὁ
Περικλέους διδάσκαλος, ὅτι τὸ φρονεῖν ἐδόκει τις εἶναι περιττός, ἐξω-
8 στρακίσθη. καὶ μὴν ἄρξαι γε τὸν Ἀριστείδην ὁ Ἰδομενεὺς οὐ κυαμευ-
τόν, ἀλλ' ἑλομένων Ἀθηναίων φησίν. εἰ δὲ καὶ μετὰ τὴν ἐν Πλαταιαῖς
μάχην ἦρξεν, ὡς αὐτὸς ὁ Δημήτριος γέγραφε, καὶ πάνυ πιθανόν ἐστιν
ἐπὶ δόξῃ τοσαύτῃ καὶ κατορθώμασι τηλικούτοις ἀξιωθῆναι δι' ἀρετὴν
9 ⟨ἀρχῆς⟩ ἧς διὰ πλοῦτον ἐτύγχανον οἱ λαγχάνοντες. ἀλλὰ γὰρ ὁ μὲν
Δημήτριος οὐ μόνον Ἀριστείδην, ἀλλὰ καὶ Σωκράτη δῆλός ἐστι τῆς
πενίας ἐξελέσθαι φιλοτιμούμενος ὡς μεγάλου κακοῦ· καὶ γὰρ ἐκείνῳ
φησὶν οὐ μόνον τὴν οἰκίαν ὑπάρχειν, ἀλλὰ καὶ μνᾶς ἑβδομήκοντα

1.6 τελευτὴν UA: ἀρχὴν S 1.8 ἀρχῆς add. Reiske

cable hostility toward gifts offered to them by friends. They may, indeed, consider it vulgar and degrading to accept presents as a means of increasing one's hoard of wealth, but they do not reject such gifts as afford a man an opportunity for acquiring a reputation for public-spirited munificence.
6 As a matter of fact, Panaetius reveals that in the matter of the tripod Demetrius was suffering from a misapprehension as a result of a confusion over names. For, from the time of the Persian Wars down to the end of the Peloponnesian War, according to Panaetius, only two men named Aristeides are officially recorded as victorious choregi. Neither of these can have been the same man as the son of Lysimachus, since the father of one of them was Xenophilus and the other one lived quite a bit later. This is clear from the style of writing, which belongs to the period after Eucleides, as well as from the fact that the name Archestratus appears on the inscription. For no poet of that name shows up on the official register at the time of the Persian Wars, while the name occurs quite often during the Peloponnesian War. Now, it would be worth while to investigate more fully the validity of Panaetius' arguments
7 but, as far as ostracism is concerned, every man who was considered to be a bit above the rest on account of his reputation or family or power of speaking was subjected to that. After all, even Pericles' teacher Damon was ostracized because he had a reputation for being too much of an intellec-
8 tual. Finally, with regard to the archonship, Idomeneus says that Aristeides was not chosen by lot, but was elected by the Athenians. And if in fact, as Demetrius himself has written, it was after the battle of Plataea that Aristeides held that office, it is quite understandable indeed, in view of his great reputation and his impressive victory, that his heroism should have earned him a position that wealth made avail-
9 able to those who were appointed by lot. But, as a matter of fact, Demetrius for his part has made it clear that he will go to great lengths to rescue not Aristeides alone from poverty (for he seems to regard poverty as a great misfortune) but even Socrates, who had, so Demetrius alleges, not only the estate which he had inherited, but also the sum of seventy

τοκιζομένας ἀπὸ Κρίτωνος.

2. Ἀριστείδης δὲ Κλεισθένους μὲν τοῦ καταστησαμένου τὴν πολιτείαν
μετὰ τοὺς τυράννους ἑταῖρος γενόμενος, ζηλώσας δὲ καὶ θαυμάσας
μάλιστα τῶν πολιτικῶν ἀνδρῶν Λυκοῦργον τὸν Λακεδαιμόνιον, ἥψατο
μὲν ἀριστοκρατικῆς πολιτείας, ἔσχε δ' ἀντιτασσόμενον ὑπὲρ τοῦ δήμου
2 Θεμιστοκλέα τὸν Νεοκλέους. ἔνιοι μὲν οὖν φασι παῖδας ὄντας αὐτοὺς
καὶ συντρεφομένους ἀπ' ἀρχῆς ἐν παντὶ καὶ σπουδῆς ἐχομένῳ καὶ παιδιᾶς πράγματι καὶ λόγῳ διαφέρεσθαι πρὸς ἀλλήλους, καὶ τὰς φύσεις
εὐθὺς ἀπὸ τῆς φιλονικίας ἐκείνης ἀνακαλύπτεσθαι, [καὶ] τὴν μὲν εὐχε-
ρῆ καὶ παράβολον καὶ πανοῦργον οὖσαν καὶ μετ' ὀξύτητος ἐπὶ πάντα
ῥᾳδίως φερομένην, τὴν δ' ἱδρυμένην ἐν ἤθει βεβαίῳ καὶ πρὸς τὸ δίκαιον
ἀτενῆ, ψεῦδος δὲ καὶ βωμολοχίαν καὶ ἀπάτην οὐδ' ἐν παιδιᾶς τινι τρό-
3 πῳ προσιεμένην. Ἀρίστων δ' ὁ Κεῖος ἐξ ἐρωτικῆς ἀρχῆς γενέσθαι φησὶ
4 καὶ προελθεῖν ἐπὶ τοσοῦτον τὴν ἔχθραν αὐτῶν. Στησίλεω γάρ, ὃς ἦν
γένει Κεῖος, ἰδέᾳ δὲ καὶ μορφῇ σώματος πολὺ τῶν ἐν ὥρᾳ λαμπρότατος,
ἀμφοτέρους ἐρασθέντας οὐ μετρίως ἐνεγκεῖν τὸ πάθος, οὐδ' ἅμα λή-
γοντι τῷ κάλλει τοῦ παιδὸς ἀποθέσθαι τὴν φιλονικίαν, ἀλλ' ὥσπερ ἐγ-
γυμνασαμένους ἐκείνῃ πρὸς τὴν πολιτείαν εὐθὺς ὁρμῆσαι, διαπύρους
5 ὄντας καὶ διαφόρως ἔχοντας. ὁ μὲν οὖν Θεμιστοκλῆς εἰς ἑταιρείαν ἐμβαλὼν ἑαυτὸν εἶχε πρόβλημα καὶ δύναμιν οὐκ εὐκαταφρόνητον, ὥστε
καὶ πρὸς τὸν εἰπόντα καλῶς ἄρξειν αὐτὸν Ἀθηναίων, ἄνπερ ἴσος ᾖ καὶ
κοινὸς ἅπασι, 'μηδέποτ',' εἰπεῖν, 'εἰς τοῦτον ἐγὼ καθίσαιμι τὸν θρόνον ἐν
6 ᾧ πλέον οὐδὲν ἕξουσιν οἱ φίλοι παρ' ἐμοὶ τῶν ἀλλοτρίων.' Ἀριστείδης δὲ

1.9 ἀπὸ Sansone: ὑπὸ SUA 2.2 καὶ del. Schaefer

minas, placed at his disposal by Crito, which he let out at interest.

2. Now, although Aristeides was an associate of Cleisthenes, the man who set the constitution to rights after the
time of the tyrants, it was Lycurgus the Spartan whom he
most admired among men of affairs and after whom he mod-
eled himself. So he became involved in politics on the side of
the aristocrats, and brought upon himself the opposition of
Themistocles, son of Neocles, who stood for the cause of the
2 people. Some say, however, that their rivalry dated from the
time they were growing up together as children when, from
the very start, they were at odds with one another, in word
and deed, over everything from the pettiest game to the
most serious matter. And furthermore it is manifest from
the very time of their earliest rivalry that the one was by
nature irresponsible, reckless and unscrupulous, and was
likely to be carried away by the slightest impulse to pursue
any and every venture, while the other was always determined to do the right thing, as he was endowed with a firm
and stable character that admitted of no falsehood, chicanery
3 or deceit, even in jest. But Ariston of Ceos says that their
antagonism arose out of a love affair and then got out of
4 hand. Both men, it seems, had fallen in love with Stesilaus, a
native of Ceos, who by the loveliness of his body far sur-
passed all the other boys, and neither of them was able to restrain his immoderate jealousy. Nor, even when the boy's
appeal began to fade, did they set aside their rivalry. Rather
it was as if that had been nothing more than a trial bout that
had warmed them up and primed them for their fight in the
5 political arena. Themistocles for his part protected himself
and gained a considerable base of power by devoting himself
to a political association. In fact, when someone said that he
would be an admirable leader of the Athenians if he could
really try to be fair and impartial to all, he went so far as to
answer, "I hope I will never take a seat on any tribunal from
which my friends cannot derive greater benefit than out-
6 siders." Aristeides, on the other hand, was his own man. He

καθ' αὑτὸν ὥσπερ ὁδὸν ἰδίαν ἐβάδιζε διὰ τῆς πολιτείας, πρῶτον μὲν οὐ βουλόμενος συναδικεῖν τοῖς ἑταίροις ἢ λυπηρὸς εἶναι μὴ χαριζόμενος, ἔπειτα τὴν ἀπὸ τῶν φίλων δύναμιν οὐκ ὀλίγους ὁρῶν ἐπαίρουσαν ἀδικεῖν ἐφυλάττετο, μόνῳ τῷ χρηστὰ καὶ δίκαια πράττειν καὶ λέγειν ἀξιῶν χαίρειν τὸν ἀγαθὸν πολίτην.

3. Οὐ μὴν ἀλλὰ καὶ πολλὰ κινουμένου τοῦ Θεμιστοκλέους παραβόλως καὶ πρὸς πᾶσαν αὐτῷ πολιτείαν ἐνισταμένου καὶ διακόπτοντος,
ἠναγκάζετό που καὶ αὐτὸς τὰ μὲν ἀμυνόμενος, τὰ δὲ κολούων τὴν
ἐκείνου δύναμιν χάριτι τῶν πολλῶν αὐξομένην ὑπεναντιοῦσθαι παρὰ
γνώμην οἷς ἔπραττεν ὁ Θεμιστοκλῆς, βέλτιον ἡγούμενος παρελθεῖν ἔνια
τῶν συμφερόντων τὸν δῆμον ἢ τῷ κρατεῖν ἐκεῖνον ἐν πᾶσιν ἰσχυρὸν γε-
2 νέσθαι. τέλος δέ ποτε τοῦ Θεμιστοκλέους πράττοντός τι τῶν δεόντων,
ἀντικρούσας καὶ περιγενόμενος, οὐ κατέσχεν, ἀλλ' εἶπεν ἀπὸ τῆς ἐκκλησίας ἀπιών, ὡς οὐκ ἔστι σωτηρία τοῖς Ἀθηναίων πράγμασιν, εἰ μὴ
3 καὶ Θεμιστοκλέα καὶ αὐτὸν εἰς τὸ βάραθρον ἐμβάλοιεν. πάλιν δὲ γράψας τινὰ γνώμην εἰς τὸν δῆμον, ἀντιλογίας οὔσης πρὸς αὐτὴν καὶ φιλονικίας, ἐκράτει· μέλλοντος δὲ τοῦ προέδρου τὸν δῆμον ἐπερωτᾶν, αἰσθόμενος ἀπὸ τῶν λόγων αὐτῶν τὸ ἀσύμφορον, ἀπέστη τοῦ ψηφίσμα-
4 τος. πολλάκις δὲ καὶ δι' ἑτέρων εἰσέφερε τὰς γνώμας, ὡς μὴ φιλονικίᾳ τῇ
πρὸς αὐτὸν ὁ Θεμιστοκλῆς ἐμπόδιος εἴη τῷ συμφέροντι. θαυμαστὴ δέ
τις ἐφαίνετο αὐτοῦ παρὰ τὰς ἐν τῇ πολιτείᾳ μεταβολὰς ἡ εὐστάθεια,
μήτε ταῖς τιμαῖς ἐπαιρομένου, πρός τε τὰς δυσημερίας ἀθορύβως καὶ

2.6 χαίρειν UA: θαρρεῖν S

kept aloof from political alliances because, in the first place, he had no desire to put himself in the position of having either to join those of his party when they acted improperly or to cause annoyance by refusing to oblige them and, in the second place, he saw that many men are enticed into misdeeds by the influence that they derive from their friends. Aristeides would have nothing to do with this sort of influence, thinking that the virtuous citizen should derive satisfaction solely from doing and saying what is right and proper.

3. It is nonetheless true that he was himself virtually compelled against his better judgment to try to thwart all of Themistocles' endeavors, in part in order to check his power, which was on the rise thanks to his popularity with the lower classes, and in part out of a need to protect himself. For not only was Themistocles agitating in an irresponsible manner on his own behalf, but he was also trying to oppose and curtail every political action of Aristeides, and Aristeides felt that it was better for the state to sacrifice its advantage in some cases than for that man to have his way and become
2 all-powerful. Eventually, when he was successful in obstructing an essential piece of legislation that Themistocles had proposed, Aristeides could not keep his feelings to himself and said, as he was leaving the assembly, that there was no hope of salvation for the Athenian state unless the people
3 threw both Themistocles and himself into the pit. On yet another occasion, when he had proposed a measure in the assembly and was securing passage of it in the face of heated opposition, he withdrew the proposal just as the chairman of the session was about to call for the vote, since the debate itself had convinced him that the measure was not in the best
4 interests of the state. On several occasions Aristeides even had his proposals introduced in the name of someone else, so that Themistocles would not be driven by personal rivalry to oppose what was advantageous. What was remarkable about him throughout these vicissitudes of political life was his equanimity. He was neither elated by the honors that he re-

πρᾴως ἔχοντος, καὶ ὁμοίως ἡγουμένου χρῆναι τῇ πατρίδι παρέχειν ἑαυτόν, οὐ χρημάτων μόνον, ἀλλὰ καὶ δόξης προῖκα καὶ ἀμισθὶ πολι-
5 τευόμενον. ὅθεν ὡς ἔοικε τῶν εἰς Ἀμφιάραον ὑπ' Αἰσχύλου πεποιημένων ἰαμβείων ἐν τῷ θεάτρῳ λεγομένων,

οὐ γὰρ δοκεῖν δίκαιος, ἀλλ' εἶναι θέλει,
βαθεῖαν ἄλοκα διὰ φρενὸς καρπούμενος,
ἀφ' ἧς τὰ κεδνὰ βλαστάνει βουλεύματα,

πάντες ἀπέβλεψαν εἰς Ἀριστείδην, ὡς ἐκείνῳ μάλιστα τῆς ἀρετῆς ταύτης προσηκούσης.

4. Οὐ μόνον δὲ πρὸς εὔνοιαν καὶ χάριν, ἀλλὰ καὶ πρὸς ὀργὴν καὶ
2 πρὸς ἔχθραν ἰσχυρότατος ἦν ὑπὲρ τῶν δικαίων ἀντιβῆναι. λέγεται γοῦν ποτε διώκων ἐχθρὸν ἐν δικαστηρίῳ, μετὰ τὴν κατηγορίαν οὐ βουλομένων ἀκούειν τοῦ κινδυνεύοντος τῶν δικαστῶν, ἀλλὰ τὴν ψῆφον εὐθὺς αἰτούντων ἐπ' αὐτόν, ἀναπηδήσας τῷ κρινομένῳ συνικετεύειν, ὅπως ἀκουσθείη καὶ τύχοι τῶν νομίμων· πάλιν δὲ κρίνων ἰδιώταις δυσί, τοῦ ἑτέρου λέγοντος ὡς πολλὰ τυγχάνει τὸν Ἀριστείδην ὁ ἀντίδικος λελυπηκώς, 'λέγ', ὦ'γαθέ,' φάναι, 'μᾶλλον εἴ τι σὲ κακὸν πεποίηκε· σοὶ γάρ,
3 οὐκ ἐμαυτῷ, δικάζω.' τῶν δὲ δημοσίων αἱρεθεὶς προσόδων ἐπιμελητής, οὐ μόνον τοὺς καθ' αὑτόν, ἀλλὰ καὶ τοὺς πρὸ αὑτοῦ γενομένους ἄρχοντας ἀπεδείκνυε πολλὰ νενοσφισμένους, καὶ μάλιστα τὸν Θεμιστοκλέα·

σοφὸς γὰρ ἀνήρ, τῆς δὲ χειρὸς οὐ κρατῶν.

4 διὸ καὶ συναγαγὼν πολλοὺς ἐπὶ τὸν Ἀριστείδην ἐν ταῖς εὐθύναις διώκων κλοπῆς καταδίκῃ περιέβαλεν, ὥς φησιν Ἰδομενεύς. ἀγανακτούντων δὲ τῶν πρώτων ἐν τῇ πόλει καὶ βελτίστων, οὐ μόνον ἀφείθη τῆς ζημίας,

ceived nor did he lose his calm self-control in times of adver-
sity, and he considered it his duty to provide his services to
his country free and without charge, forgoing rewards alike
5 of money and esteem. For this reason they say that, when
the famous verses that Aeschylus composed to describe Amphiaraus were recited in the theater,

Not to seem just he seeketh, but to be.
The fruit of a deep furrow reapeth he
in a rich heart, whence his good counsels rise,

all eyes turned toward Aristeides, as though this virtue belonged especially to him.

4. In taking up the standard of justice he withstood with
all his force not only the promptings of favoritism and parti-
sanship but also those of vengefulness and personal enmity.
2 They say, for example, that once when he was prosecuting a
political adversary before a court of law, the judges refused
to listen to the accused once they had heard Aristeides' in-
dictment and, although they were demanding an immediate
vote of condemnation, Aristeides leapt to his feet and joined
the defendant in imploring the judges that he be granted the
hearing to which he was entitled under the law. On another
occasion, when he was arbitrating the conflicting claims of
two individuals, one of them mentioned the fact that, as it
happened, his adversary had more than once done injury to
Aristeides. "Sir," he said, "tell me rather if he has done injury
to you. For it is your case, not mine, that I am adjudicating."
3 When he was elected supervisor of public revenues, he exposed not only the current magistrates as guilty of widespread corruption, but those of previous years as well, especially Themistocles.

There's nothing wrong with that man's brain;
It's just his fingers he can't restrain.

4 And for this reason, according to Idomeneus, when Aristeides
presented his accounts, Themistocles gathered considerable
support and secured a conviction against him on a charge of
embezzlement. But the most influential men in the state took
umbrage at this and not only was his fine annulled, but he

5 ἀλλὰ καὶ πάλιν ἄρχων ἐπὶ τὴν αὐτὴν διοίκησιν ἀπεδείχθη. προσποι-
ούμενος δὲ τῶν προτέρων μεταμέλειν αὐτῷ καὶ μαλακώτερον ἐνδιδοὺς
ἑαυτόν, ἤρεσκε τοῖς τὰ κοινὰ κλέπτουσιν οὐκ ἐξελέγχων οὐδ' ἀκριβο-
λογούμενος, ὥστε καταπιμπλαμένους τῶν δημοσίων ὑπερεπαινεῖν τὸν
Ἀριστείδην καὶ δεξιοῦσθαι τὸν δῆμον ὑπὲρ αὐτοῦ, σπουδάζοντας
6 ἄρχοντα πάλιν αἱρεθῆναι. μελλόντων δὲ χειροτονεῖν, ἐπετίμησε τοῖς
Ἀθηναίοις· 'ὅτε μὲν γάρ,' ἔφη, 'πιστῶς καὶ καλῶς ὑμῖν ἦρξα, προεπηλα-
κίσθην· ἐπεὶ δὲ πολλὰ τῶν κοινῶν καταπροεῖμαι τοῖς κλέπτουσι, θαυ-
7 μαστὸς εἶναι δοκῶ πολίτης. αὐτὸς μὲν οὖν αἰσχύνομαι τῇ νῦν τιμῇ
μᾶλλον τῆς πρῴην καταδίκης, συνάχθομαι δ' ὑμῖν, παρ' οἷς ἐνδοξότε-
8 ρόν ἐστι τοῦ σῴζειν τὰ δημόσια τὸ χαρίζεσθαι τοῖς πονηροῖς.' ταῦτα δ'
εἰπὼν καὶ τὰς κλοπὰς ἐξελέγξας, τοὺς μὲν τότε βοῶντας ὑπὲρ αὐτοῦ καὶ
μαρτυροῦντας ἐπεστόμισε, τὸν δ' ἀληθινὸν καὶ δίκαιον ἀπὸ τῶν βελτίστων ἔπαινον εἶχεν.

5. Ἐπεὶ δὲ Δᾶτις ὑπὸ Δαρείου πεμφθείς, λόγῳ μὲν ἐπιθεῖναι δίκην
Ἀθηναίοις, ὅτι Σάρδεις ἐνέπρησαν, ἔργῳ δὲ καταστρέψασθαι τοὺς
Ἕλληνας, εἰς Μαραθῶνα παντὶ τῷ στόλῳ κατεσχήκει καὶ τὴν χώραν
ἐπόρθει, τῶν δέκα καθεστώτων τοῖς Ἀθηναίοις ἐπὶ τὸν πόλεμον στρατηγῶν μέγιστον μὲν εἶχεν ἀξίωμα Μιλτιάδης, δόξῃ δὲ καὶ δυνάμει δεύτε-
2 ρος ἦν Ἀριστείδης, καὶ τότε περὶ τῆς μάχης γνώμῃ τῇ Μιλτιάδου προσθέμενος, οὐ μικρὰν ῥοπὴν ἐποίησε, καὶ παρ' ἡμέραν ἑκάστου στρατηγοῦ τὸ κράτος ἔχοντος, ὡς περιῆλθεν εἰς αὐτὸν ἡ ἀρχή, παρέδωκε
Μιλτιάδῃ, διδάσκων τοὺς συνάρχοντας ὅτι τὸ πείθεσθαι καὶ ἀκολου-

5.1 κατεσχήκει Sauppe: κατέσχηκε S: κατέσχε UA

5 was re-elected to the same magistracy. Thereupon he pretended that he had repented of his former ways and showed
every sign of being more compliant, winning the favor of
those who were embezzling state funds by not insisting upon
a strict audit and by not exposing their crimes. With their
pockets full of the money that belonged to the people, they
went before the people and praised Aristeides to the skies,
campaigning on his behalf and doing everything they could
6 to ensure his re-election. But when the vote was about to be
taken, he delivered a severe reprimand to the Athenian people saying, "When I provided you with fair and honest leadership you treated me contemptibly, but now that I have
surrendered a good portion of the public funds to the embez-
7 zlers, I am considered a first-rate citizen. For my part I am
less ashamed of my former condemnation than I am of the
esteem in which now I am held. But I really feel sorry for
you because, as far as you are concerned, it is more admirable to indulge criminals than to preserve what belongs
8 to the state." By saying these things and by thus exposing
their thefts he muzzled those who were clamoring and testi-
fying on his behalf. But by the same token he secured true
and sincere praise from the most worthy citizens.

5. The time came when Datis landed with his entire force
at Marathon and began to ravage the countryside. He had
been sent by Darius ostensibly for the purpose of punishing
the Athenians because they were responsible for the burning
of Sardis, but in fact in order to subjugate the Greeks. At this
time it was Miltiades who was held in greatest esteem among
the ten generals chosen by the Athenians to prosecute the
war, but Aristeides was next after him in reputation and in-
2 fluence. Indeed, on that occasion he played no small role in
tipping the balance in favor of Miltiades' strategy for the
battle. Not only did he share Miltiades' view of the matter
but, since each general held the command on a daily basis, he
handed over his power to Miltiades when it came to be his
turn to take command. In doing this he taught his fellow
commanders an important lesson, that it is no disgrace to

θεῖν τοῖς εὖ φρονοῦσιν οὐκ αἰσχρόν, ἀλλὰ σεμνόν ἐστι καὶ σωτήριον.
3 οὕτω δὲ πραΰνας τὴν φιλονεικίαν καὶ προτρεψάμενος αὐτοὺς ἀγαπᾶν
μιᾷ γνώμῃ τῇ κρατίστῃ χρωμένους, ἔρρωσε τὸν Μιλτιάδην, τῷ ἀπερι-
σπάστῳ τῆς ἐξουσίας ἰσχυρὸν γενόμενον. χαίρειν γὰρ ἐῶν ἕκαστος ἤδη
4 τὸ παρ' ἡμέραν ἄρχειν, ἐκείνῳ προσεῖχεν. ἐν δὲ τῇ μάχῃ μάλιστα τῶν
Ἀθηναίων τοῦ μέσου πονήσαντος καὶ πλεῖστον ἐνταῦθα τῶν βαρβάρων χρόνον ἀντερεισάντων κατὰ τὴν Λεοντίδα καὶ τὴν Ἀντιοχίδα
φυλήν, ἠγωνίσαντο λαμπρῶς τεταγμένοι παρ' ἀλλήλους ὅ τε Θεμιστο-
5 κλῆς καὶ ὁ Ἀριστείδης· ὁ μὲν γὰρ Λεοντίδος ἦν, ὁ δ' Ἀντιοχίδος. ἐπεὶ δὲ
τρεψάμενοι τοὺς βαρβάρους εἰς τὰς ναῦς ἐνέβαλον, καὶ πλέοντας οὐκ
ἐπὶ νήσων ἑώρων, ἀλλ' ὑπὸ τοῦ πνεύματος καὶ τῆς θαλάσσης εἴσω πρὸς
τὴν Ἀττικὴν ἀποβιαζομένους, φοβηθέντες μὴ τὴν πόλιν ἔρημον λάβωσι
τῶν ἀμυνομένων, ταῖς μὲν ἐννέα φυλαῖς ἠπείγοντο πρὸς τὸ ἄστυ, καὶ
6 κατήνυσαν αὐθημερόν· ἐν δὲ τῷ Μαραθῶνι μετὰ τῆς ἑαυτοῦ φυλῆς
Ἀριστείδης ἀπολειφθεὶς φύλαξ τῶν αἰχμαλώτων καὶ τῶν λαφύρων, οὐκ
ἐψεύσατο τὴν δόξαν, ἀλλὰ χύδην μὲν ἀργύρου καὶ χρυσοῦ παρόντος,
ἐσθῆτος δὲ παντοδαπῆς καὶ χρημάτων ἄλλων ἀμυθήτων ἐν ταῖς σκη-
ναῖς καὶ τοῖς ἡλωκόσι σκάφεσιν ὑπαρχόντων, οὔτ' αὐτὸς ἐπεθύμησε
θιγεῖν, οὔτ' ἄλλον εἴασε, πλὴν εἴ τινες ἐκεῖνον λαθόντες ὠφελήθησαν.
7 ὧν ἦν καὶ Καλλίας ὁ δᾳδοῦχος· τούτῳ γάρ τις ὡς ἔοικε τῶν βαρβάρων
προσέπεσεν, οἰηθεὶς βασιλέα διὰ τὴν κόμην καὶ τὸ στρόφιον εἶναι·
προσκυνήσας δὲ καὶ λαβόμενος τῆς δεξιᾶς, ἔδειξε πολὺ χρυσίον ἐν
8 λάκκῳ τινὶ κατορωρυγμένον· ὁ δὲ Καλλίας ὠμότατος ἀνθρώπων καὶ
παρανομώτατος γενόμενος, τὸν μὲν χρυσὸν ἀνείλετο, τὸν δ' ἄνθρωπον,

5.3 φιλονεικίαν UA: προθυμίαν S

obey men of good sense and to be led by them, but rather it
3 is conduct both noble and salutary. Thus he allayed their
contentiousness and he inspired them to embrace the one
policy that had the best chance of success. And so he fortified Miltiades' authority, making it secure and free from dis-
traction. For, from that point on, each of the generals renounced the practice of holding the command on a daily basis
4 and began to take orders from Miltiades. When the battle
occurred, it was the center of the Athenian line that bore the
brunt of the action and it was there, at the point to which the
tribes Leontis and Antiochis were assigned, that the Persians
offered the most prolonged resistance. Themistocles and
Aristeides, being representatives of Leontis and Antiochis respectively, were stationed side by side and fought with great
5 distinction. When they had routed the enemy and had driv-
en them onto their ships they perceived that, rather than
sailing off in the direction of the islands, they were being
forced off course by the wind and the current and were
headed toward land, specifically, toward Attica. This
alarmed the Athenians, who were afraid that their city, now
deprived of its defenders, would be captured. So, with a
force consisting of nine of the tribes, they hastened to reach
6 town and arrived that very day, while Aristeides, along with
the rest of his tribe, was left behind at Marathon to guard the
prisoners and the booty that had been taken. Nor did he fail
to live up to his reputation for, although gold and silver could
be seen strewn everywhere, and although fabric of every description as well as other goods beyond number were to be
had in the tents and the ships that had been captured, he
neither desired to lay his hands on it himself nor would he
allow anyone else to do so. There were some, however, who
helped themselves to the loot without Aristeides' knowledge,
7 one of whom was Callias the Torchbearer. It is said that one
of the Persians, thinking that he was the king on account of
his long hair and headband, prostrated himself at his feet
and then, taking him by the hand, showed him a large hoard
8 of gold that lay buried somewhere in a storage-pit. Callias,
who was an exceptionally savage and violent man, took the

ὡς μὴ κατείποι πρὸς ἑτέρους, ἀπέκτεινεν. ἐκ τούτου φασὶ καὶ λακκο-
πλούτους ὑπὸ τῶν κωμικῶν τοὺς ἀπὸ τῆς οἰκίας λέγεσθαι, σκωπτόντων
9 εἰς τὸν τόπον ἐν ᾧ τὸ χρυσίον ὁ Καλλίας εὗρεν. Ἀριστείδης δὲ τὴν ἐπώνυμον εὐθὺς ἀρχὴν ἦρξε. καίτοι φησὶν ὁ Φαληρεὺς Δημήτριος ἄρξαι
τὸν ἄνδρα μικρὸν ἔμπροσθεν τοῦ θανάτου μετὰ τὴν ἐν Πλαταιαῖς
10 μάχην. ἐν δὲ ταῖς ἀναγραφαῖς μετὰ μὲν Ξανθιππίδην, ἐφ' οὗ Μαρδόνιος
ἡττήθη Πλαταιᾶσιν, οὐδ' ὁμώνυμον Ἀριστείδην ἐν πάνυ πολλοῖς λαβεῖν ἔστι, μετὰ δὲ Φαίνιππον, ἐφ' οὗ τὴν ἐν Μαραθῶνι μάχην ἐνίκων,
εὐθὺς Ἀριστείδης ἄρχων ἀναγέγραπται.

6. Πασῶν δὲ τῶν περὶ αὐτὸν ἀρετῶν ἡ δικαιοσύνη μάλιστα τοῖς πολλοῖς αἴσθησιν παρεῖχε διὰ τὸ τὴν χρείαν ἐνδελεχεστάτην αὐτῆς καὶ
2 κοινοτάτην ὑπάρχειν. ὅθεν ἀνὴρ πένης καὶ δημοτικὸς ἐκτήσατο τὴν
βασιλικωτάτην καὶ θειοτάτην προσηγορίαν τὸν Δίκαιον· ὃ τῶν βασιλέων καὶ τυράννων οὐδεὶς ἐζήλωσεν, ἀλλὰ Πολιορκηταὶ καὶ Κεραυνοὶ
καὶ Νικάτορες, ἔνιοι δ' Ἀετοὶ καὶ Ἱέρακες ἔχαιρον προσαγορευόμενοι,
τὴν ἀπὸ τῆς βίας καὶ τῆς δυνάμεως ὡς ἔοικε μᾶλλον ἢ τὴν ἀπὸ τῆς ἀρε-
3 τῆς δόξαν ἀγαπῶντες. καίτοι τὸ θεῖον, ᾧ γλίχονται συνοικειοῦν καὶ
συναφομοιοῦν ἑαυτούς, τρισὶ δοκεῖ διαφέρειν, ἀφθαρσίᾳ καὶ δυνάμει
καὶ ἀρετῇ, ὧν καὶ σεμνότατον ἡ ἀρετὴ καὶ θειότατόν ἐστιν· ἀφθάρτῳ
μὲν γὰρ εἶναι καὶ τῷ κενῷ καὶ τοῖς στοιχείοις συμβέβηκε· δύναμιν δὲ καὶ
σεισμοὶ καὶ κεραυνοὶ καὶ πνευμάτων ὁρμαὶ καὶ ῥευμάτων ἐπιφοραὶ μεγάλην ἔχουσι· δίκης δὲ καὶ θέμιδος οὐδέν, ὅτι μὴ τῷ φρονεῖν καὶ λογίζε-
4 σθαι θεῖόν ἐστι, μεταλαγχάνει. διὸ καὶ τριῶν ὄντων ἃ πεπόνθασιν οἱ
πολλοὶ πρὸς τὸ θεῖον, ζήλου καὶ φόβου καὶ τιμῆς, ζηλοῦν μὲν αὐτοὺς
καὶ μακαρίζειν ἐοίκασι κατὰ τὸ ἄφθαρτον καὶ ἀίδιον, ἐκπλήττεσθαι δὲ
καὶ δεδιέναι κατὰ τὸ κύριον καὶ δυνατόν, ἀγαπᾶν δὲ καὶ τιμᾶν καὶ σέ-

6.2 τὸν Δίκαιον UA: τὸ Δίκαιον S: fort. τὸ Δίκαιος? 6.3 τῷ φρονεῖν SA: τὸ φρονεῖν U| θεῖον S[1]: τὸ θεῖον S[2]UA| ἐστι Bernardakis: ἔτι S: om. UA

money for himself and, to prevent the man from revealing
his secret to others, murdered him. This is the reason, they
say, that the members of his family are called "Pitriches" by
the comic poets, who thus mockingly refer to the place where
9 Callias found his gold. It was immediately following this that
Aristeides entered office as archon eponymous, although
Demetrius of Phalerum contends that he held office after the
10 battle of Plataea, shortly before his death. But in the official
register, after the name of Xanthippides, who was archon
when Mardonius was defeated at Plataea, not a single Aristeides can be found among the scores of names that are giv-
en. The name of Aristeides is recorded, however, right after
that of Phaenippus, during whose term of office the Athenians won the battle at Marathon.

6. Of all his virtues it was his adherence to justice that
especially brought him to the attention of the people, since
2 that virtue's exercise is the most persistent and general. And
this is how a poor man and a man of the people acquired that
most kingly and divine appellation, The Just, a title which no
king or tyrant ever coveted. They delighted instead in being
addressed by names like The Besieger, The Thunderbolt and
The Conqueror, or like The Eagle and The Hawk, apparently
preferring a reputation based upon violence and power to
3 one based upon virtue. And yet it is generally thought that
the divine, with which these men strive to identify and associate themselves, is transcendent by reason of three charac-
teristics, eternal existence, power and virtue, the last being
the most lofty and divine. For eternal existence is an attribute of space and the elements also, while vast power is
exhibited by earthquakes and thunderbolts, by blasts of
wind and torrents of rushing water, but nothing partakes of
justice and right except that which is divine by virtue of rea-
4 son and understanding. Thus it seems that, of the three responses, envy, fear and reverence, that the gods evoke
among the general public, envy and the consciousness that
they are exquisitely happy result from their immortality and
everlasting existence, awe and fear from their authority and

5 βεσθαι κατὰ τὴν δικαιοσύνην. ἀλλὰ καίπερ οὕτω διακείμενοι, τῆς μὲν ἀθανασίας, ἣν ἡ φύσις ἡμῶν οὐ δέχεται, καὶ τῆς δυνάμεως, ἧς ἐν τῇ τύχῃ κεῖται τὸ πλεῖστον, ἐπιθυμοῦσι, τὴν δ᾽ ἀρετήν, ὃ μόνον ἐστὶ τῶν θείων ἀγαθῶν ἐφ᾽ ἡμῖν, ἐν ὑστέρῳ τίθενται, κακῶς φρονοῦντες, ὡς τὸν ἐν δυνάμει καὶ τύχῃ μεγάλῃ καὶ ἀρχῇ βίον ἡ μὲν δικαιοσύνη ποιεῖ θεῖον, ἡ δ᾽ ἀδικία θηριώδη.

7. Τῷ δ᾽ οὖν Ἀριστείδῃ συνέβη τὸ πρῶτον ἀγαπωμένῳ διὰ τὴν ἐπωνυμίαν ὕστερον φθονεῖσθαι, μάλιστα μὲν τοῦ Θεμιστοκλέους λόγον εἰς τοὺς πολλοὺς διαδιδόντος, ὡς Ἀριστείδης, ἀνῃρηκὼς τὰ δικαστήρια τῷ κρίνειν ἅπαντα καὶ δικάζειν, λέληθε μοναρχίαν ἀδορυφόρητον αὑτῷ κατεσκευασμένος· ἤδη δέ που καὶ ὁ δῆμος, ἐπὶ τῇ νίκῃ μέγα φρονῶν καὶ τῶν μεγίστων ἀξιῶν ἑαυτόν, ἤχθετο τοῖς ὄνομα καὶ δόξαν ὑπὲρ τοὺς
2 πολλοὺς ἔχουσι, καὶ συνελθόντες εἰς ἄστυ πανταχόθεν ἐξοστρακίζουσι τὸν Ἀριστείδην, ὄνομα τῷ φθόνῳ τῆς δόξης φόβον τυραννίδος θέμενοι. μοχθηρίας γὰρ οὐκ ἦν κόλασις ὁ ἐξοστρακισμός, ἀλλ᾽ ἐκαλεῖτο μὲν δι᾽ εὐπρέπειαν ὄγκου καὶ δυνάμεως βαρυτέρας ταπείνωσις καὶ κόλουσις, ἦν δὲ φθόνου παραμυθία φιλάνθρωπος, εἰς ἀνήκεστον οὐδέν, ἀλλ᾽ εἰς μετάστασιν ἐτῶν δέκα τὴν πρὸς τὸ λυποῦν ἀπερειδομένου δυσμένειαν.
3 ἐπεὶ δ᾽ ἤρξαντό τινες ἀνθρώπους ἀγεννεῖς καὶ πονηροὺς ὑποβάλλειν τῷ πράγματι, τελευταῖον ἁπάντων Ὑπέρβολον, ἐξοστρακίσαντες ἐπαύσαντο. λέγεται δὲ τὸν Ὑπέρβολον ἐξοστρακισθῆναι διὰ τοιαύτην αἰτίαν· Ἀλκιβιάδης καὶ Νικίας μέγιστον ἐν τῇ πόλει δυνάμενοι διεστα-
4 σίαζον. ὡς οὖν ὁ δῆμος ἔμελλεν ἐπιφέρειν τὸ ὄστρακον καὶ δῆλος ἦν τὸν ἕτερον γράψων, διαλεχθέντες ἀλλήλοις καὶ τὰς στάσεις ἑκατέρας εἰς ταὐτὸ συναγαγόντες, τὸν Ὑπέρβολον ἐξοστρακισθῆναι παρεσκεύα-

6.5 ἐφ᾽ ἡμῖν S: ἐν ἡμῖν UA 7.1 ἤχθετο τῇ ὀνομασίᾳ δόξαν . . . ἐχούσῃ S 7.2 κόλουσις Faehse: κόλασις SUA 7.4 ἐπιφέρειν Sansone: ἐκφέρειν UA: φέρειν S

power, and affection, reverence and respect from their jus-
5 tice. But, despite this attitude, men covet immortality and
power, though our nature does not admit of the one and the
other rests for the most part with fortune, while virtue, the
lone admirable feature of the gods which we can attain, is assigned to last place. This is a mistake, for it is justice that
renders divine the life of a man involved in power and great
fortune and positions of authority, while injustice renders
such a life brutish.

7. At any rate, Aristeides found that, while his nickname
at first inspired affection, it later gave rise to jealousy. The
principal reason for this was that Themistocles was going
around to the people, saying that Aristeides, by pronouncing
judgment and adjudicating in all matters, had abolished the
courts of law and had surreptitiously set himself up as dic-
tator, lacking only the bodyguard. But it seems that the
Athenians, puffed up by their victory and thinking nothing
too good for themselves, were already becoming irritated by
those whose names and reputations marked them out from
2 the crowd. And so they came into town from all over and
ostracized Aristeides, nominally from fear of despotism, but
in fact because they were jealous of his reputation. For ostracism was not a punishment for wrongdoing. Rather, while
it was ostensibly a means of abasing and curtailing oppressive pride and power, it was in reality a humane method of
assuaging envy, which could direct its malicious desire to in-
jure, not toward some irreparable harm, but toward a
3 penalty consisting of a ten-year expulsion. But they ceased
the practice of ostracism when some men began inflicting
this punishment on low and lawless individuals. Last of all
was Hyperbolus, who was said to have been banished for the
following reason. Alcibiades and Nicias, the most powerful
4 men in the state, were the leaders of rival factions. So, when
the people were about to impose ostracism, and when it was
clear that they were going to decree the banishment of one
or the other of them, the two men called a conference, recon-
ciled their respective factions and brought about the banish-

σαν. ἐκ δὲ τούτου δυσχεράνας ὁ δῆμος ὡς καθυβρισμένον τὸ πρᾶγμα
5 καὶ προπεπηλακισμένον ἀφῆκε παντελῶς καὶ κατέλυσεν. ἦν δὲ τοιοῦτον ὡς τύπῳ φράσαι τὸ γινόμενον· ὄστρακον λαβὼν ἕκαστος καὶ γράψας ὃν ἐβούλετο μεταστῆσαι τῶν πολιτῶν, ἔφερεν εἰς ἕνα τόπον τῆς
6 ἀγορᾶς περιπεφραγμένον ἐν κύκλῳ δρυφάκτοις. οἱ δ' ἄρχοντες πρῶτον
μὲν διηρίθμουν τὸ σύμπαν ἐν ταὐτῷ τῶν ὀστράκων πλῆθος· εἰ γὰρ ἑξα-
κισχιλίων ἐλάττονες οἱ φέροντες εἶεν, ἀτελὴς ἦν ὁ ἐξοστρακισμός· ἔπειτα
τῶν ὀνομάτων ἕκαστον ἰδίᾳ θέντες, τὸν ὑπὸ τῶν πλείστων γεγραμμένον
7 ἐξεκήρυττον εἰς ἔτη δέκα, καρπούμενον τὰ αὑτοῦ. γραφομένων οὖν
τότε τῶν ὀστράκων, λέγεταί τινα τῶν ἀγραμμάτων καὶ παντελῶς ἀγροί-
κων ἀναδόντα τῷ Ἀριστείδῃ τὸ ὄστρακον ὡς ἑνὶ τῶν τυχόντων παρα-
καλεῖν, ὅπως Ἀριστείδην ἐγγράψειε. τοῦ δὲ θαυμάσαντος καὶ πυθομέ-
νου μή τι κακὸν αὐτὸν Ἀριστείδης πεποίηκεν, 'οὐδέν,' εἰπεῖν, 'οὐδὲ γινώ-
σκω τὸν ἄνθρωπον, ἀλλ' ἐνοχλοῦμαι πανταχοῦ τὸν Δίκαιον ἀκούων.'
8 ταῦτ' ἀκούσαντα τὸν Ἀριστείδην ἀποκρίνασθαι μὲν οὐδέν, ἐγγράψαι δὲ
τοὔνομα τῷ ὀστράκῳ καὶ ἀποδοῦναι. τῆς δὲ πόλεως ἀπαλλαττόμενος
ἤδη, τὰς χεῖρας ἀνατείνας πρὸς τὸν οὐρανὸν ηὔξατο τὴν ἐναντίαν ὡς
ἔοικεν εὐχὴν τῷ Ἀχιλλεῖ, μηδένα καιρὸν Ἀθηναίους καταλαβεῖν ὃς
ἀναγκάσει τὸν δῆμον Ἀριστείδου μνησθῆναι.

8. Τρίτῳ δ' ἔτει Ξέρξου διὰ Θετταλίας καὶ Βοιωτίας ἐλαύνοντος ἐπὶ τὴν Ἀττικήν, λύσαντες τὸν νόμον ἐψηφίσαντο τοῖς μεθεστῶσι κάθοδον, μάλιστα φοβούμενοι τὸν Ἀριστείδην μὴ προσθέμενος τοῖς πολεμίοις διαφθείρῃ καὶ μεταστήσῃ πολλοὺς τῶν πολιτῶν πρὸς τὸν βάρβαρον, οὐκ ὀρθῶς στοχαζόμενοι τοῦ ἀνδρός, ὅς γε καὶ πρὸ τοῦ δόγματος τούτου διετέλει προτρέπων καὶ παροξύνων τοὺς Ἕλληνας ἐπὶ τὴν ἐλευθερίαν, καὶ μετὰ τὸ δόγμα, Θεμιστοκλέους στρατηγοῦντος αὐτο-

7.6 ἰδίᾳ θέντες UA: ἰδίᾳ τιθέντες Z: διατιθέντες S 7.7 εἰπεῖν Schaefer: εἶπεν SUA

ment of Hyperbolus. As a result of this, the people, upset because the institution of ostracism had been abused and de-
5 based, entirely gave up the practice and abolished it. Here,
in outline, is the procedure. Each person would take a potsherd, write the name of a citizen whom he wished to remove from the city, and bring it to a particular spot in the
6 market place that was encircled by a railing. First the archons would count up the total number of potsherds for, if
those voting were fewer than six thousand, the ostracism was
inconclusive. Then, after separating out each of the names,
they would make proclamation that the man receiving the
largest number of votes was to be banished for a period of
ten years, while still enjoying the income from his estate.
7 Now, we are told that, on that occasion, while the potsherds
were being inscribed, some illiterate and ill-bred peasant
held up his potsherd to Aristeides and demanded, as if he
were just anybody, that he write the name of Aristeides on
it. When he expressed surprise and asked what harm Aristeides could possibly have done him, the man replied: "None.
I don't even know the man. But I can't stand hearing every-
8 one call him The Just." When he heard this, Aristeides without saying a word wrote his name on the potsherd and handed it back. At last, when he was taking his departure from
the city, he raised up his hands toward heaven and made a
prayer quite different from that which Achilles is supposed
to have made, namely that no crisis overtake the Athenians
such as to remind them perforce of Aristeides.

8. But, within three years, at the time when Xerxes, in his march against Athens, was passing through Thessaly and Boeotia, the Athenians repealed the enactment and voted to repatriate those who were in exile. Their primary concern was over Aristeides who, they feared, might take up the enemy's cause and seduce many of the citizens, inspiring them to shift their allegiance to the Persians. But their estimation of the man was wide of the mark. For, even before this resolution, he never ceased urging the Greeks and inciting them to strike a blow for freedom and, once the resolution passed,

κράτορος, πάντα συνέπραττε καὶ συνεβούλευεν, ἐνδοξότατον ἐπὶ
2 σωτηρίᾳ κοινῇ ποιῶν τὸν ἔχθιστον. ὡς γὰρ ἀπολιπεῖν τὴν Σαλαμῖνα
βουλευομένων τῶν περὶ Εὐρυβιάδην αἱ βαρβαρικαὶ τριήρεις νύκτωρ
ἀναχθεῖσαι καὶ περιβαλοῦσαι τόν τε πόρον ἐν κύκλῳ καὶ τὰς νήσους
κατεῖχον, οὐδενὸς προειδότος τὴν κύκλωσιν, ἧκεν ὁ Ἀριστείδης ἀπ'
3 Αἰγίνης παραβόλως διὰ τῶν πολεμίων νεῶν διεκπλεύσας, καὶ νυκτὸς
ἐλθὼν ἐπὶ τὴν σκηνὴν τοῦ Θεμιστοκλέους καὶ καλέσας αὐτὸν ἔξω μόνον, 'ἡμεῖς,' εἶπεν, 'ὦ Θεμιστόκλεις, εἰ σωφρονοῦμεν, ἤδη τὴν κενὴν καὶ
μειρακιώδη στάσιν ἀφέντες ἀρξώμεθα σωτηρίου καὶ καλῆς φιλονεικίας,
πρὸς ἀλλήλους ἁμιλλώμενοι σῶσαι τὴν Ἑλλάδα, σὺ μὲν ἄρχων καὶ
στρατηγῶν, ἐγὼ δ' ὑπουργῶν καὶ συμβουλεύων· ἐπεὶ καὶ νῦν σε πυνθά-
νομαι μόνον ἅπτεσθαι τῶν ἀρίστων λογισμῶν, κελεύοντα διαναυμαχεῖν
4 ἐν τοῖς στενοῖς τὴν ταχίστην, καί σοι τῶν συμμάχων ἀντιπραττόντων οἱ
πολέμιοι συνεργεῖν ἐοίκασι· τὸ γὰρ ἐν κύκλῳ καὶ κατόπιν ἤδη πέλαγος
ἐμπέπλησται νεῶν πολεμίων, ὥστε καὶ τοὺς μὴ θέλοντας ἀνάγκη κατεί-
ληφεν ἀγαθοὺς ἄνδρας εἶναι καὶ μάχεσθαι· φυγῆς γὰρ ὁδὸς οὐ λείπεται.'
5 πρὸς ταῦθ' ὁ Θεμιστοκλῆς εἶπεν· 'οὐκ ἂν ἐβουλόμην, ὦ Ἀριστείδη, σὲ
κατὰ τοῦτο κρείττονά μου γενέσθαι, πειράσομαι δὲ πρὸς καλὴν ἀρχὴν
ἁμιλλώμενος ὑπερβαλέσθαι τοῖς ἔργοις.' ἅμα δ' αὐτῷ φράσας τὴν ὑπ'
αὐτοῦ κατασκευασθεῖσαν ἀπάτην ἐπὶ τὸν βάρβαρον, παρεκάλει πείθειν τὸν Εὐρυβιάδην καὶ διδάσκειν ὡς ἀμήχανόν ἐστι σωθῆναι μὴ ναυ-
6 μαχήσαντας· εἶχε γὰρ μᾶλλον αὐτοῦ πίστιν. ὅθεν ἐν τῷ συλλόγῳ τῶν
στρατηγῶν εἰπόντος Κλεοκρίτου τοῦ Κορινθίου πρὸς τὸν Θεμιστοκλέα,
μηδ' Ἀριστείδῃ τὴν γνώμην ἀρέσκειν αὐτοῦ, παρόντα γὰρ σιωπᾶν, ἀντ-
εῖπεν ὁ Ἀριστείδης ὡς οὐκ ἂν ἐσιώπα μὴ λέγοντος τὰ ἄριστα τοῦ Θεμι-
στοκλέους· νυνὶ δ' ἡσυχίαν ἄγειν οὐ δι' εὔνοιαν τοῦ ἀνδρός, ἀλλὰ τὴν
γνώμην ἐπαινῶν.

he did everything he could to assist and advise Themistocles, who was then commander in chief, thus enabling his bitterest enemy to win supreme public acclaim for bringing about the
2 deliverance of all. For, when Eurybiades was contemplating abandoning Salamis, and the Persian warships, which had under cover of darkness put out to sea, set up a blockade around the straits and were taking possession of the islands, Aristeides was the first to know of the encirclement and he returned from Aegina, sailing without regard for his own
3 safety through the line of enemy ships. During the night he came to Themistocles' tent and, summoning him to come outside by himself, said, "If we are men of good sense, Themistocles, we will put aside our futile and childish rivalry. From this point on let us engage in a noble and salutary competition. Let us vie with each other for the deliverance of Greece, you by leading and commanding, I by helping and advising. Even now I find that there is no one who follows the most advantageous line of reasoning except you. For you urge that the decisive battle be fought as soon as possible in the straits
4 and, while the allies are setting up obstacles, the enemy seem to be giving you support. Already the waters behind us and all about are full of enemy ships. Consequently, compulsion has overtaken even the faint of heart to prove their mettle
5 and fight. No path of escape remains." To these words Themistocles replied, "In this matter, Aristeides, I should not have wished you to have the better of me but, challenged by the noble initiative that you have taken, I shall attempt to surpass you by my deeds." And with that he told Aristeides of the plan that he had contrived to deceive the Persians. He begged him to prevail upon Eurybiades (for Aristeides was more readily trusted than Themistocles) and to show him
6 that deliverance was impossible without a battle at sea. And so, during the council of war, when Cleocritus the Corinthian said to Themistocles that his opinion did not even secure the approval of Aristeides who, though present, held his tongue, Aristeides contradicted him, saying, "I would not hold my tongue if Themistocles were not offering the best advice. As it is, I am keeping quiet, not out of goodwill toward the man,

9. Οἱ μὲν οὖν ναύαρχοι τῶν Ἑλλήνων ταῦτ' ἔπραττον. Ἀριστείδης δ'
ὁρῶν τὴν Ψυττάλειαν, ἣ πρὸ τῆς Σαλαμῖνος ἐν τῷ πόρῳ κεῖται νῆσος οὐ
μεγάλη, πολεμίων ἀνδρῶν μεστὴν οὖσαν, ἐμβιβάσας εἰς ὑπηρετικὰ τοὺς
προθυμοτάτους καὶ μαχιμωτάτους τῶν πολιτῶν, προσέμειξε τῇ Ψυτταλείᾳ, καὶ μάχην πρὸς τοὺς βαρβάρους συνάψας ἀπέκτεινε πάντας,
2 πλὴν ὅσοι τῶν ἐπιφανῶν ζῶντες ἥλωσαν. ἐν δὲ τούτοις ἦσαν ἀδελφῆς
βασιλέως ὄνομα Σανδάκης τρεῖς παῖδες, οὓς εὐθὺς ἀπέστειλε πρὸς τὸν
Θεμιστοκλέα, καὶ λέγονται κατά τι λόγιον τοῦ μάντεως Εὐφραντίδου
3 κελεύσαντος ὠμηστῇ Διονύσῳ πρὸ τῆς μάχης καθιερευθῆναι. τὴν δὲ
νησῖδα τοῖς ὅπλοις πανταχόθεν ὁ Ἀριστείδης περιστέψας, ἐφήδρευε τοῖς
ἐκφερομένοις πρὸς αὐτήν, ὡς μήτε τῶν φίλων τινὰ διαφθαρῆναι μήτε τῶν
4 πολεμίων διαφυγεῖν. ὁ γὰρ πλεῖστος ὠθισμὸς τῶν νεῶν καὶ τῆς μάχης τὸ
καρτερώτατον ἔοικε περὶ τὸν τόπον ἐκεῖνον γενέσθαι· διὸ καὶ τρόπαιον
5 ἕστηκεν ἐν τῇ Ψυτταλείᾳ. μετὰ δὲ τὴν μάχην ὁ Θεμιστοκλῆς ἀποπειρώ-
μενος τοῦ Ἀριστείδου καλὸν μὲν εἶναι καὶ τὸ πεπραγμένον ἔργον αὐτοῖς
ἔλεγε, κρεῖττον δὲ λείπεσθαι τὸ λαβεῖν ἐν τῇ Εὐρώπῃ τὴν Ἀσίαν, ἀνα-
πλεύσαντας εἰς Ἑλλήσποντον τὴν ταχίστην καὶ τὰ ζεύγματα διακό-
6 ψαντας. ἐπεὶ δ' Ἀριστείδης ἀνακραγὼν τοῦτον μὲν ἐκέλευε τὸν λόγον
καταβαλεῖν, σκοπεῖν δὲ καὶ ζητεῖν ὅπως τὴν ταχίστην ἐκβάλωσι τὸν
Μῆδον ἐκ τῆς Ἑλλάδος, μὴ κατακλεισθεὶς ἀπορίᾳ φυγῆς μετὰ τοσαύτης
δυνάμεως τραπῇ πρὸς ἄμυναν ὑπ' ἀνάγκης, οὕτω πέμπει πάλιν Ἀρνά-
κην εὐνοῦχον ὁ Θεμιστοκλῆς ἐκ τῶν αἰχμαλώτων κρύφα, φράσαι βασιλεῖ κελεύσας ὅτι πλεῖν ἐπὶ τὰς γεφύρας ὡρμημένους τοὺς Ἕλληνας
αὐτὸς ἀποτρέψειε, σῴζεσθαι βασιλέα βουλόμενος.

10. Ἐκ τούτου Ξέρξης μὲν περίφοβος γενόμενος εὐθὺς ἐπὶ τὸν Ἑλλήσποντον ἠπείγετο, Μαρδόνιος δὲ τοῦ στρατοῦ τὸ δοκιμώτατον ἔχων,

10.1 δοκιμώτατον S: μαχιμώτατον S (marg.) UA

but because I applaud his advice."

9. Now, while the commanders of the Greek fleet were
thus occupied, Aristeides noticed that Psyttaleia, the small
island situated in the straits between Salamis and the mainland, was occupied by hostile troops. He put on board some
noncombat vessels the most willing and able of the citizens
and made a landing on Psyttaleia. There he joined battle
with the Persians, killing all of them except those men of
2 rank who could be captured alive. Among these were three
sons of Sandaces, the sister of the king, whom Aristeides immediately sent off to Themistocles. (It is reported that, in accordance with some oracle and at the urging of the prophet
Euphrantides, they were offered up before the battle as a
3 human sacrifice to Dionysus Omestes.) Then Aristeides stationed his troops all around the islet, on the alert for anyone
being driven ashore there, that no friend might perish and no
4 foe manage to escape. For it seems that the greater part of
the naval engagement and the most serious fighting occurred
in that place. For this reason a trophy was in fact set up on
5 Psyttaleia. Following the battle Themistocles, making trial of
Aristeides, said that, while it was a fine deed that they had
accomplished, something of greater significance remained as
well, namely to trap Asia within Europe by setting sail as
soon as possible for the Hellespont and cutting through the
6 bridges of boats. But Aristeides, with a shout of dismay, told
him to repudiate that proposal and to seek rather how they
might cast the Persians out of Greece as soon as possible, and
not compel them to direct so large a force toward self-de-
fense by cutting them off without any means of escape. So
Themistocles secretly dispatched the eunuch Arnaces, who
was one of the prisoners of war, ordering him to go back to
the king and tell him that he, Themistocles, out of a desire
that the king be saved, had turned back the Greeks when
they were intent upon steering for the bridges.

10. Under these circumstances Xerxes took fright and lost no time making for the Hellespont, leaving Mardonius

περὶ τριάκοντα μυριάδας, ὑπελείπετο, καὶ φοβερὸς ἦν ἀπ' ἰσχυρᾶς τῆς
περὶ τὸ πεζὸν ἐλπίδος, ἀπειλῶν τοῖς Ἕλλησι καὶ γράφων τοιαῦτα· 'νενι-
κήκατε θαλασσίοις ξύλοις χερσαίους ἀνθρώπους, οὐκ ἐπισταμένους
κώπην ἐλαύνειν· ἀλλὰ νῦν πλατεῖα μὲν ἡ Θετταλῶν γῆ, καλὸν δὲ τὸ
2 Βοιώτιον πεδίον ἀγαθοῖς ὁπλίταις καὶ ἱππεῦσιν ἐναγωνίσασθαι.' πρὸς δ'
Ἀθηναίους ἔπεμψεν ἰδίᾳ γράμματα καὶ λόγους παρὰ βασιλέως, τήν τε
πόλιν αὐτοῖς ἀναστήσειν ἐπαγγελλομένου καὶ χρήματα πολλὰ δώσειν
καὶ τῶν Ἑλλήνων κυρίους καταστήσειν, ἐκποδὼν τοῦ πολέμου γενομέ-
3 νους. οἱ δὲ Λακεδαιμόνιοι πυθόμενοι ταῦτα καὶ δείσαντες, ἔπεμψαν
Ἀθήναζε πρέσβεις, δεόμενοι τῶν Ἀθηναίων ὅπως παῖδας μὲν καὶ γυναῖ-
κας εἰς Σπάρτην ἀποστείλωσι, τοῖς δὲ πρεσβυτέροις τροφὰς παρ' αὐτῶν
λαμβάνωσιν· ἰσχυρὰ γὰρ ἦν ἀπορία περὶ τὸν δῆμον, ἀπολωλεκότα καὶ
4 τὴν χώραν καὶ τὴν πόλιν. οὐ μὴν ἀλλὰ τῶν πρέσβεων ἀκούσαντες,
Ἀριστείδου ψήφισμα γράψαντος, ἀπεκρίναντο θαυμαστὴν ἀπόκρισιν,
τοῖς μὲν πολεμίοις συγγνώμην ἔχειν φάσκοντες, εἰ πάντα πλούτου καὶ
χρημάτων ὤνια νομίζοιεν, ὧν κρεῖττον οὐδὲν ἴσασιν, ὀργίζεσθαι δὲ
Λακεδαιμονίοις, ὅτι τὴν πενίαν καὶ τὴν ἀπορίαν τὴν νῦν παροῦσαν
Ἀθηναίοις μόνον ὁρῶσι, τῆς δ' ἀρετῆς καὶ τῆς φιλοτιμίας ἀμνημονοῦ-
5 σιν, ἐπὶ σιτίοις ὑπὲρ τῆς Ἑλλάδος ἀγωνίζεσθαι παρακαλοῦντες. ταῦτα
γράψας Ἀριστείδης καὶ τοὺς πρέσβεις εἰς ἐκκλησίαν παραγαγών, Λακεδαιμονίοις μὲν ἐκέλευσε φράζειν, ὡς οὐκ ἔστι χρυσοῦ τοσοῦτον πλῆθος
οὔθ' ὑπὲρ γῆς οὔθ' ὑπὸ γῆν, ὅσον Ἀθηναῖοι δέξαιντο ἂν πρὸ τῆς τῶν
6 Ἑλλήνων ἐλευθερίας. τοῖς δὲ παρὰ Μαρδονίου τὸν ἥλιον δείξας, 'ἄχρι
ἂν οὗτος,' ἔφη, 'ταύτην πορεύηται τὴν πορείαν, Ἀθηναῖοι πολεμήσουσι
Πέρσαις ὑπὲρ τῆς δεδῃωμένης χώρας καὶ τῶν ἠσεβημένων καὶ κατακε-
καυμένων ἱερῶν.' ἔτι δ' ἀρὰς θέσθαι τοὺς ἱερεῖς ἔγραψεν, εἴ τις ἐπικηρυ-

10.5 ὑπὲρ γῆς Blass: ὑπὲρ γῆν SUA

behind with the pick of the fighting force, approximately
300,000 men. On account of his unwavering confidence in
his infantry, Mardonius was an intimidating presence, and he
wrote a threatening letter to the Greeks, saying, "Thanks to
some bits of lumber on the seas you are victorious over
landsmen who know nothing of pushing an oar. Now, however, Thessaly provides open country, while the Boeotian
plain is ideal for a contest of first-rate men at arms and
2 horsemen." But to the Athenians he sent a separate letter
bearing a message from the king, who promised that he
would rebuild their city, give them large sums of money and
make them masters of the Greeks once they had withdrawn
3 from the war. When the Lacedaemonians learned of this
they were alarmed. So they sent a delegation to Athens,
begging the Athenians to dispatch women and children to
Sparta and to receive from them provisions for the elderly.
For the populace was beset by severe privation, having had
4 both its fields and its city destroyed. The Athenians listened
to what the delegation had to say but, in spite of everything,
they responded in the form of a remarkable decree that
Aristeides had proposed. They said that they could pardon
the enemy for thinking that everything had a price in terms
of wealth and money, for the enemy knew of no higher values than these; but they were indignant that the Lacedaemonians, considering only the want and privation that now
faced the Athenians and forgetting about their valor and
dedication, were trying to induce them to fight for Greece by
5 bribing them with bread. After making this proposal, Aristeides brought the delegation before a meeting of the assembly and instructed it to inform the Lacedaemonians that
nowhere, either above the earth or under it, was there an
abundance of gold so great that the Athenians would accept
6 it in preference to the freedom of the Greeks. Then, pointing
to the sun, he said to the men sent by Mardonius, "As long as
that keeps its present course, so long will the Athenians fight
against the Persians to protect their ravaged land and their
temples, now desecrated and reduced to ashes." Furthermore, he proposed that the priests should call down impre-

7 κεύσαιτο Μήδοις ἢ τὴν συμμαχίαν ἀπολίποι τῶν Ἑλλήνων. ἐμβαλόν-
τος δὲ Μαρδονίου τὸ δεύτερον εἰς τὴν Ἀττικήν, αὖθις εἰς Σαλαμῖνα
διεπέρασαν. Ἀριστείδης δὲ πεμφθεὶς εἰς Λακεδαίμονα τῆς μὲν βραδυ-
τῆτος αὐτοῖς ἐνεκάλει καὶ τῆς ὀλιγωρίας, προεμένοις αὖθις τῷ βαρβάρῳ
τὰς Ἀθήνας, ἠξίου δὲ πρὸς τὰ ἔτι σῳζόμενα τῆς Ἑλλάδος βοηθεῖν.
8 ταῦτ' ἀκούσαντες οἱ ἔφοροι μεθ' ἡμέραν μὲν ἐδόκουν παίζειν καὶ ῥᾳθυ-
μεῖν ἑορτάζοντες· ἦν γὰρ αὐτοῖς Ὑακίνθια· νυκτὸς δὲ πεντακισχιλίους
Σπαρτιατῶν ἐπιλέξαντες, ὧν ἕκαστος ἑπτὰ περὶ αὑτὸν εἵλωτας εἶχεν,
9 ἐξέπεμψαν οὐκ εἰδότων τῶν Ἀθηναίων. ἐπεὶ δὲ πάλιν ἐγκαλῶν ὁ Ἀριστείδης προσῆλθεν, οἱ δὲ σὺν γέλωτι ληρεῖν αὐτὸν ἔφασαν καὶ καθεύδειν, ἤδη γὰρ ἐν Ὀρεστείῳ τὸν στρατὸν εἶναι, πορευόμενον ἐπὶ τοὺς
ξένους (ξένους γὰρ ἐκάλουν τοὺς Πέρσας), οὐ κατὰ καιρὸν ἔφη παίζειν
αὐτοὺς ὁ Ἀριστείδης, ἀντὶ τῶν πολεμίων τοὺς φίλους ἐξαπατῶντας.
10 ταῦθ' οἱ περὶ τὸν Ἰδομενέα λέγουσιν· ἐν δὲ τῷ ψηφίσματι τοῦ Ἀριστείδου
πρεσβευτὴς οὐκ αὐτός, ἀλλὰ Κίμων καὶ Ξάνθιππος καὶ Μυρωνίδης
φέρονται.

11. Χειροτονηθεὶς δὲ στρατηγὸς αὐτοκράτωρ ἐπὶ τὴν μάχην, καὶ τῶν
2 Ἀθηναίων ὀκτακισχιλίους ὁπλίτας ἀναλαβών, ἧκεν εἰς Πλαταιάς. ἐκεῖ
δὲ καὶ Παυσανίας ὁ τοῦ σύμπαντος ἡγούμενος Ἑλληνικοῦ συνέμειξεν,
ἔχων τοὺς Σπαρτιάτας, καὶ τῶν ἄλλων Ἑλλήνων ἐπέρρει τὸ πλῆθος.
τῶν δὲ βαρβάρων τὸ μὲν ὅλον τῆς στρατοπεδείας παρὰ τὸν Ἀσωπὸν
ποταμὸν παρεκτεταμένης οὐδεὶς ἦν ὅρος διὰ τὸ μέγεθος, περὶ δὲ τὰς
ἀποσκευὰς καὶ τὰ κυριώτατα τεῖχος περιεφράξαντο τετράγωνον, οὗ
3 τῶν πλευρῶν ἑκάστη μῆκος ἦν δέκα σταδίων. Παυσανίᾳ μὲν οὖν καὶ
τοῖς Ἕλλησι κοινῇ Τεισαμενὸς ὁ Ἠλεῖος ἐμαντεύσατο, καὶ προεῖπε
νίκην ἀμυνομένοις καὶ μὴ προεπιχειροῦσιν· Ἀριστείδου δὲ πέμψαντος

cations upon anyone of the Greeks who negotiated with the
7 Persians or abandoned the alliance. When for the second time Mardonius invaded Athenian territory, they crossed over again to Salamis and sent Aristeides on a mission to Lacedaemon. There he reproached the Spartans for their dilatoriness and negligence, saying that they had once again abandoned Athens to the Persians, and he indicated that he expected them to come to the aid of that part of Greece that
8 was still free. The ephors listened to this and, so long as it was daytime, they gave the impression of relaxing and being idle, since it was their festival of the Hyacinthia. But during the night, and without the knowledge of the Athenians, they dispatched five thousand Spartans, whom they had previously selected, each one of them attended by seven helots.
9 When Aristeides came before them, renewing his accusations, they laughed and said that he was still asleep and talking nonsense, for their army had already reached Oresteium in its march against the foreigners. ("Foreigners" was the word they used to use to refer to the Persians.) Aristeides replied that it was an inopportune pleasantry for them to mislead their allies instead of the enemy. This is the account that
10 Idomeneus gives. But in Aristeides' proposal, he himself is not named as ambassador. Instead, Cimon, Xanthippus and Myronides are named.

11. In anticipation of the battle, Aristeides was elected commander in chief, and he arrived at Plataea leading eight
2 thousand Athenian men at arms. He was joined there by Pausanias, the leader of the combined Greek forces, with his Spartans, and by the rest of the Greeks, who kept streaming in in large numbers. The Persian army was encamped along the Asopus river but, because of its great size, it was not altogether enclosed. The baggage train and the headquarters, however, were fortified by a rectangular wall, each side of
3 which was ten stades in length. Now, to Pausanias and to the Greeks in general Teisamenus of Elis prophesied, foretelling victory for them if they remained on the defensive and did not initiate hostilities. But as for Aristeides, when he sent to

εἰς Δελφούς, ἀνεῖλεν ὁ θεὸς Ἀθηναίους καθυπερτέρους ἔσεσθαι τῶν
ἐναντίων εὐχομένους τῷ Διὶ καὶ τῇ Ἥρᾳ τῇ Κιθαιρωνίᾳ καὶ Πανὶ καὶ
Νύμφαις Σφραγίτισι, καὶ θύοντας ἥρωσιν Ἀνδροκράτει Λεύκωνι Πει-
σάνδρῳ Δαμοκράτει Ὑψίονι Ἀκταίωνι Πολυείδῳ, καὶ τὸν κίνδυνον ἐν
γᾷ ἰδίᾳ ποιουμένους ἐν τῷ πεδίῳ τᾶς Δάματρος τᾶς Ἐλευσινίας καὶ τᾶς
4 Κόρας. οὗτος ὁ χρησμὸς ἀνενεχθεὶς ἀπορίαν τῷ Ἀριστείδῃ παρεῖχεν.
οἱ μὲν γὰρ ἥρωες οἷς ἐκέλευε θύειν ἀρχηγέται Πλαταιέων ἦσαν, καὶ τὸ
τῶν Σφραγιτίδων Νυμφῶν ἄντρον ἐν μιᾷ κορυφῇ τοῦ Κιθαιρῶνός ἐστιν,
εἰς δυσμὰς ἡλίου θερινὰς τετραμμένον, ἐν ᾧ καὶ μαντεῖον ἦν πρότερον
ὥς φασι καὶ πολλοὶ κατείχοντο τῶν ἐπιχωρίων, οὓς νυμφολήπτους
5 προσηγόρευον. τὸ δὲ τῆς Ἐλευσινίας Δήμητρος πεδίον, καὶ τὸ τὴν
μάχην ἐν ἰδίᾳ χώρᾳ ποιουμένοις τοῖς Ἀθηναίοις νίκην δίδοσθαι, πάλιν
εἰς τὴν Ἀττικὴν ἀνεκαλεῖτο καὶ μεθίστη τὸν πόλεμον. ἔνθα τῶν Πλαταιέων ὁ στρατηγὸς Ἀρίμνηστος ἔδοξε κατὰ τοὺς ὕπνους ὑπὸ τοῦ Διὸς
τοῦ Σωτῆρος ἐπερωτώμενον αὐτόν, ὅτι δὴ πράττειν δέδοκται τοῖς Ἕλλησιν, εἰπεῖν, 'αὔριον εἰς Ἐλευσῖνα τὴν στρατιὰν ἀπάξομεν, ὦ δέσποτα,
6 καὶ διαμαχούμεθα τοῖς βαρβάροις ἐκεῖ κατὰ τὸ πυθόχρηστον.' τὸν
οὖν θεὸν φάναι διαμαρτάνειν αὐτοὺς τοῦ παντός· αὐτόθι γὰρ εἶναι περὶ
τὴν Πλαταϊκὴν τὰ πυθόχρηστα, καὶ ζητοῦντας ἀνευρήσειν. τούτων
ἐναργῶς τῷ Ἀριμνήστῳ φανέντων, ἐξεγρόμενος τάχιστα μετεπέμψατο
τοὺς ἐμπειροτάτους καὶ πρεσβυτάτους τῶν πολιτῶν, μεθ' ὧν διαλεγόμενος καὶ συνδιαπορῶν εὗρεν ὅτι τῶν Ὑσιῶν πλησίον ὑπὸ τὸν Κιθαι-
ρῶνα ναός ἐστιν ἀρχαῖος πάνυ Δήμητρος Ἐλευσινίας καὶ Κόρης
7 προσαγορευόμενος. εὐθὺς οὖν παραλαβὼν τὸν Ἀριστείδην ἦγεν ἐπὶ
τὸν τόπον, εὐφυέστατον ὄντα παρατάξαι φάλαγγα πεζὴν ἱπποκρατου-
μένοις διὰ τὰς ὑπωρείας τοῦ Κιθαιρῶνος, ἄφιππα ποιούσας τὰ καταλή-

11.4 ἀνενεχθεὶς Schaefer: ἀπενεχθεὶς SUA 11.6 Ὑσιῶν Amyot: νυσίων SUA

Delphi, he received the following oracular response from the
god: "The Athenians will be victorious over their opponents if
they pray to Zeus, Cithaeronian Hera, Pan and the Sphragitic
Nymphs, if they sacrifice to the heroes Androcrates, Leucon,
Peisander, Damocrates, Hypsion, Actaeon and Polyeidus, and
if they take upon themselves the risk of fighting in their own
4 territory, in the plain of Eleusinian Demeter and Kore." When
this oracle was reported to Aristeides it posed a dilemma.
For on the one hand the heroes to whom they were ordered
to make sacrifice were venerated figures of Plataean legend,
and the cave of the Sphragitic Nymphs is to be found on one
of the peaks of Cithaeron, facing in a northwesterly direction.
(It is said that there had formerly been an oracle in this cave,
and that a number of the inhabitants were possessed by
what was called "nympholepsy," that is, a prophetic inspira-
5 tion granted by the Nymphs.) On the other hand, the "plain
of Eleusinian Demeter" and the promise of victory to the
Athenians "if they take upon themselves the risk of fighting
in their own territory" transplanted the war and summoned
it back to Athenian soil. At this point, the Plataean general
Arimnestus had a dream in which Zeus the Savior appeared
to him and asked him just what the Greeks had decided to
do. "Tomorrow, master," he had replied, "we shall lead our
forces off to Eleusis and there, in accordance with the Pythian
6 pronouncement, we shall engage with the Persians." Thereupon the god had said that they were completely mistaken,
since right there near Plataea was the place mentioned in the
pronouncement, which they would find if they looked for it.
The dream was quite vivid, and as soon as Arimnestus awak-
ened he sent for the oldest and most knowledgeable of the
citizens, whom he interviewed in hopes of resolving his
dilemma. He discovered that at the foot of Mount Cithaeron
near Hysiae was quite an ancient temple, called that of
7 Eleusinian Demeter and Kore. So he took along Aristeides
with him and immediately led him to the spot, which is ide-
ally suited for the deployment of an infantry phalanx by an
army deficient in cavalry, since the foothills of Cithaeron
render that part of the plain that terminates near the temple

8 γοντα καὶ συγκυροῦντα τοῦ πεδίου πρὸς τὸ ἱερόν. ταύτῃ δ' ἦν καὶ τὸ
τοῦ Ἀνδροκράτους ἡρῷον ἐγγύς, ἄλσει πυκνῶν καὶ συσκίων δένδρων
περιεχόμενον. ὅπως δὲ μηδὲν ἐλλιπὲς ἔχῃ πρὸς τὴν ἐλπίδα τῆς νίκης ὁ
χρησμός, ἔδοξε τοῖς Πλαταιεῦσιν, Ἀριμνήστου γνώμην εἰπόντος, ἀνελεῖν τὰ πρὸς τὴν Ἀττικὴν ὅρια τῆς Πλαταιίδος καὶ τὴν χώραν ἐπιδοῦ-
ναι τοῖς Ἀθηναίοις, ὑπὲρ τῆς Ἑλλάδος ἐν οἰκείᾳ κατὰ τὸ χρησμὸν
9 ἐναγωνίσασθαι. ταύτην μὲν οὖν τὴν φιλοτιμίαν τῶν Πλαταιέων οὕτω
συνέβη περιβόητον γενέσθαι, ὥστε καὶ Ἀλέξανδρον ἤδη βασιλεύοντα
τῆς Ἀσίας ὕστερον πολλοῖς ἔτεσι τειχίζοντα τὰς Πλαταιὰς ἀνειπεῖν
Ὀλυμπίασιν ὑπὸ κήρυκος ὅτι 'ταύτην ὁ βασιλεὺς ἀποδίδωσι Πλαται-
εῦσι τῆς ἀνδραγαθίας καὶ μεγαλοψυχίας χάριν, ἐπειδὴ τοῖς Ἕλλησιν ἐν
τῷ Μηδικῷ πολέμῳ τὴν χώραν ἐπέδωκαν καὶ παρέσχον αὑτοὺς προθυμοτάτους.

12. Ἀθηναίοις δὲ Τεγεᾶται περὶ τάξεως ἐρίσαντες ἠξίουν, ὥσπερ αἰεί,
Λακεδαιμονίων τὸ δεξιὸν ἐχόντων κέρας, αὐτοὶ τὸ εὐώνυμον ἔχειν,
πολλὰ τοὺς αὑτῶν προγόνους ἐγκωμιάζοντες. ἀγανακτούντων δὲ τῶν
2 Ἀθηναίων, παρελθὼν ὁ Ἀριστείδης εἶπε· 'Τεγεάταις μὲν ἀντειπεῖν περὶ
εὐγενείας καὶ ἀνδραγαθίας ὁ παρὼν καιρὸς οὐ δίδωσι· πρὸς δ' ὑμᾶς, ὦ
Σπαρτιᾶται, καὶ τοὺς ἄλλους Ἕλληνας λέγομεν, ὅτι τὴν ἀρετὴν οὐκ
ἀφαιρεῖται τόπος οὐδὲ δίδωσιν· ἣν δ' ἂν ὑμεῖς ἡμῖν τάξιν ἀποδῶτε,
πειρασόμεθα κοσμοῦντες καὶ φυλάττοντες μὴ καταισχύνειν τοὺς
3 προηγωνισμένους ἀγῶνας. ἥκομεν γὰρ οὐ τοῖς συμμάχοις στασιά-
σοντες, ἀλλὰ μαχούμενοι τοῖς πολεμίοις, οὐδ' ἐπαινεσόμενοι τοὺς
πατέρας, ἀλλ' αὐτοὺς ἄνδρας ἀγαθοὺς τῇ Ἑλλάδι παρέξοντες· ὡς
οὗτος ὁ ἀγὼν δείξει καὶ πόλιν καὶ ἄρχοντα καὶ ἰδιώτην ὁπόσου τοῖς
4 Ἕλλησιν ἄξιός ἐστι.' ταῦτ' ἀκούσαντες οἱ σύνεδροι καὶ ἡγεμόνες
ἀπεδέξαντο τοὺς Ἀθηναίους καὶ θάτερον αὐτοῖς κέρας ἀπέδοσαν.

8 unsatisfactory for the use of cavalry. Furthermore, there was nearby the shrine of Androcrates, in the midst of a thick and shady grove. And, to make sure that every provision of the oracle conduced to the expectation of success, Arimnestus proposed, and the citizens of Plataea voted, that the boundary markers between the territories of Athens and Plataea be removed, and that their land be consigned to the Athenians so that, in accordance with the oracle, the contest for the freedom of Greece might take place in the Athenians' own
9 territory. This magnanimous gesture of the Plataeans brought them such widespread renown that, even at a much later date, when Alexander had just made himself king of Asia, he fortified Plataea and had a herald proclaim at the Olympic Games, "Whereas the Plataeans, at the time of the Persian War, consigned their territory to the Greeks and exhibited utmost devotion, the king hereby rewards them for their heroism and unselfishness."

12. The Tegeans began a quarrel with the Athenians concerning the disposition of troops. They expatiated at length regarding the virtues of their ancestors and claimed that they should occupy the left wing, as they regularly did when the Lacedaemonians occupied the right. At this the Athenians were indignant, and Aristeides came forward to speak.
2 "As to the Tegeans," he said, "the present crisis does not allow us to debate matters of valor and pedigree with them. But to you, men of Sparta, and to the rest of the Greeks we address ourselves: a position neither removes nor confers nobility. We shall strive to fill honorably and defend whatever post you assign us, nor will we bring dishonor upon our previous
3 campaigns. We are here not to vie with our allies but to face the enemy, not to extol our forefathers but to prove ourselves in the service of Greece. For you can be sure that this contest will display to the Greeks the worth of each state,
4 each captain, each citizen." When they heard these words, the commanders and the members of the council endorsed the claims of the Athenians, and assigned them the other wing.

13. Οὔσης δὲ μετεώρου τῆς Ἑλλάδος, καὶ μάλιστα τοῖς Ἀθηναίοις τῶν
πραγμάτων ἐπισφαλῶς ἐχόντων, ἄνδρες ἐξ οἴκων ἐπιφανῶν καὶ χρημάτων μεγάλων πένητες ὑπὸ τοῦ πολέμου γεγονότες, καὶ πᾶσαν ἅμα τῷ
πλούτῳ τὴν ἐν τῇ πόλει δύναμιν αὐτῶν καὶ δόξαν οἰχομένην ὁρῶντες,
ἑτέρων τιμωμένων καὶ ἀρχόντων, συνῆλθον εἰς οἰκίαν τινὰ τῶν ἐν Πλαταιαῖς κρύφα καὶ συνωμόσαντο καταλύσειν τὸν δῆμον· εἰ δὲ μὴ προχω-
2 ροίη, λυμανεῖσθαι τὰ πράγματα καὶ τοῖς βαρβάροις προδώσειν. πραττομένων δὲ τούτων ἐν τῷ στρατοπέδῳ, καὶ συχνῶν ἤδη διεφθαρμένων,
αἰσθόμενος ὁ Ἀριστείδης καὶ φοβηθεὶς τὸν καιρόν, ἔγνω μήτ' ἐᾶν ἀμε-
λούμενον τὸ πρᾶγμα μήθ' ἅπαν ἐκκαλύπτειν, ἀγνοούμενον εἰς ὅσον
ἐκβήσεται πλῆθος ὁ ἔλεγχος τὸν τοῦ δικαίου ζητῶν ὅρον ἀντὶ τοῦ συμ-
3 φέροντος. ὀκτὼ δή τινας ἐκ πολλῶν συνέλαβε, καὶ τούτων δύο μέν, οἷς
πρώτοις ἡ κρίσις προεγράφη [οἳ] καὶ πλείστην αἰτίαν εἶχον, Αἰσχίνης
Λαμπτρεὺς καὶ Ἀγασίας Ἀχαρνεύς, ᾤχοντο φεύγοντες ἐκ τοῦ στρατο-
πέδου· τοὺς δ' ἄλλους ἀφῆκε, θαρρῆσαι διδοὺς καὶ μεταγνῶναι τοῖς ἔτι
λανθάνειν οἰομένοις, ὑπειπὼν ὡς μέγα δικαστήριον ἔχουσι τὸν πόλεμον
ἀπολύσασθαι τὰς αἰτίας ὀρθῶς καὶ δικαίως τῇ πατρίδι βουλευόμενοι.

14. Μετὰ ταῦτα Μαρδόνιος, ᾧ πλεῖστον ἐδόκει διαφέρειν, τῶν Ἑλλήνων ἀπεπειρᾶτο, τὴν ἵππον ἀθρόαν αὐτοῖς ἐφεὶς καθεζομένοις ὑπὸ τὸν
πρόποδα τοῦ Κιθαιρῶνος ἐν χωρίοις ὀχυροῖς καὶ πετρώδεσι, πλὴν
2 Μεγαρέων. οὗτοι δὲ τρισχίλιοι τὸ πλῆθος ὄντες ἐν τοῖς ἐπιπέδοις μᾶλλον ἐστρατοπεδεύοντο. διὸ καὶ κακῶς ἔπασχον ὑπὸ τῆς ἵππου, ῥυείσης
3 ἐπ' αὐτοὺς καὶ προσβολὰς ἐχούσης πανταχόθεν. ἔπεμπον οὖν ἄγγελον
κατὰ τάχος πρὸς Παυσανίαν βοηθεῖν κελεύοντες, ὡς οὐ δυνάμενοι

13.2 ἀγνοούμενον UA: ἀγνοοῦντας S 13.3 οἳ del. Sansone| Λαμπτρεὺς Keil: Λαμπρεὺς SUA| Ἀγασίας S: Ἀγησίας UA 14.1 ᾧ S: ὃς UA

13. While Greece was in a state of turmoil, and the situation at Athens in particular was most unstable, some men of distinguished families who had lost great fortunes as a result of the war, realizing that all their political power and prestige had vanished along with their wealth, and that another group of men now held positions of respect and authority, held a clandestine meeting in a house at Plataea, where they entered into a conspiracy to overthrow the democratic government. If their plan did not succeed, they were prepared to
2 ruin the state and sell out to the Persians. Aristeides found out that these things were going on in the camp and that a number of men had already been led astray. He was alarmed by the seriousness of the situation and he resolved neither to overlook the matter nor to uncover it altogether, since it was unclear how many men the investigation would implicate if it pursued justice to the limit and did not stop
3 short at expediency. So he arrested a mere eight out of many. Two of them, Aeschines of Lamptrae and Agasias of Acharnae, whose indictments were the first to be made public and who bore the greatest responsibility, fled from camp and went into exile. Aristeides did not prosecute the rest. He wished to give those who were under the impression that they were still undetected the opportunity to rally and repent, and he suggested that the war represented a great tribunal where they could disprove their guilt if their intentions toward their fatherland were proper and honorable.

14. After this Mardonius put the Greeks to the test. He thought that his superiority lay most of all in his cavalry, so he launched it en masse against the Greeks who, with the exception of the Megarians, were occupying a secure and
2 rugged position beneath the foothills of Cithaeron. The Megarians, numbering three thousand, were encamped instead on the level ground, and for this reason were hard pressed by the cavalry, which streamed in upon them and
3 found avenues of attack on all sides. Inasmuch as they could not on their own withstand the strength of the enemy, they

4 καθ' αὑτοὺς ὑποστῆναι τὸ τῶν βαρβάρων πλῆθος. ταῦτα Παυσανίας
ἀκούων, ἤδη δὲ καὶ καθορῶν ἀποκεκρυμμένον ἀκοντισμάτων καὶ
τοξευμάτων πλήθει τὸ στρατόπεδον τῶν Μεγαρέων καὶ συνεσταλμέ-
νους αὐτοὺς εἰς ὀλίγον, αὐτὸς μὲν ἀμήχανος ἦν ἱππότας ἀμύνειν ὁπλι-
τικῇ φάλαγγι καὶ βαρείᾳ τῇ Σπαρτιατῶν, τοῖς δ' ἄλλοις στρατηγοῖς καὶ
λοχαγοῖς τῶν Ἑλλήνων περὶ αὐτὸν οὖσι προύθετο ζῆλον ἀρετῆς καὶ
φιλοτιμίας, εἰ δή τινες ἑκόντες ἀναδέξαιντο προαγωνίσασθαι καὶ βοη-
5 θῆσαι τοῖς Μεγαρεῦσι. τῶν δ' ἄλλων ὀκνούντων, Ἀριστείδης ἀναδεξά-
μενος ὑπὲρ τῶν Ἀθηναίων τὸ ἔργον, ἀποστέλλει τὸν προθυμότατον τῶν
λοχαγῶν Ὀλυμπιόδωρον, ἔχοντα τοὺς ὑπ' αὐτῷ τεταγμένους λογάδας
τριακοσίους καὶ τοξότας ἀναμεμειγμένους σὺν αὐτοῖς. τούτων ὀξέως
διασκευασαμένων καὶ προσφερομένων δρόμῳ, Μασίστιος ὁ τῶν βαρβάρων ἵππαρχος, ἀνὴρ ἀλκῇ τε θαυμαστὸς μεγέθει τε καὶ κάλλει σώματος περιττός, ὡς κατεῖδεν, ἐναντίον ἐπιστρέψας τὸν ἵππον εἰς αὐτοὺς
6 ἤλαυνε. τῶν δ' ἀνασχομένων καὶ συμβαλόντων, ἦν ἀγὼν καρτερός, ὡς
πεῖραν ἐν τούτῳ λαμβανόντων τοῦ παντός. ἐπεὶ δὲ τοξευθεὶς ὁ ἵππος
τὸν Μασίστιον ἀπέρριψε, καὶ πεσὼν ὑπὸ βάρους τῶν ὅπλων αὐτός τε
δυσκίνητος ἦν ἀναφέρειν καὶ τοῖς Ἀθηναίοις ἐπικειμένοις καὶ παίουσι
δυσμεταχείριστος, οὐ μόνον στέρνα καὶ κεφαλήν, ἀλλὰ καὶ τὰ γυῖα
χρυσῷ καὶ χαλκῷ καὶ σιδήρῳ καταπεφραγμένος, τοῦτον μὲν ᾗ τὸ κρά-
νος ὑπέφαινε τὸν ὀφθαλμὸν ἀκοντίου στύρακι παίων τις ἀνεῖλεν, οἱ δ'
7 ἄλλοι Πέρσαι προέμενοι τὸν νεκρὸν ἔφευγον. ἐγνώσθη δὲ τοῦ κατορ-
θώματος τὸ μέγεθος τοῖς Ἕλλησιν οὐκ ἀπὸ τῶν νεκρῶν τοῦ πλήθους
8 (ὀλίγοι γὰρ οἱ πεσόντες ἦσαν), ἀλλὰ τῷ πένθει τῶν βαρβάρων. καὶ γὰρ
ἑαυτοὺς ἔκειραν ἐπὶ τῷ Μασιστίῳ καὶ ἵππους καὶ ἡμιόνους, οἰμωγῆς τε
καὶ κλαυθμοῦ τὸ πεδίον ἐνεπίμπλασαν, ὡς ἄνδρα πολὺ πρῶτον ἀρετῇ

14.4 ἱππότας S: πρὸς ἱππότας UA

sent a messenger immediately to Pausanias and called for
4 him to come to their rescue. When he heard this, Pausanias
could already see that the Megarian camp was hidden from
sight by the great number of javelins and arrows, and that
the Megarians themselves were compressed in a small area.
While there was no way that he himself, with his slow phalanx of armored Spartans, could repulse cavalrymen, he
turned to the other Greek generals and captains standing
around him and laid down a challenge to their spirit of heroism and ambition, to see whether anyone might undertake
willingly to fight in the forefront and go to the aid of the
5 Megarians. While the others were hesitating, Aristeides undertook the mission in the name of the Athenians, and he
dispatched Olympiodorus, the most enterprising of the captains, along with the elite corps of three hundred men under
his command and some archers incorporated into their ranks.
Quickly these men equipped themselves and charged at a
run. When Masistius, the commander of the enemy cavalry
and a man of remarkable courage and exceptional physical
stature and grace, noticed them, he wheeled his horse to face
6 them and rode to the attack. They held their ground, however, and took on the enemy, whereupon a fierce struggle en-
sued, with everyone treating this as the decisive encounter of
the war. But Masistius' horse was struck by an arrow and
threw its rider. The weight of his armor made it difficult for
Masistius himself to recover from his fall and at the same
time frustrated the Athenians, who were pressing in upon
him and hacking at him, for not only his head and chest, but
also his limbs were encased in gold, bronze and silver. He
was dispatched, however, by someone who stabbed him in
the eye-hole of his helmet with the spike at the butt end of
his spear. At this, the rest of the Persians abandoned his
7 body and fled. The magnitude of their success was brought
home to the Greeks not by the number of the slain (for the
casualties were few), but by the mourning displayed by the
8 enemy. For in honor of Masistius they cut short not only
their own hair but that of their horses and mules, and the
plain rang out with their wailing and lamentation, making it

καὶ δυνάμει μετά γε Μαρδόνιον αὐτὸν ἀποβαλόντες.

15. Μετὰ δὲ τὴν ἱππομαχίαν ἀμφότεροι μάχης ἔσχοντο χρόνον πο-
λύν· ἀμυνομένοις γὰρ οἱ μάντεις νίκην προὔφαινον ἐκ τῶν ἱερῶν ὁμοίως
2 καὶ τοῖς Πέρσαις καὶ τοῖς Ἕλλησιν, εἰ δ' ἐπιχειροῖεν, ἧτταν. ἔπειτα
Μαρδόνιος, ὡς αὐτῷ μὲν ἡμερῶν ὀλίγων τὰ ἐπιτήδεια περιῆν, οἱ δ'
Ἕλληνες ἀεί τινων ἐπιρρεόντων πλείονες ἐγίγνοντο, δυσανασχετῶν ἔγνω
μηκέτι μένειν, ἀλλὰ διαβὰς ἅμα φάει τὸν Ἀσωπὸν ἐπιθέσθαι τοῖς Ἕλλησιν ἀπροσδοκήτως, καὶ παράγγελμα τοῖς ἡγεμόσιν ἑσπέρας ἔδωκε.
3 μεσούσης δὲ μάλιστα τῆς νυκτὸς ἀνὴρ ἵππον ἔχων ἀτρέμα προσεμεί-
γνυε τῷ στρατοπέδῳ τῶν Ἑλλήνων, ἐντυχὼν δὲ ταῖς φυλακαῖς, ἐκέλευεν
αὐτῷ προσελθεῖν Ἀριστείδην τὸν Ἀθηναῖον. ὑπακούσαντος δὲ ταχέως,
ἔφησεν· 'εἰμὶ μὲν Ἀλέξανδρος ὁ Μακεδόνων βασιλεύς, ἥκω δὲ κινδύνων
τὸν μέγιστον εὐνοίᾳ τῇ πρὸς ὑμᾶς αἰρόμενος, ὡς μὴ τὸ αἰφνίδιον ἐκπλή-
4 ξειεν ὑμᾶς χεῖρον ἀγωνίσασθαι. μαχεῖται γὰρ ὑμῖν Μαρδόνιος αὔριον,
οὐχ ὑπ' ἐλπίδος χρηστῆς οὐδὲ θάρσους, ἀλλ' ἀπορίας τῶν παρόντων,
ἐπεὶ καὶ μάντεις ἐκεῖνον ἀπαισίοις ἱεροῖς καὶ λογίοις χρησμῶν εἴργουσι
μάχης, καὶ τὸν στρατὸν ἔχει δυσθυμία πολλὴ καὶ κατάπληξις. ἀλλ'
ἀνάγκη τολμῶντα πειρᾶσθαι τῆς τύχης ἢ τὴν ἐσχάτην ὑπομένειν ἀπο-
5 ρίαν καθεζόμενον.' ταῦτα φράσας ὁ Ἀλέξανδρος ἐδεῖτο τὸν Ἀριστείδην αὐτὸν εἰδέναι καὶ μνημονεύειν, ἑτέρῳ δὲ μὴ κατειπεῖν. ὁ δ' οὐ καλῶς ἔχειν ἔφη ταῦτα Παυσανίαν ἀποκρύψασθαι· ἐκείνῳ γὰρ ἀνακεῖ-
σθαι τὴν ἡγεμονίαν· πρὸς δὲ τοὺς ἄλλους ἄρρητα πρὸ τῆς μάχης [ἔδο-
ξεν] ἔσεσθαι, νικώσης δὲ τῆς Ἑλλάδος οὐδένα τὴν Ἀλεξάνδρου προ-
6 θυμίαν καὶ ἀρετὴν ἀγνοήσειν. λεχθέντων δὲ τούτων ὅ τε βασιλεὺς τῶν

15.3 δὲ κινδύνων τὸν μέγιστον UA: δὲ ἐκ κινδύνων τῶν μεγίστων S
15.4 ἀλλ' ἀνάγκη UA: τὰ πολλὰ ἀνάγκη S 15.5 ἔδοξεν del. Blass

clear that the man they had lost was, with the exception of Mardonius himself, by far the foremost in valor and strength.

15. After the cavalry battle, both sides refused for a long
time to initiate an engagement for, as a result of the sacrifices, the prophets kept promising the Persians and the
Greeks alike that they would be victorious if they remained
on the defensive and that they would suffer defeat if they
2 acted as the aggressor. But then Mardonius, realizing that his
supplies would hold out only for a few days and that the
Greeks' numbers were increasing as fresh troops were constantly streaming in, could not restrain himself and he determined not to wait any longer. Instead, he would cross the
Asopus at daybreak and fall upon the Greeks without warning. And so, during the evening, he gave orders to his offi-
3 cers. Just about midnight, however, a man on horseback approached the Greek camp without making a sound and, when
he encountered the sentinels, he requested that Aristeides
the Athenian come to him. Aristeides promptly complied,
and the man said, "I am Alexander, king of the Macedonians.
Out of sympathy with your cause I have exposed myself to
the utmost danger and have come to insure that the unex-
pected not cause you to fight at a disadvantage by throwing
4 your troops into disarray. Tomorrow Mardonius will fight
you. This is not because of any hope of success or confidence,
but out of frustration at his present situation. For prophets
are restraining him too, saying that sacrifices and oracles are
unfavorable for battle, and considerable despondency and
consternation prevail over the army. But he is forced either
to steel himself and make trial of his fate, or to sit still and
5 suffer extreme privation." When he finished, Alexander
begged Aristeides to bear his words in mind, but to keep
them to himself and not reveal them to anyone else. But
Aristeides said that it was not right to keep this from Pausanias, since the command lay with him. As far as the others
were concerned, however, he would tell them nothing before
the battle but, if the Greeks were victorious, everyone would
6 learn of Alexander's unselfishness and valor. When their

Μακεδόνων ἀπήλαυνεν ὀπίσω πάλιν, ὅ τ' Ἀριστείδης ἀφικόμενος ἐπὶ τὴν σκηνὴν τοῦ Παυσανίου διηγεῖτο τοὺς λόγους, καὶ μετεπέμποντο τοὺς ἄλλους ἡγεμόνας καὶ παρήγγελλον ἐν κόσμῳ τὸν στρατὸν ἔχειν, ὡς μάχης ἐσομένης.

16. Ἐν τούτῳ δ', ὡς Ἡρόδοτος ἱστορεῖ, Παυσανίας Ἀριστείδῃ προσέ-
φερε λόγον, ἀξιῶν τοὺς Ἀθηναίους ἐπὶ τὸ δεξιὸν μεταγαγόντα κατὰ
τοὺς Πέρσας ἀντιταχθῆναι, βέλτιον γὰρ ἀγωνιεῖσθαι τῆς τε μάχης ἐμ-
πείρους γεγονότας καὶ τῷ προνενικηκέναι θαρροῦντας, αὐτῷ δὲ παρα-
δοῦναι τὸ εὐώνυμον, ὅπου τῶν Ἑλλήνων οἱ μηδίζοντες ἐπιβάλλειν
2 ἔμελλον. οἱ μὲν οὖν ἄλλοι στρατηγοὶ τῶν Ἀθηναίων ἀγνώμονα καὶ
φορτικὸν ἡγοῦντο τὸν Παυσανίαν, εἰ τὴν ἄλλην ἐῶν τάξιν ἐν χώρᾳ
μόνους ἄνω καὶ κάτω μεταφέρει σφᾶς ὥσπερ εἵλωτας, κατὰ τὸ μαχιμώ-
3 τατον προβαλλόμενος· ὁ δ' Ἀριστείδης διαμαρτάνειν αὐτοὺς ἔφασκε
τοῦ παντός, εἰ πρῴην μὲν ὑπὲρ τοῦ τὸ εὐώνυμον κέρας ἔχειν διεφιλο-
τιμοῦντο Τεγεάταις καὶ προκριθέντες ἐσεμνύνοντο, νῦν δὲ Λακεδαιμονίων ἑκουσίως ἐξισταμένων αὐτοῖς τοῦ δεξιοῦ καὶ τρόπον τινὰ τὴν
ἡγεμονίαν παραδιδόντων, οὔτε τὴν δόξαν ἀγαπῶσιν, οὔτε κέρδος
ἡγοῦνται τὸ μὴ πρὸς ὁμοφύλους καὶ συγγενεῖς, ἀλλὰ βαρβάρους φύσει
4 πολεμίους ἀγωνίσασθαι. ἐκ τούτου πάνυ προθύμως οἱ Ἀθηναῖοι διη-
μείβοντο τοῖς Σπαρτιάταις τὴν τάξιν, καὶ λόγος ἐχώρει δι' αὐτῶν πολὺς
ἀλλήλοις παρεγγυώντων, ὡς οὔθ' ὅπλα βελτίω λαβόντες οὔτε ψυχὰς
ἀμείνους οἱ πολέμιοι τῶν ἐν Μαραθῶνι προσίασιν, ἀλλὰ τὰ αὐτὰ μὲν
ἐκείνοις τόξα, τὰ αὐτὰ δ' ἐσθῆτος ποικίλματα καὶ χρυσὸς ἐπὶ σώμασι
5 μαλακοῖς καὶ ψυχαῖς ἀνάνδροις. ἡμῖν δ' ὅπλα μὲν ὅμοια καὶ σώματα,
μεῖζον δὲ ταῖς νίκαις τὸ θάρσος· ὁ δ' ἀγὼν οὐχ ὑπὲρ χώρας καὶ πόλεως

16.2 ἀγνώμονα S: πολυπράγμονα UA 16.3 φύσει S: καὶ φύσει UA

conversation ended, the king of the Macedonians rode off again and Aristeides went to Pausanias' tent and told him what Alexander had said. Then they summoned the other commanders and gave orders that the army be kept in good array, since a battle was imminent.

16. At this point, according to Herodotus, Pausanias made a proposal to Aristeides. He thought that, inasmuch as the Athenians were likely to put up a better fight, since they were experienced in combat and their spirits were buoyed by the fact of their earlier success, Aristeides should move them to the right wing and station them opposite the Persian position. Further, Aristeides was to hand over to him the left wing, where those of the Greeks who had joined forces with
2 the enemy were going to attack. Now the other Athenian generals thought it crass and inconsiderate of Pausanias to leave the rest of the formation in place while he singled them out and, treating them as though they were helots, shifted them up and down and placed them where they would bear
3 the brunt of the attack. But Aristeides said that they were completely mistaken. Why, just the other day they were engaged in an all-out fight with the Tegeans for the honor of occupying the left wing and were pretty proud of themselves when they were chosen. And now here were the Lacedaemonians voluntarily relinquishing the right wing and practically handing over the command to them, and they neither welcomed the honor nor realized that it was all to the good to fight, not against kinsfolk and brothers, but against their
4 natural enemy, the barbarians. After this the Athenians were quite eager to change places with the Spartans in the line of battle, and throughout the ranks words of encouragement circulated in abundance. "The enemy are approaching," they said, "having no better equipment than at Marathon and no firmer spirits. Instead, they have the same bows and arrows as before, the same embroidered trappings and gold to
5 cloak delicate bodies and unmanly hearts. But we, while our equipment and our bodies are the same, have greater confidence as a result of our victories. Nor are we fighting, as we

μόνον ὡς ἐκείνοις, ἀλλ' ὑπὲρ τῶν ἐν Μαραθῶνι καὶ Σαλαμῖνι τροπαίων,
6 ὡς μηδ' ἐκεῖνα Μιλτιάδου δοκῇ καὶ τύχης, ἀλλ' Ἀθηναίων. οὗτοι μὲν
οὖν σπεύδοντες ἐν ἀμείψει τῶν τάξεων ἦσαν· αἰσθόμενοι δὲ Θηβαῖοι
παρ' αὐτομόλων, Μαρδονίῳ φράζουσι, κἀκεῖνος εὐθύς, εἴτε δεδιὼς τοὺς
Ἀθηναίους εἴτε τοῖς Λακεδαιμονίοις συμπεσεῖν φιλοτιμούμενος, ἀντι-
παρεξῆγε τοὺς Πέρσας ἐπὶ τὸ δεξιόν, τοὺς δ' Ἕλληνας ἐκέλευε τοὺς σὺν
7 αὐτῷ κατὰ τοὺς Ἀθηναίους ἵστασθαι. γενομένης δὲ τῆς μετακοσμή-
σεως καταφανοῦς, ὅ τε Παυσανίας ἀποτραπεὶς αὖθις ἐπὶ τοῦ δεξιοῦ
κατέστη, καὶ Μαρδόνιος, ὥσπερ εἶχεν ἐξ ἀρχῆς, ἀνέλαβε τὸ εὐώνυμον
8 κατὰ τοὺς Λακεδαιμονίους γενόμενος, ἥ θ' ἡμέρα διεξῆλθεν ἀργή, καὶ
τοῖς Ἕλλησι βουλευομένοις ἔδοξε πορρωτέρω μεταστρατοπεδεῦσαι καὶ
καταλαβεῖν εὔυδρον χωρίον, ἐπεὶ τὰ πλησίον νάματα καθύβριστο καὶ
διέφθαρτο τῶν βαρβάρων ἱπποκρατούντων.

17. Ἐπελθούσης δὲ νυκτὸς καὶ τῶν στρατηγῶν ἀγόντων ἐπὶ τὴν ἀπο-
δεδειγμένην στρατοπεδείαν, οὐ πάνυ πρόθυμον ἦν ἕπεσθαι καὶ συμμέ-
νειν τὸ πλῆθος, ἀλλ' ὡς ἀνέστησαν ἐκ τῶν πρώτων ἐρυμάτων, ἐφέροντο
πρὸς τὴν πόλιν τῶν Πλαταιέων οἱ πολλοί, καὶ θόρυβος ἦν ἐκεῖ δια-
σκιδναμένων καὶ κατασκηνούντων ἀτάκτως. Λακεδαιμονίοις δὲ συν-
2 έβαινεν ἄκουσι μόνοις ἀπολείπεσθαι τῶν ἄλλων· Ἀμομφάρετος γάρ,
ἀνὴρ θυμοειδὴς καὶ φιλοκίνδυνος, ἔκπαλαι πρὸς τὴν μάχην σπαργῶν
καὶ βαρυνόμενος τὰς πολλὰς ἀναβολὰς καὶ μελλήσεις, τότε δὴ παντάπασι τὴν μετανάστασιν φυγὴν ἀποκαλῶν καὶ ἀπόδρασιν, οὐκ ἔφη
λείψειν τὴν τάξιν, ἀλλ' αὐτόθι μένων μετὰ τῶν αὐτοῦ λοχιτῶν ὑποστή-
3 σεσθαι Μαρδόνιον. ὡς δὲ Παυσανίας ἐπελθὼν ἔλεγε ταῦτα πράττειν
ἐψηφισμένα καὶ δεδογμένα τοῖς Ἕλλησιν, ἀράμενος ταῖν χεροῖν πέτρον

16.7 ἀνέλαβε UA: εὐθὺς ἀνέλαβε S 16.8 εὔυδρον S: ἔνυδρον UA
17.1 συνέβαινεν Sintenis: συνέβη μὲν SUA| ἄκουσι μόνοις UA:
ἄκουσιν S

did then, merely for the sake of our land and our city, but for the sake of the trophies at Marathon and Salamis, to prove that they were the product, not of Miltiades and good for-
6 tune, but of the Athenians." Now, while these were hastening to change their position in the line, the Thebans found out about it from some deserters and told Mardonius. Immediately he, whether out of fear of the Athenians or because he nourished the ambition of pitting himself against the Lacedaemonians, countered by leading out his Persians to the right wing to face them, and he ordered those Greeks who were fighting on his side to stand and face the Athenians.
7 When it became clear that this change of disposition had been made, Pausanias did an about-face and once again took up his position on the right wing, while Mardonius resumed his original position on the left facing the Lacedaemonians.
8 So the day passed without an engagement. The Greeks meanwhile took counsel and decided to move their camp a bit further on and to take possession of an area that was well furnished with fresh water, since the nearby springs were contaminated and ruined by the enemy and their superior cavalry.

17. When night came on the generals led the way to the site that had been fixed on for the camp, but the men in the ranks did not exactly prove eager to keep together and follow along. Instead, once they had left the defenses of their earlier position, the majority rushed off toward the town of Plataea, creating turmoil there as they dispersed and pitched their tents wherever they wished. It turned out also that the Lacedaemonians were unwillingly being left behind by them-
2 selves. For Amompharetus, a mettlesome, defiant man who had all along been seething with eagerness for the fray and irritated by the numerous postponements and delays, this time had had enough. He absolutely denounced the move as retreat and desertion, and he refused to leave his position. Instead, he would stay right there with his company and
3 await Mardonius' attack. When Pausanias came up and tried to explain that this action had been decided by vote of the

μέγαν ὁ Ἀμομφάρετος καὶ καταβαλὼν πρὸ τῶν ποδῶν τοῦ Παυσανίου,
ταύτην ἔφη ψῆφον αὐτὸς περὶ τῆς μάχης τίθεσθαι, τὰ δὲ τῶν ἄλλων
4 δειλὰ βουλεύματα καὶ δόγματα χαίρειν ἐᾶν. ἀπορούμενος δὲ Παυσανίας τῷ παρόντι, πρὸς μὲν τοὺς Ἀθηναίους ἔπεμψεν ἀπιόντας ἤδη,
περιμεῖναι δεόμενος καὶ κοινῇ βαδίζειν, αὐτὸς δὲ τὴν ἄλλην δύναμιν ἦγε
5 πρὸς τὰς Πλαταιὰς ὡς ἀναστήσων τὸν Ἀμομφάρετον. ἐν τούτῳ δὲ κατ-
ελάμβανεν ἡμέρα, καὶ Μαρδόνιος (οὐ γὰρ ἔλαθον τὴν στρατοπεδείαν
ἐκλελοιπότες οἱ Ἕλληνες) ἔχων συντεταγμένην τὴν δύναμιν ἐπεφέρετο
τοῖς Λακεδαιμονίοις βοῇ πολλῇ καὶ πατάγῳ τῶν βαρβάρων, ὡς οὐ
μάχης γενησομένης, ἀλλὰ φεύγοντας ἀναρπασομένων τοὺς Ἕλληνας.
6 ὃ μικρᾶς ῥοπῆς ἐδέησε γενέσθαι. κατιδὼν γὰρ τὸ γιγνόμενον ὁ Παυσανίας, ἔσχετο μὲν τῆς πορείας καὶ τὴν ἐπὶ μάχῃ τάξιν ἐκέλευσε λαμβά-
νειν ἕκαστον, ἔλαθε δ' αὐτόν, εἴθ' ὑπὸ τῆς πρὸς τὸν Ἀμομφάρετον ὀργῆς
εἴτε τῷ τάχει θορυβηθέντα τῶν πολεμίων, σύνθημα δοῦναι τοῖς Ἕλλη-
7 σιν. ὅθεν οὔτ' εὐθὺς οὔτ' ἀθρόοι, κατ' ὀλίγους δὲ καὶ σποράδην, ἤδη
τῆς μάχης ἐν χερσὶν οὔσης, προσεβοήθουν. ὡς δὲ θυόμενος οὐκ ἐκαλ-
λιέρει, προσέταξε τοῖς Λακεδαιμονίοις τὰς ἀσπίδας πρὸ τῶν ποδῶν
θεμένους ἀτρέμα καθέζεσθαι καὶ προσέχειν αὐτῷ, μηδένα τῶν πολεμί-
8 ων ἀμυνομένους, αὐτὸς δὲ πάλιν ἐσφαγιάζετο. καὶ προσέπιπτον οἱ
ἱππεῖς, ἤδη δὲ καὶ βέλος ἐξικνεῖτο καί τις ἐπέπληκτο τῶν Σπαρτιατῶν. ἐν
τούτῳ δὲ καὶ Καλλικράτης, ὃν ἰδέᾳ τε κάλλιστον Ἑλλήνων καὶ σώματι
μέγιστον ἐν ἐκείνῳ τῷ στρατῷ γενέσθαι λέγουσι, τοξευθεὶς καὶ θνῄσκων
οὐκ ἔφη τὸν θάνατον ὀδύρεσθαι, καὶ γὰρ ἐλθεῖν οἴκοθεν ὑπὲρ τῆς Ἑλ-
9 λάδος ἀποθανούμενος, ἀλλ' ὅτι θνῄσκει τῇ χειρὶ μὴ χρησάμενος. ἦν
οὖν τὸ μὲν πάθος δεινόν, ἡ δ' ἐγκράτεια θαυμαστὴ τῶν ἀνδρῶν. οὐ γὰρ

17.4 ἀπιόντας UA: ἀπόντας S 17.6 δοῦναι UA: μὴ δοῦναι S 17.8 ἀποθανούμενος Bryan: ἀποθανούμενον SUA

Greeks, Amompharetus picked up a huge rock in both his
hands and flung it down at Pausanias' feet. "Here," he said,
"is my ballot for war. I don't give a damn about the others'
gutless deliberations and decisions." Pausanias did not know
how to deal with the situation that confronted him. First he
sent a message to the Athenians, who were already moving
off, begging them to wait and march with him. Then he led
the rest of his forces in person toward Plataea, thinking that
this would cause Amompharetus to move. While this was
happening, day dawned and Mardonius became aware that
the Greeks had abandoned their camp. So he marshaled his
forces and attacked the Lacedaemonians with a great shouting and clashing of arms on the part of the Persians, who
thought that, instead of having to fight, they would merely
sweep up the Greeks as they fled. And this is very nearly
what in fact occurred. For, when Pausanias noticed what was
happening, though he halted his march and gave the order
that his men should take up battle positions, he forgot, either
by reason of his anger toward Amompharetus or because he
was confused by the suddenness of the enemy's attack, to
7 give a battle-signal to the Greeks. (For this reason they did
not immediately come to his assistance, nor did they come in
a body; rather they came in small groups and at intervals,
after the battle had already been joined.) Then, since he was
not able to obtain favorable omens when he sacrificed, he ordered the Lacedaemonians to place their shields on the
ground in front of them and sit still. They were not to retaliate against a single enemy soldier, but were to await his or-
8 ders while he attempted a second sacrifice. The cavalry were
actually charging, and already missiles were reaching them
and here and there a Spartan soldier was struck. In the
midst of all this Callicrates, said to have been the tallest and
most handsome man at that time in the Greek army, was hit
by an arrow. As he died he said that he did not grieve over
his death (for he had left home precisely that he might lay
down his life on behalf of Greece), but over the fact that he
9 was dying without having struck a blow. In short, the self-
control of those men, in spite of their awful situation, was

ἠμύνοντο τοὺς πολεμίους ἐπιβαίνοντας, ἀλλὰ τὸν παρὰ τοῦ θεοῦ κα
τοῦ στρατηγοῦ καιρὸν ἀναμένοντες, ἠνείχοντο βαλλόμενοι καὶ πί
πτοντες ἐν ταῖς τάξεσιν. ἔνιοι δέ φασι τῷ Παυσανίᾳ μικρὸν ἔξω τῆ
παρατάξεως θύοντι καὶ κατευχομένῳ τῶν Λυδῶν τινας ἄφνω προσπε
σόντας ἁρπάζειν καὶ διαρρίπτειν τὰ περὶ τὴν θυσίαν, τὸν δὲ Παυσανία
καὶ τοὺς περὶ αὐτὸν οὐκ ἔχοντας ὅπλα ῥάβδοις καὶ μάστιξι παίειν· διὸ
καὶ νῦν ἐκείνης τῆς ἐπιδρομῆς μίμημα τὰς περὶ τὸν βωμὸν ἐν Σπάρτῃ
πληγὰς τῶν ἐφήβων καὶ τὴν μετὰ ταῦτα Λυδῶν πομπὴν συντελεῖσθαι.

18. Δυσφορῶν οὖν ὁ Παυσανίας τοῖς παροῦσιν, ἄλλα τοῦ μάντεως ἐπ'
ἄλλοις ἱερεῖα καταβάλλοντος, τρέπεται πρὸς τὸ Ἡραῖον τῇ ὄψει δεδα-
κρυμένος, καὶ τὰς χεῖρας ἀνασχὼν εὔξατο Κιθαιρωνίᾳ ⟨θ'⟩ Ἥρᾳ καὶ
θεοῖς ἄλλοις οἳ Πλαταιίδα γῆν ἔχουσιν, εἰ μὴ πέπρωται τοῖς Ἕλλησι
νικᾶν, ἀλλὰ δράσαντάς γέ τι παθεῖν καὶ δείξαντας ἔργῳ τοῖς πολεμίοις,
ὡς ἐπ' ἄνδρας ἀγαθοὺς καὶ μάχεσθαι μεμαθηκότας ἐστράτευσαν.
2 ταῦτα τοῦ Παυσανίου θεοκλυτοῦντος, ἅμα ταῖς εὐχαῖς ἐφάνη τὰ ἱερὰ
καὶ νίκην ὁ μάντις ἔφραζε, καὶ δοθέντος εἰς ἅπαντας τοῦ παραγγέλ-
ματος καθίστασθαι πρὸς τοὺς πολεμίους ἥ τε φάλαγξ ὄψιν ἔσχεν αἰφνι-
δίως ἑνὸς ζῴου θυμοειδοῦς πρὸς ἀλκὴν τρεπομένου καὶ φρίξαντος, τοῖς
τε βαρβάροις τότε παρέστη λογισμός, ὡς πρὸς ἄνδρας αὐτοῖς ὁ ἀγὼν
3 ἔσοιτο μαχουμένους ἄχρι θανάτου. διὸ καὶ πολλὰ προθέμενοι τῶν
γέρρων ἐτόξευον εἰς τοὺς Λακεδαιμονίους, οἱ δὲ τηροῦντες ἅμα τὸν
συνασπισμὸν ἐπέβαινον, καὶ προσπεσόντες ἐξεώθουν τὰ γέρρα, καὶ τοῖς
δόρασι τύπτοντες πρόσωπα καὶ στέρνα τῶν Περσῶν πολλοὺς κατέβαλ-

18.1 θ' add. Sauppe 18.2 ὁ μάντις ἔφραζε S: οἱ μάντεις ἐμήνυον UA| ἔσοιτο UA: ἔσται S

astonishing. They offered no resistance to the enemy when
they attacked, but rather allowed themselves to be struck
and to fall where they stood in their ranks as they waited for
the signal from the gods and their general that the time was
0 right. According to some authorities, Pausanias was engaged
in sacrifice and prayer at a short distance from the line of
battle when a band of Lydians suddenly fell upon him and
began snatching up and scattering the sacrificial offerings.
Since Pausanias and the men with him had no weapons, they
used rods and whips to beat off the enemy. This is supposed
to be the reason that even today the beating of the ephebes
at the altar in Sparta and the procession of Lydians that follows it are celebrated, as a reenactment of that attack.

18. Pausanias was provoked by the circumstances in
which he found himself (for the seer was slaughtering one
sacrificial victim after another) and in tears he turned his
face toward the temple of Hera and, raising his hands to
heaven, prayed to Cithaeronian Hera and to the other gods
who watch over the Plataean land, "If the Greeks are not
destined to be victorious, at least before they perish let them
accomplish something and show the enemy by their deeds
that they have engaged with brave men who know how to
2 fight." Such was the appeal that Pausanias made to the gods.
At the very time he was making his prayer, the omens
proved favorable and the seer foretold victory. When the
general order was given to make a stand against the enemy,
the phalanx all of a sudden took on the appearance of a single, spirited creature, bristling and turning to defend itself.
At that point the enemy could not help thinking that they
were faced with a struggle against real men who were ready
3 to fight to the death, so they set up a large number of their
wicker-work shields in front of themselves and began
shooting arrows into the Lacedaemonian ranks. The latter
meanwhile advanced to the attack, all the time keeping their
formation together with their shields locked. Falling upon
the enemy they thrust aside their wicker-work shields and
set about striking them in the face and chest with their

4 λον, οὐκ ἀπράκτως οὐδ᾽ ἀθύμως πίπτοντας. καὶ γὰρ ἀντιλαμβανό
μενοι τῶν δοράτων ταῖς χερσὶ γυμναῖς συνέθραυον τὰ πλεῖστα, κα
πρὸς τὰς ξιφουλκίας ἐχώρουν οὐκ ἀργῶς, ταῖς τε κοπίσι καὶ τοῖς ἀκινά
καις χρώμενοι καὶ τὰς ἀσπίδας παρασπῶντες, καὶ συμπλεκόμενο
5 χρόνον πολὺν ἀντεῖχον. οἱ δ᾽ Ἀθηναῖοι τέως μὲν ἠτρέμουν ἀναμένον
τες τοὺς Λακεδαιμονίους, ἐπεὶ δὲ κραυγή τε προσέπιπτε πολλὴ μαχομέ
νων καὶ παρῆν ὥς φασιν ἄγγελος παρὰ Παυσανίου τὰ γιγνόμενο
6 φράζων, ὥρμησαν κατὰ τάχος βοηθεῖν, καὶ προχωροῦσιν αὐτοῖς διὰ
τοῦ πεδίου πρὸς τὴν βοὴν ἐπεφέροντο τῶν Ἑλλήνων οἱ μηδίζοντες.
Ἀριστείδης δὲ πρῶτον μὲν ὡς εἶδε, πολὺ προελθὼν ἐβόα, μαρτυρόμενος
Ἑλληνίους θεούς, ἔχεσθαι μάχης καὶ μὴ σφίσιν ἐμποδὼν εἶναι μηδὲ
κωλύειν ἐπαμύνοντας τοῖς προκινδυνεύουσιν ὑπὲρ τῆς Ἑλλάδος· ἐπεὶ δ
ἑώρα μὴ προσέχοντας αὐτῷ καὶ συντεταγμένους ἐπὶ μάχην, οὕτω τῆς
ἐκεῖ βοηθείας ἀποτραπόμενος συνέβαλλε τούτοις, περὶ πεντακισμυρί-
7 ους οὖσιν. ἀλλὰ τὸ μὲν πλεῖστον εὐθὺς ἐνέδωκε καὶ ἀπεχώρησεν, ἅτε
δὴ καὶ τῶν βαρβάρων ἀπηλλαγμένων, ἡ δὲ μάχη λέγεται μάλιστα κατὰ
Θηβαίους γενέσθαι, προθυμότατα τῶν πρώτων καὶ δυνατωτάτων τότε
παρ᾽ αὐτοῖς μηδιζόντων καὶ τὸ πλῆθος οὐ κατὰ γνώμην ἀλλ᾽ ὀλιγαρ-
χούμενον ἀγόντων.

19. Οὕτω δὲ τοῦ ἀγῶνος δίχα συνεστῶτος, πρῶτοι μὲν ἐώσαντο τοὺς Πέρσας οἱ Λακεδαιμόνιοι, καὶ τὸν Μαρδόνιον ἀνὴρ Σπαρτιάτης ὄνομα Ἀρίμνηστος ἀποκτίννυσι, λίθῳ τὴν κεφαλὴν πατάξας, ὥσπερ αὐτῷ

18.4 ταῖς τε S: ἀλλὰ ταῖς UA 18.6 ἔχεσθαι S: ἀπέχεσθαι UA| συνέβαλλε UA: συνέβαλε S 19.1 πρῶτοι S: πρῶτον UA| Ἀρίμνηστος UA (et sic pars codicum Herod. 9.64.2): διάπνηστος S: Ἀειμν- Aristodem. et alii codices Herodoti

spears, laying low a large number of Persians, who displayed
4 no lack of energy and spirit before they fell. For they would
lay hold of the spears with their bare hands and, after they
had broken most of them, would proceed actively to hand-to-
hand combat. They engaged and held out for quite some
time, pulling away the Greeks' shields and making use of
5 their own scimitars and short swords. As to the Athenians,
for a while they had kept still, waiting for the Lacedaemonians. But, when their ears were assailed by the cries of many
combatants and when (as is alleged to have happened) a
messenger arrived from Pausanias and reported what was
happening, they dashed off at full speed to bring assistance.
6 As they were advancing across the plain in the direction of
the shouting, those of the Greeks who had gone over to the
enemy began to rush down upon them. When Aristeides
caught sight of them, at first he went out far in advance and
called out to them, appealing to them in the name of the Gre-
cian gods to abstain from combat, and not to hinder them or
prevent them from coming to the aid of those who were laying their lives on the line for Greece. When he observed,
however, that they were not paying attention to him and
were ranged in battle-array, he abandoned the mission to assist the Lacedaemonians and turned his attention to engaging
with these men, who were approximately fifty thousand in
7 number. But the better part of them quickly gave in and
withdrew—after all, even the Persians were in retreat—and it
is reported that the struggle was primarily with the Thebans.
Now, among the Thebans at that time it was the most influential and powerful citizens who were especially fervent
supporters of the Persian cause; the populace at large followed along, not of their own accord, but because they were
governed by an oligarchic administration.

19. And thus it happened that the contest took place in two locations, with the Lacedaemonians being the first to drive back the Persians. Mardonius was killed by a Spartan man named Arimnestus, who struck him in the head with a stone. This was just as it had been foretold to him by the or-

2 προεσήμηνε τὸ Ἀμφιάρεω μαντεῖον. ἔπεμψε γὰρ ἄνδρα Λυδὸν ἐνταῦθα, Κᾶρα δ' ἕτερον εἰς τὸ Πτῷον ὁ Μαρδόνιος, καὶ τοῦτον μὲν ὁ προφήτης Καρικῇ γλώσσῃ προσεῖπεν, ὁ δὲ Λυδὸς ἐν τῷ σηκῷ τοῦ Ἀμφιάρεω κατευνασθεὶς ἔδοξεν ὑπηρέτην τινὰ τοῦ θεοῦ παραστῆναι καὶ κελεύειν αὐτὸν ἀπιέναι, μὴ βουλομένῳ δὲ λίθον εἰς τὴν κεφαλὴν ἐμβαλεῖν μέγαν, ὥστε δόξαι πληγέντα τεθνάναι τὸν ἄνθρωπον· καὶ ταῦτα μὲν οὕτω γε-
3 νέσθαι λέγεται. τοὺς δὲ φεύγοντας εἰς τὰ ξύλινα τείχη καθεῖρξαν. ὀλίγῳ δ' ὕστερον Ἀθηναῖοι τοὺς Θηβαίους τρέπονται, τριακοσίους τοὺς ἐπιφανεστάτους καὶ πρώτους διαφθείραντες ἐν αὐτῇ τῇ μάχῃ. γεγενημένης γὰρ τῆς τροπῆς ἧκεν αὐτοῖς ἄγγελος πολιορκεῖσθαι τὸ βαρβαρικὸν εἰς
4 τὰ τείχη κατακεκλειμένον. οὕτω δὴ σῴζεσθαι τοὺς Ἕλληνας ἐάσαντες ἐβοήθουν πρὸς τὰ τείχη, καὶ τοῖς Λακεδαιμονίοις παντάπασιν ἀργῶς πρὸς τειχομαχίαν καὶ ἀπείρως ἔχουσιν ἐπιφανέντες, αἱροῦσι τὸ στρατό-
5 πεδον φόνῳ πολλῷ τῶν πολεμίων. λέγονται γὰρ ἀπὸ τῶν τριάκοντα μυριάδων τετρακισμύριοι φυγεῖν σὺν Ἀρταβάζῳ, τῶν δ' ὑπὲρ τῆς Ἑλλάδος ἀγωνισαμένων ἔπεσον οἱ πάντες ἐπὶ χιλίοις ἑξήκοντα καὶ τριακό-
6 σιοι. τούτων Ἀθηναῖοι μὲν ἦσαν δύο καὶ πεντήκοντα, πάντες ἐκ τῆς Αἰαντίδος φυλῆς, ὥς φησι Κλείδημος, ἀγωνισαμένης ἄριστα (διὸ καὶ ταῖς Σφραγίτισι νύμφαις ἔθυον Αἰαντίδαι τὴν πυθόχρηστον θυσίαν ὑπὲρ τῆς νίκης, ἐκ δημοσίου τὸ ἀνάλωμα λαμβάνοντες), Λακεδαιμόνιοι δ' ἑνὶ
7 πλείους τῶν ἐνενήκοντα, Τεγεᾶται δ' ἑκκαίδεκα. θαυμαστὸν οὖν τὸ Ἡροδότου, πῶς μόνους τούτους φησὶν εἰς χεῖρας ἐλθεῖν τοῖς πολεμίοις, τῶν δ' ἄλλων Ἑλλήνων μηδένα. καὶ γὰρ τὸ πλῆθος τῶν πεσόντων καὶ τὰ μνήματα μαρτυρεῖ κοινὸν γενέσθαι τὸ κατόρθωμα, καὶ τὸν βωμὸν οὐκ ἂν ἐπέγραψαν οὕτως, εἰ μόναι τρεῖς πόλεις ἠγωνίσαντο, τῶν ἄλλων ἀτρέμα καθεζομένων·

19.2 τὸ Πτῷον S: Τροφωνίου UA| βουλομένῳ S: βουλομένου UA (cf. *mor.* 412a ἐπιμένοντος)

2 acle of Amphiaraus. For Mardonius had sent a Lydian man
there (he also sent a second man, a Carian, to the Ptoon
sanctuary, where the prophet addressed him in the Carian
language) and, when this Lydian lay down to sleep in the
precinct of Amphiaraus, he dreamed that one of the god's
attendants was standing beside him and ordering him to
leave. When he refused, the attendant hurled a great stone
at his head and, in his dream, the man was killed by the
blow. Well, this is what is reported to have occurred. At any
rate, the Lacedaemonians penned the routed Persians within
3 their wooden walls. Not long after, the Athenians put the
Thebans to flight, killing three hundred of the foremost citizens. This was during the engagement itself; once the tide
had turned in favor of the Athenians, a messenger came to
them to announce that the invading forces were shut up
4 within their walls and were under siege. And so they allowed the Greeks to save themselves, and they rushed toward the walls to provide support. The Lacedaemonians
were inexperienced in conducting siege operations and were
not proceeding with much industry, but the Athenians on
their arrival captured the encampment with much loss of en-
5 emy life. It is reported that 40,000 of the 300,000 escaped
with Artabazus, while the total number of those who fell
6 fighting for Greece was 1,360. Fifty-two of these were Athenians, all of them, according to Cleidemus, from the tribe
Aeantis, which especially distinguished itself in the fighting.
(This is why members of that tribe used to perform the vic-
tory-sacrifice to the Sphragitic Nymphs that was demanded
by the Delphic oracle, although the expense was borne by the
public treasury.) Ninety-one were Lacedaemonians and six-
7 teen Tegeans. One wonders, therefore, how Herodotus can
say that only these, and none of the other Greeks, engaged
with the enemy. The numbers of those who fell and their
monuments testify to the fact that the victory was indeed
shared by all. Furthermore, if only three states had been involved in the fighting while the rest sat around doing nothing, they could not have placed the following inscription on
the altar:

τόνδε ποθ' Ἕλληνες νίκας κράτει, ἔργῳ Ἄρηος,
Πέρσας ἐξελάσαντες ἐλευθέρᾳ Ἑλλάδι κοινὸν
ἱδρύσαντο Διὸς βωμὸν Ἐλευθερίου.

8 ταύτην τὴν μάχην ἐμαχέσαντο τῇ τρίτῃ τοῦ Βοηδρομιῶνος ἱσταμένου
κατ' Ἀθηναίους, κατὰ δὲ Βοιωτοὺς τετράδι τοῦ Πανήμου φθίνοντος, ᾗ
καὶ νῦν ἔτι τὸ Ἑλληνικὸν ἐν Πλαταιαῖς ἀθροίζεται συνέδριον καὶ θύ-
9 ουσι τῷ Ἐλευθερίῳ Διὶ Πλαταιεῖς ὑπὲρ τῆς νίκης. τὴν δὲ τῶν ἡμερῶν
ἀνωμαλίαν οὐ θαυμαστέον, ὅπου καὶ νῦν διηκριβωμένων τῶν ἐν
ἀστρολογίᾳ μᾶλλον ἄλλην ἄλλοι μηνὸς ἀρχὴν καὶ τελευτὴν ἄγουσιν.

20. Ἐκ τούτου τῶν Ἀθηναίων τὸ ἀριστεῖον οὐ παραδιδόντων τοῖς
Σπαρτιάταις οὐδὲ τρόπαιον ἱστάναι συγχωρούντων ἐκείνοις, παρ' οὐδὲν
ἂν ἦλθεν εὐθὺς ἀπολέσθαι τὰ πράγματα τῶν Ἑλλήνων ἐν τοῖς ὅπλοις
διαστάντων, εἰ μὴ πολλὰ παρηγορῶν καὶ διδάσκων τοὺς συστρατήγους
ὁ Ἀριστείδης, μάλιστα δὲ Λεωκράτη καὶ Μυρωνίδην, ἔσχε καὶ συνέπεισε
2 τὴν κρίσιν ἐφεῖναι τοῖς Ἕλλησιν. ἐνταῦθα βουλευομένων τῶν Ἑλλήνων
Θεογείτων μὲν ὁ Μεγαρεὺς εἶπεν, ὡς ἑτέρᾳ πόλει δοτέον εἴη τὸ ἀριστεῖον,
εἰ μὴ βούλονται συνταράξαι πόλεμον ἐμφύλιον· ἐπὶ τούτῳ δ' ἀναστὰς
Κλεόκριτος ὁ Κορίνθιος, δόξαν μὲν παρέσχεν ὡς Κορινθίοις αἰτήσων τὸ
ἀριστεῖον (ἦν γὰρ ἐν ἀξιώματι μεγίστῳ μετὰ τὴν Σπάρτην καὶ τὰς Ἀθήνας ἡ Κόρινθος), εἶπε δὲ πᾶσιν ἀρέσαντα καὶ θαυμαστὸν λόγον ὑπὲρ
Πλαταιέων, καὶ συνεβούλευσε τὴν φιλονικίαν ἀνελεῖν, ἐκείνοις τὸ ἀρι-
3 στεῖον ἀποδόντας, οἷς οὐδετέρους τιμωμένοις ἀχθέσεσθαι. ῥηθέντων δὲ
τούτων, πρῶτος μὲν Ἀριστείδης συνεχώρησεν ὑπὲρ τῶν Ἀθηναίων,
ἔπειτα Παυσανίας ὑπὲρ τῶν Λακεδαιμονίων. οὕτω δὲ διαλλαγέντες,
ἐξεῖλον ὀγδοήκοντα τάλαντα τοῖς Πλαταιεῦσιν, ἀφ' ὧν τὸ τῆς Ἀθηνᾶς

19.7 ἐλευθέρᾳ S: ἐλεύθερον UA 19.8 τρίτῃ] τετράδι SUA, sed cf. *Cam.* 19.5, *mor.* 349f 20.2 ἑτέρᾳ] οὐδετέρᾳ Muretl ἀχθέσεσθαι Sintenis: ἄχ(θ)εσθαι SUA

The Greeks by force of arms, the war god's travail,
repulsed the Persians and did prevail.
For Liberator Zeus this altar they did here prepare,
for all the liberated Greeks to share.

8 This battle was fought on the third day of Boedromion, according to the Athenian calendar. According to the Boeotian calendar, however, it was on the twenty-seventh of Panemus, and it is on this date that, even today, the Hellenic Council convenes at Plataea and sacrifice is offered by the Plataeans
9 to Zeus Eleutherius in honor of the victory. The discrepancy in the dates is not surprising when one considers that, even today, when the science of astronomy has advanced to a point of much greater accuracy, people cannot agree regarding the time at which a month begins or ends.

20. When, after this, the Athenians were unwilling to surrender the award of valor to the Spartans or even allow them the right to erect a trophy, the Greek nation might very well have divided itself into contending armed camps and perished then and there, had not Aristeides gone to great lengths to calm down his fellow generals and teach them a lesson. In particular he restrained Leocrates and Myronides, and he convinced them to refer the decision to the Greeks.
2 Then, while the Greeks were deliberating, Theogeiton of Megara proposed that, unless they wished to provoke civil war, the award should be given to a different state altogether. At this point Cleocritus of Corinth arose to speak. Everyone expected that he would claim that the Corinthians deserved the award, since Corinth had the greatest prestige after Sparta and Athens. But he surprised and satisfied everyone by delivering a speech in favor of the Plataeans. He advised that the contention be put to rest by granting the award to them, since neither of the contending parties would
3 feel offended if they were honored. When this proposal was made, first Aristeides expressed assent in the name of the Athenians, then Pausanias followed suit in the name of the Lacedaemonians. Once this reconciliation had been effected, they set aside the sum of eighty talents for the Plataeans,

ᾠκοδόμησαν ἱερὸν καὶ τὸ ἕδος ἔστησαν καὶ γραφαῖς τὸν νεὼν διεκό-
σμησαν, αἳ μέχρι νῦν ἀκμάζουσαι διαμένουσιν· ἔστησαν δὲ τρόπαιον
4 ἰδίᾳ μὲν Λακεδαιμόνιοι, χωρὶς δ' Ἀθηναῖοι. περὶ δὲ θυσίας ἐρομένοις
αὐτοῖς ἀνεῖλεν ὁ Πύθιος Διὸς Ἐλευθερίου βωμὸν ἱδρύσασθαι, θῦσαι δὲ
μὴ πρότερον ἢ τὸ κατὰ τὴν χώραν πῦρ ἀποσβέσαντας ὡς ὑπὸ τῶν
βαρβάρων μεμιασμένον ἐναύσασθαι καθαρὸν ἐκ Δελφῶν ἀπὸ τῆς
5 κοινῆς ἑστίας. οἱ μὲν οὖν ἄρχοντες τῶν Ἑλλήνων περιιόντες εὐθὺς
ἠνάγκαζον ἀποσβεννύναι τὰ πυρὰ πάντα τοὺς χρωμένους· εἷς δὲ
Πλαταιέων Εὐχίδας ὑποσχόμενος ὡς ἐνδέχεται τάχιστα κομιεῖν τὸ
παρὰ τοῦ θεοῦ πῦρ, ἧκεν εἰς Δελφούς, ἁγνίσας δὲ τὸ σῶμα καὶ περιρ-
ρανάμενος ἐστεφανώσατο δάφνῃ, καὶ λαβὼν ἀπὸ τοῦ βωμοῦ τὸ πῦρ,
δρόμῳ πάλιν εἰς τὰς Πλαταιὰς ἐχώρει καὶ πρὸ ἡλίου δυσμῶν ἐπανῆλθε,
6 τῆς αὐτῆς ἡμέρας χιλίους σταδίους κατανύσας. ἀσπασάμενος δὲ τοὺς
πολίτας καὶ τὸ πῦρ παραδούς, εὐθὺς ἔπεσε καὶ μετὰ μικρὸν ἐξέπνευσεν.
ἀγάμενοι δ' αὐτὸν οἱ Πλαταιεῖς ἔθαψαν ἐν τῷ ἱερῷ τῆς Εὐκλείας Ἀρτέ-
μιδος, ἐπιγράψαντες τὸ τετράμετρον τοῦτο·

Εὐχίδας Πυθῶδε θρέξας ⟨αὖτις⟩ ἦλθ' αὐθημερόν.

7 τὴν δ' Εὔκλειαν οἱ μὲν πολλοὶ καὶ καλοῦσι καὶ νομίζουσιν Ἄρτεμιν,
ἔνιοι δέ φασιν Ἡρακλέους μὲν θυγατέρα καὶ Μυρτοῦς γενέσθαι, τῆς
Μενοιτίου θυγατρός, Πατρόκλου δ' ἀδελφῆς, τελευτήσασαν δὲ παρθέ-
8 νον ἔχειν παρά τε Βοιωτοῖς καὶ Λοκροῖς τιμάς. βωμὸς γὰρ αὐτῇ καὶ
ἄγαλμα κατὰ πᾶσαν ἀγορὰν ἵδρυται, καὶ προθύουσιν αἵ τε γαμούμε-
ναι καὶ οἱ γαμοῦντες.

21. Ἐκ τούτου γενομένης ἐκκλησίας κοινῆς τῶν Ἑλλήνων, ἔγραψεν Ἀριστείδης ψήφισμα συνιέναι μὲν εἰς Πλαταιὰς καθ' ἕκαστον ἐνιαυτὸν ἀπὸ τῆς Ἑλλάδος προβούλους καὶ θεωρούς, ἄγεσθαι δὲ πενταετηρικὸν

20.3 ᾠκοδόμησαν UA: ἀνῳκοδόμησεν S 20.5 εἷς Schaefer: ἐκ SUA 20.6 ἀγάμενοι S: ἀράμενοι UAl ⟨αὖτις⟩ ἦλθ' Sansone: ἦλθε ⟨τᾷδ'⟩ Aldina: ἦλθε ⟨δεῦρ'⟩ Herwerden

and with these funds they built the sanctuary of Athena, set
up the statue of her and decorated her temple with paintings
which to this very day retain their freshness and vigor. The
Lacedaemonians erected their own trophy, and the Athenians
4 erected their own in a separate place. In response to their
inquiry regarding sacrifice, Pythian Apollo directed them to
set up an altar of Zeus Eleutherius, but not to make sacrifice
until they had extinguished all fire in the land (on the
grounds that it was contaminated by the foreigners) and had
borrowed untainted fire from the common hearth at Delphi.
5 The leaders of the Greeks immediately began going around
and requiring that all those who had fires lit extinguish them.
Meanwhile Euchidas, a Plataean, came to Delphi with a
promise that he would convey the sacred fire by the fastest
possible means. First he purified his body by sprinkling
himself with lustral water and he placed on his head a crown
of laurel. Then, taking the fire from the altar, he ran back to
Plataea and reached home before sunset, having covered a
6 distance of one thousand stades in one day. He gave greet-
ings to the citizens and handed over the fire. Thereupon he
collapsed and, after a while, expired. To honor him the
Plataeans buried him in the sanctuary of Artemis Eucleia and
set up the following inscription in trochaic meter:

Euchidas sped to Delphi, running all the way.
He came back here the selfsame day.

7 Now, as to this Eucleia, most people identify her with Artemis
and so call her. But there are some who claim that she was
the daughter of Heracles and Myrto (Myrto being the
daughter of Menoetius and the sister of Patroclus) and that,
after dying a virgin, she became an object of devotion among
8 the Boeotians and Locrians. In fact, an altar and a statue
stand in her honor in every market-place, and brides and
grooms make their preliminary sacrifices there.

21. After this, the Greeks held a general assembly, where Aristeides drafted a motion to the effect that delegates and envoys from the cities of Greece should convene once each year at Plataea, that every fourth year contests called the

2 ἀγῶνα τῶν Ἐλευθερίων, εἶναι δὲ σύνταξιν Ἑλληνικὴν μυρίας μὲν ἀσπίδας, χιλίους δ' ἵππους, ναῦς δ' ἑκατὸν ἐπὶ τὸν πρὸς τοὺς βαρβάρους
πόλεμον, Πλαταιεῖς δ' ἀσύλους καὶ ἱεροὺς ἀφίεσθαι τῷ θεῷ θύοντας
ὑπὲρ τῆς Ἑλλάδος. κυρωθέντων δὲ τούτων, οἱ Πλαταιεῖς ὑπεδέξαντο
τοῖς πεσοῦσι καὶ κειμένοις αὐτόθι τῶν Ἑλλήνων ἐναγίζειν καθ' ἕκαστον
3 ἐνιαυτόν. καὶ τοῦτο μέχρι νῦν δρῶσι τόνδε τὸν τρόπον· τοῦ Μαιμακτη-
ριῶνος μηνός, ὅς ἐστι παρὰ Βοιωτοῖς Ἀλαλκομένιος, τῇ ἕκτῃ ἐπὶ δέκα
πέμπουσι πομπήν, ἧς προηγεῖται μὲν ἅμ' ἡμέρᾳ σαλπιγκτὴς ἐγκελευό-
μενος τὸ πολεμικόν, ἕπονται δ' ἅμαξαι μυρρίνης μεσταὶ καὶ στεφανω-
μάτων καὶ μέλας ταῦρος καὶ χοὰς οἴνου καὶ γάλακτος ἐν ἀμφορεῦσιν
4 ἐλαίου τε καὶ μύρου κρωσσοὺς νεανίσκοι κομίζοντες ἐλεύθεροι (δούλῳ
γὰρ οὐδενὸς θέμις ἐστὶ τῶν περὶ τὴν διακονίαν ἐκείνην προσάψασθαι
διὰ τὸ τοὺς ἄνδρας ἀποθανεῖν ὑπὲρ ἐλευθερίας), ἐπὶ πᾶσι δὲ τῶν Πλαταιέων ὁ ἄρχων, ᾧ τὸν ἄλλον χρόνον οὔτε σιδήρου θιγεῖν ἔξεστιν οὔθ'
ἑτέραν ἐσθῆτα πλὴν λευκῆς ἀναλαβεῖν, τότε χιτῶνα φοινικοῦν ἐνδεδυ-
κώς, ἀράμενός θ' ὑδρίαν ἀπὸ τοῦ γραμματοφυλακίου ξιφήρης ἐπὶ τοὺς
5 τάφους προάγει διὰ μέσης τῆς πόλεως. εἶτα λαβὼν ὕδωρ ἀπὸ τῆς κρή-
νης αὐτὸς ἀπολούει τε τὰς στήλας καὶ μύρῳ χρίει, καὶ τὸν ταῦρον εἰς
τὴν πυρὰν σφάξας καὶ κατευξάμενος Διὶ καὶ Ἑρμῇ χθονίῳ, παρακαλεῖ
τοὺς ἀγαθοὺς ἄνδρας τοὺς ὑπὲρ τῆς Ἑλλάδος ἀποθανόντας ἐπὶ τὸ
6 δεῖπνον καὶ τὴν αἱμακουρίαν. ἔπειτα κρατῆρα κεράσας οἴνου καὶ
χεάμενος ἐπιλέγει, 'προπίνω τοῖς ἀνδράσι τοῖς ὑπὲρ τῆς ἐλευθερίας τῶν
Ἑλλήνων ἀποθανοῦσι.' ταῦτα μὲν οὖν ἔτι καὶ νῦν διαφυλάττουσιν οἱ
Πλαταιεῖς.

21.2-3 ἐναγίζειν καὶ καθ' ἕκαστον ἐνιαυτὸν ἔτι καὶ νῦν δρῶσι S
21.4 θέμις ἐστὶ S: ἔξεστι UA 21.5 αἱμακουρίαν Xylander:
αἱμ(αχ)οκουρίαν SUA

2 Eleutheria should be held, that there should be a levy to prosecute the war against the Persians, consisting of Greek forces in the amount of 10,000 infantry, 1,000 cavalry and 100 ships, and that the Plataeans should be exempted and should be regarded as sacred and inviolable so long as they perform the sacrifices to the god on behalf of the Greeks. This motion passed, and the Plataeans took it upon themselves to make annual offerings to those of the Greeks who
3 had fallen and were buried at the site of the battle. They continue to do this to this day, the manner of the rite being as follows. On the sixteenth of Maemacterion (which month is called Alalcomenius among the Boeotians) there is a procession that begins at daybreak, at the head of which is a trumpet player sounding the signal for attack. Behind him are wagons loaded with branches of myrtle and with wreaths, one black bull and young men bringing libations of wine and milk in jars and carrying pitchers of olive oil and
4 aromatics. (The young men are free-born, as it is not proper for a slave to become involved with any feature of this ritual, inasmuch as it was on behalf of freedom that the men had died.) Last of all is the archon of the Plataeans, to whom it is at other times forbidden to touch iron or to wear any but white clothing, but who dresses on that occasion in a purple tunic and carries a sword. He takes from the records office a water pitcher and wends his way through the middle of the
5 city to the place of burial. Then, with his own hands he washes off the tombstones with water from the fountain and he anoints them with aromatic oil, after which he slaughters the bull over the altar on which it is to be burned. Next, he makes prayer to Zeus and Hermes of the Underworld, and he summons those valiant men who died on behalf of Greece to
6 partake of the meal and the blood-offerings. Then he mixes a bowl of wine and pours it out as he recites the following words: "I hereby honor the men who died fighting for the freedom of the Greeks." This ritual is still observed by the Plataeans to this very day.

22. Ἐπεὶ δ' ἀναχωρήσαντας εἰς τὸ ἄστυ τοὺς Ἀθηναίους ὁ Ἀριστείδης
ἑώρα ζητοῦντας τὴν δημοκρατίαν ἀπολαβεῖν, ἅμα μὲν ἄξιον ἡγούμενος διὰ τὴν ἀνδραγαθίαν ἐπιμελείας τὸν δῆμον, ἅμα δ' οὐκέτι ῥᾴδιον
ἰσχύοντα τοῖς ὅπλοις καὶ μέγα φρονοῦντα ταῖς νίκαις ἐκβιασθῆναι,
γράφει ψήφισμα κοινὴν εἶναι τὴν πολιτείαν καὶ τοὺς ἄρχοντας ἐξ Ἀθη-
2 ναίων πάντων αἱρεῖσθαι. Θεμιστοκλέους δὲ πρὸς τὸν δῆμον εἰπόντος,
ὡς ἔχει τι βούλευμα καὶ γνώμην ἀπόρρητον, ὠφέλιμον δὲ τῇ πόλει καὶ
σωτήριον, ἐκέλευσαν Ἀριστείδην μόνον ἀκοῦσαι καὶ συνδοκιμάσαι.
3 φράσαντος δὲ τῷ Ἀριστείδῃ τοῦ Θεμιστοκλέους, ὡς διανοεῖται τὸ ναύσταθμον ἐμπρῆσαι τῶν Ἑλλήνων, οὕτω γὰρ ἔσεσθαι μεγίστους καὶ
κυρίους ἁπάντων τοὺς Ἀθηναίους, παρελθὼν εἰς τὸν δῆμον ὁ Ἀριστείδης ἔφη τῆς πράξεως ἣν Θεμιστοκλῆς πράττειν διανοεῖται μήτε λυσιτε-
4 λεστέραν ἄλλην μήτ' ἀδικωτέραν εἶναι. ταῦτ' ἀκούσαντες οἱ Ἀθηναῖοι
παύσασθαι τὸν Θεμιστοκλέα προσέταξαν. οὕτω μὲν οὖν ὁ δῆμος ἦν
φιλοδίκαιος, οὕτω δὲ τῷ δήμῳ πιστὸς ὁ ἀνὴρ καὶ βέβαιος.

23. Ἐπεὶ δὲ στρατηγὸς ἐκπεμφθεὶς μετὰ Κίμωνος ἐπὶ τὸν πόλεμον ἑώρα
τόν τε Παυσανίαν καὶ τοὺς ἄλλους ἄρχοντας τῶν Σπαρτιατῶν ἐπαχθεῖς
καὶ χαλεποὺς τοῖς συμμάχοις ὄντας, αὐτός τε πρᾴως καὶ φιλανθρώπως
ὁμιλῶν, καὶ τὸν Κίμωνα παρέχων εὐάρμοστον αὐτοῖς καὶ κοινὸν ἐν ταῖς
στρατείαις, ἔλαθε τῶν Λακεδαιμονίων οὐχ ὅπλοις οὐδὲ ναυσὶν οὐδ'
ἵπποις, εὐγνωμοσύνῃ δὲ καὶ πολιτείᾳ τὴν ἡγεμονίαν παρελόμενος.
2 προσφιλεῖς γὰρ ὄντας τοῖς Ἕλλησι τοὺς Ἀθηναίους διὰ τὴν Ἀριστείδου
δικαιοσύνην καὶ τὴν Κίμωνος ἐπιείκειαν ἔτι μᾶλλον ἡ τοῦ Παυσανίου

22.1 ταῖς νίκαις S: τὸν δῆμον UA 22.3 τὸ ναύσταθ. S: τὸν ναύσταθ. UA 22.4 πιστὸς ὁ ἀνὴρ Koraes: πιστὸς ἀνὴρ UA: ὁ ἀνὴρ πιστὸς S

22. When Aristeides noticed that the Athenians, on their return to the city, sought as their due the adoption of a democratic form of government, he considered that, in the first place, the people were worthy, because of the bravery they had displayed, of solicitous consideration and, in the second place, it was no longer an easy matter to browbeat them, fortified as they were by the possession of arms and filled with presumption as a result of their military success-es. So he drafted a motion to the effect that the business of government should be shared by everyone and that public officials should be elected from among all the Athenians.
2 And, when Themistocles said publicly that he had a certain secret project in mind that was conducive to the welfare and security of the state, they prevailed upon him to disclose it to
3 Aristeides alone for his approval. Themistocles then revealed to Aristeides that his idea was to set fire to the Greeks' fleet, since by doing so the Athenians would become supreme in power and authority, whereupon Aristeides made a public statement to the effect that, while there was no plan more advantageous than the one Themistocles had in
4 mind, there was none more wicked. When the Athenians heard this, they ordered Themistocles to cease and desist. This indicates, on the one hand, how devoted the people were to the pursuit of justice and, on the other hand, how trustworthy and dependable the man was in promoting the interests of the people.

23. When, during his generalship, he was dispatched along with Cimon to prosecute the war, he noticed that Pausanias and the other Spartan officials were overbearing and harsh toward the allies, while he himself treated them with forbearance and compassion, and likewise induced Cimon to be cooperative and to act in concert with them on their campaigns. In this way he deprived the Spartans, without their knowing it, of their leadership, not by means of arms or ships or horses, but by means of thoughtfulness and diplomacy.
2 For the Athenians, who won the affections of the Greeks through the fair-mindedness of Aristeides and the reason-

πλεονεξία καὶ βαρύτης ποθεινοὺς ἐποίει. τοῖς τε γὰρ ἄρχουσι τῶν
συμμάχων ἀεὶ μετ' ὀργῆς ἐνετύγχανε καὶ τραχέως, τούς τε πολλοὺς
ἐκόλαζε πληγαῖς, ἢ σιδηρᾶν ἄγκυραν ἐπιτιθεὶς ἠνάγκαζεν ἑστάναι δι'
3 ὅλης τῆς ἡμέρας. στιβάδα δ' οὐκ ἦν λαβεῖν οὐδὲ χόρτον οὐδὲ κρήνῃ
προσελθεῖν ὑδρευσόμενον οὐδένα πρὸ τῶν Σπαρτιατῶν, ἀλλὰ μάστιγας
ἔχοντες ὑπηρέται τοὺς προσιόντας ἀπήλαυνον. ὑπὲρ ὧν τοῦ Ἀριστείδου ποτὲ βουληθέντος ἐγκαλέσαι καὶ διδάξαι, συναγαγὼν τὸ πρόσωπον
4 ὁ Παυσανίας οὐκ ἔφη σχολάζειν οὐδ' ἤκουσεν. ἐκ τούτου προσιόντες
οἱ ναύαρχοι καὶ στρατηγοὶ τῶν Ἑλλήνων, μάλιστα δὲ Χῖοι καὶ Σάμιοι
καὶ Λέσβιοι, τὸν Ἀριστείδην ἔπειθον ἀναδέξασθαι τὴν ἡγεμονίαν καὶ
προσαγαγέσθαι τοὺς συμμάχους, πάλαι δεομένους ἀπαλλαγῆναι τῶν
5 Σπαρτιατῶν καὶ μετατάξασθαι πρὸς τοὺς Ἀθηναίους. ἀποκριναμένου
δ' ἐκείνου τοῖς μὲν λόγοις αὐτῶν τό τ' ἀναγκαῖον ἐνορᾶν καὶ τὸ δίκαιον,
ἔργου δὲ δεῖσθαι τὴν πίστιν ὃ πραχθὲν οὐκ ἐάσει πάλιν μεταβαλέσθαι
τοὺς πολλούς, οὕτως οἱ περὶ τὸν Σάμιον Οὐλιάδην καὶ τὸν Χῖον Ἀντα-
γόραν συνομοσάμενοι περὶ Βυζάντιον ἐμβάλλουσιν εἰς τὴν τριήρη τοῦ
6 Παυσανίου προεκπλέουσαν ἐν μέσῳ λαβόντες. ὡς δὲ κατιδὼν ἐκεῖνος
ἐξανέστη καὶ μετ' ὀργῆς ἠπείλησεν ὀλίγῳ χρόνῳ τοὺς ἄνδρας ἐπιδείξειν
οὐκ εἰς τὴν αὑτοῦ ναῦν ἐμβεβληκότας, ἀλλ' εἰς τὰς ἰδίας πατρίδας,
ἐκέλευον αὐτὸν ἀπιέναι καὶ ἀγαπᾶν τὴν συναγωνισαμένην Τύχην ἐν
Πλαταιαῖς· ἐκείνην γὰρ ἔτι τοὺς Ἕλληνας αἰσχυνομένους μὴ λαμβά-
νειν ἀξίαν δίκην παρ' αὐτοῦ. τέλος δ' ἀποστάντες ᾤχοντο πρὸς τοὺς
7 Ἀθηναίους. ἔνθα δὴ καὶ τὸ φρόνημα τῆς Σπάρτης διεφάνη θαυμαστόν·
ὡς γὰρ ᾔσθοντο τῷ μεγέθει τῆς ἐξουσίας διαφθειρομένους αὐτῶν τοὺς
ἄρχοντας, ἀφῆκαν ἑκουσίως τὴν ἡγεμονίαν καὶ πέμποντες ἐπὶ τὸν
πόλεμον ἐπαύσαντο στρατηγούς, μᾶλλον αἱρούμενοι σωφρονοῦντας

23.3 ὑδρευσόμενον UA: ὑδρευόμενον S| ποτ' ἐγκαλέσαι καὶ διδάξαι βουλομένου UA 23.7 τῷ μεγέθει S: διὰ τὰ μεγέθη UA| ἐπαύσαντο Reiske: ἔπαυσαν τοὺς SA: ἐπαύσαντο τοὺς U

ableness of Cimon, were made even more attractive by the ambition and arrogance of Pausanias. His dealings with the leaders of the allies were always heated and rude, and he would punish common soldiers with floggings, or compel
3 them to stand all day long holding an iron anchor. No one could secure bedding or fodder or approach a fountain to draw water for himself before the Spartans; their servants, armed with whips, would drive off any who made the attempt. And on one occasion, when Aristeides determined to take him to task for these incidents and show him the error of his ways, Pausanias glowered at him and, saying that he
4 was too busy, would not even listen to him. As a result of this, the naval and military commanders of the Greeks, especially those from Chios, Samos and Lesbos, approached Aristeides and sought to convince him to assume the leadership and win over the allies to his cause, since they had long desired to rid themselves of the Spartans and join forces with
5 the Athenians. He replied that, while he could see that their arguments were both compelling and just, it was necessary to demonstrate their good faith by performing some deed which would prevent the men in the ranks from changing their minds. And so the Samian Ouliades and Antagoras of Chios conspired to intercept Pausanias' trireme near Byzantium as
6 it sailed out at the head of the fleet and attack it. When Pausanias saw what was happening, he leapt to his feet and in a rage threatened that before long he would make it clear that these men were not so much attacking his ship as their own homelands. They told him to begone and to give thanks to Lady Luck, who fought by his side at Plataea, for it was only the reverence that the Greeks still felt toward her that prevented them from punishing him as he deserved. Thus, in
7 the end, they rose up and went over to the Athenians. It was then that the Spartan character displayed itself admirably. When they realized that their leaders were being corrupted by the extent of their powers, they voluntarily renounced the leadership and ceased dispatching commanders to prosecute the war. In preference to the rule over all of Greece they chose to ensure that their citizens maintain decency and

ἔχειν καὶ τοῖς ἔθεσιν ἐμμένοντας τοὺς πολίτας ἢ τῆς Ἑλλάδος ἄρχειν ἁπάσης.

24. Οἱ δ᾽ Ἕλληνες ἐτέλουν μέν τινα καὶ Λακεδαιμονίων ἡγουμένων ἀποφορὰν εἰς τὸν πόλεμον, ταχθῆναι δὲ βουλόμενοι καὶ κατὰ πόλιν ἑκάστοις τὸ μέτριον, ᾐτήσαντο παρὰ τῶν Ἀθηναίων Ἀριστείδην, καὶ προσέταξαν αὐτῷ χώραν τε καὶ προσόδους ἐπισκεψάμενον ὁρίσαι τὸ
2 κατ᾽ ἀξίαν ἑκάστῳ καὶ δύναμιν. ὁ δὲ τηλικαύτης ἐξουσίας κύριος γενόμενος, καὶ τρόπον τινὰ τῆς Ἑλλάδος ἐπ᾽ αὐτῷ μόνῳ τὰ πράγματα πάντα θεμένης, πένης μὲν ἐξῆλθεν, ἐπανῆλθε δὲ πενέστερος, οὐ μόνον καθαρῶς καὶ δικαίως, ἀλλὰ καὶ προσφιλῶς πᾶσι καὶ ἁρμοδίως τὴν
3 ἀπογραφὴν τῶν χρημάτων ποιησάμενος. ὡς γὰρ οἱ παλαιοὶ τὸν ἐπὶ Κρόνου βίον, οὕτως οἱ σύμμαχοι τῶν Ἀθηναίων τὸν ἐπ᾽ Ἀριστείδου φόρον εὐποτμίαν τινὰ τῆς Ἑλλάδος ὀνομάζοντες ὕμνουν, καὶ μάλιστα μετ᾽ οὐ πολὺν χρόνον διπλασιασθέντος, εἶτ᾽ αὖθις τριπλασιασθέντος.
4 ὃν μὲν γὰρ Ἀριστείδης ἔταξεν ἦν εἰς ἑξήκοντα καὶ τετρακοσίων ταλάντων λόγον· τούτῳ δὲ Περικλῆς μὲν ἐπέθηκεν ὀλίγου δεῖν τὸ τρίτον μέρος (ἑξακόσια γὰρ τάλαντα Θουκυδίδης φησὶν ἀρχομένου τοῦ πολέμου
5 προσιέναι τοῖς Ἀθηναίοις ἀπὸ τῶν συμμάχων), Περικλέους δ᾽ ἀποθανόντος, ἐπιτείνοντες οἱ δημαγωγοὶ κατὰ μικρὸν εἰς χιλίων καὶ τριακοσίων ταλάντων κεφάλαιον ἀνήγαγον, οὐχ οὕτω τοῦ πολέμου διὰ μῆκος καὶ τύχας δαπανηροῦ γενομένου καὶ πολυτελοῦς, ὡς τὸν δῆμον εἰς διανομὰς καὶ θεωρικὰ καὶ κατασκευὰς ἀγαλμάτων καὶ ἱερῶν προαγα-
6 γόντες. μέγα δ᾽ οὖν ὄνομα τοῦ Ἀριστείδου καὶ θαυμαστὸν ἔχοντος ἐπὶ τῇ διατάξει τῶν φόρων ὁ Θεμιστοκλῆς λέγεται καταγελᾶν, ὡς οὐκ ἀνδρὸς ὄντα τὸν ἔπαινον, ἀλλὰ θυλάκου χρυσοφύλακος, ἀνομοίως

23.7 ἄρχειν S: ἔχειν τὴν ἀρχὴν UA 24.2 ἁρμοδίως UA: ἁρμονίως S| ἀπογραφὴν Schaefer: ἐπιγραφὴν SUA 24.4 τούτῳ Περικλῆς UA| Περικλῆς ἐπέθηκεν S

abide by their ancestral ways.

24. Even when the Spartans held the command, the
Greeks were accustomed to making some financial contribution to the war, but now they desired that a determination of
the appropriate amount to be assessed in each instance be
made also city by city, so they solicited from the Athenians
the services of Aristeides, and they gave him the task of sur-
veying each city's territory and revenues, thereby deter-
2 mining each city's obligations and capacity to pay. He embarked on this mission a poor man and, despite the fact that
he was now master of such vast resources, what with Greece
virtually placing its fortunes in his hands alone, he returned
a poorer man. Not only did he keep himself free from all
dishonesty and corruption, but he managed even to draw up
the assessment list in a manner that everyone found agree-
3 able and appropriate. This is shown by the fact that, just as
the ancients used to sing the praises of life in the "Era of
Cronus," so the allies of the Athenians would refer glowingly
to the assessment in the "Era of Aristeides" as a piece of good
fortune for Greece. This was especially the case when, a
short time later, the assessment was doubled and then, on
4 another occasion, tripled. For the amount assessed by Aristeides totaled 460 talents. Then Pericles increased this
amount by nearly a third (for Thucydides says that at the
beginning of the war the Athenians were receiving an income
5 of six hundred talents from their allies) and then, after the
death of Pericles, the popular leaders outdid themselves by
gradually bringing the amount up to a total of 1,300 talents.
This was not so much because the war proved costly and expensive on account of its length and vicissitudes; rather these
leaders took the people down the path that led to public
doles, subsidies of festival performances and the erection of
6 statues and temples. At any rate, Aristeides possessed a
widespread and splendid reputation for his assignment of the
tributes, but Themistocles is supposed to have said derisively
that the praise heaped on him was appropriate not to a man
but to a money-bag. This was said in inadequate retaliation

7 ἀμυνόμενος τὴν Ἀριστείδου παρρησίαν· ἐκείνῳ γὰρ εἰπόντος ποτὲ τοῦ Θεμιστοκλέους ἀρετὴν ἡγεῖσθαι μεγίστην στρατηγοῦ τὸ γιγνώσκειν καὶ προαισθάνεσθαι τὰ βουλεύματα τῶν πολεμίων, 'τοῦτο μέν,' εἰπεῖν, 'ἀναγκαῖόν ἐστιν, ὦ Θεμιστόκλεις, καλὸν δὲ καὶ στρατηγικὸν ἀληθῶς ἡ περὶ τὰς χεῖρας ἐγκράτεια.'

25. Ὁ δ' Ἀριστείδης ὥρκισε μὲν τοὺς Ἕλληνας καὶ ὤμοσεν ὑπὲρ τῶν Ἀθηναίων, μύδρους ἐμβαλὼν ἐπὶ ταῖς ἀραῖς εἰς τὴν θάλατταν· ὕστερον δὲ τῶν πραγμάτων ἄρχειν ἐγκρατέστερον ὡς ἔοικεν ἐκβιαζομένων, ἐκέλευε τοὺς Ἀθηναίους τὴν ἐπιορκίαν τρέψαντας εἰς αὑτὸν ᾗ συμφέρει
2 χρῆσθαι τοῖς πράγμασι. καθ' ὅλου δ' ὁ Θεόφραστός φησι τὸν ἄνδρα τοῦτον περὶ τὰ οἰκεῖα καὶ τοὺς πολίτας ἄκρως ὄντα δίκαιον, ἐν τοῖς κοινοῖς τὰ πολλὰ πρᾶξαι πρὸς τὴν ὑπόθεσιν τῆς πατρίδος, ὡς συχνῆς
3 καὶ ἀδικίας δεομένην. καὶ γὰρ τὰ χρήματά φασιν ἐκ Δήλου βουλευομένων Ἀθήναζε κομίσαι παρὰ τὰς συνθήκας καὶ Σαμίων εἰσηγουμένων, εἰπεῖν ἐκεῖνον ὡς οὐ δίκαιον μέν, συμφέρον δὲ τοῦτ' ἐστί· καὶ τέλος εἰς τὸ ἄρχειν ἀνθρώπων τοσούτων καταστήσας τὴν πόλιν, αὐτὸς ἐνέμεινε τῇ πενίᾳ, καὶ τὴν ἀπὸ τοῦ πένης εἶναι δόξαν οὐδὲν ἧττον ἀγαπῶν τῆς ἀπὸ
4 τῶν τροπαίων διετέλεσε. δῆλον δ' ἐκεῖθεν· Καλλίας ὁ δᾳδοῦχος ἦν αὐτῷ γένει προσήκων· τοῦτον οἱ ἐχθροὶ θανάτου διώκοντες, ἐπεὶ περὶ ὧν ἐγράψαντο μετρίως κατηγόρησαν, ἔξωθεν εἶπόν τινα λόγον τοιοῦτον
5 πρὸς τοὺς δικαστάς· 'Ἀριστείδην,' ἔφησαν, 'ἴστε τὸν Λυσιμάχου θαυμαζόμενον ἐν τοῖς Ἕλλησι· τούτῳ πῶς ἔχειν οἴεσθε τὰ κατ' οἶκον, ὁρῶντες

24.7 ἐκεῖνος UA (quo servato εἶπεν pro εἰπεῖν legit Sintenis)
25.2 τὰ πολλὰ S: πολλὰ UA| καὶ ἀδικίας Sauppe: καὶ οὐ δικαίας S: ἀδικίας UA 25.3 φασιν S: φησιν UA

7 to the outspoken comment of Aristeides who, when Themistocles once told him that he thought the best quality a commander can have is the ability to recognize and anticipate the
enemy's strategy, said, "That is indeed indispensable, Themistocles, but the true mark of a gentleman and a commander is the ability to restrain his fingers."

25. Aristeides administered the oath of allegiance to the
Greeks, and it was he who took the oath on behalf of the
Athenians, casting pieces of metal into the sea as he pronounced the curses. Later on, however, when circumstances
apparently required that a more firm rule be imposed, he
would tell the Athenians to conduct their affairs in the manner that best suited their own interests and to allow the re-
2 sponsibility for committing perjury to rest with him. And in
general Theophrastus says that this man, who was the very
model of respectability when it came to his personal life and
to his relations with his fellow citizens, for the most part acted, when it came to matters of state, in accordance with his
country's objectives (implying thereby that these objectives
3 often involve actual dishonesty). For example, they say that,
when deliberations were taking place at the instigation of the
Samians as to whether the treasury should be transferred,
contrary to the terms of the agreement, from Delos to Athens,
Aristeides commented that the proposal was dishonest, but
advantageous. And finally, though he was responsible for
giving his city the power to rule so many men, he himself
persevered in his impoverished state, and he continued to
cherish the reputation that his poverty conferred on him just
4 as much as that conferred on him by his victories. This is
clear from the following account. Callias the Torchbearer was
a relative of his who was being prosecuted by his enemies on
a capital charge. After they had presented a reasonably good
case against him based upon the actual terms of the indict-
ment, they went on to introduce irrelevant considerations by
making a speech to the jurors in which they said something
5 like the following: "You know Aristeides, the son of Lysimachus, who has excited the admiration of the Greeks. When

αὐτὸν ἐν τρίβωνι τοιούτῳ προερχόμενον εἰς τὸ δημόσιον; ἆρ' οὐκ εἰκός
ἐστι τὸν ῥιγοῦντα φανερῶς καὶ πεινῆν οἴκοι καὶ τῶν ἄλλων ἐπιτηδείων
6 σπανίζειν; τοῦτον μέντοι Καλλίας ἀνεψιὸν ὄντα, πλουσιώτατος ὢν
Ἀθηναίων, περιορᾷ μετὰ τέκνων καὶ γυναικὸς ἐνδεόμενον, πολλὰ
κεχρημένος τῷ ἀνδρὶ καὶ πολλάκις αὐτοῦ τῆς παρ' ὑμῖν δυνάμεως
7 ἀπολελαυκώς.' ὁ δὲ Καλλίας ὁρῶν ἐπὶ τούτῳ μάλιστα θορυβοῦντας
τοὺς δικαστὰς καὶ χαλεπῶς πρὸς αὐτὸν ἔχοντας, ἐκάλει τὸν Ἀριστείδην, ἀξιῶν μαρτυρῆσαι πρὸς τοὺς δικαστάς, ὅτι πολλάκις αὐτοῦ
πολλὰ καὶ διδόντος καὶ δεομένου λαβεῖν οὐκ ἠθέλησεν, ἀποκρινάμε-
νος ὡς μᾶλλον αὐτῷ διὰ πενίαν μέγα φρονεῖν ἢ Καλλίᾳ διὰ πλοῦτον
8 προσήκει· πλούτῳ μὲν γὰρ ἔστι πολλοὺς ἰδεῖν εὖ τε καὶ καλῶς χρωμένους, πενίαν δὲ φέροντι γενναίως οὐ ῥᾴδιον ἐντυχεῖν· αἰσχύνεσθαι δὲ
πενίαν τοὺς ἀκουσίως πενομένους. ταῦτα τοῦ Ἀριστείδου τῷ Καλλίᾳ
προσμαρτυρήσαντος, οὐδεὶς ἦν τῶν ἀκουσάντων ὃς οὐκ ἀπῄει πένης
μᾶλλον ὡς Ἀριστείδης εἶναι βουλόμενος ἢ πλουτεῖν ὡς Καλλίας.
9 ταῦτα μὲν οὖν Αἰσχίνης ὁ Σωκρατικὸς ἀναγέγραφε. Πλάτων δὲ τῶν
μεγάλων δοκούντων καὶ ὀνομαστῶν Ἀθήνησι μόνον ἄξιον λόγου
τοῦτον ἀποφαίνει τὸν ἄνδρα· Θεμιστοκλέα μὲν γὰρ καὶ Κίμωνα καὶ
Περικλέα στοῶν καὶ χρημάτων καὶ φλυαρίας πολλῆς ἐμπλῆσαι τὴν πό-
10 λιν, Ἀριστείδην δὲ πολιτεύσασθαι πρὸς ἀρετήν. μεγάλα δ' αὐτοῦ καὶ
τὰ πρὸς Θεμιστοκλέα τῆς ἐπιεικείας σημεῖα· χρησάμενος γὰρ αὐτῷ
παρὰ πᾶσαν ὁμοῦ τὴν πολιτείαν ἐχθρῷ καὶ δι' ἐκεῖνον ἐξοστρακισθείς,
ἐπεὶ τὴν αὐτὴν λαβὴν παρέσχεν ὁ ἀνὴρ ἐν αἰτίᾳ γενόμενος πρὸς τὴν
πόλιν, οὐκ ἐμνησικάκησεν, ἀλλ' Ἀλκμαίωνος καὶ Κίμωνος καὶ πολλῶν
ἄλλων ἐλαυνόντων καὶ κατηγορούντων, μόνος Ἀριστείδης οὔτ' ἔπρα-

25.5 προερχόμενον Reiske: προσερχόμενον SUA| πεινῆν] πεινᾶν UA: ῥιγᾶν S 25.8 καλῶς C. F. Hermann: κακῶς SUA

you see him appearing in such a threadbare cloak in public, what do you suppose his personal circumstances are like? Is it not likely that the man who can be seen shivering in public and who makes no secret of his poverty lacks at home the
6 other necessities of life as well? And yet Callias, this man's cousin and the wealthiest of the Athenians, allows him and his wife and children to suffer in poverty, though he has himself often taken advantage of this man's services and has on several occasions enjoyed the benefits of his influence
7 with you." When Callias saw that the jurors were more agitated over this than over anything else and that they were inclined to condemn him, he summoned Aristeides and asked him to testify before the jurors that he had on numerous occasions offered him large sums and had begged him to accept the money, but that Aristeides had on each occasion refused, saying that he had more cause to be proud of his
8 poverty than Callias of his wealth. It was not difficult, he said, to point to men who took full and appropriate advantage of their wealth, but it was not easy to find a man who bore poverty with dignity. To be ashamed of poverty was a mark of those who could not help but be poor. Of those who heard Aristeides' testimony for Callias there was not one who went away feeling that he would rather be wealthy like Cal-
9 lias than be poor like Aristeides. This is what Aeschines, the follower of Socrates, has recorded. And Plato proclaims that, of the men who were generally considered great and notable in Athens, this man was the only one who was truly worthy. For, while Themistocles, Cimon and Pericles filled the city with porticoes and riches and all sorts of nonsense, Aristeides
10 made virtue the hallmark of his public career. There are even good indications of his gentlemanly treatment of Themistocles. For, although he treated Aristeides as an enemy throughout his entire career and was responsible for his banishment, when Themistocles was publicly prosecuted, thereby giving Aristeides an opportunity to turn the tables on him, the latter refused to bear a grudge. Instead, while Alcmaeon and Cimon and a number of others were hounding him and accusing him, Aristeides alone refrained from doing

ξεν οὔτ' εἶπέ τι φαῦλον, οὐδ' ἀπέλαυσεν ἐχθροῦ δυστυχοῦντος, ὥσπερ οὐδ' εὐημεροῦντι πρότερον ἐφθόνησε.

26. Τελευτῆσαι δ' Ἀριστείδην οἱ μὲν ἐν Πόντῳ φασὶν ἐκπλεύσαντα
πράξεων ἕνεκα δημοσίων, οἱ δ' Ἀθήνησι γήρᾳ, τιμώμενον καὶ θαυμαζόμενον ὑπὸ τῶν πολιτῶν. Κρατερὸς δ' ὁ Μακεδὼν τοιαῦτά τινα περὶ
2 τῆς τελευτῆς τοῦ ἀνδρὸς εἴρηκε· μετὰ γὰρ τὴν Θεμιστοκλέους φυγήν
φησιν ὥσπερ ἐξυβρίσαντα τὸν δῆμον ἀναφῦσαι πλῆθος συκοφαντῶν, οἳ
τοὺς ἀρίστους καὶ δυνατωτάτους ἄνδρας διώκοντες ὑπέβαλλον τῷ
3 φθόνῳ τῶν πολλῶν, ἐπαιρομένων ὑπ' εὐτυχίας καὶ δυνάμεως. ἐν τούτοις
καὶ Ἀριστείδην ἁλῶναι δωροδοκίας, Διοφάντου τοῦ Ἀμφιτροπῆθεν
κατηγοροῦντος, ὡς ὅτε τοὺς φόρους ἔπραττε παρὰ τῶν Ἰώνων χρήματα
λαβόντος, ἐκτεῖσαι δ' οὐκ ἔχοντα τὴν καταδίκην πεντήκοντα μνῶν
4 οὖσαν, ἐκπλεῦσαι καὶ περὶ τὴν Ἰωνίαν ἀποθανεῖν. τούτων δ' οὐδὲν
ἔγγραφον ὁ Κρατερὸς τεκμήριον παρέσχηκεν, οὔτε δίκην οὔτε ψήφισμα,
καίπερ εἰωθὼς ἐπιεικῶς γράφειν τὰ τοιαῦτα καὶ παρατίθεσθαι τοὺς
5 ἱστοροῦντας. οἱ δ' ἄλλοι πάντες, ὡς ἔπος εἰπεῖν, ὅσοι τὰ πλημμεληθέντα
τῷ δήμῳ περὶ τοὺς στρατηγοὺς διεξίασι, τὴν μὲν Θεμιστοκλέους φυγὴν
καὶ τὰ Μιλτιάδου δεσμὰ καὶ τὴν Περικλέους ζημίαν καὶ τὸν Πάχητος
ἐν τῷ δικαστηρίῳ θάνατον, ἀνελόντος ἑαυτὸν ἐπὶ τοῦ βήματος ὡς
ἡλίσκετο, καὶ πολλὰ τοιαῦτα συνάγουσι καὶ θρυλοῦσιν, Ἀριστείδου δὲ
τὸν μὲν ἐξοστρακισμὸν παρατίθενται, καταδίκης δὲ τοιαύτης οὐδαμοῦ
μνημονεύουσι.

27. Καὶ μέντοι καὶ τάφος ἐστὶν αὐτοῦ Φαληροῖ δεικνύμενος, ὅν φασι
2 κατασκευάσαι τὴν πόλιν αὐτῷ μηδ' ἐντάφια καταλιπόντι, καὶ τὰς μὲν
θυγατέρας ἱστοροῦσιν ἐκ τοῦ πρυτανείου τοῖς νυμφίοις ἐκδοθῆναι,

or saying anything cheap. Just as he had not previously been envious of a rival's good fortune, so he did not enjoy the sight of a rival in distress.

26. Some say that Aristeides died in the territory near
the Black Sea, when he made a voyage there on state business, but according to others he died in Athens of old age,
honored and admired by his fellow citizens. Concerning the
man's death Craterus the Macedonian tells a story that goes
2 something like this. After Themistocles had gone into exile,
the people began to luxuriate and sprouted an abundant crop
of informers, who went about prosecuting the most prominent and influential men, subjecting them to the malice of
the masses, who were carried away by their own success and
3 power. Among these men was Aristeides, who was convicted
of accepting bribes. He was charged by Diophantus, of the
deme Amphitrope, with taking money from some Ionians at
the time when he was collecting the tribute. He could not
afford to pay the fine of fifty minas, so he left the city and
4 sailed for Ionia, where he died. But Craterus has provided no
documentary proof, either in the form of a sentence or a decree, of these matters, in spite of the fact that it is his usual
custom to transcribe such things and to cite his authorities.
5 But the other writers who describe the indignities inflicted
by the people upon their generals and who drone on and on,
compiling any number of anecdotes, about the exile of Themistocles, for example, or the imprisonment of Miltiades, or
the fine imposed on Pericles, or the death in court of Paches, who committed suicide on the podium when he was convicted, all these writers, if I may say so, while they cite Aristeides' ostracism, nowhere make mention of a conviction of
this sort.

27. And, as a matter of fact, at Phalerum a tomb of Aristeides can be seen which, they say, was set up in his honor
by the city, since he had not left even enough money for fu-
2 neral expenses. Furthermore, it is said that his daughters
were given in marriage to their bridegrooms from the town

δημοσίᾳ τῆς πόλεως τὸν γάμον ἐγγυώσης καὶ προῖκα τρισχιλίας δραχμὰς ἑκατέρᾳ ψηφισαμένης, Λυσιμάχῳ δὲ τῷ υἱῷ μνᾶς μὲν ἑκατὸν
ἀργυρίου καὶ γῆς τοσαῦτα πλέθρα πεφυτευμένης ἔδωκεν ὁ δῆμος,
ἄλλας δὲ δραχμὰς τέσσαρας εἰς ἡμέραν ἑκάστην ἀπέταξεν, Ἀλκιβιά-
3 δου τὸ ψήφισμα γράψαντος. ἔτι δὲ Λυσιμάχου θυγατέρα Πολυκρίτην
ἀπολιπόντος, ὡς Καλλισθένης φησί, καὶ ταύτῃ σίτησιν ὅσην καὶ τοῖς
Ὀλυμπιονίκαις ὁ δῆμος ἐψηφίσατο. Δημήτριος δ' ὁ Φαληρεὺς καὶ
Ἱερώνυμος ὁ Ῥόδιος καὶ Ἀριστόξενος ὁ μουσικὸς καὶ Ἀριστοτέλης (εἴ
γε δὴ τὸ Περὶ εὐγενείας βιβλίον ἐν τοῖς γνησίοις Ἀριστοτέλους θετέον)
ἱστοροῦσι Μυρτὼ θυγατριδῆν Ἀριστείδου Σωκράτει τῷ σοφῷ συνοικῆ-
σαι, γυναῖκα μὲν ἑτέραν ἔχοντι, ταύτην δ' ἀναλαβόντι χηρεύουσαν διὰ
4 πενίαν καὶ τῶν ἀναγκαίων ἐνδεομένην. πρὸς μὲν οὖν τούτους ἱκανῶς ὁ
Παναίτιος ἐν τοῖς Περὶ Σωκράτους ἀντείρηκεν· ὁ δὲ Φαληρεὺς ἐν τῷ
Σωκράτει φησὶ μνημονεύειν Ἀριστείδου θυγατριδοῦν εὖ μάλα πένητα
Λυσίμαχον, ὃς ἑαυτὸν μὲν ἐκ πινακίου τινὸς ὀνειροκριτικοῦ παρὰ τὸ
5 Ἰακχεῖον λεγόμενον καθεζόμενος ἔβοσκε, τῇ δὲ μητρὶ καὶ τῇ ταύτης
ἀδελφῇ ψήφισμα γράψας ἔπεισε τὸν δῆμον τροφὴν διδόναι τριώβολον
ἑκάστης ἡμέρας. αὐτὸς μέντοι φησὶν ὁ Δημήτριος νομοθετῶν ἀντὶ τριω-
6 βόλου δραχμὴν ἑκατέρᾳ τάξαι τῶν γυναικῶν. καὶ οὐδέν ἐστι θαυμαστὸν οὕτω φροντίσαι τῶν ἐν ἄστει τὸν δῆμον, ὅπου θυγατριδῆν Ἀριστο-
γείτονος ἐν Λήμνῳ πυθόμενοι ταπεινὰ πράττειν ἀνδρὸς ἀποροῦσαν διὰ
πενίαν κατήγαγον Ἀθήναζε καὶ συνοικίσαντες ἀνδρὶ τῶν εὖ γεγονότων
7 τὸ Ποταμοῖ χωρίον εἰς φερνὴν ἐπέδωκαν. ἧς φιλανθρωπίας καὶ χρηστό-

27.3 εἴ γε δὴ τὸ Ziegler: εἰ δὴ τό γε S: εἰ δὴ τὸ UA 27.5 γράψας ἔπεισε τὸν δ. τροφὴν διδόναι S: γράψας δωρεὰν ἔπεισε τὸν δ. διδόναι UA| φησὶν ὁ Δ. νομ. ἀντὶ τριωβόλου S: ὁ Δ. νομ. ἐψηφίσατο UA

hall—arrangements for the betrothal were made at public expense by the city and a dowry was decreed amounting to three thousand drachmas for each daughter—and the community gave Aristeides' son Lysimachus one hundred minas in silver and one hundred acres of cultivated land, as well as an additional appropriation of four drachmas per day. (The
3 proposer of this measure was Alcibiades.) Moreover, according to Callisthenes, when Lysimachus died and was survived by a daughter Polycrite, the people approved a measure to give public maintenance to her as well, in an amount equal to that granted to victors in the Olympic Games. Now, according to Demetrius of Phalerum, Hieronymus of Rhodes, Aristoxenus the writer of musical treatises and Aristotle (provided, that is, the book On Nobility deserves a place among the genuine works of Aristotle), Aristeides' granddaughter Myrto lived with the philosopher Socrates, who had another wife at the time but who took her in when she was a widow in need of life's necessities and unable to remarry be-
4 cause of her poverty. But of course Panaetius has amply refuted these men in his work On Socrates. In his own book entitled "Socrates," Demetrius of Phalerum says that he can remember an impoverished descendant of Aristeides named Lysimachus, who supported himself by sitting outside the building called the "Iaccheium" and using some sort of tablet
5 that interpreted dreams, and who convinced the people to approve his proposal that his mother and her sister be given an allowance of three obols per day. Demetrius says, however, that when he was in charge of the government he himself assigned an allowance of one drachma to each of the women
6 instead of three obols. Nor is it in any way surprising that the people had such regard for their fellow citizens when one considers the fact that, when they learned that a granddaughter of Aristogeiton was living on Lemnos in obscurity and was unable to marry because of her poverty, they brought her back to Athens, gave her in marriage to a man of the upper classes and included as her dowry the estate in
7 Potamus. Inasmuch as Athens gives abundant indication even today of its nobility and compassion, it is with some

τητος ἔτι πολλὰ καὶ καθ' ἡμᾶς ἡ πόλις ἐκφέρουσα δείγματα θαυμάζεται καὶ ζηλοῦται δικαίως.

ΒΙΟΣ ΚΑΤΩΝΟΣ

28(1). Μάρκῳ δὲ Κάτωνί φασιν ἀπὸ Τούσκλου τὸ γένος εἶναι, δίαιταν δὲ καὶ βίον ἔχειν πρὸ τῶν στρατειῶν καὶ τῆς πολιτείας ἐν χωρίοις πατρῴοις περὶ τοὺς Σαβίνους. τῶν δὲ προγόνων παντάπασιν ἀγνώστων γεγονέναι δοκούντων αὐτὸς ὁ Κάτων καὶ τὸν πατέρα Μᾶρκον ὡς ἀγαθὸν ἄνδρα καὶ στρατιωτικὸν ἐπαινεῖ, καὶ Κάτωνα τὸν πρόπαππον ἀριστείων πολλάκις τυχεῖν φησι καὶ πέντε πολεμιστὰς ἵππους ἐν μάχαις ἀποβαλόντα τὴν τιμὴν ἀπολαβεῖν ἐκ τοῦ δημοσίου δι' ἀνδραγαθίαν.
2 εἰωθότων δὲ τῶν Ῥωμαίων τοὺς ἀπὸ γένους μὲν δόξαν οὐκ ἔχοντας, ἀρχομένους δὲ γνωρίζεσθαι δι' αὑτῶν, καινοὺς προσαγορεύειν ἀνθρώπους, ὥσπερ καὶ τὸν Κάτωνα προσηγόρευον, αὐτὸς ἔλεγε καινὸς εἶναι πρὸς ἀρχὴν καὶ δόξαν, ἔργοις δὲ προγόνων καὶ ἀρεταῖς παμπάλαιος.
3 ἐκαλεῖτο δὲ τῷ τρίτῳ τῶν ὀνομάτων πρότερον οὐ Κάτων, ἀλλὰ Πρῖσκος, ὕστερον δὲ τὸν Κάτωνα τῆς δυνάμεως ἐπώνυμον ἔσχε· Ῥωμαῖοι
4 γὰρ τὸν ἔμπειρον κάτον ὀνομάζουσιν. ἦν δὲ τὸ μὲν εἶδος ὑπόπυρρος καὶ γλαυκός, ὡς ὁ ποιήσας τὸ ἐπιγραμμάτιον οὐκ εὐμενῶς παρεμφαίνει·

πυρρόν, πανδακέτην, γλαυκόμματον, οὐδὲ θανόντα
Πόρκιον εἰς ἀίδην Φερσεφόνη δέχεται.

5 τὴν δὲ τοῦ σώματος ἕξιν, αὐτουργίᾳ καὶ διαίτῃ σώφρονι καὶ στρατείαις ἀπ' ἀρχῆς συντρόφου γεγονότος, πάνυ χρηστικὴν εἶχε καὶ πρὸς ἰσχὺν καὶ πρὸς ὑγίειαν ὁμαλῶς συνεστῶσαν. τὸν δὲ λόγον, ὥσπερ δεύτερον

28.3 κάτον anonymus: Κάτωνα SUA

justification that it is admired and stands as a model for others.

LIFE OF MARCUS CATO

28(1). Marcus Cato belonged to a family that, it is said, came from Tusculum. Before he embarked on his military and political career, however, he resided in and supported himself by means of an ancestral estate in the territory of the Sabines. Although his ancestors are generally regarded as having been entirely without distinction, Cato himself extols the bravery and martial expertise of his father Marcus and he claims that his paternal great-grandfather often won prizes for valor and on five occasions, when his charger was killed out from under him in battle, he was awarded from the public treasury the cost of the steed on account of his
2 courageousness. It is the Roman custom to use the expression "new men" to refer to those whose distinction is not conferred on them by their birth, but who first attract recognition because of their own merits. And this is how they referred to Cato, but he himself used to say that, while he was a new man from the point of view of political office and prestige, he was quite well established from the point of
3 view of his ancestors' deeds and acts of valor. Now his third name was not originally "Cato." Rather it was "Priscus," and he received the name "Cato" later on as a nickname because of his ability. (The Romans use the word *catus* to mean
4 "clever.") As far as his appearance is concerned, his hair was reddish and his eyes grey. This is indicated rather unkindly by the author of the little epigram:

Cato's quite snappish, has grey eyes and red head.
He's unwelcome in Hades, even when dead.

5 As to his constitution, it was quite adaptable and also solid, from the point of view of both strength and health, since his body was inured from the start to manual labor, austerity and military campaigns. He acquired a capacity for and trained himself in public speaking, regarding it as a sort of

σῶμα καὶ τῶν καλῶν μονονοὺκ ἀναγκαῖον ὄργανον ἀνδρὶ μὴ ταπεινῶς
βιωσομένῳ μηδ' ἀπράκτως, ἐξηρτύετο καὶ παρεσκεύαζεν, ἐν ταῖς περι-
οικίσι κώμαις καὶ τοῖς πολιχνίοις ἑκάστοτε συνδικῶν τοῖς δεομένοις καὶ
6 πρῶτον ἀγωνιστὴς εἶναι δοκῶν πρόθυμος, εἶτα καὶ ῥήτωρ ἱκανός. ἐκ δὲ
τούτου μᾶλλον τοῖς χρωμένοις κατεφαίνετο βάρος τι καὶ φρόνημα περὶ
αὐτὸν ἤθους, πραγμάτων μεγάλων καὶ πολιτείας δεόμενον ἡγεμονικῆς.
7 οὐ γὰρ μόνον ὡς ἔοικε μισθαρνίας καθαρὸν αὐτὸν ἐπὶ τὰς δίκας καὶ
τοὺς ἀγῶνας παρεῖχεν, ἀλλ' οὐδὲ τὴν δόξαν ὡς μέγιστον ἀγαπῶν ἐφαίνετο τὴν ἀπὸ τῶν τοιούτων ἀγώνων, πολὺ δὲ μᾶλλον ἐν ταῖς μάχαις ταῖς
πρὸς τοὺς πολεμίους καὶ ταῖς στρατείαις βουλόμενος εὐδοκιμεῖν, ἔτι
8 μειράκιον ὢν τραυμάτων τὸ σῶμα μεστὸν ἐναντίων εἶχε. φησὶ γὰρ αὐτὸς ἑπτακαίδεκα γεγονὼς ἔτη τὴν πρώτην στρατεύσασθαι στρατείαν,
περὶ ὃν Ἀννίβας χρόνον εὐτυχῶν ἐπέφλεγε τὴν Ἰταλίαν. παρεῖχε δ'
αὑτὸν ἐν ταῖς μάχαις τῇ μὲν χειρὶ πλήκτην, τῷ δὲ ποδὶ μόνιμον καὶ βέ-
βαιον, γαῦρον δὲ τῷ προσώπῳ. λόγου δ' ἀπειλῇ καὶ τραχύτητι φωνῆς
πρὸς τοὺς πολεμίους ἐχρῆτο, ὀρθῶς καὶ διανοούμενος καὶ διδάσκων ὅτι
πολλάκις τὰ τοιαῦτα τοῦ ξίφους μᾶλλον καταπλήττεται τὸν ἐναντίον.
9 ἐν δὲ ταῖς πορείαις αὐτὸς ἐβάδιζε φέρων τὰ ὅπλα, καὶ θεράπων εἷς εἵπε-
το τὰ πρὸς τὴν δίαιταν αὐτῷ κομίζων, ᾧ λέγεται μηδέποτε δυσκολᾶναι
μηδὲ μέμψασθαι παραθέντος ἄριστον ἢ δεῖπνον, ἀλλὰ καὶ συλλαμβά-
νειν αὐτὸς τὰ πλεῖστα καὶ συμπαρασκευάζειν ἀπὸ τῶν στρατιωτικῶν
10 γενόμενος ἔργων. ὕδωρ δ' ἔπινεν ἐπὶ στρατείας πλὴν εἴποτε διψήσας
περιφλεγῶς ὄξος αἰτήσειεν ἢ τῆς ἰσχύος ἐνδιδούσης ἐπιλάβοι μικρὸν
οἰνάριον.

29(2). Ἦν δὲ πλησίον αὐτοῦ τῶν ἀγρῶν ἡ γενομένη Μανίου Κουρί-
ου τοῦ τρὶς θριαμβεύσαντος ἔπαυλις. ἐπὶ ταύτην συνεχῶς βαδίζων καὶ

28.5 μονονοὺκ Orelli: οὐ μόνον SUA 28.8 τὸν ἐναντίον S: τοὺς ἐναντίους UA 28.10 αἰτήσειεν Bekker: ᾔτησεν SUA

second body and as an instrument for good that is all but indispensable to a man intent upon avoiding a life of obscurity
and inactivity. He was constantly serving as advocate for
those who required his services in the neighboring towns and
villages, first acquiring a reputation as an ardent pleader,
6 then as a capable orator as well. As a result of this, those
with whom he associated increasingly formed the impression
that there was about him a certain seriousness of character
and determination that made inevitable his involvement in
7 public affairs and in positions of leadership. For he seems
not only to have avoided any mercenary tendencies in connection with his lawsuits and legal contests, but he appears
not even to have cherished as of paramount importance the
reputation that such contests confer. He much preferred to
distinguish himself in engagements with the enemy and on
campaigns. Even as a youth, his body was covered with
8 wounds suffered while facing the enemy. He himself says
that he was seventeen years old when he served on his first
campaign, that being at the time when Italy was being elec-
trified by Hannibal's successes. In battle he displayed an aggressive hand, a steady and stable foot, an unperturbed
countenance. He would address the enemy with threatening
words and a harsh tone of voice, correctly recognizing (and
instructing others as well) that this sort of thing is often
more effective than the sword in intimidating one's adver-
9 sary. When on the march he would carry his military gear
himself, and a single servant would follow along with his
camp supplies. It is said that he never even became annoyed
or found fault with this man when he served him his breakfast or supper. On the contrary, most of the time Cato would
himself lend a hand and help prepare the meals when he had
10 finished with his military duties. On campaign he drank
water, except that on occasion, when he was burning with
thirst, he would ask for some vinegar-water or, when his
strength was flagging, he would add a little ordinary wine.

29(2). Near his farm was the villa that had belonged to Manius Curius, a man who had celebrated three triumphs.

θεώμενος τοῦ τε χωρίου τὴν μικρότητα καὶ τῆς οἰκήσεως τὸ λιτόν, ἔν-
νοιαν ἐλάμβανε τοῦ ἀνδρὸς ὅτι Ῥωμαίων μέγιστος γενόμενος καὶ τὰ
μαχιμώτατα τῶν ἐθνῶν ὑπαγαγόμενος καὶ Πύρρον ἐξελάσας Ἰταλίας,
τοῦτο τὸ χωρίδιον αὐτὸς ἔσκαπτε καὶ ταύτην τὴν ἔπαυλιν ᾤκει μετὰ
2 τρεῖς θριάμβους. ἐνταῦθα πρὸς ἐσχάρᾳ καθήμενον αὐτὸν ἕψοντα
γογγυλίδας εὑρόντες οἱ Σαυνιτῶν πρέσβεις ἐδίδοσαν πολὺ χρυσίον, ὁ δ'
ἀπεπέμψατο φήσας οὐδὲν χρυσίου δεῖν ᾧ δεῖπνον ἀρκεῖ τοιοῦτον· αὐτῷ
3 μέντοι τοῦ χρυσίον ἔχειν κάλλιον εἶναι τὸ νικᾶν τοὺς ἔχοντας. ταῦθ' ὁ
Κάτων ἐνθυμούμενος ἀπῄει, καὶ τὸν αὑτοῦ πάλιν οἶκον ἐφορῶν καὶ
χωρία καὶ θεράποντας καὶ δίαιταν, ἐπέτεινε τὴν αὐτουργίαν καὶ περιέ-
κοπτε τὴν πολυτέλειαν. Φαβίου δὲ Μαξίμου τὴν Ταραντίνων πόλιν
ἑλόντος, ἔτυχε μὲν ὁ Κάτων στρατευόμενος ὑπ' αὐτῷ κομιδῇ μειράκιον
ὤν, Νεάρχῳ δέ τινι τῶν Πυθαγορικῶν ξένῳ χρησάμενος, ἐσπούδασε τῶν
4 λόγων μεταλαβεῖν. ἀκούσας δὲ ταῦτα διαλεγομένου τοῦ ἀνδρὸς οἷς
καὶ Πλάτων κέχρηται, τὴν μὲν 'ἡδονὴν' ἀποκαλῶν 'μέγιστον κακοῦ
δέλεαρ,' συμφορὰν δὲ τῇ ψυχῇ τὸ σῶμα πρώτην, λύσιν δὲ καὶ καθαρ-
μὸν οἷς μάλιστα χωρίζει καὶ ἀφίστησιν αὑτὴν τῶν περὶ τὸ σῶμα παθη-
μάτων λογισμοῖς, ἔτι μᾶλλον ἠγάπησε τὸ λιτὸν καὶ τὴν ἐγκράτειαν.
5 ἄλλως δὲ παιδείας Ἑλληνικῆς ὀψιμαθὴς λέγεται γενέσθαι, καὶ πόρρω
παντάπασιν ἡλικίας ἐληλακὼς Ἑλληνικὰ βιβλία λαβὼν εἰς χεῖρας,
βραχέα μὲν ἀπὸ Θουκυδίδου, πλείονα δ' ἀπὸ Δημοσθένους εἰς τὸ ῥη-
6 τορικὸν ὠφεληθῆναι. τὰ μέντοι συγγράμματα καὶ δόγμασιν Ἑλληνικοῖς
καὶ ἱστορίαις ἐπιεικῶς διαπεποίκιλται, καὶ μεθηρμηνευμένα πολλὰ

29.2 ἀπεπέμψατο UA: ἀπέπεμψε S

He would always wander over to this place and gaze at the grounds and the dwelling. The insignificance of the one and the simplicity of the other gave him some idea of the character of this man who, though he had attained pre-eminence among the Romans by subjugating the most war-like tribes and by driving Pyrrhus from Italy, with his own hands used to cultivate this plot of ground and, after three triumphs,
2 lived in this farmhouse. Here it was that the ambassadors of the Samnites found him, seated in front of the fire, engaged in boiling turnips. They had come to offer him a large sum of money, but he sent them away saying, "A man who can be satisfied with such a meal has no need of gold. As far as I am concerned, possessing gold is less attractive than con-
3 quering those who possess it." With his head full of these things Cato would return home and, when he contemplated instead his own house, his estate, his servants, his way of life, he would exert himself all the more and would cut back inessential expenses. When Fabius Maximus took the city of Tarentum, Cato, who was then quite young, happened to be serving under his command and was staying at the home of a certain Nearchus. This man was a Pythagorean, and Cato
4 conceived an interest in partaking of his teachings. In the course of conversation he heard from him those doctrines which Plato too had formulated, namely that the greatest enticement to wrongdoing is pleasure, that the soul's chief encumbrance is the body, that those exercises of reason that most successfully sunder and divorce the soul from corporeal sensation are the true liberators and purifiers of the soul. This caused him to espouse still more fondly the life of sim-
5 plicity and self-discipline. In other respects, though, it is said that it was only late in life that he was exposed to Greek education, not taking up a Greek book until he was well advanced in years, at which time, though his reading of Thucydides provided him with some benefit in developing his rhetorical technique, it was from Demosthenes that he de-
6 rived greater profit. His writings are, however, fairly well laced with Greek ideas and anecdotes, and a number of literal translations from the Greek are ranged among his sayings

κατὰ λέξιν ἐν τοῖς ἀποφθέγμασι καὶ ταῖς γνωμολογίαις τέτακται.

30(3). Ἦν δέ τις ἀνὴρ εὐπατρίδης μὲν ἐν τοῖς μάλιστα Ῥωμαίων καὶ
δυνατός, ἀρετὴν δὲ φυομένην μὲν αἰσθάνεσθαι δεινός, εὐμενὴς δὲ καὶ
2 θρέψαι καὶ προαγαγεῖν εἰς δόξαν, Οὐαλέριος Φλάκκος. οὗτος εἶχεν
ὁμοροῦντα χωρία τοῖς Κάτωνος, πυνθανόμενος δὲ τὴν αὐτουργίαν καὶ
δίαιταν αὐτοῦ παρὰ τῶν οἰκετῶν καὶ θαυμάσας ἐξηγουμένων ὅτι πρωὶ
μὲν εἰς ἀγορὰν βαδίζει καὶ παρίσταται τοῖς δεομένοις, ἐπανελθὼν δ᾽ εἰς
τὸ χωρίον, ἂν μὲν ᾖ χειμὼν ἐξωμίδα λαβών, θέρους δὲ γυμνὸς ἐργασά-
μενος μετὰ τῶν οἰκετῶν ἐσθίει τὸν αὐτὸν ἄρτον ὁμοῦ καθήμενος καὶ
πίνει τὸν αὐτὸν οἶνον, ἄλλην τε πολλὴν ἐπιείκειαν αὐτοῦ καὶ μετριό-
τητα καί τινας καὶ λόγους ἀποφθεγματικοὺς διαμνημονευόντων, ἐκέ-
3 λευσε κληθῆναι πρὸς τὸ δεῖπνον. ἐκ δὲ τούτου χρώμενος καὶ κατανοῶν
ἥμερον καὶ ἀστεῖον ἦθος, ὥσπερ φυτὸν ἀσκήσεως καὶ χώρας ἐπιφανοῦς
δεόμενον, προετρέψατο καὶ συνέπεισεν ἅψασθαι τῆς ἐν Ῥώμῃ πολιτείας. κατελθὼν οὖν εὐθὺς τοὺς μὲν αὐτὸς ἐκτᾶτο θαυμαστὰς καὶ φίλους
διὰ τῶν συνηγοριῶν, πολλὴν δὲ τοῦ Οὐαλερίου τιμήν τε καὶ δύναμιν
4 αὐτῷ προστιθέντος, χιλιαρχίας ἔτυχε πρῶτον, εἶτ᾽ ἐταμίευσεν. ἐκ τούτου δὲ λαμπρὸς ὢν ἤδη καὶ περιφανής, αὐτῷ τῷ Οὐαλερίῳ πρὸς τὰς
μεγίστας συνεξέδραμεν ἀρχάς, ὕπατός τε μετ᾽ ἐκείνου καὶ πάλιν τιμητὴς
γενόμενος. τῶν δὲ πρεσβυτέρων πολιτῶν Μαξίμῳ Φαβίῳ προσένειμεν
ἑαυτόν, ἐνδοξοτάτῳ μὲν ὄντι καὶ μεγίστην ἔχοντι δύναμιν, μᾶλλον δὲ
τὸν τρόπον αὐτοῦ καὶ τὸν βίον ὡς κάλλιστα παραδείγματα προθέμε-
5 νος. διὸ καὶ Σκιπίωνι τῷ μεγάλῳ, νέῳ μὲν ὄντι τότε, πρὸς δὲ τὴν Φαβίου
δύναμιν ἀνταίροντι καὶ φθονεῖσθαι δοκοῦντι, παρ᾽ οὐδὲν ἐποιήσατο

30.4 πρὸς Reiske: περὶ SUA 30.5 τότε, πρὸς δὲ τὴν UA: τότε δὲ πρὸς τὴν S

and aphorisms.

30(3). There was a certain man named Valerius Flaccus, who was among the most nobly born and influential of the Romans. This man had a rare ability to discern budding excellence, and he took an interest in fostering its growth and
2 promoting it to public view. This man possessed land that bordered on Cato's, and he learned from his servants about his strenuous way of life. He was amazed to hear them recount how he would walk to the forum early in the day to represent those who needed his help and then, returning to his estate, he would work by the side of his servants, wearing a short tunic in winter and stripped in summer, and would take refreshment by their side as well, eating the same bread and drinking the same wine. When they went on to relate many further examples of his proper and restrained conduct, including even some of his choice sayings, Valerius
3 gave word that he should be invited to dinner, and from that day they were friends. When Valerius saw that he was dealing with a cultivated and refined temperament that, like some plant, needed training and a place in the sun, he urged him and encouraged him to enter the political life of Rome. No sooner did he come into the city than he acquired a number of clients and friends by his own efforts as an advocate. At the same time, his association with Valerius bestowed upon him considerable prestige and influence, and he first obtained a military tribuneship and then became quaestor.
4 As a result of this, he was now a distinguished and prominent figure, and he set out, in company with Valerius himself, in pursuit of the highest offices, serving as his colleague in the consulship and again in the censorship. As to the older citizens, he attached himself to Fabius Maximus, not only because he was exceptionally renowned and possessed tremendous influence, but even more because of his character and conduct, which Cato regarded as the finest models to follow.
5 It was for this reason that he did not think twice about setting himself at variance with the great Scipio, who was at that time, despite his youth, rebelling against the authority of

γενέσθαι διάφορος, ἀλλὰ καὶ ταμίας αὐτῷ πρὸς τὸν ἐν Λιβύῃ συνεκ-
πεμφθεὶς πόλεμον, ὡς ἑώρα τῇ συνήθει πολυτελείᾳ χρώμενον τὸν ἄνδρα
καὶ καταχορηγοῦντα τοῖς στρατεύμασιν ἀφειδῶς τῶν χρημάτων, ἐπαρ-
ρησιάζετο πρὸς αὐτόν, οὐ τὸ τῆς δαπάνης μέγιστον εἶναι φάσκων, ἀλλ'
ὅτι διαφθείρει τὴν πάτριον εὐτέλειαν τῶν στρατιωτῶν, εἰς ἡδονὰς καὶ
6 τρυφὰς τῷ περιόντι τῆς χρείας τρεπομένων. εἰπόντος δὲ τοῦ Σκιπίωνος
ὡς οὐδὲν δέοιτο ταμίου λίαν ἀκριβοῦς πλησίστιος ἐπὶ τὸν πόλεμον
φερόμενος (πράξεων γάρ, οὐ χρημάτων, τῇ πόλει λόγον ὀφείλειν),
ἀπῆλθεν ὁ Κάτων ἐκ Σικελίας καὶ μετὰ τοῦ Φαβίου καταβοῶν ἐν τῷ
συνεδρίῳ φθοράν τε χρημάτων ἀμύθητον ὑπὸ τοῦ Σκιπίωνος καὶ δια-
τριβὰς αὐτοῦ μειρακιώδεις ἐν παλαίστραις καὶ θεάτροις, ὥσπερ οὐ
στρατηγοῦντος, ἀλλὰ πανηγυρίζοντος, ἐξειργάσατο πεμφθῆναι δημάρ-
χους ἐπ' αὐτὸν ἄξοντας εἰς Ῥώμην, ἄνπερ ἀληθεῖς αἱ κατηγορίαι φα-
7 νῶσιν. ὁ μὲν οὖν Σκιπίων ἐν τῇ παρασκευῇ τοῦ πολέμου τὴν νίκην
ἐπιδειξάμενος καὶ φανεὶς ἡδὺς μὲν ἐπὶ σχολῆς συνεῖναι φίλοις, οὐδαμῇ
δὲ τῷ φιλανθρώπῳ τῆς διαίτης εἰς τὰ σπουδαῖα καὶ μεγάλα ῥᾴθυμος,
ἐξέπλευσεν ἐπὶ τὸν πόλεμον.

31(4). Τῷ δὲ Κάτωνι πολλὴ μὲν ἀπὸ τοῦ λόγου δύναμις ηὔξητο καὶ
Ῥωμαίων αὐτὸν οἱ πολλοὶ Δημοσθένη προσηγόρευον, ὁ δὲ βίος μᾶλλον
2 ὀνομαστὸς ἦν αὐτοῦ καὶ περιβόητος. ἡ μὲν γὰρ ἐν τῷ λέγειν δεινότης
προέκειτο τοῖς νέοις ἀγώνισμα κοινὸν ἤδη καὶ περισπούδαστον, ὁ δὲ τὴν
πάτριον αὐτουργίαν ὑπομένων καὶ δεῖπνον ἀφελὲς καὶ ἄριστον ἄπυρον
καὶ λιτὴν ἐσθῆτα καὶ δημοτικὴν ἀσπαζόμενος οἴκησιν καὶ τὸ μὴ δεῖσθαι τῶν περιττῶν μᾶλλον ἢ τὸ κεκτῆσθαι θαυμάζων σπάνιος ἦν, ἤδη

30.5 διαφθείρει UA: διατρίβει S 30.6 ἀμύθητον S: ἀμυθήτων UA
31.1 ηὔξητο S: ηὔξατο U: ηὔξετο A| Ῥωμαίων UA^{2}: Ῥωμαῖον SA^{1}

Fabius and of whom Fabius was thought to be jealous. In fact, when he was dispatched along with Scipio to serve as his quaestor in the war in Libya, seeing him display his customary prodigality and squander money without restraint on his campaigns, he was outspoken in his criticism of him, saying that it was not so much the expenses that mattered, but that he was undermining the frugality that his soldiers had inherited from their ancestors and was introducing them to diversions and luxuries by supplying them with more than
6 the bare necessities. Scipio replied by saying that he had no need of a quaestor who was excessively strict when he was sailing into war at full speed. For he owed the city, he said, an accounting not of his expenses but of his performance. So Cato left Sicily and, along with Fabius, denounced in the senate Scipio's unprecedented squandering of funds and the amount of time he spent in palaestras and theaters engaged in juvenile pursuits, as though he were attending some festival rather than leading an army. Cato's efforts brought it about that tribunes were sent to Scipio for the purpose of bringing him to Rome to determine if the accusations bore
7 any semblance of truth. For his part, Scipio painted a picture of the victory that his preparations for war entailed and he made it clear that, while he was affable in his dealings with friends in his leisure moments, he was by no means debilitated by his convivial ways when it came to serious and weighty matters. And so he sailed off to the war.

31(4). As a result of his eloquence, Cato's influence had grown considerably, and most of the Romans used to call him "Demosthenes," but it was more for his personal conduct that
2 he was celebrated and renowned. For skill in public speaking was an object for which the young were already striving eagerly and in large numbers, whereas it was most unusual to see a man who shunned neither the kind of manual labor that his ancestors engaged in nor a simple meal nor a cold breakfast nor plain clothing, who could be happy with an undistinguished residence, who thought it more admirable to dispense with luxuries than to possess them. At that time al-

τότε τῆς πολιτείας τὸ καθαρὸν ὑπὸ μεγέθους οὐ φυλαττούσης, ἀλλὰ τῷ
κρατεῖν πραγμάτων πολλῶν καὶ ἀνθρώπων πρὸς πολλὰ μειγνυμένης
3 ἔθη καὶ βίων παραδείγματα παντοδαπῶν ὑποδεχομένης. εἰκότως οὖν
ἐθαύμαζον τὸν Κάτωνα, τοὺς μὲν ἄλλους ὑπὸ τῶν πόνων θραυομένους
καὶ μαλασσομένους ὑπὸ τῶν ἡδονῶν ὁρῶντες, ἐκεῖνον δ' ὑπ' ἀμφοῖν
ἀήττητον, οὐ μόνον ἕως ἔτι νέος καὶ φιλότιμος ἦν, ἀλλὰ καὶ γέροντα
πολὺν ἤδη μεθ' ὑπατείαν καὶ θρίαμβον, ὥσπερ ἀθλητὴν νικηφόρον,
ἐγκαρτεροῦντα τῇ τάξει τῆς ἀσκήσεως καὶ διομαλίζοντα μέχρι τῆς τε-
4 λευτῆς. ἐσθῆτα μὲν γὰρ οὐδέποτέ φησι φορέσαι πολυτελεστέραν ἑκατὸν δραχμῶν, πιεῖν δὲ καὶ στρατηγῶν καὶ ὑπατεύων τὸν αὐτὸν οἶνον
τοῖς ἐρέταις, ὄψον δὲ παρασκευάζεσθαι πρὸς τὸ δεῖπνον ἐξ ἀγορᾶς
ἀσσαρίων τριάκοντα, καὶ τοῦτο διὰ τὴν πόλιν, ὅπως ἰσχύοι τὸ σῶμα
5 πρὸς τὰς στρατείας, ἐπίβλημα δὲ τῶν ποικίλων Βαβυλώνιον ἐκ κληρο-
νομίας κτησάμενος εὐθὺς ἀποδόσθαι, τῶν δ' ἐπαύλεων αὐτοῦ μηδεμίαν
εἶναι κεκονιαμένην, οὐδένα δὲ πώποτε πρίασθαι δοῦλον ὑπὲρ τὰς χιλίας δραχμὰς καὶ πεντακοσίας, ὡς ἂν οὐ τρυφερῶν οὐδ' ὡραίων, ἐργατι-
κῶν δὲ καὶ στερεῶν οἷον ἱπποκόμων καὶ βοηλατῶν δεόμενος· καὶ τούτους δὲ πρεσβυτέρους γενομένους ᾤετο δεῖν ἀποδίδοσθαι καὶ μὴ βό-
6 σκειν ἀχρήστους. ὅλως δὲ μηδὲν εὔωνον εἶναι τῶν περιττῶν, ἀλλ' οὗ τις
οὐ δεῖται, κἂν ἀσσαρίου πιπράσκηται, πολλοῦ νομίζειν· κτᾶσθαι δὲ τὰ
σπειρόμενα καὶ νεμόμενα μᾶλλον ἢ τὰ ῥαινόμενα καὶ σαιρόμενα.

32(5). Ταῦτα δ' οἱ μὲν εἰς μικρολογίαν ἐτίθεντο τοῦ ἀνδρός, οἱ δ' ὡς ἐπὶ διορθώσει καὶ σωφρονισμῷ τῶν ἄλλων ἐνδοτέρω συστέλλοντος ἑαυτὸν ἀπεδέχοντο. πλὴν τὸ τοῖς οἰκέταις ὡς ὑποζυγίοις ἀποχρησάμε-

31.4 ἐρέταις S: ἐργάταις UA 32.1 ἀπεδέχοντο S: ἀποδέχονται UA

ready Rome was, on account of its size, unable to preserve its purity; because of its domination over many lands and peoples it was coming into contact with various races and was
3 exposed to patterns of behavior of every description. It is therefore not surprising that the people admired Cato, particularly when they saw that, while the rest were either ruined by their exertions or enervated by a life of luxury, he could be mastered neither by the one nor the other. And this was true not only while he was still young and ambitious but, even when he was quite an old man and had a consulship and a triumph behind him, like some champion athlete he persisted in his training routine and continued, with regular-
4 ity, to the end. He claims, indeed, that he never wore a garment worth more than one hundred drachmas; that he drank the same wine, even when he was praetor and consul, as the rowers; that he would spend thirty asses at the market on meat or fish for his dinner, and that only for the sake of the state, so that his body would be strong enough for campaigns;
5 that he had inherited a fancy Babylonian rug, but had sold it immediately; that none of his houses had plastered walls; that he had never purchased a slave for more than 1,500 drachmas, as he would not be likely to need dainty ones in the bloom of youth, but rather robust ones who were good workers, to serve as grooms, for instance, or herdsmen. (He thought that one should sell off even these when they reached a certain age and not bother supporting them when
6 they were useless.) In a word, he regarded nothing as a bargain if it was inessential. On the contrary, he thought that if one paid even an as for something one did not need, it was too high a price. And he would say that he acquired real estate for sowing and pasturing rather than for sprinkling and sweeping.

32(5). While this was regarded by some as a sign of the man's parsimony, some accepted it rather as the behavior of a man who was tightening his own belt as a means of providing guidance to, and instilling discipline in, the rest. As far as I am concerned, treating servants as though they were

νον ἐπὶ γήρως ἐξελαύνειν καὶ πιπράσκειν ἀτενοῦς ἄγαν ἤθους ἔγωγε
τίθεμαι καὶ μηδὲν ἀνθρώπῳ πρὸς ἄνθρωπον οἰομένου κοινώνημα τῆς
2 χρείας πλέον ὑπάρχειν. καίτοι τὴν χρηστότητα τῆς δικαιοσύνης πλα-
τύτερον τόπον ὁρῶμεν ἐπιλαμβάνουσαν· νόμῳ μὲν γὰρ καὶ τῷ δικαίῳ
πρὸς ἀνθρώπους μόνον χρῆσθαι πεφύκαμεν, πρὸς εὐεργεσίας δὲ καὶ
χάριτας ἔστιν ὅτε καὶ μέχρι τῶν ἀλόγων ζῴων ὥσπερ ἐκ πηγῆς πλουσίας
ἀπορρεῖ τῆς ἡμερότητος. καὶ γὰρ ἵππων ἀπειρηκότων ὑπὸ χρόνου τρο-
φαὶ καὶ κυνῶν οὐ σκυλακεῖαι μόνον ἀλλὰ καὶ γηροκομίαι τῷ χρηστῷ
3 προσήκουσιν. ὁ δὲ τῶν Ἀθηναίων δῆμος οἰκοδομῶν τὸν Ἑκατόμπεδον,
ὅσας κατενόησεν ἡμιόνους μάλιστα τοῖς πόνοις ἐγκαρτερούσας, ἀπέ-
λυσεν ἐλευθέρας νέμεσθαι καὶ ἀφέτους, ὧν μίαν φασὶ καταβαίνουσαν
ἀφ᾽ ἑαυτῆς πρὸς τὰ ἔργα τοῖς ἀνάγουσι τὰς ἁμάξας ὑποζυγίοις εἰς
ἀκρόπολιν συμπαρατρέχειν καὶ προηγεῖσθαι καθάπερ ἐγκελευομένην
καὶ συνεξορμῶσαν, ἣν καὶ τρέφεσθαι δημοσίᾳ μέχρι τελευτῆς ἐψηφί-
4 σαντο. τῶν δὲ Κίμωνος ἵππων αἷς Ὀλύμπια τρὶς ἐνίκησε καὶ ταφαὶ πλησίον εἰσὶ τῶν ἐκείνου μνημάτων. κύνας δὲ συντρόφους γενομένους καὶ
συνήθεις ἄλλοι τε πολλοὶ καὶ Ξάνθιππος ὁ παλαιὸς τὸν εἰς Σαλαμῖνα
τῇ τριήρει παρανηξάμενον, ὅτε τὴν πόλιν ὁ δῆμος ἐξέλιπεν, ἐπὶ τῆς
5 ἄκρας ἐκήδευσεν ἣν Κυνὸς σῆμα μέχρι νῦν καλοῦσιν. οὐ γὰρ ὡς ὑπο-
δήμασιν ἢ σκεύεσι τοῖς ψυχὴν ἔχουσι χρηστέον, κοπέντα καὶ κατατρι-
βέντα ταῖς ὑπηρεσίαις ἀπορριπτοῦντας, ἀλλ᾽ ἢ διὰ μηδὲν ἄλλο μελέτης
οὕνεκα τοῦ φιλανθρώπου προεθιστέον ἑαυτὸν ἐν τούτοις πρᾶον εἶναι
6 καὶ μειλίχιον. ἐγὼ μὲν οὖν οὐδὲ βοῦν ἂν ἐργάτην διὰ γῆρας ἀποδοίμην,
μή τί γε πρεσβύτερον ἄνθρωπον, ἐκ χώρας συντρόφου καὶ διαίτης συν-

32.1 ἀτενοῦς UA et Thom. Magist. *Ecl.* p. 21 Ritschl: ἀγεννοῦς S
32.2 χρόνου S: πόνου UA 32.5 ἀπορριπτοῦντας UA:
ἀπορρίπτοντας S| μειλίχιον UA: μείλιχον S

beasts of burden, driving them away and selling them in their old age, indicates a spirit of unrelenting insensitivity and one which thinks that there is no relationship between
2 men higher than one based on expediency. We can see, however, that humane behavior extends over a greater range of activity than does justice for, while we naturally bring law and justice into play with regard only to our dealings with men, it often happens that, through benevolence and charity, there flows from our good nature as from a copious spring a stream that reaches even to the creatures that are deprived of reason. For it is the part of the humane master to provide support for horses that are past their prime and to maintain his hounds not only when they are vigorous but in their old
3 age as well. When the Athenian people were engaged in the construction of the Parthenon, they took those mules that they noticed to be particularly hard-working and set them free, to roam and pasture as they wished. The story goes that one of them would of her own accord go down to the stone-yards and would run alongside the teams pulling the wagons to the acropolis and lead the way, just as if she were urging them on and encouraging them. The people passed a decree that she should be maintained at public expense for
4 the rest of her days. And the horses with which Cimon won victories on three occasions at the Olympic Games have graves next to his own monument. Likewise there are many stories of men who gave the honor of burial to dogs who had grown up with them and with whom they had become familiar. Xanthippus of old, for instance, buried on the promontory that is still today called Houndsgrave the dog that swam alongside his trireme to Salamis at the time when
5 the people abandoned the city. We should not, after all, treat living creatures as though they were shoes or tools, tossing them aside after they have been beaten down and ravaged by their servitude. Instead, if for no reason other than for the sake of exercising our feelings of compassion, we should use these in order to practice being forbearing and gentle.
6 For my part, I would not even sell a draft ox on account of old age, much less an aged human being, sending him, as it

ἤθους ὥσπερ ἐκ πατρίδος μεθιστάμενον ἀντὶ κερμάτων μικρῶν, ἄχρη-
7 στόν γε τοῖς ὠνουμένοις ὥσπερ τοῖς πιπράσκουσι γενησόμενον. ὁ δὲ
Κάτων, ὥσπερ νεανιευόμενος ἐπὶ τούτοις, καὶ τὸν ἵππον ᾧ παρὰ τὰς
στρατείας ὑπατεύων ἐχρῆτό φησιν ἐν Ἰβηρίᾳ καταλιπεῖν, ἵνα μὴ τῇ
πόλει λογίσηται τὸ ναῦλον αὐτοῦ. ταῦτα μὲν οὖν εἴτε μεγαλοψυχίας
εἴτε μικρολογίας θετέον, ἔξεστι τῷ πείθοντι χρῆσθαι λογισμῷ.

33(6). Τῆς δ' ἄλλης ἐγκρατείας ὑπερφυῶς θαυμαστὸς ὁ ἀνήρ, ὅστις
στρατηγῶν ἐλάμβανεν ἑαυτῷ καὶ τοῖς περὶ αὐτὸν οὐ πλέον εἰς τὸν μῆνα
πυρῶν ἢ τρεῖς Ἀττικοὺς μεδίμνους, εἰς δὲ τὴν ἡμέραν κριθῶν τοῖς ὑπο-
2 ζυγίοις ἔλαττον τριῶν ἡμιμεδίμνων. ἐπαρχίαν δὲ λαβὼν Σαρδόνα, τῶν
πρὸ αὐτοῦ στρατηγῶν εἰωθότων χρῆσθαι καὶ σκηνώμασι δημοσίοις καὶ
κλίναις καὶ ἱματίοις, πολλῇ δὲ θεραπείᾳ καὶ φίλων πλήθει καὶ περὶ δεῖ-
πνα δαπάναις καὶ παρασκευαῖς βαρυνόντων, ἐκεῖνος ἄπιστον ἐποίησε
3 τὴν διαφορὰν τῆς εὐτελείας· δαπάνης μὲν γὰρ εἰς οὐδὲν οὐδεμιᾶς προσ-
εδεήθη δημοσίας, ἐπεφοίτα δὲ ταῖς πόλεσιν αὐτὸς μὲν ἄνευ ζεύγους πο-
ρευόμενος, εἷς δ' ἠκολούθει δημόσιος ἐσθῆτα καὶ σπονδεῖον αὐτῷ πρὸς
4 ἱερουργίαν κομίζων. ἐν δὲ τούτοις οὕτως εὔκολος καὶ ἀφελὴς τοῖς ὑπὸ
χεῖρα φαινόμενος, αὖθις ἀνταπεδίδου τὴν σεμνότητα καὶ τὸ βάρος, ἀ-
παραίτητος ὢν ἐν τῷ δικαίῳ καὶ τοῖς ὑπὲρ τῆς ἡγεμονίας προστάγμασιν
ὄρθιος καὶ αὐθέκαστος, ὥστε μηδέποτε τὴν Ῥωμαίων ἀρχὴν ἐκείνοις
μήτε φοβερωτέραν μήτε προσφιλεστέραν γενέσθαι.

34(7). Τοιαύτην δέ τινα φαίνεται καὶ ὁ λόγος τοῦ ἀνδρὸς ἰδέαν ἔχειν·
εὔχαρις γὰρ ἅμα καὶ δεινὸς ἦν, ἡδὺς καὶ καταπληκτικός, φιλοσκώμμων

32.6 γε τοῖς UA: τε τοῖς Sl γενησόμενον S: γεγενημένον UA 32.7 παρὰ S: πρὸς UA 33.1 ὅστις S: οἷον ὅτι UA

were, into exile in exchange for a couple of pieces of copper
and depriving him of the place where he had grown up and
the routine that had become familiar. After all, he is going to
7 be no more useful to the buyer than to the seller. But Cato,
giving the impression that he takes some kind of adolescent
pride in these things, even says that he left behind in Spain
the horse that he had used on his campaigns during his consulship, in order to avoid charging the state for its trans-
portation by boat. Now, it is possible to use convincing arguments to prove either that all of this is to be ascribed to
magnanimity or to parsimony.

33(6). His austerity, however, was otherwise admirable
in the extreme. As commander he would take no more than
three Attic bushels of wheat per month for himself and his
staff, and less than one and a half bushels of barley per day
2 for his pack animals. He obtained as his province Sardinia
and, whereas the praetors before him were accustomed to
availing themselves of living quarters, couches and clothing
provided at public expense, and used to make oppressive
demands for large numbers of servants, accommodation for a
host of companions, expenses and furnishings for banquets,
he marked an incredible contrast to them with his frugality.
3 He made no demands on public funds for any supplemental
expenditures whatever. He would make his rounds of the
municipalities on foot, with no chariot, but a single servant,
provided by the state, would attend him carrying vestments
4 and a vessel for his use in religious ceremonies. In all of this
he appeared so congenial and unpretentious to those under
his jurisdiction, and at the same time he balanced this with
the appropriate authority and seriousness, being so relentless
in his dispensation of justice and so direct and forthright
with regard to the rulings he issued on behalf of his administration, that those people never felt Roman rule to be more
intimidating, or more welcome.

34(7). The man's powers of public speaking apparently
made very much the same sort of impression as well. For his

καὶ αὐστηρός, ἀποφθεγματικὸς καὶ ἀγωνιστικός, ὥσπερ ὁ Πλάτων τὸν
Σωκράτους φησὶν ἔξωθεν ἰδιώτην καὶ σατυρικὸν καὶ ὑβριστὴν τοῖς ἐν-
τυγχάνουσι φαινόμενον, ἔνδοθεν σπουδῆς καὶ πραγμάτων μεστὸν εἶναι
δάκρυα κινούντων τοῖς ἀκροωμένοις καὶ τὴν καρδίαν στρεφόντων.
2 ὅθεν οὐκ οἶδ' ὅτι πεπόνθασιν οἱ τῷ Λυσίου λόγῳ τὰ μάλιστα προσεοι-
3 κέναι φάμενοι τὸν Κάτωνος. οὐ μὴν ἀλλὰ ταῦτα μὲν οἷς μᾶλλον ἰδέας
λόγων Ῥωμαϊκῶν αἰσθάνεσθαι προσήκει διακρινοῦσιν, ἡμεῖς δὲ τῶν
ἀπομνημονευομένων βραχέα γράψομεν, οἳ τῷ λόγῳ πολὺ μᾶλλον ἢ τῷ
προσώπῳ, καθάπερ ἔνιοι νομίζουσι, τῶν ἀνθρώπων φαμὲν ἐμφαίνεσθαι
τὸ ἦθος.

35(8). Μέλλων ποτὲ τὸν Ῥωμαίων δῆμον ὡρμημένον ἀκαίρως ἐπὶ
σιτομετρίας καὶ διανομὰς ἀποτρέπειν, ἤρξατο τῶν λόγων οὕτως· 'χαλε-
2 πὸν μέν ἐστιν, ὦ πολῖται, πρὸς γαστέρα λέγειν ὦτα μὴ ἔχουσαν.' κατη-
γορῶν δὲ τῆς πολυτελείας ἔφη χαλεπὸν εἶναι σωθῆναι πόλιν ἐν ᾗ πωλεῖ-
3 ται πλείονος ἰχθὺς ἢ βοῦς. ἐοικέναι δὲ προβάτοις ἔφη τοὺς Ῥωμαίους·
'ὡς γὰρ ἐκεῖνα καθ' ἕκαστον μὲν οὐ πείθεται, σύμπαντα δ' ἕπεται μετ'
ἀλλήλων τοῖς ἄγουσιν, οὕτω καὶ ὑμεῖς,' εἶπεν, 'οἷς οὐκ ἂν ἀξιώσαιτε
συμβούλοις χρήσασθαι κατ' ἰδίαν, ὑπὸ τούτων εἰς ἓν συνελθόντες ἄγε-
4 σθε.' περὶ δὲ τῆς γυναικοκρατίας διαλεγόμενος, 'πάντες,' εἶπεν, 'ἄνθρωποι τῶν γυναικῶν ἄρχουσιν, ἡμεῖς δὲ πάντων ἀνθρώπων, ἡμῶν δ' αἱ
γυναῖκες.' τοῦτο μὲν οὖν ἐστιν ἐκ τῶν Θεμιστοκλέους μετενηνεγμένον
5 ἀποφθεγμάτων· ἐκεῖνος γὰρ ἐπιτάττοντος αὐτῷ πολλὰ τοῦ υἱοῦ διὰ τῆς
μητρός, 'ὦ γύναι,' εἶπεν, ''Αθηναῖοι μὲν ἄρχουσι τῶν Ἑλλήνων, ἐγὼ δ'
Ἀθηναίων, ἐμοῦ δὲ σύ, σοῦ δ' ὁ υἱός· ὥστε φειδέσθω τῆς ἐξουσίας, δι' ἣν
6 ἀνόητος ὢν πλεῖστον Ἑλλήνων δύναται.' τὸν δὲ δῆμον ὁ Κάτων ἔφη τὸν

34.1 Σωκράτους A (et primitus U?): Σωκράτην nunc U: Σωκράτη S| ἔνδοθεν UA: ἔνδοθεν δὲ S 34.3 Ῥωμαϊκῶν S: ῥητορικῶν UA 35.1 μὴ *mor.* 131d, 198d, 996d, Stob. 3.6.61: οὐκ SUA

speech was at one and the same time both elegant and tough,
smooth and intimidating, jocular and stern, magisterial and
contentious. It is rather like what Plato says about Socrates'
speech, that on the outside it appeared to those who came in
contact with it to be somewhat uncouth, ribald and aggressive, but on the inside to abound with seriousness and with
profound ideas that move listeners to tears and that trans-
2 form the way they feel. It is for this reason that I cannot
understand what entered the minds of those people who
claim that Cato's manner of speaking resembled so closely
3 that of Lysias. Be that as it may, this matter will be settled
by those who are in a better position than I am to appreciate
the character of Roman oratory. For my part, I propose to
record briefly some of his sayings, for I maintain that, contrary to what some people believe, men's character is much
more clearly reflected in their speech than in their features.

35(8). On one occasion, when it was his intention to di-
vert the people of Rome from their inopportune enthusiasm
for doles and distributions of grain, he began his comments
by saying, "Fellow citizens, it is not an easy task addressing a
2 belly that has no ears." In his denunciation of luxury he said
that it was difficult for a city to find salvation in which a fish
3 sold for more than an ox. He compared the Romans to sheep:
"Just as they cannot be prevailed upon individually, but as a
group flock together and follow their leaders, in the same
manner you," he said, "when you hold a meeting, allow your-
selves to be led by men whose advice you would not be
4 willing to follow in private." When he was discussing the
power of women he said, "All men rule their wives; we rule
all men; our wives rule us." This saying, however, is a trans-
5 lation of one of Themistocles'. For he once said, when his son
kept using his mother's influence to tell Themistocles what to
do, "My dear wife, the Athenians rule the Greeks; I rule the
Athenians; you rule me; and our son rules you. Make sure,
therefore, that he does not abuse the power that enables him,
immature though he is, to have the greatest influence among
6 the Greeks." Cato said that the Roman people established not

Ῥωμαίων οὐ μόνον ταῖς πορφύραις, ἀλλὰ καὶ τοῖς ἐπιτηδεύμασι τὰς
τιμὰς ἐπιγράφειν· 'ὡς γὰρ οἱ βαφεῖς,' ἔφη, 'ταύτην μάλιστα βάπτουσιν ᾗ
χαίροντας ὁρῶσιν, οὕτως οἱ νέοι ταῦτα μανθάνουσι καὶ ζηλοῦσιν οἷς
7 ἂν ὁ παρ' ὑμῶν ἔπαινος ἕπηται.' παρεκάλει δ' αὐτούς, εἰ μὲν ἀρετῇ καὶ
σωφροσύνῃ γεγόνασι μεγάλοι, μηδὲν μεταβάλλεσθαι πρὸς τὸ χεῖρον, εἰ
δ' ἀκρασίᾳ καὶ κακίᾳ, μεταβάλλεσθαι πρὸς τὸ βέλτιον· ἱκανῶς γὰρ ἤδη
8 μεγάλους ἀπ' ἐκείνων γεγονέναι. τοὺς δὲ πολλάκις ἄρχειν σπουδάζοντας ἔφη καθάπερ ἀγνοοῦντας τὴν ὁδὸν ἀεὶ μετὰ ῥαβδούχων ζητεῖν πο-
9 ρεύεσθαι, μὴ πλανηθῶσιν. ἐπετίμα δὲ τοῖς πολίταις τοὺς αὐτοὺς αἱρου-
μένοις πολλάκις ἄρχοντας· 'δόξετε γάρ,' ἔφη, 'ἢ μὴ πολλοῦ τὸ ἄρχειν
10 ἄξιον ἢ μὴ πολλοὺς τοῦ ἄρχειν ἀξίους ἡγεῖσθαι.' περὶ δὲ τῶν ἐχθρῶν
τινος αἰσχρῶς καὶ ἀδόξως βιοῦν δοκοῦντος, 'ἡ τούτου μήτηρ,' ἔφη,
11 'κατάραν, οὐκ εὐχήν, ἡγεῖται τὸ τοῦτον ὑπὲρ γῆς ἀπολιπεῖν.' τὸν δὲ
πεπρακότα τοὺς πατρῴους ἀγροὺς παραλίους ὄντας ἐπιδεικνύμενος
προσεποιεῖτο θαυμάζειν ὡς ἰσχυρότερον τῆς θαλάττης· 'ἃ γὰρ ἐκείνη
12 μόλις ἐπέκλυζεν, οὗτος,' ἔφη, 'ῥᾳδίως καταπέπωκεν.' ἐπεὶ δ' Εὐμένους
τοῦ βασιλέως ἐπιδημήσαντος εἰς Ῥώμην ἥ τε σύγκλητος ὑπερφυῶς
ἀπεδέξατο καὶ τῶν πρώτων ἅμιλλα καὶ σπουδὴ περὶ αὐτὸν ἐγίνετο,
13 δῆλος ἦν ὁ Κάτων ὑφορώμενος καὶ φυλαττόμενος αὐτόν. εἰπόντος δέ
τινος, 'ἀλλὰ μὴν χρηστός ἐστι καὶ φιλορώμαιος,' 'ἔστω,' εἶπεν· 'ἀλλὰ
14 φύσει τοῦτο τὸ ζῷον ὁ βασιλεὺς σαρκοφάγον ἐστίν.' οὐδένα δὲ τῶν
εὐδαιμονιζομένων ἔφη βασιλέων ἄξιον εἶναι παραβάλλειν πρὸς Ἐπα-
μεινώνδαν ἢ Περικλέα ἢ Θεμιστοκλέα ἢ Μάνιον Κούριον ἢ Ἀμίλκαν
15 τὸν ἐπικληθέντα Βάρκαν. αὐτῷ δ' ἔλεγε τοὺς ἐχθροὺς φθονεῖν, ὅτι καθ'
ἡμέραν ἐκ νυκτὸς ἀνίσταται καὶ τῶν ἰδίων ἀμελῶν τοῖς δημοσίοις σχο-
16 λάζει. βούλεσθαι δ' ἔλεγε μᾶλλον εὖ πράξας ἀποστερηθῆναι χάριν ἢ

35.6 ἕπηται UA: γίνηται S 35.7 μηδὲν S: μὴ UA 35.9 τοῦ ἄρχειν *mor.* 199a: τοὺς ἄρχειν SUA 35.11 ἐπέκλυζεν Flacelière: ἔκλυζεν SUA: ἐπικλύζει *mor.* 199b

only the value of purple fabric but of morals as well. For he
said, "Just as dyers make especial use of that color which
they recognize has especial appeal, so the young learn and
7 emulate whatever behavior attracts your commendation." He
would exhort them to make no change for the worse if they
had achieved eminence through virtue and prudence but, if
they had achieved it through licentiousness and vice, to make
a change for the better, since they had achieved already suf-
8 ficient eminence on those grounds. He said that those who
sought frequent election to public office were like men who
had lost their way and were constantly looking to have lic-
9 tors to escort them and keep them on the right path. He used
to take the citizens to task for electing the same men again
and again to public office, saying, "You will give people the
impression either that you do not consider public office
worth much or that you do not consider many men worthy of
10 public office." Concerning one of his opponents who had a
reputation for leading a life of debauchery and shame he
said, "This man's mother considers that she will be cursed,
11 not blessed, if she is survived by him." Pointing to a man
who had sold off his inherited holdings along the coast, he
affected to be amazed that the man was more powerful than
the sea and said, "With the greatest of ease he has lapped up
12 what the sea's assaults could barely reach." When King
Eumenes was visiting Rome, the senate gave him an effu-
sively lavish welcome and each of the leading citizens was
trying to outdo the other in making a great fuss over him,
but it was observed that Cato viewed him with suspicion and
13 kept out of his way. Someone then remarked to Cato, "But
you cannot deny that he is a man of distinction and is partial
to the Romans." To which Cato replied, "True. But the nature
14 of this beast called 'king' is to eat meat." He said that none of
the kings then being celebrated could stand comparison with
Epameinondas or Pericles or Themistocles or Manius Curius
15 or Hamilcar "Barca." He would say that his opponents jeal-
ously held it against him that he arose every day before
dawn and devoted his time to matters of state, to the neglect
16 of his own affairs. He used to say that he would rather act

17 κακῶς μὴ τυχεῖν κολάσεως, καὶ συγγνώμην ἔφη διδόναι πᾶσι τοῖς ἀ-
μαρτάνουσι πλὴν αὑτοῦ.

36(9). Τῶν δὲ Ῥωμαίων εἰς Βιθυνίαν τρεῖς ἑλομένων πρέσβεις, ὧν ὁ
μὲν ποδαγρικὸς ἦν, ὁ δὲ τὴν κεφαλὴν ἐξ ἀνατρήσεως καὶ περικοπῆς
κοίλην εἶχεν, ὁ δὲ τρίτος ἐδόκει μωρὸς εἶναι, καταγελῶν ὁ Κάτων ἔλεγε
πρεσβείαν ὑπὸ Ῥωμαίων ἀποστέλλεσθαι μήτε πόδας μήτε κεφαλὴν μήτε
2 καρδίαν ἔχουσαν. ὑπὲρ δὲ τῶν ἐξ Ἀχαΐας φυγάδων ἐντευχθεὶς διὰ Πολύβιον ὑπὸ Σκιπίωνος, ὡς πολὺς ἐν τῇ συγκλήτῳ λόγος ἐγίνετο, τῶν μὲν
διδόντων κάθοδον αὐτοῖς, τῶν δ' ἐνισταμένων, ἀναστὰς ὁ Κάτων, 'ὥσπερ οὐκ ἔχοντες,' εἶπεν, 'ὃ πράττωμεν, καθήμεθα τὴν ἡμέραν ὅλην περὶ
γεροντίων Γραικῶν ζητοῦντες, πότερον ὑπὸ τῶν παρ' ἡμῖν ἢ τῶν ἐν
3 Ἀχαΐᾳ νεκροφόρων ἐκκομισθῶσι.' ψηφισθείσης δὲ τῆς καθόδου τοῖς
ἀνδράσιν, ἡμέρας ὀλίγας οἱ περὶ τὸν Πολύβιον διαλιπόντες αὖθις ἐπε-
χείρουν εἰς τὴν σύγκλητον εἰσελθεῖν, ὅπως ἃς πρότερον εἶχον ἐν Ἀχαΐᾳ
τιμὰς οἱ φυγάδες ἀναλάβοιεν, καὶ τοῦ Κάτωνος ἀπεπειρῶντο τῆς γνώμης. ὁ δὲ μειδιάσας ἔφη τὸν Πολύβιον ὥσπερ τὸν Ὀδυσσέα βούλεσθαι
πάλιν εἰς τὸ τοῦ Κύκλωπος σπήλαιον εἰσελθεῖν, τὸ πιλίον ἐκεῖ καὶ τὴν
4 ζώνην ἐπιλελησμένον. τοὺς δὲ φρονίμους ἔλεγε μᾶλλον ὑπὸ τῶν ἀφρό-
νων ἢ τοὺς ἄφρονας ὑπὸ τῶν φρονίμων ὠφελεῖσθαι· τούτους μὲν γὰρ
φυλάττεσθαι τὰς ἐκείνων ἁμαρτίας, ἐκείνους δὲ τὰς τούτων μὴ μιμεῖσθαι
5 κατορθώσεις. τῶν δὲ νέων ἔφη χαίρειν τοῖς ἐρυθριῶσι μᾶλλον ἢ τοῖς
ὠχριῶσι, στρατιώτου δὲ μὴ δεῖσθαι τὰς μὲν χεῖρας ἐν τῷ βαδίζειν, τοὺς
δὲ πόδας ἐν τῷ μάχεσθαι κινοῦντος, μεῖζον δὲ ῥέγχοντος ἢ ἀλαλά-
6 ζοντος. τὸν δ' ὑπέρπαχυν κακίζων, 'ποῦ δ' ἄν,' ἔφη, 'τῇ πόλει σῶμα
τοιοῦτο γένοιτο χρήσιμον, οὗ τὸ μεταξὺ λαιμοῦ καὶ βουβώνων ἅπαν
7 ὑπὸ τῆς γαστρὸς κατέχεται;' τῶν δὲ φιληδόνων τινὰ βουλόμενον αὐτῷ

36.2 πράττωμεν *mor.* 199e: πράττομεν SUA 36.7 τινὰ βουλόμενον UA: τινὸς βουλομένου S

honorably and not be appreciated than act dishonorably and
17 escape punishment. And he said that he had forgiveness for
everyone who made a mistake, except himself.

36(9). When the Romans chose as ambassadors to Bithynia three men of whom one was afflicted with gout, one had
undergone an operation in which part of his skull was removed with a trepan and the third was considered mentally
deficient, Cato made the derisive comment that the Roman
state was dispatching an embassy that was missing feet, a
2 head and a heart. When, at the instigation of Polybius, Scipio
made an appeal for Cato's support in behalf of the exiles from
Achaea and there was considerable debate in the senate
between those who were in favor of granting them repatria-
tion and those who were opposed, Cato stood up and said,
"We are sitting around all day long as though we do not know
what to do with ourselves, and we are trying to decide
whether a pack of Greek grandfathers should receive their
3 last rites from the undertakers here or in Greece." A few
days after the voting took place, as a result of which repatri-
ation was granted to the men, Polybius once again ventured
to enter the senate in order to restore to the exiles the rights
that they formerly possessed in Greece. When he tried to
explore how Cato felt about the matter, Cato said with a smile
that Polybius reminded him of Odysseus, wishing to return to
the Cyclops' cave because he had forgotten his cap and his
4 belt there. He used to say that wise men derived greater
benefit from fools than vice versa, since the former paid attention to the latter's mistakes while the latter were unable
5 to reproduce the former's accomplishments. He said that it
pleased him more to see those young men who blushed than
those who blanched, and that he had no use for a soldier
whose hands were exercised on the march and whose feet
were exercised on the battlefield, or for one whose snore was
6 louder than his battle cry. When reviling an obese man he
said, "What use could the state possibly make of a body like
that? Why, from gullet to groin there is nothing but belly."
7 When a certain hedonist invited him to join his circle of ac-

συνεῖναι παραιτούμενος, ἔφη μὴ δύνασθαι ζῆν μετ' ἀνθρώπου τῆς καρ-
8 δίας τὴν ὑπερῴαν εὐαισθητοτέραν ἔχοντος. τοῦ δ' ἐρῶντος ἔλεγε τὴν
9 ψυχὴν ἐν ἀλλοτρίῳ σώματι ζῆν. μεταμεληθῆναι δ' αὐτὸς ἐν παντὶ τῷ
βίῳ τρεῖς μεταμελείας· μίαν μὲν ἐπὶ τῷ γυναικὶ πιστεῦσαι λόγον ἀπόρρητον, ἑτέραν δὲ πλεύσας ὅπου δυνατὸν ἦν πεζεῦσαι, τὴν δὲ τρίτην ὅτι
10 μίαν ἡμέραν ἀδιάθετος ἔμεινε. πρὸς δὲ πρεσβύτην πονηρευόμενον,
'ἄνθρωπε,' εἶπε, 'πολλὰ ἔχοντι τῷ γήρᾳ τὰ αἰσχρὰ μὴ προστίθει τὴν ἀπὸ
11 τῆς κακίας αἰσχύνην.' πρὸς δὲ δήμαρχον ἐν διαβολῇ μὲν φαρμακείας
γενόμενον, φαῦλον δὲ νόμον εἰσφέροντα καὶ βιαζόμενον, 'ὦ μειράκιον,'
εἶπεν, 'οὐκ οἶδα πότερον χεῖρόν ἐστιν ὃ κίρνης πιεῖν ἢ ὃ γράφεις κυρῶ-
12 σαι.' βλασφημούμενος δ' ὑπ' ἀνθρώπου βεβιωκότος ἀσελγῶς καὶ κακῶς, 'ἄνισος,' εἶπεν, 'ἡ πρὸς σέ μοι μάχη ἐστί· καὶ γὰρ ἀκούεις τὰ κακὰ
ῥᾳδίως καὶ λέγεις εὐχερῶς, ἐμοὶ δὲ καὶ λέγειν ἀηδὲς καὶ ἀκούειν ἄηθες.'
τὸ μὲν οὖν τῶν ἀπομνημονευμάτων γένος τοιοῦτόν ἐστιν.

37(10). Ὕπατος δὲ μετὰ Φλάκκου Οὐαλερίου τοῦ φίλου καὶ συνή-
θους ἀποδειχθείς, ἔλαχε τῶν ἐπαρχιῶν ἣν Ἐντὸς Ἱσπανίαν Ῥωμαῖοι
καλοῦσιν. ἐνταῦθα δ' αὐτῷ τὰ μὲν καταστρεφομένῳ τῶν ἐθνῶν, τὰ δ'
οἰκειουμένῳ διὰ λόγου, πολλὴ στρατιὰ τῶν βαρβάρων ἐπέπεσε, καὶ
κίνδυνος ἦν αἰσχρῶς ἐκβιασθῆναι· διὸ τῶν ἐγγὺς Κελτιβήρων ἐπεκαλεῖ-
2 το συμμαχίαν. αἰτούντων δ' ἐκείνων τῆς βοηθείας διακόσια τάλαντα
μισθόν, οἱ μὲν ἄλλοι πάντες οὐκ ἀνασχετὸν ἐποιοῦντο Ῥωμαίους βαρβάροις ἐπικουρίας ὁμολογῆσαι μισθόν, ὁ δὲ Κάτων οὐδὲν ἔφη δεινὸν
εἶναι· νικῶντας μὲν γὰρ ἀποδώσειν παρὰ τῶν πολεμίων, οὐ παρ' αὐτῶν,
ἡττωμένων δὲ μήτε τοὺς ἀπαιτουμένους ἔσεσθαι μήτε τοὺς ἀπαιτοῦν-
3 τας. ταύτην δὲ τὴν μάχην κατὰ κράτος ἐνίκησε, καὶ τὰ ἄλλα προυχώ-

36.12 ἄηθες om. S 37.1 διὰ λόγου S: διὰ λόγων UA

quaintances, Cato declined, saying that he could not put up
with a man whose palate was more refined than his intellect.
8,9 He said that a lover's soul lives in someone else's body. He
said that there were three things he regretted in his entire
life; one was that he had confided a secret to a woman, the
second was that he had sailed when he could have gone by
land and the third was that he allowed himself to remain in-
10 testate for one day. To an old man who was behaving dis-
gracefully he said, "Sir, old age has indignities enough; you
11 need not add the indignity that is born of depravity." When
a certain tribune, who had been charged with administering
poison, was proposing a worthless law and was vehement in
his efforts to have it passed, Cato said, "Young man, I do not
know which is worse, to drink your brew or to pass your
12 bill." When he was being reviled by a man who had been
living a life of licentiousness and vice, he said, "I am at a disadvantage when I contend with you. For you are used to
hearing insults and you voice them with ease, whereas I
neither take pleasure in using insulting language nor am I
accustomed to hear it." This gives some idea of the character
of his sayings.

37(10). He was elected consul along with his friend and
companion Valerius Flaccus, and he was assigned to the province that the Romans call "Inner Spain." While he was engaged there in subduing a number of the tribes by force of
arms and in winning over others by diplomacy, he was attacked by a large army of natives and he risked suffering the
humiliation of being forcibly dislodged from his position. So
he solicited the cooperation of the neighboring Celtiberi who,
2 however, demanded a payment of two hundred talents in
return for their support. Now, everyone else regarded it as
intolerable that Romans should agree to pay foreigners for
assistance, but Cato said that it was not so terrible. For, if
they were victorious, they would use the enemy's money,
rather than their own, to make the payment. If, on the other
hand, they were defeated, there would be no one left stand-
3 ing either to make or demand payment. In the battle that

ρει λαμπρῶς. Πολύβιος μέν γέ φησι τῶν ἐντὸς Βαίτιος ποταμοῦ πόλεων
ἡμέρᾳ μιᾷ τὰ τείχη κελεύσαντος αὐτοῦ περιαιρεθῆναι (πάμπολλαι δ'
ἦσαν αὗται καὶ γέμουσαι μαχίμων ἀνδρῶν)· αὐτὸς δέ φησιν ὁ Κάτων
πλείονας εἰληφέναι πόλεις ὧν διήγαγεν ἡμερῶν ἐν Ἰβηρίᾳ· καὶ τοῦτο
4 κόμπος οὐκ ἔστιν, εἴπερ ὡς ἀληθῶς τετρακόσιαι τὸ πλῆθος ἦσαν. τοῖς
μὲν οὖν στρατιώταις πολλὰ παρὰ τὴν στρατείαν ὠφεληθεῖσιν ἔτι καὶ
λίτραν ἀργυρίου κατ' ἄνδρα προσδιένειμεν, εἰπὼν ὡς κρεῖττον εἴη πολλοὺς Ῥωμαίων ἀργύριον ἢ χρυσίον ὀλίγους ἔχοντας ἐπανελθεῖν· εἰς δ'
αὐτὸν ἐκ τῶν ἁλισκομένων οὐδὲν ἐλθεῖν λέγει πλὴν ὅσα πέπωκεν ἢ βέ-
5 βρωκε, καὶ 'οὐκ αἰτιῶμαι,' φησί, 'τοὺς ὠφελεῖσθαι ζητοῦντας ἐκ τούτων,
ἀλλὰ βούλομαι μᾶλλον περὶ ἀρετῆς τοῖς ἀρίστοις ἢ περὶ χρημάτων τοῖς
πλουσιωτάτοις ἁμιλλᾶσθαι καὶ τοῖς φιλαργυρωτάτοις περὶ φιλαργυρί-
6 ας.' οὐ μόνον δ' αὐτόν, ἀλλὰ καὶ τοὺς περὶ αὐτὸν ἐφύλαττε καθαροὺς
παντὸς λήμματος. ἦσαν δὲ πέντε θεράποντες ἐπὶ στρατείας σὺν αὐτῷ·
τούτων εἷς ὄνομα Πάκκιος ἠγόρασε τρία τῶν αἰχμαλώτων παιδάρια·
τοῦ δὲ Κάτωνος αἰσθομένου, πρὶν εἰς ὄψιν ἐλθεῖν ἀπήγξατο. τοὺς δὲ
παῖδας ὁ Κάτων ἀποδόμενος, εἰς τὸ δημόσιον ἀνήνεγκε τὴν τιμήν.

38(11). Ἔτι δ' αὐτοῦ διατρίβοντος ἐν Ἰβηρίᾳ, Σκιπίων ὁ μέγας,
ἐχθρὸς ὢν καὶ βουλόμενος ἐνστῆναι κατορθοῦντι καὶ τὰς Ἰβηρικὰς
πράξεις ὑπολαβεῖν, διεπράξατο τῆς ἐπαρχίας ἐκείνης ἀποδειχθῆναι
διάδοχος· σπεύσας δ' ὡς ἐνῆν τάχιστα κατέπαυσε τὴν ἀρχὴν τοῦ Κά-
2 τωνος. ὁ δὲ λαβὼν σπείρας ὁπλιτῶν πέντε καὶ πεντακοσίους ἱππεῖς
προπομπούς, κατεστρέψατο μὲν τὸ Λακετανῶν ἔθνος, ἑξακοσίους δὲ
3 τῶν ηὐτομοληκότων κομισάμενος ἀπέκτεινεν· ἐφ' οἷς σχετλιάζοντα τὸν
Σκιπίωνα κατειρωνευόμενος, οὕτως ἔφη τὴν Ῥώμην ἔσεσθαι μεγίστην,
τῶν μὲν ἐνδόξων καὶ μεγάλων τὰ τῆς ἀρετῆς πρωτεῖα μὴ μεθιέντων τοῖς

37.3 Βαίτιος Stephanus: βαιτίου UA: βέλτιος S 37.4 εἴη S: ἦν UA

followed he won a resounding victory and he carried out the
rest of his duties with success and distinction. Indeed, Polybius says that on his orders the fortifications of the cities this
side of the Baetis River were torn down in a single day.
(These were quite numerous and abounded in armed troops.)
And Cato himself claims that he captured more cities in Spain
than he spent days there. Nor is this an idle boast, if indeed
4 it is true that they numbered four hundred. In the course of
the campaign the men helped themselves to a large amount
of booty. He ordered that an additional pound of silver be
distributed to each man, saying that it was better for a large
number of Romans to return with silver than a small number
with gold. As for himself, he says that the only booty he ac-
5 cepted was what he ate or drank. "It is not that I blame
those who wish to help themselves to these things," he said,
"but I would rather rival the best men for virtue than the
6 wealthiest for money or the greediest for avarice." And he
made sure that not only he himself, but those around him as
well, were untainted by any profit. He had five attendants
along with him on campaign, one of whom was named Paccius. This man had bought three boys who were among the
captives and, when Cato found out about it, he hanged himself rather than face him. Cato sold the boys and returned
the price to the treasury.

38(11). While he was still in Spain, no less a figure than
his adversary Scipio, who wished to forestall his success and
to take over the command of operations in Spain, managed to
have himself appointed his successor in the administration of
that province, and he made all possible speed in relieving
2 him of his command. But Cato took an escort consisting of
five companies of infantry and five hundred horse and subdued the tribe of the Lacetani by force of arms. In addition,
he recovered and put to death six hundred of those who had
3 gone over to the enemy. Scipio bitterly protested these actions, but Cato teased him, saying that this was how Rome
would attain supremacy, when its foremost citizens refused
to surrender the prize for virtue to those who were less dis-

ἀσημοτέροις, τῶν δ' ὥσπερ αὐτός ἐστι δημοτικῶν ἁμιλλωμένων ἀρετῇ
4 πρὸς τοὺς τῷ γένει καὶ τῇ δόξῃ προήκοντας. οὐ μὴν ἀλλὰ τῆς συγκλήτου ψηφισαμένης μηδὲν ἀλλάττειν μηδὲ κινεῖν τῶν διῳκημένων ὑπὸ τοῦ
Κάτωνος, ἡ μὲν ἀρχὴ τῷ Σκιπίωνι τῆς αὑτοῦ μᾶλλον ἢ τῆς Κάτωνος
ἀφελοῦσα δόξης ἐν ἀπραξίᾳ καὶ σχολῇ μάτην διῆλθεν, ὁ δὲ Κάτων
θριαμβεύσας οὐχ, ὥσπερ οἱ πλεῖστοι τῶν μὴ πρὸς ἀρετήν, ἀλλὰ πρὸς
δόξαν ἁμιλλωμένων, ὅταν εἰς τὰς ἄκρας τιμὰς ἐξίκωνται καὶ τύχωσιν
ὑπατείας καὶ θριάμβων, ἤδη τὸ λοιπὸν εἰς ἡδονὴν καὶ σχολὴν συσκευ-
ασάμενοι τὸν βίον ἐκ τῶν κοινῶν ἀπίασιν, οὕτω καὶ αὐτὸς ἐξανῆκε καὶ
κατέλυσε τὴν ἀρετήν, ἀλλ' ὅμοια τοῖς πρῶτον ἁπτομένοις πολιτείας καὶ
διψῶσι τιμῆς καὶ δόξης ἀφ' ἑτέρας ἀρχῆς συντείνας ἑαυτὸν ἐν μέσῳ
παρεῖχε καὶ φίλοις χρῆσθαι καὶ πολίταις, οὔτε τὰς συνηγορίας οὔτε τὰς
στρατείας ἀπειπάμενος.

39(12). Τιβερίῳ μὲν οὖν Σεμπρωνίῳ τὰ περὶ Θρᾴκην καὶ Ἴστρον
ὑπατεύοντι πρεσβεύων συγκατειργάσατο, Μανίῳ δ' Ἀκιλίῳ χιλιαρχῶν
ἐπ' Ἀντίοχον τὸν μέγαν συνεξῆλθεν εἰς τὴν Ἑλλάδα, φοβήσαντα Ῥω-
2 μαίους ὡς οὐδένα ἕτερον μετ' Ἀννίβαν. τὴν γὰρ Ἀσίαν ὅσην ὁ Νικάτωρ
Σέλευκος εἶχεν ὀλίγου δεῖν ἅπασαν ἐξ ὑπαρχῆς ἀνειληφώς, ἔθνη τε
πάμπολλα καὶ μάχιμα βαρβάρων ὑπήκοα πεποιημένος, ἐπῆρτο συμ-
3 πεσεῖν Ῥωμαίοις ὡς μόνοις ἔτι πρὸς αὐτὸν ἀξιομάχοις οὖσιν. εὐπρεπῆ
δὲ τοῦ πολέμου ποιησάμενος αἰτίαν τοὺς Ἕλληνας ἐλευθεροῦν, οὐδὲν
δεομένους, ἀλλ' ἐλευθέρους καὶ αὐτονόμους χάριτι τῇ Ῥωμαίων ἀπὸ
Φιλίππου καὶ Μακεδόνων νεωστὶ γεγονότας, διέβη μετὰ δυνάμεως, καὶ
σάλον εὐθὺς ἡ Ἑλλὰς εἶχε καὶ μετέωρος ἦν, ἐλπίσι διαφθειρομένη βα-
4 σιλικαῖς ὑπὸ τῶν δημαγωγῶν. ἔπεμπεν οὖν πρεσβείας ὁ Μάνιος ἐπὶ τὰς

38.4 τῆς αὑτοῦ Sauppe: τῆς αὐτοῦ SUA 39.3 οὐδὲν S et *Flam.* 15.1: μηδὲν UA| ἀλλ' S: ἀλλὰ καὶ UA 39.4 πρεσβείας S: πρέσβεις UA

tinguished, and when common men like himself sought to rival the virtue of those who had the advantage of them in
4 birth and renown. At any rate, the senate voted that no
change or modification should be made in the administrative
policies set by Cato and, while Scipio's term of office did more
to detract from his own than from Cato's reputation, as it was
frittered away in idleness and inactivity, Cato was accorded a
triumph. But he did not give up or bring to an end his commitment to virtue, the way most people, who strive not for
virtue but for renown, once they have achieved the highest
honors and have attained a consulship and triumphs, from
that point on take leave of public affairs and arrange for
themselves a life given over to enjoyment and leisure. On
the contrary, like those just entering public life, with their
thirst for esteem and renown, he made a fresh start, going
out of his way to make himself available for use by friends
and fellow citizens, and not hesitating to offer his services
both in the courts of law and on the battlefield.

39(12). And so he assisted the consul Tiberius Sempronius in his tour of duty in Thrace and the region near the
Danube, serving as his legate, and as military tribune he accompanied Manius Acilius to Greece on his campaign against
Antiochus the Great, who struck terror into the hearts of the
2 Romans as no one else had done since Hannibal. For he had
secured anew nearly the whole of that part of Asia that Seleucus the Conqueror possessed and, now that he had made
quite a large number of warlike foreign nations his subjects,
he was inspired to join battle with the Romans, feeling that
3 only they remained as a challenge to him. He manufactured
as a plausible motive for the war the liberation of the Greeks,
although there was no need for this, as they had recently
been liberated from Philip and the Macedonians through the
kind offices of the Romans and had been made autonomous.
When he crossed over with his army, Greece was immediately thrown into a state of confusion and uncertainty, since
the country was being undermined by expectations, stirred
4 up by the popular leaders, regarding the king's intentions. So

πόλεις, καὶ τὰ μὲν πλεῖστα τῶν νεωτεριζόντων Τίτος Φλαμινῖνος ἔσχεν ἄνευ ταραχῆς καὶ κατεπράυνεν, ὡς ἐν τοῖς περὶ ἐκείνου γέγραπται, Κά-
5 των δὲ Κορινθίους καὶ Πατρεῖς, ἔτι δ' Αἰγιεῖς παρεστήσατο. πλεῖστον δὲ χρόνον ἐν Ἀθήναις διέτριψε, καὶ λέγεται μέν τις αὐτοῦ φέρεσθαι λόγος ὃν Ἑλληνιστὶ πρὸς τὸν δῆμον εἶπεν, ὡς ζηλῶν τε τὴν ἀρετὴν τῶν παλαιῶν Ἀθηναίων, τῆς τε πόλεως διὰ τὸ κάλλος καὶ τὸ μέγεθος ἡδέως γεγονὼς θεατής· τὸ δ' οὐκ ἀληθές ἐστιν, ἀλλὰ δι' ἑρμηνέως ἐνέτυχε τοῖς Ἀθηναίοις, δυνηθεὶς ἂν αὐτὸς εἰπεῖν, ἐμμένων δὲ τοῖς πατρίοις καὶ
6 καταγελῶν τῶν τὰ Ἑλληνικὰ τεθαυμακότων. (Ποστούμιον γοῦν Ἀλβῖνον ἱστορίαν Ἑλληνιστὶ γράψαντα καὶ συγγνώμην αἰτούμενον ἐπέσκωψεν, εἰπὼν δοτέον εἶναι τὴν συγγνώμην, εἰ τῶν Ἀμφικτυόνων ψηφι-
7 σαμένων ἀναγκασθεὶς ὑπέμεινε τὸ ἔργον.) θαυμάσαι δέ φησι τοὺς Ἀθηναίους τὸ τάχος αὐτοῦ καὶ τὴν ὀξύτητα τῆς φράσεως· ἃ γὰρ αὐτὸς ἐξέφερε βραχέως, τὸν ἑρμηνέα μακρῶς καὶ διὰ πολλῶν ἀπαγγέλλειν· τὸ δ' ὅλον οἴεσθαι τὰ ῥήματα τοῖς μὲν Ἕλλησιν ἀπὸ χειλῶν, τοῖς δὲ Ῥωμαίοις ἀπὸ καρδίας φέρεσθαι.

40(13). Ἐπεὶ δ' Ἀντίοχος ἐμφράξας τὰ περὶ Θερμοπύλας στενὰ τῷ στρατοπέδῳ καὶ τοῖς αὐτοφυέσι τῶν τόπων ἐρύμασι προσβαλὼν χαρακώματα καὶ διατειχίσματα, καθῆστο τὸν πόλεμον ἐκκεκλεικέναι νομίζων, τὸ μὲν κατὰ στόμα βιάζεσθαι παντάπασιν ἀπεγίνωσκον οἱ Ῥωμαῖοι, τὴν δὲ Περσικὴν ἐκείνην περιήλυσιν καὶ κύκλωσιν ὁ Κάτων εἰς νοῦν
2 βαλόμενος, ἐξώδευσε νύκτωρ, ἀναλαβὼν μέρος τι τῆς στρατιᾶς. ἐπεὶ δ' ἄνω προελθόντων ὁ καθοδηγῶν αἰχμάλωτος ἐξέπεσε τῆς ὁδοῦ καὶ πλανώμενος ἐν τόποις ἀπόροις καὶ κρημνώδεσι δεινὴν ἀθυμίαν καὶ φόβον ἐνειργάσατο τοῖς στρατιώταις, ὁρῶν ὁ Κάτων τὸν κίνδυνον ἐκέ-

39.5 ἡδέως S: ἡδέως εἴη UA| τὸ δ' UA: τοῦτο δ' S 39.7 φησι S: φασι UA

Manius dispatched embassies to the cities and, while it was
Titus Flamininus, as has been described in the account devoted to him, who was primarily responsible for calming down
and placating the parties that favored revolt, it was Cato who
won over the inhabitants of Corinth and Patrae, and of Aegi-
5 um as well. He spent a great deal of time in Athens, and it is
claimed that a speech of his exists which he delivered in
public in the Greek language, to the effect that he was an
admirer of the ancient Athenians' virtue and that he took
pleasure in viewing the city, because of its beauty and its
size. But this is not true. Rather he addressed the Athenians
through an interpreter and, although he could have spoken
on his own, he preferred to follow Roman precedent, thereby
holding up to ridicule those who had become infatuated with
6 Greek culture. (He made fun, for example, of Postumius Albinus, who had written a historical work in Greek and begged
indulgence for doing so, saying that it would be right to grant
him indulgence if he were submitting to the task under com-
7 pulsion of a decree of the Amphictyons.) He says that the
Athenians were impressed with the rapidity and concision of
his delivery, for the interpreter conveyed at length and using
many words what he himself expressed briefly. And he says
that, in general, he is of the opinion that the Greeks produce
words with their lips, the Romans with their minds.

40(13). Antiochus blocked the pass at Thermopylae with
his troops and, once he had enhanced the natural defenses of
the place by constructing ramparts and fortifications, he re-
laxed, thinking that he had closed the door on war. But,
while the Romans were despairing altogether of the likelihood of forcing the position by means of a frontal attack, Cato
bethought himself of that famous detour and circling movement of the Persians, and he marched out, taking a portion of
2 the army with him, under cover of darkness. When they had
advanced to high ground, the captive who was leading the
way strayed from the path and, when he began wandering
about in impenetrable and precipitous terrain, he filled the
troops with severe despondency and alarm. Cato saw the

λευσε τοὺς ἄλλους ἅπαντας ἀτρεμεῖν καὶ περιμένειν, αὐτὸς δὲ Λεύκιόν
τινα Μάλλιον, ἄνδρα δεινὸν ὀρειβατεῖν, παραλαβὼν ἐχώρει πολυπό-
νως καὶ παραβόλως, ἐν ἀσελήνῳ νυκτὶ καὶ βαθείᾳ, κοτίνοις καὶ πάγοις
ἀνατεταμένοις διασπάσματα πολλὰ τῆς ὄψεως καὶ ἀσάφειαν ἐχούσης,
ἕως ἐμβαλόντες εἰς ἀτραπόν, ὡς ᾤοντο κάτω περαίνουσαν ἐπὶ τὸ στρατόπεδον τῶν πολεμίων, ἔθεντο σημεῖα πρός τινας εὐσκόπους κεραίας
3 ὑπὲρ τὸ Καλλίδρομον ἀνεχούσας. οὕτω δὲ πάλιν ἐπανελθόντες ὀπίσω,
τὴν στρατιὰν ἀνέλαβον καὶ πρὸς τὰ σημεῖα προαγαγόντες ἥψαντο μὲν
ἐκείνης τῆς ἀτραποῦ καὶ κατεστήσαντο τὴν πορείαν, μικρὸν δὲ προελ-
θοῦσιν αὐτοῖς ἐπέλιπε φάραγγος ὑπολαμβανούσης, καὶ πάλιν ἦν ἀπορία καὶ δέος, οὐκ ἐπισταμένων οὐδὲ συνορώντων ὅτι πλησίον ἐτύγχα-
4 νον τῶν πολεμίων γεγονότες. ἤδη δὲ διέλαμπεν ἡμέρα, καὶ φθογγῆς τις
ἔδοξεν ἐπακοῦσαι, τάχα δὲ καὶ καθορᾶν Ἑλληνικὸν χάρακα καὶ προ-
φυλακὴν ὑπὸ τὸ κρημνῶδες. οὕτως οὖν ἐπιστήσας ἐνταῦθα τὴν στρατιὰν ὁ Κάτων, ἐκέλευσεν αὐτῷ προσελθεῖν ἄνευ τῶν ἄλλων τοὺς Φιρ-
5 μανούς, οἷς ἀεὶ πιστοῖς ἐχρῆτο καὶ προθύμοις. συνδραμόντων δὲ καὶ
περιστάντων αὐτὸν ἀθρόων, εἶπεν, 'ἀλλ' ἄνδρα χρῄζω λαβεῖν τῶν πολεμίων ζῶντα καὶ πυθέσθαι, τίνες οἱ προφυλάττοντες οὗτοι, καὶ πόσον
πλῆθος αὐτῶν, τίς ὁ τῶν ἄλλων διάκοσμος ἢ τάξις καὶ παρασκευὴ μεθ'
ἧς ὑπομένουσιν ἡμᾶς. τὸ δ' ἔργον ἅρπασμα δεῖ τάχους γενέσθαι καὶ
τόλμης, ᾗ καὶ λέοντες ἄνοπλοι θαρροῦντες ἐπὶ τὰ δειλὰ τῶν θηρίων
6 βαδίζουσι.' ταῦτ' εἰπόντος τοῦ Κάτωνος, αὐτόθεν ὁρούσαντες ὥσπερ
εἶχον οἱ Φιρμανοὶ κατὰ τῶν ὀρῶν ἔθεον ἐπὶ τὰς προφυλακάς, καὶ
προσπεσόντες ἀπροσδόκητοι πάντας μὲν διετάραξαν καὶ διεσκέδασαν,
7 ἕνα δ' αὐτοῖς ὅπλοις ἁρπάσαντες ἐνεχείρισαν τῷ Κάτωνι. παρὰ τούτου

40.2 κοτίνοις UA: σκοτεινοῖς S 40.4 φθογγῆς UA: φθογγὴν S 40.5 καὶ πόσον S: πόσον UA| ἢ τάξις καὶ S: ἢ τάξις ἢ UA| ἅ. δεῖ τάχους γενέσθαι S: ἅ. τάχους γενέσθω UA| ᾗ UA: εἰ S

plight they were in and ordered all the rest to stay calm and wait there while he set out accompanied only by a certain Lucius Mallius, who was an experienced mountain-climber. He made his way with great difficulty and at great risk to himself, since there was no moon and it was late at night, and his vision was in many places cut off and obscured by wild olive trees and looming outcrops of rock. Finally they reached a path which they thought led down to the enemy camp, and they set markers up by some readily visible crags
3 that rise up over Callidromum. When they had done this, they turned around and went back to camp. Then, taking the army, they led the way to the markers, where they found the path and resumed their march. But, after they had advanced but a short distance, the path gave out and they were faced with a gaping ravine. Once again there was despair and fright, for they had no way of knowing or realizing that they
4 were in fact near the enemy. But by now day was beginning to break, and one or two soldiers thought that they could hear voices. Presently, they thought that they could even make out Greek fortifications and an outpost at the foot of the cliffs. At this point Cato halted his forces on the spot, and he ordered his Firmian troops, which he considered ever loyal and full of spirit, to come to him apart from the rest of the
5 army. They came on the double and thronged about him, and he said, "All right, what I need is to capture alive one of the enemy and to find out who these men are at the outpost and what their number is, what is the disposition of the rest of the troops, with what battle plans and what degree of readiness they are awaiting us. The success of this mission requires that you pounce upon them with the speed and daring of lions who, though unarmed, boldly move in upon
6 those among their prey who lack spirit." No sooner had Cato finished his speech than the Firmians coursed down the mountain-side without delay and ran toward the outpost, which they fell upon without any warning. All the troops there were thrown into utter confusion and were completely routed, although one of them was captured, together with his
7 arms, and handed over to Cato. From this man Cato learned

μαθὼν ὡς ἡ μὲν ἄλλη δύναμις ἐν τοῖς στενοῖς κάθηται μετ' αὐτοῦ τοῦ βασιλέως, οἱ δὲ φρουροῦντες οὗτοι τὰς ὑπερβολὰς Αἰτωλῶν εἰσιν ἑξακόσιοι λογάδες, καταφρονήσας τῆς ὀλιγότητος ἅμα καὶ τῆς ὀλιγωρίας, εὐθὺς ἐπῆγεν ἅμα σάλπιγξι καὶ ἀλαλαγμῷ, πρῶτος σπασάμενος τὴν μάχαιραν. οἱ δ' ὡς εἶδον ἀπὸ τῶν κρημνῶν ἐπιφερομένους, φεύγοντες εἰς τὸ μέγα στρατόπεδον κατεπίμπλασαν ταραχῆς ἅπαντας.

41(14). Ἐν τούτῳ δὲ καὶ τοῦ Μανίου κάτωθεν πρὸς τὰ διατειχίσματα βιαζομένου καὶ τοῖς στενοῖς προσβάλλοντος ἀθρόαν τὴν δύναμιν, ὁ μὲν Ἀντίοχος εἰς τὸ στόμα λίθῳ πληγείς, ἐκτιναχθέντων αὐτοῦ τῶν ὀδόντων, ἀπέστρεψεν ὀπίσω τὸν ἵππον περιαλγὴς γενόμενος, τοῦ δὲ στρατοῦ μέρος οὐδὲν ὑπέμεινε τοὺς Ῥωμαίους, ἀλλὰ καίπερ ἀπόρους καὶ ἀμηχάνους τῆς φυγῆς ὁδοὺς καὶ πλάνας ἐχούσης, ἑλῶν βαθέων καὶ πετρῶν ἀποτόμων τὰ πτώματα καὶ τὰς ὀλισθήσεις ὑποδεχομένων, εἰς ταῦτα διὰ τῶν στενῶν ὑπερχεόμενοι καὶ συνωθοῦντες ἀλλήλους φόβῳ
2 πληγῆς καὶ σιδήρου πολεμίων αὐτοὺς διέφθειρον. ὁ δὲ Κάτων ἀεὶ μέν τις ἦν ὡς ἔοικε τῶν ἰδίων ἐγκωμίων ἀφειδὴς καὶ τὴν ἄντικρυς μεγαλαυχίαν ὡς ἐπακολούθημα τῆς μεγαλουργίας οὐκ ἔφευγε, πλεῖστον δὲ ταῖς πράξεσι ταύταις ὄγκον περιτέθεικε, καί φησι τοῖς ἰδοῦσιν αὐτὸν τότε διώκοντα καὶ παίοντα τοὺς πολεμίους παραστῆναι μηδὲν ὀφείλειν Κάτωνα τῷ δήμῳ τοσοῦτον ὅσον Κάτωνι τὸν δῆμον, αὐτόν τε Μάνιον τὸν ὕπατον θερμὸν ἀπὸ τῆς νίκης ἔτι θερμῷ περιπλακέντα πολὺν χρόνον ἀσπάζεσθαι καὶ βοᾶν ὑπὸ χαρᾶς ὡς οὔτ' ἂν αὐτὸς οὔθ' ὁ σύμπας δῆ-
3 μος ἐξισώσειε τὰς ἀμοιβὰς ταῖς Κάτωνος εὐεργεσίαις. μετὰ δὲ τὴν μάχην εὐθὺς εἰς Ῥώμην ἐπέμπετο τῶν ἠγωνισμένων αὐτάγγελος, καὶ διέ-

40.7 μετ' αὐτοῦ τοῦ S: μετὰ τοῦ UA| κατεπίμπλασαν ταραχῆς ἅπαντας S: ταραχῆς ἐνεπίμπλασαν ἅπαντα UA

that the remaining forces, along with the king himself, had taken up their position in the pass, and that these men who were guarding the mountain-passes were a select body of six hundred Aetolians. Cato was the first to draw his saber and immediately, with contempt for their small numbers as well as for their carelessness, he led the charge amidst the sounds of trumpets and shouting. When the enemy caught sight of them rushing toward them from the cliffs, they fled to the main camp, where they filled everyone with trepidation.

41(14). At this point, while Manius was trying to force his way toward the fortifications from his position down below and was making a concentrated assault upon the pass with all his forces, Antiochus was struck in the face with a stone, which dashed out his teeth. Because of the sudden and severe pain he quickly wheeled his horse about. Not a single division of the army stood fast to resist the Romans. Instead, despite the fact that the only hope of escape was along all but impenetrable paths on which one could easily become lost (for deep marshes and sheer cliffs afforded them only the prospect of either slipping on the ground or falling from a height), they streamed through the passes in that direction and, pushing one another aside from fear of the blows of the enemy's weapons, they brought about their own destruction.
2 Now Cato was, as it seems, always one for being unstinting in his own praise. He did not even shun thoroughly vainglorious boasting, since he regarded it as merely the corollary of glorious achievements. But it was this action of his that he emphasized most dramatically, saying that it occurred to those who saw him on that occasion pursuing and smiting the enemy that the people of Rome owed a greater debt to Cato than he owed to them. Further, he says that the consul Manius, when the two of them were still fresh from their victory, threw his arms about him and hugged him for the longest time, crying out joyfully that neither he himself nor the people as a whole could adequately repay Cato for the service
3 that he had performed. Immediately following the battle he was dispatched to Rome so that he could announce in person

πλευσε μὲν εἰς Βρεντέσιον εὐτυχῶς, μιᾷ δ' ἐκεῖθεν ἡμέρᾳ διελάσας εἰς Τάραντα καὶ τέσσαρας ἄλλας ὁδεύσας πεμπταῖος εἰς Ῥώμην ἀπὸ θα-
4 λάσσης ἀφίκετο καὶ πρῶτος ἀπήγγειλε τὴν νίκην, καὶ τὴν μὲν πόλιν ἐνέπλησεν εὐφροσύνης καὶ θυσιῶν, φρονήματος δὲ τὸν δῆμον ὡς πάσης γῆς καὶ θαλάττης κρατεῖν δυνάμενον.

42(15). Τῶν μὲν οὖν πολεμικῶν πράξεων τοῦ Κάτωνος αὗται σχεδόν εἰσιν ἐλλογιμώταται· τῆς δὲ πολιτείας φαίνεται τό τε περὶ τὰς κατηγορίας καὶ τοὺς ἐλέγχους τῶν πονηρῶν μόριον οὐ μικρᾶς ἄξιον σπουδῆς ἡγησάμενος. αὐτός τε γὰρ ἐδίωξε πολλούς, καὶ διώκουσιν ἑτέροις συνηγωνίσατο, καὶ παρεσκεύασεν ὅλως διώκοντας, ὡς ἐπὶ Σκιπίωνα
2 τοὺς περὶ Πετίλιον. τοῦτον μὲν οὖν ἀπ' οἴκου τε μεγάλου καὶ φρονήματος ἀληθινοῦ ποιησάμενον ὑπὸ πόδας τὰς διαβολὰς μὴ ἀποκτεῖναι δυνηθεὶς ἀφῆκε, Λεύκιον δὲ τὸν ἀδελφὸν αὐτοῦ μετὰ τῶν κατηγόρων συστὰς καταδίκῃ περιέβαλε χρημάτων πολλῶν πρὸς τὸ δημόσιον, ἣν οὐκ ἔχων ἐκεῖνος ἀπολύσασθαι καὶ κινδυνεύων δεθῆναι, μόλις ἐπικλή-
3 σει τῶν δημάρχων ἀφείθη. λέγεται δὲ καὶ νεανίσκῳ τινὶ τεθνηκότος πατρὸς ἐχθρὸν ἠτιμωκότι καὶ πορευομένῳ δι' ἀγορᾶς μετὰ τὴν δίκην ἀπαντήσας ὁ Κάτων δεξιώσασθαι καὶ εἰπεῖν ὅτι ταῦτα χρὴ τοῖς γονεῦσιν ἐναγίζειν, οὐκ ἄρνας οὐδ' ἐρίφους, ἀλλ' ἐχθρῶν δάκρυα καὶ καταδίκας.
4 οὐ μὴν οὐδ' αὐτὸς ἐν τῇ πολιτείᾳ περιῆν ἀθῷος, ἀλλ' ὅπου τινὰ λαβὴν τοῖς ἐχθροῖς παράσχοι, κρινόμενος καὶ κινδυνεύων διετέλει. λέγεται

42.1 τό τε Sansone: τότε SUA

the results of the engagement. He met with good fortune in
his crossing to Brundisium; from there he reached Tarentum
in a single day and, after traveling four more days, he arrived in Rome on the fifth day from his landing. He was the
4 first to give the news of the victory, and he filled the city
with cause for thanksgiving and sacrifices, while he filled the
people with the conviction that they had it within their power to dominate every land and every sea.

42(15). Now, as far as Cato's military service is concerned, the foregoing exploits are the ones that are pretty
much the most celebrated. As to his political activity, he
makes it clear that he regarded that aspect of it that was
concerned with the arraignment and conviction of miscreants
as of some considerable importance. For, not only did he
himself prosecute a large number of individuals, but he
joined the fray when others were involved in the prosecution
and in general he incited people to undertake prosecutions.
Such was the case with Petilius' prosecution of Scipio who,
2 however, coming as he did from a noble line and being possessed of unaffected sensibilities, saw to it that the slanders
against him were stamped out. When Cato was unable to secure his execution, he left him alone and joined forces instead
with the accusers of Scipio's brother Lucius, upon whom he
managed to have a large fine imposed, payable to the public
treasury. (Lucius could not afford to pay this fine and was in
danger of being thrown into prison, but he was eventually let
3 off when an appeal was made to the tribunes.) It is said that
a certain young man, who had brought charges that resulted
in the disfranchisement of an enemy of the young man's deceased father, was walking through the forum after the trial,
when Cato ran up to him and congratulated him, saying, "This
is the right way to honor one's parents: not with the sacrifice
of lambs and kids, but by convicting their enemies and
4 causing them grief." That is not to say that he was himself
able to survive unscathed throughout his political career, but
he was always being brought to trial and constantly risking
conviction whenever he gave his enemies an opportunity to

γὰρ ὀλίγον ἀπολιπούσας τῶν πεντήκοντα φυγεῖν δίκας, μίαν δὲ τὴν τε-
λευταίαν ἓξ ἔτη καὶ ὀγδοήκοντα γεγονώς, ἐν ᾗ καὶ τὸ μνημονευόμενον
εἶπεν, ὡς χαλεπόν ἐστιν ἐν ἄλλοις βεβιωκότα ἀνθρώποις ἐν ἄλλοις
5 ἀπολογεῖσθαι. καὶ τοῦτο πέρας οὐκ ἐποιήσατο τῶν ἀγώνων, τεσσάρων
δ' ἄλλων ἐνιαυτῶν διελθόντων Σερουίου Γάλβα κατηγόρησεν, ἐνενήκοντα γεγονὼς ἔτη. κινδυνεύει γὰρ ὡς ὁ Νέστωρ εἰς τριγονίαν τῷ βίῳ καὶ
6 ταῖς πράξεσι κατελθεῖν· Σκιπίωνι γὰρ ὡς λέλεκται τῷ μεγάλῳ πολλὰ διερεισάμενος ἐν τῇ πολιτείᾳ, διέτεινεν εἰς Σκιπίωνα τὸν νέον, ὃς ἦν ἐκείνου κατὰ ποίησιν υἱωνός, υἱὸς δὲ Παύλου τοῦ Περσέα καὶ Μακεδόνας
καταπολεμήσαντος.

43(16). Τῆς δ' ὑπατείας κατόπιν ἔτεσι δέκα τιμητείαν ὁ Κάτων παρ-
ήγγειλε. κορυφὴ δέ τίς ἐστι τιμῆς ἁπάσης ἡ ἀρχὴ καὶ τρόπον τινὰ τῆς
πολιτείας ἐπιτελείωσις, ἄλλην τε πολλὴν ἐξουσίαν ἔχουσα καὶ τὴν περὶ
2 τὰ ἤθη καὶ τοὺς βίους ἐξέτασιν. οὔτε γὰρ γάμον οὔτε παιδοποιίαν τινὸς
οὔτε δίαιταν οὔτε συμπόσιον ᾤοντο δεῖν ἄκριτον καὶ ἀνεξέταστον, ὡς
ἕκαστος ἐπιθυμίας ἔχοι καὶ προαιρέσεως, ἀφεῖσθαι, πολὺ δὲ μᾶλλον ἐν
τούτοις νομίζοντες ἢ ταῖς ὑπαίθροις καὶ πολιτικαῖς πράξεσι τρόπον ἀνδρὸς ἐνορᾶσθαι, φύλακα καὶ σωφρονιστὴν καὶ κολαστὴν τοῦ μηδένα
καθ' ἡδονὰς ἐκτρέπεσθαι καὶ παρεκβαίνειν τὸν ἐπιχώριον καὶ συνήθη
βίον ᾑροῦντο τῶν καλουμένων πατρικίων ἕνα καὶ τῶν δημοτικῶν ἕνα.
3 τιμητὰς δὲ τούτους προσηγόρευον, ἐξουσίαν ἔχοντας ἀφελέσθαι μὲν
ἵππον, ἐκβαλεῖν δὲ συγκλήτου τὸν ἀκολάστως βιοῦντα καὶ ἀτάκτως.
οὗτοι δὲ καὶ τὰ τιμήματα τῶν οὐσιῶν λαμβάνοντες ἐπεσκόπουν καὶ ταῖς

42.6 διερεισάμενος Reiske: διερισάμενος SUA 43.3 οὐσιῶν Amyot: θυσιῶν SUA

secure some hold on him. Indeed, it is said that he was the
defendant in nearly fifty cases, the last of which was when
he was eighty-six years old. (It was in the course of this trial, by the way, that he made the famous remark, that it was
difficult for a man to defend himself before the men of one
generation when he had lived his life among the men of an-
5 other.) And not even here did he put an end to his judicial
contests; four years later, when he was ninety, he brought an
action against Servius Galba. He seems, indeed, like Nestor,
to have remained vital and active down through three gener-
6 ations for, as I have mentioned, he had a number of encoun-
ters with the great Scipio during his political career, and he
lasted until the time of the younger Scipio, who was the
grandson of the earlier Scipio by adoption and the son of
Paullus, the conqueror of Perseus and the Macedonians.

43(16). Ten years after his consulship Cato sought election as censor. This position is, so to speak, the crown of all
public offices and represents in a sense the culmination of
one's political career, since it involves the exercise of considerable power, including in particular the responsibility of
2 scrutinizing morals and conduct. For they believed that no
person ought to be allowed either to undertake marriage and
the begetting of children or to spend money on himself and
on the entertainment of his friends without being subject to
examination and scrutiny into the character of the impulses
and motivations involved. And, inasmuch as they considered
that these actions give much better insight into a man's
ethics than does a man's public and civic behavior, they used
to elect one man from among the so-called patricians and one
from among the plebeians to serve as guardians and correctors and scourges, to prevent anyone from following his own
inclinations and departing or deviating from the traditional
3 Roman way of life. These men were called "censors," and
they had the power to demote an individual from the rank of
knight and to banish from the senate anyone whose conduct
was incontinent and improper. In addition, they had charge
of supervising the assessment of property, and they kept the

ἀπογραφαῖς τὰ γένη καὶ τὰς πολιτείας διέκρινον, ἄλλας τε μεγάλας ἔχει
4 δυνάμεις ἡ ἀρχή. διὸ καὶ τῷ Κάτωνι πρὸς τὴν παραγγελίαν ἀπήντησαν
ἐνιστάμενοι σχεδὸν οἱ γνωριμώτατοι καὶ πρῶτοι τῶν συγκλητικῶν. τοὺς
μὲν γὰρ εὐπατρίδας ὁ φθόνος ἐλύπει, παντάπασιν οἰομένους προπηλα-
κίζεσθαι τὴν εὐγένειαν ἀνθρώπων ἀπ' ἀρχῆς ἀδόξων εἰς τὴν ἄκραν τιμὴν καὶ δύναμιν ἀναβιβαζομένων, οἱ δὲ μοχθηρὰ συνειδότες ἑαυτοῖς
ἐπιτηδεύματα καὶ τῶν πατρίων ἐκδιαίτησιν ἐθῶν ἐφοβοῦντο τὴν αὐστη-
5 ρίαν τοῦ ἀνδρὸς ἀπαραίτητον ἐν ἐξουσίᾳ καὶ χαλεπὴν ἐσομένην. διὸ
συμφρονήσαντες καὶ παρασκευάσαντες ἑπτὰ κατῆγον ἐπὶ τὴν παραγγελίαν ἀντιπάλους τῷ Κάτωνι, θεραπεύοντας ἐλπίσι χρησταῖς τὸ πλῆ-
6 θος, ὡς δὴ μαλακῶς καὶ πρὸς ἡδονὴν ἄρχεσθαι δεόμενον. τοὐναντίον
δ' ὁ Κάτων οὐδεμίαν ἐνδιδοὺς ἐπιείκειαν, ἀλλ' ἄντικρυς ἀπειλῶν τε τοῖς
πονηροῖς ἀπὸ τοῦ βήματος καὶ κεκραγὼς μεγάλου καθαρμοῦ χρῄζειν
τὴν πόλιν, ἠξίου τοὺς πολλοὺς εἰ σωφρονοῦσι μὴ τὸν ἥδιστον, ἀλλὰ τὸν
7 σφοδρότατον αἱρεῖσθαι τῶν ἰατρῶν· τοῦτον δ' αὐτὸν εἶναι καὶ τῶν πατρικίων ἕνα Φλάκκον Οὐαλέριον· μετ' ἐκείνου γὰρ οἴεσθαι μόνου τὴν
τρυφὴν καὶ τὴν μαλακίαν ὥσπερ ὕδραν τέμνων καὶ ἀποκαίων προὔρ-
γου τι ποιήσειν, τῶν δ' ἄλλων ὁρᾶν ἕκαστον ἄρξαι κακῶς βιαζόμενον,
8 ὅτι τοὺς καλῶς ἄρξοντας δέδοικεν. οὕτω δ' ἄρα μέγας ἦν ὡς ἀληθῶς
καὶ μεγάλων ἄξιος δημαγωγῶν ὁ Ῥωμαίων δῆμος, ὥστε μὴ φοβηθῆναι
τὴν ἀνάτασιν καὶ τὸν ὄγκον τοῦ ἀνδρός, ἀλλὰ τοὺς ἡδεῖς ἐκείνους καὶ
πρὸς χάριν ἅπαντα ποιήσειν δοκοῦντας ἀπορρίψας ἑλέσθαι μετὰ τοῦ
Κάτωνος τὸν Φλάκκον, ὥσπερ οὐκ αἰτοῦντος ἀρχήν, ἀλλ' ἄρχοντος
ἤδη καὶ προστάττοντος ἀκροώμενος.

43.5 θεραπεύοντας UA: θεραπεύοντες S 43.8 ὥστε UA: ὃς ᾤετο S

census-rolls in which the citizens were distinguished according to family and political status. The office involves the ex-
4 ercise of other important powers as well. For this reason
many of the most distinguished and influential of the senators stood for the office in order to thwart the candidacy of
Cato. For the members of the best families were racked with
envy, particularly because they felt that nobility of birth was
being debased by allowing men of obscure origins to rise to
the pinnacle of esteem and power, while those who had
guilty consciences because of their wicked ways and their
abandonment of traditional values feared the man's severity
which, they thought, was likely to become unremitting and
5 oppressive once he was in a position of authority. So they
organized and conspired to throw their support behind the
candidacy of seven men in opposition to Cato. These men
attempted to ingratiate themselves with the people by instilling in them fine hopes, under the illusion that what the
people wanted was to be governed in a slack and complaisant
6 manner. Quite to the contrary, Cato made no effort to be affable. Instead, uttering open threats from the speaker's
platform against reprobates and crying out that the city was
in need of a great purgation, he told the people that, if they
were wise, they should choose for themselves not the most
7 agreeable physicians but the most effective. And these, he
said, were himself and, of the patricians, Valerius Flaccus.
For only with the aid of that man did he think he could make
progress toward cropping and searing the luxury and laxity
that had sprung up like some Hydra. Further, he said that, as
far as he could see, the remaining candidates were doing everything in their power to be able to govern badly, because
8 they were all afraid of those who would govern well. In the
event, the Roman people were so truly noble and so deserving of noble leaders that, so far from being intimidated by
the man's intensity and gravity, they repudiated those nice
men who gave the impression that there was nothing they
would not do to please them, and they elected Flaccus along
with Cato, to whom they listened, not as one seeking office,
but as one already in office and directing their affairs.

44(17). Προέγραψε μὲν οὖν ὁ Κάτων τῆς συγκλήτου τὸν συνάρ-
χοντα καὶ φίλον Λεύκιον Οὐαλέριον Φλάκκον, ἐξέβαλε δὲ τῆς βουλῆς
ἄλλους τε συχνοὺς καὶ Λεύκιον Κοΐντιον, ὕπατον μὲν ἑπτὰ πρότερον
ἐνιαυτοῖς γεγενημένον, ὃ δ' ἦν αὐτῷ πρὸς δόξαν ὑπατείας μεῖζον, ἀδελ-
2 φὸν Τίτου Φλαμινίνου τοῦ καταπολεμήσαντος Φίλιππον. αἰτίαν δὲ τῆς
ἐκβολῆς ἔσχε τοιαύτην· μειράκιον ἐκ τῆς παιδικῆς ὥρας ἑταιροῦν ἀνει-
ληφὼς ὁ Λεύκιος ἀεὶ περὶ αὑτὸν εἶχε, καὶ συνεπήγετο στρατηγῶν ἐπὶ τιμῆς καὶ δυνάμεως τοσαύτης ὅσην οὐδεὶς εἶχε τῶν πρώτων παρ' αὐτῷ φί-
3 λων καὶ οἰκείων. ἐτύγχανε μὲν οὖν ἡγούμενος ὑπατικῆς ἐπαρχίας· ἐν δὲ
συμποσίῳ τινὶ τὸ μειράκιον ὥσπερ εἰώθει συγκατακείμενον ἄλλην τε
κολακείαν ἐκίνει πρὸς ἄνθρωπον ἐν οἴνῳ ῥᾳδίως ἀγόμενον καὶ φιλεῖν
αὐτὸν οὕτως ἔλεγεν, 'ὥστ',' ἔφη, 'θέας οὔσης οἴκοι μονομάχων οὐ τεθε-
αμένος πρότερον ἐξώρμησα πρὸς σέ, καίπερ ἐπιθυμῶν ἰδεῖν ἄνθρωπον
4 σφαττόμενον.' ὁ δὲ Λεύκιος ἀντιφιλοφρονούμενος, 'ἀλλὰ τούτου γε χάριν,' εἶπε, 'μή μοι κατάκεισο λυπούμενος· ἐγὼ γὰρ ἰάσομαι.' καὶ κελεύσας ἕνα τῶν ἐπὶ θανάτῳ κατακρίτων εἰς τὸ συμπόσιον ἀχθῆναι καὶ τὸν
ὑπηρέτην ἔχοντα πέλεκυν παραστῆναι, πάλιν ἠρώτησε τὸν ἐρώμενον εἰ
βούλεται τυπτόμενον θεάσασθαι. φήσαντος δὲ βούλεσθαι, προσέταξεν
5 ἀποκόψαι τοῦ ἀνθρώπου τὸν τράχηλον. οἱ μὲν οὖν πλεῖστοι ταῦθ'
ἱστοροῦσι, καὶ ὅ γε Κικέρων αὐτὸν τὸν Κάτωνα διηγούμενον ἐν τῷ Περὶ
γήρως διαλόγῳ πεποίηκεν· ὁ δὲ Λίβιος αὐτόμολον εἶναί φησι Γαλάτην
τὸν ἀναιρεθέντα, τὸν δὲ Λεύκιον οὐ δι' ὑπηρέτου κτεῖναι τὸν ἄνθρωπον,
ἀλλ' αὐτὸν ἰδίᾳ χειρί, καὶ ταῦτ' ἐν λόγῳ γεγράφθαι Κάτωνος. ἐκβλη-
θέντος οὖν τοῦ Λευκίου τῆς βουλῆς ὑπὸ τοῦ Κάτωνος, ὁ ἀδελφὸς αὐ-

44.1 προέγραψε ed. Iuntina: προσέγραψε SUA 44.3 πρὸς ἄνθρωπον S: πρὸς τὸν ἄνθρωπον UA 44.4 παραστῆναι S: εἰσαχθῆναι UA 44.5 ἐν λόγῳ S: ἐν τῷ (ἔν τῳ volebant?) λόγῳ UA

44(17). Accordingly, Cato set his colleague and friend
Lucius Valerius Flaccus at the head of the list of senators, and
he banished a number of men from the senate, not least of
whom was Lucius Quinctius. This man had been consul seven
years before, but his claim to fame rested not so much on his
consulship as on the fact that he was the brother of Titus
2 Flamininus, the conqueror of Philip. The following is the reason for the expulsion. Lucius always kept with him a boy
whom he had taken into his company and who made his living on the basis of his youthful good looks. Even when he
went on campaign he brought him along in a position of hon-
or and power such as none of his most important friends and
3 relatives had with him. It happened that, while Lucius was
serving as governor of his consular province, the boy was re-
clining next to him, as he customarily did, at some drinking-
party. He took advantage of the fact that, since Lucius had
been drinking, he could easily be influenced, and he began to
set blandishments in motion against him. At one point he
said that he loved him so much that, even though there was a
gladiatorial show taking place at home, and even though he
longed to see a man being killed, he had rushed to Lucius'
4 side rather than stay and watch. Lucius returned the com-
pliment and said, "Well, as far as that is concerned, you need
not lie here in distress to please me. For I shall cure you."
With that he gave orders that one of the men who were condemned to death be brought into the gathering and that his
lictor stand by with an axe. Then he turned again to the boy
and asked if he wished to see a deathblow being administered. When the boy said yes, he ordered that the man be
5 beheaded. Such, at any rate, is the account that most authorities give, and Cicero goes so far as to represent Cato
himself in the dialogue On Old Age as telling the story. Livy,
however, alleges that the man who was killed was a Gallic
deserter, that Lucius did not have the man killed by his lictor
but did the deed himself with his own hand, and that all of
this is recorded in a speech of Cato's. At any rate, after Lucius had been banished from the senate by Cato, Lucius'

τοῦ βαρέως φέρων ἐπὶ τὸν δῆμον κατέφυγε καὶ τὴν αἰτίαν ἐκέλευσεν εἰ-
6 πεῖν τὸν Κάτωνα τῆς ἐκβολῆς. εἰπόντος δὲ καὶ διηγησαμένου τὸ συμπόσιον, ἐπεχείρει μὲν ὁ Λεύκιος ἀρνεῖσθαι, προκαλουμένου δὲ τοῦ Κάτωνος εἰς ὁρισμὸν ἀνεδύετο. καὶ τότε μὲν ἄξια παθεῖν κατεγνώσθη· θέας δ' οὔσης ἐν θεάτρῳ, τὴν ὑπατικὴν χώραν παρελθὼν καὶ πορρωτάτω
που καθεσθεὶς οἶκτον ἔσχε παρὰ τῷ δήμῳ, καὶ βοῶντες ἠνάγκασαν αὐτὸν μετελθεῖν, ὡς ἦν δυνατὸν ἐπανορθούμενοι καὶ θεραπεύοντες τὸ γε-
7 γενημένον. ἄλλον δὲ βουλῆς ἐξέβαλεν ὑπατεύσειν ἐπίδοξον ὄντα Μα-
νίλιον, ὅτι τὴν αὑτοῦ γυναῖκα μεθ' ἡμέραν ὁρώσης τῆς θυγατρὸς κατε-
φίλησεν. αὑτῷ δ' ἔφη τὴν γυναῖκα μηδέποτε πλὴν βροντῆς μεγάλης γενομένης περιπλακῆναι, καὶ μετὰ παιδιᾶς εἰπεῖν αὐτὸν ὡς μακάριός ἐστι
τοῦ Διὸς βροντῶντος.

45(18). Ἤνεγκε δέ τινα τῷ Κάτωνι καὶ Λεύκιος ὁ Σκιπίωνος ἀδελφὸς
ἐπίφθονον αἰτίαν, θριαμβικὸς ἀνὴρ ἀφαιρεθεὶς ὑπ' αὐτοῦ τὸν ἵππον·
ἔδοξε γὰρ οἷον ἐφυβρίζων Ἀφρικανῷ Σκιπίωνι τεθνηκότι τοῦτο ποιῆσαι.
2 τοὺς δὲ πλείστους ἠνίασε μάλιστα τῇ περικοπῇ τῆς πολυτελείας, ἣν
ἄντικρυς μὲν ἀφελέσθαι, νενοσηκότων ἤδη καὶ διεφθαρμένων ὑπ' αὐτῆς
τῶν πολλῶν, ἀδύνατον ἦν, κύκλῳ δὲ περιιὼν ἠνάγκαζεν ἐσθῆτος, ὀχή-
ματος, κόσμου γυναικείου, σκευῶν τῶν περὶ δίαιταν, ὧν ἑκάστου τὸ
τίμημα χιλίας καὶ πεντακοσίας δραχμὰς ὑπερέβαλλεν, ἀποτιμᾶσθαι
τὴν ἀξίαν εἰς τὸ δεκαπλάσιον, βουλόμενος ἀπὸ μειζόνων τιμημάτων

44.6 ὁρισμὸν SUA et *Flam.* 19.4: ὁρκισμὸν superscriptum in A

45.1 τεθνηκότι S: om. UA

brother, to whom this came as quite a blow, made an appeal
to the people and demanded that Cato give an explanation for
6 the expulsion. Cato gave his explanation and recounted the
story concerning the drinking-party. Lucius tried to deny
the story but, when Cato challenged him to a formal wager
under the law, he backed down. At that point, it was generally recognized that the penalty that had been imposed was
just. When, however, at a public performance in the theater,
Lucius passed by the section reserved for those of consular
rank and took his seat somewhere at the farthest possible
remove, he stirred up feelings of compassion among the people. The outcry that they raised compelled him to change his
seat and, to the extent that it was possible, made amends for
7 and eased the pain of what had happened. Another man
whom Cato banished from the senate was Manilius, who was
likely to be elected to the consulship. The reason was that he
had kissed his own wife in broad daylight and in sight of his
daughter. As far as Cato himself is concerned, he claimed
that he never embraced his wife except after a loud thunderclap, adding that he made the facetious comment that he considered himself blessed whenever Jupiter thundered.

45(18). Lucius, Scipio's brother, also gave rise to a certain amount of resentment directed against Cato. For, although Lucius had celebrated a triumph, he was demoted by
Cato from the rank of knight, and it was thought that Cato
had done this to give an affront of sorts to the dead Scipio
2 Africanus. What gave the greatest offense, however, to the
largest number of people was his attempt to cut back the
proliferation of luxury. There was no way to eliminate it altogether, as the general public had by this time already been
corrupted by it and were now in a thoroughly diseased state,
so he tried to circumvent it, and he imposed a reassessment
according to which all articles of clothing, all vehicles, all
items of feminine adornment and all furnishings of the house
whose value exceeded 1,500 drachmas each, were to be assessed at ten times their value. His intention was that, as a
result of increased valuations, people would find that the

3 αὐτοῖς μείζονας καὶ τὰς εἰσφορὰς εἶναι, καὶ προσετίμησε τρεῖς χαλκοῦς
πρὸς τοῖς χιλίοις, ὅπως βαρυνόμενοι ταῖς ἐπιβολαῖς, καὶ τοὺς εὐσταλεῖς
καὶ λιτοὺς ὁρῶντες ἀπὸ τῶν ἴσων ἐλάττονα τελοῦντας εἰς τὸ δημόσιον,
ἀπαγορεύωσιν. ἦσαν οὖν αὐτῷ χαλεποὶ μὲν οἱ τὰς εἰσφορὰς διὰ τὴν
τρυφὴν ὑπομένοντες, χαλεποὶ δ' αὖ πάλιν οἱ τὴν τρυφὴν ἀποτιθέμενοι
4 διὰ τὰς εἰσφοράς. πλούτου γὰρ ἀφαίρεσιν οἱ πολλοὶ νομίζουσι τὴν
κώλυσιν αὐτοῦ τῆς ἐπιδείξεως· ἐπιδείκνυσθαι δὲ τοῖς περιττοῖς, οὐ τοῖς
ἀναγκαίοις. ὃ δὴ καὶ μάλιστά φασι τὸν φιλόσοφον Ἀρίστωνα θαυμάζειν, ὅτι τοὺς τὰ περιττὰ κεκτημένους μᾶλλον ἡγοῦνται μακαρίους ἢ
5 τοὺς τῶν ἀναγκαίων καὶ χρησίμων εὐποροῦντας. Σκόπας δ' ὁ Θεσσα-
λός, αἰτουμένου τινὸς τῶν φίλων παρ' αὐτοῦ τι τοιοῦτον ὃ μὴ σφόδρ' ἦν
χρήσιμον ἐκείνῳ, καὶ λέγοντος ὡς οὐδὲν αἰτεῖ τῶν ἀναγκαίων καὶ χρησίμων, 'καὶ μὴν ἐγὼ τούτοις,' εἶπεν, 'εὐδαίμων καὶ πλούσιός εἰμι, τοῖς ἀ-
χρήστοις καὶ περιττοῖς.' οὕτως ὁ τοῦ πλούτου ζῆλος οὐδενὶ πάθει φυσι-
κῷ συνημμένος ἐκ τῆς ὀχλώδους καὶ θυραίου δόξης ἐπεισόδιός ἐστιν.

46(19). Οὐ μὴν ἀλλὰ τῶν ἐγκαλούντων ἐλάχιστα φροντίζων ὁ Κάτων ἔτι μᾶλλον ἐπέτεινεν, ἀποκόπτων μὲν ὀχετοὺς οἳ τὸ παραρρέον δημόσιον ὕδωρ ὑπολαμβάνοντες ἀπῆγον εἰς οἰκίας ἰδίας καὶ κήπους, ἀνατρέπων δὲ καὶ καταβάλλων ὅσα προὔβαινεν εἰς τὸ δημόσιον οἰκοδομήματα, συστέλλων δὲ τοῖς μισθοῖς τὰς ἐργολαβίας, τὰ δὲ τέλη ταῖς

45.5 καὶ χρησίμων UA: om. S| ἐπεισόδιός UA: ἐπεισόδιόν S 46.1 οἳ . . . ἀπῆγον S: οἷς . . . ὑπῆγον UA

3 amount of their payments was increased as well. Furthermore, he imposed an additional assessment on these items of three asses per thousand, in hopes that the people would renounce their ways when they saw that, while they themselves were suffering from these burdensome imposts, those who possessed the same means but who lived in a modest and frugal manner made smaller contributions to the state. As it turned out, he incurred the hostility not only of those who had to put up with these payments on account of their extravagance, but also of those who made the effort to put
4 aside their extravagance on account of the payments. For people generally consider that being prevented from showing off their wealth is tantamount to having their wealth taken from them, since inessentials, rather than necessities, are regarded as the means of showing off. It is precisely this, they say, that the philosopher Ariston found most surprising, that those who possess inessentials are thought to have attained a more blissful state than those who possess an abundant sup-
5 ply of those things that are necessary and useful. When one of his friends asked Scopas the Thessalian to give him an object which was the sort of thing that was of no particular use to him, saying that he was not asking for anything essential or useful, Scopas replied by saying, "Yet it is just these things, these useless and inessential things, that are the source of my well-being and prosperity." This goes to show that obsession with wealth is not connected with any natural impulse, but is imposed from outside, prompted by that vulgar and adventitious force, public opinion.

46(19). In spite of everything, Cato paid not the least bit of attention to his critics. He became, in fact, even more stringent, cutting off pipes that were tapping the nearby public water supply and diverting water to private houses and gardens, tearing down and demolishing any buildings that encroached upon public property, minimizing the cost of public works contracts by keeping a rein on wages while at the same time driving up to the highest possible level the amount at which contracts for the collection of revenues

2 πράσεσιν ἐπὶ τὰς ἐσχάτας ἐλαύνων τιμάς. ἀφ' ὧν αὐτῷ πολὺ συνήχθη
μῖσος. οἱ δὲ περὶ τὸν Τίτον συστάντες ἐπ' αὐτὸν ἔν τε τῇ βουλῇ τὰς γεγενημένας ἐκδόσεις καὶ μισθώσεις τῶν ἱερῶν καὶ δημοσίων ἔργων ἔλυσαν
ὡς γεγενημένας ἀλυσιτελῶς, καὶ τῶν δημάρχων τοὺς θρασυτάτους
παρώξυνον ἐν δήμῳ προσκαλέσασθαι τὸν Κάτωνα καὶ ζημιῶσαι δυσὶ
3 ταλάντοις. πολλὰ δὲ καὶ πρὸς τὴν τῆς βασιλικῆς κατασκευὴν ἠναντι-
ώθησαν, ἣν ἐκεῖνος ἐκ χρημάτων κοινῶν ὑπὸ τὸ βουλευτήριον τῇ ἀγο-
4 ρᾷ παρέβαλε καὶ Πορκία βασιλικὴ προσηγορεύθη. φαίνεται δὲ θαυ-
μαστῶς ἀποδεξάμενος αὐτοῦ τὴν τιμητείαν ὁ δῆμος. ἀνδριάντα γοῦν
ἀναθεὶς ἐν τῷ ναῷ τῆς Ὑγιείας ἐπέγραψεν οὐ τὰς στρατηγίας οὐδὲ τὸν
θρίαμβον τοῦ Κάτωνος, ἀλλ', ὡς ἄν τις μεταφράσειε τὴν ἐπιγραφήν, ὅτι
'τὴν Ῥωμαίων πολιτείαν ἐγκεκλιμένην καὶ ῥέπουσαν ἐπὶ τὸ χεῖρον τιμητὴς γενόμενος χρησταῖς ἀγωγαῖς καὶ σώφροσιν ἐθισμοῖς καὶ διδασκαλί-
5 αις εἰς ὀρθὸν αὖθις ἀποκατέστησε.' καίτοι πρότερον αὐτὸς κατεγέλα
τῶν ἀγαπώντων τὰ τοιαῦτα, καὶ λανθάνειν αὐτοὺς ἔλεγεν ἐπὶ χαλκέων
καὶ ζωγράφων ἔργοις μέγα φρονοῦντας, αὐτοῦ δὲ καλλίστας εἰκόνας ἐν
6 ταῖς ψυχαῖς περιφέρειν τοὺς πολίτας. πρὸς δὲ τοὺς θαυμάζοντας ὅτι
πολλῶν ἀδόξων ἀνδριάντας ἐχόντων ἐκεῖνος οὐκ ἔχει, 'μᾶλλον γάρ,'
ἔφη, 'βούλομαι ζητεῖσθαι, διὰ τί μου ἀνδριὰς οὐ κεῖται ἢ διὰ τί κεῖται.'
τὸ δ' ὅλον οὐδ' ἐπαινούμενον ἠξίου τὸν ἀγαθὸν πολίτην ὑπομένειν, εἰ
7 μὴ τοῦτο χρησίμως γίγνοιτο τῷ κοινῷ. καίτοι πλεῖστα πάντων ἑαυτὸν
ἐγκεκωμίακεν, ὅς γε καὶ τοὺς ἁμαρτάνοντάς τι περὶ τὸν βίον, εἶτ' ἐλεγ-
χομένους, λέγειν φησὶν ὡς οὐκ ἄξιον ἐγκαλεῖν αὐτοῖς· οὐ γὰρ Κάτωνές
εἰσι· καὶ τοὺς ἔνια μιμεῖσθαι τῶν ὑπ' αὐτοῦ πραττομένων οὐκ ἐμμελῶς
ἐπιχειροῦντας ἐπαριστέρους καλεῖσθαι Κάτωνας· ἀφορᾶν δὲ τὴν βου-

46.2 παρώξυνον . . . προσκαλ. UA: παρώξυναν . . . προκαλ. S
46.3 Πορκία βασιλικὴ προσηγορεύθη S: Πορκίαν βασιλικὴν
προσηγόρευσεν UA 46.4 ἐπὶ τὸ χεῖρον S: ἐπὶ τὰ χείρω UA 46.7
καίτοι Blass: καὶ SUA| περὶ τὸν βίον S: παρὰ τὸν βίον UA

were sold. As a result of these measures, he became the fo-
cus of considerable animosity. The supporters of Titus
Flamininus banded together and brought about a repeal in
the senate of the measures that had been taken in connection
with the farming out of contracts for the construction of temples and for public works, on the grounds that these measures had not proved profitable, and they tried to incite the
brashest of the tribunes to have Cato summoned before the
3 people and fined two talents. In addition, they put up considerable resistance to the construction, at public expense, of
the basilica that he built next to the forum, at the foot of the
4 Curia, which was known as the Basilica Porcia. The people,
on the other hand, made it clear that they held his censorship
in extraordinarily high esteem. For example, when they set
up a statue of him in the temple of Health, the inscription
recorded neither Cato's military commands nor his triumph;
instead it bore a statement that may be translated as follows:
"When Rome was in a state of decline and decay, he became
censor and, by providing sound leadership and by the example of his sober conduct, set it on the proper path again."
5 And yet on earlier occasions he himself used to ridicule people who prized honors like this, saying that, without being
aware of it, they were swelling with pride over the work of
mere sculptors and painters, whereas he knew that his fellow
citizens carried about the finest images of him in their hearts.
6 When people expressed surprise that, although there were
statues of any number of undistinguished men, there was
none of him, he replied, "Well, I would rather have people
ask why there is no statue of me than why there is one."
And in general he thought that the good citizen ought not
even to allow himself to be praised, unless this was done in
7 such a manner as to be beneficial to the state. And yet there
was no one more ready to sing his own praises. It is he who
says that, when people were found to be guilty of some
delinquency in their conduct, they would respond by saying,
"It is not fair to blame us. We are no Catos." And he says
that people who try without success to imitate some of his
achievements are known as "left-handed Catos." Finally, he

λὴν πρὸς αὐτὸν ἐν τοῖς ἐπισφαλεστάτοις καιροῖς ὥσπερ ἐν πλῷ πρὸς
κυβερνήτην, καὶ πολλάκις μὴ παρόντος ὑπερτίθεσθαι τὰ πλείστης ἄξια
8 σπουδῆς. ἃ δὴ παρὰ τῶν ἄλλων αὐτῷ μαρτυρεῖται· μέγα γὰρ ἔσχεν ἐν
τῇ πόλει καὶ διὰ τὸν βίον καὶ διὰ τὸν λόγον καὶ διὰ τὸ γῆρας ἀξίωμα.

47(20). Γέγονε δὲ καὶ πατὴρ ἀγαθὸς καὶ περὶ γυναῖκα χρηστὸς ἀνὴρ
καὶ χρηματιστὴς οὐκ εὐκαταφρόνητος οὐδ᾿ ὥς τι μικρὸν ἢ φαῦλον ἐν
παρέργῳ μεταχειρισάμενος τὴν τοιαύτην ἐπιμέλειαν. ὅθεν οἶμαι δεῖν
2 καὶ περὶ τούτων ὅσα καλῶς ἔχει διελθεῖν. γυναῖκα μὲν γὰρ εὐγενεστέ-
ραν ἢ πλουσιωτέραν ἔγημεν, ἡγούμενος ὁμοίως μὲν ἀμφοτέρας ἔχειν
βάρος καὶ φρόνημα, τὰς δὲ γενναίας αἰδουμένας τὰ αἰσχρὰ μᾶλλον
3 ὑπηκόους εἶναι πρὸς τὰ καλὰ τοῖς γεγαμηκόσι. τὸν δὲ τύπτοντα γαμε-
τὴν ἢ παῖδα τοῖς ἁγιωτάτοις ἔλεγεν ἱεροῖς προσφέρειν τὰς χεῖρας· ἐν ἐπαίνῳ δὲ μείζονι τίθεσθαι τὸ γαμέτην ἀγαθὸν ἢ τὸ μέγαν εἶναι συγκλητι-
κόν· ἐπεὶ καὶ Σωκράτους οὐδὲν ἄλλο θαυμάζειν τοῦ παλαιοῦ πλὴν ὅτι
γυναικὶ χαλεπῇ καὶ παισὶν ἀποπλήκτοις χρώμενος ἐπιεικῶς καὶ πρᾴως
4 διετέλεσε. γενομένου δὲ τοῦ παιδὸς οὐδὲν ἦν ἔργον οὕτως ἀναγκαῖον, εἰ
μή τι δημόσιον, ὡς μὴ παρεῖναι τῇ γυναικὶ λουούσῃ καὶ σπαργανούσῃ
5 τὸ βρέφος. αὐτὴ γὰρ ἔτρεφεν ἰδίῳ γάλακτι· πολλάκις δὲ καὶ τὰ τῶν δού-
λων παιδάρια τῷ μαστῷ προσιεμένη κατεσκεύαζεν εὔνοιαν ἐκ τῆς συν-
τροφίας πρὸς τὸν υἱόν. ἐπεὶ δ᾿ ἤρξατο συνιέναι, παραλαβὼν αὐτὸς ἐδίδασκε γράμματα. καίτοι χαρίεντα δοῦλον εἶχε γραμματιστὴν ὄνομα

47.1 διελθεῖν S: διεξελθεῖν UA 47.2 μὲν γὰρ S: μὲν οὖν UA

states that the members of the senate look to him in the most
desperate crises as though he were the helmsman on a voyage, and that they frequently postpone deliberating on mat-
3 ters of utmost urgency when he is not present. To be sure,
all of this is vouched for by the other authorities, for he was
held in great esteem in the city because of his conduct, his
eloquence and his age.

47(20). He was in addition an excellent father and a fine
husband, and his ability to provide for his family was by no
means negligible, nor did he attend casually to affairs of this
sort, with the attitude that they were of little or no importance. For this reason I feel that I am obligated to give an
account of the admirable features of his behavior in this re-
2 gard as well. He married a woman who was distinguished
rather for nobility of birth than for affluence, for he considered that, while both circumstances to the same degree confer upon women dignity and sensibility, those who are well
born, because of their inbred desire to avoid disgrace, are
more disposed to be guided by their husbands to pursue
3 what is honorable. He used to say that any man who beat his
wife or child was laying violent hands upon the most inviolable of sacred objects, and that he regarded it as more
praiseworthy to be a good husband than to be a great senator. This is borne out by the fact that, even in the case of
Socrates of old, he said that the only thing he admired about
him was his abiding civility and restraint in his dealings with
4 a shrewish wife and retarded children. After his son was
born, there was no business, with the exception of affairs of
state, so pressing as to keep him from home when his wife
5 was bathing and swaddling the baby. (She nursed it herself,
in fact, with her own milk, and she commonly gave the priv-
ilege of sucking at her breast to the children of their slaves
as well, inspiring in them feelings of good will toward their
son as a result of this shared nurturing.) As the boy reached
the age when he could take instruction, Cato himself undertook to teach him to read. He had, to be sure, a cultivated
slave in his employ by the name of Chilo, who was an experi-

6 Χίλωνα, πολλοὺς διδάσκοντα παῖδας· οὐκ ἠξίου δὲ τὸν υἱόν, ὥς φησιν
αὐτός, ὑπὸ δούλου κακῶς ἀκούειν ἢ τοῦ ὠτὸς ἀνατείνεσθαι μανθά-
νοντα βράδιον, οὐδέ γε μαθήματος τηλικούτου [τῷ] δούλῳ χάριν ὀφείλειν, ἀλλ' αὐτὸς μὲν ἦν γραμματιστής, αὐτὸς δὲ νομοδιδάκτης, αὐτὸς δὲ
γυμναστής, οὐ μόνον ἀκοντίζειν οὐδ' ὁπλομαχεῖν οὐδ' ἱππεύειν διδάσκων τὸν υἱόν, ἀλλὰ καὶ τῇ χειρὶ πὺξ παίειν καὶ καῦμα καὶ ψῦχος ἀν-
έχεσθαι καὶ τὰ δινώδη καὶ τραχύνοντα τοῦ ποταμοῦ διανηχόμενον
7 ἀποβιάζεσθαι. καὶ τὰς ἱστορίας δὲ συγγράψαι φησὶν αὐτὸς ἰδίᾳ χειρὶ
καὶ μεγάλοις γράμμασιν, ὅπως οἴκοθεν ὑπάρχοι τῷ παιδὶ πρὸς ἐμπει-
ρίαν τῶν παλαιῶν καὶ πατρίων ὠφελεῖσθαι· τὰ δ' αἰσχρὰ τῶν ῥημάτων
οὐχ ἧττον ἐξευλαβεῖσθαι τοῦ παιδὸς παρόντος ἢ τῶν ἱερῶν παρθένων
8 ἃς Ἑστιάδας καλοῦσι· συλλούσασθαι δὲ μηδέποτε. (καὶ τοῦτο κοινὸν
ἔοικε Ῥωμαίων ἔθος εἶναι· καὶ γὰρ πενθεροὶ γαμβροῖς ἐφυλάττοντο
συλλούεσθαι, δυσωπούμενοι τὴν ἀποκάλυψιν καὶ γύμνωσιν. εἶτα μέντοι παρ' Ἑλλήνων τὸ γυμνοῦσθαι μαθόντες, αὐτοὶ πάλιν τοῦ καὶ μετὰ
9 γυναικῶν τοῦτο πράσσειν ἀναπεπλήκασι τοὺς Ἕλληνας.) οὕτω δὲ
καλὸν ἔργον εἰς ἀρετὴν τῷ Κάτωνι πλάττοντι καὶ δημιουργοῦντι τὸν
υἱόν, ἐπεὶ τὰ τῆς προθυμίας ἦν ἄμεμπτα καὶ δι' εὐφυΐαν ὑπήκουεν ἡ ψυχή, τὸ δὲ σῶμα μαλακώτερον ἐφαίνετο τοῦ πονεῖν, ἐπανῆκεν αὐτῷ τὸ
10 σύντονον ἄγαν καὶ κεκολασμένον τῆς διαίτης. ὁ δὲ καίπερ οὕτως ἔχων
ἀνὴρ ἀγαθὸς ἦν ἐν ταῖς στρατείαις, καὶ τὴν πρὸς Περσέα μάχην ἠγωνί-

47.6 δούλῳ Hercher: τῷ δούλῳ UA: om. S 47.8 πενθεροὶ γαμβροῖς Sintenis: πενθεροῖς γαμβροὶ SUA 47.9 πλάττοντι UA: καὶ πράττοντι S

enced teacher of reading and writing and who had a large number of pupils. But, as he himself says, he did not feel that it was right for his son to be subjected to verbal abuse or have his ear pulled by a slave when he was a bit slow to learn his lessons, still less that he should feel indebted to a slave for instruction in a subject of such importance. Instead, he himself served as his instructor in reading and writing, as his instructor in the law and as his instructor in physical education, teaching his son not only how to throw the spear, how to fight in armor and how to manage a horse, but also how to fight barehanded, how to tolerate extremes of heat and cold and how to endure the exertion of swimming across the river at a point where it is rough and turbulent. Further, he says that, when he composed his historical books, he wrote them out himself with his own hand in large letters, so that his son might have in his own home the opportunity to enrich himself from the point of view of gaining familiarity with his ancient heritage. And he says that he was no less careful to avoid foul language in the presence of his son than in the presence of the sacrosanct maidens known as the Vestal Virgins and, further, that he never attended the bath in the company of his son. (In fact, this seems to have been a general habit of the Romans. For even men who were related to one another by marriage used to take care to avoid bathing together, since they were embarrassed at the sight of undressing and nakedness. Subsequently, however, when the Romans learned from the Greeks to go naked, they for their part reinfected the Greeks and passed on to them the practice of doing this even in the presence of women.) Now, while Cato was engaged so productively in shaping and moulding his son into a man of quality, he found that, while the boy's enthusiasm left nothing to be desired and his spirit was by nature inclined to be obedient to his father, his body was apparently not strong enough for great exertion, so for the boy's benefit he moderated the excessively rigorous and grueling aspects of his regimen. In spite of his constitution, the boy proved to be an excellent soldier in the field, and he fought with conspicuous valor under the command of Paullus

σατο λαμπρῶς Παύλου στρατηγοῦντος. εἶτα μέντοι τοῦ ξίφους ἐκ-
κρουσθέντος ὑπὸ πληγῆς ἢ δι' ὑγρότητα τῆς χειρὸς ἐξολισθόντος,
ἀχθεσθεὶς τρέπεται πρός τινας τῶν συνήθων καὶ παραλαβὼν ἐκείνους
11 αὖθις εἰς τοὺς πολεμίους ἐνέβαλε. πολλῷ δ' ἀγῶνι καὶ βίᾳ μεγάλῃ δια-
φωτίσας τὸν τόπον, ἀνεῦρε μόγις ἐν πολλοῖς σάγμασιν ὅπλων καὶ σώμασι νεκρῶν ὁμοῦ φίλων τε καὶ πολεμίων κατασεσωρευμένων. ἐφ' ᾧ καὶ
Παῦλος ὁ στρατηγὸς ἠγάσθη τὸ μειράκιον, καὶ Κάτωνος αὐτοῦ φέρεταί
τις ἐπιστολὴ πρὸς τὸν υἱόν, ὑπερφυῶς ἐπαινοῦντος τὴν περὶ τὸ ξίφος φι-
12 λοτιμίαν αὐτοῦ καὶ σπουδήν. ὕστερον δὲ καὶ Παύλου θυγατέρα Τερτί-
αν ἔγημεν ὁ νεανίας, ἀδελφὴν Σκιπίωνος, οὐχ ἧττον ἤδη δι' αὐτὸν ἢ τὸν
πατέρα καταμειγνύμενος εἰς γένος τηλικοῦτον. ἡ μὲν οὖν περὶ τὸν υἱὸν
ἐπιμέλεια τοῦ Κάτωνος ἄξιον ἔσχε τέλος.

48(21). Οἰκέτας δὲ πολλοὺς ἐκτᾶτο, τῶν αἰχμαλώτων ὠνούμενος
μάλιστα τοὺς μικροὺς καὶ δυναμένους ἔτι τροφὴν καὶ παίδευσιν ὡς
σκύλακας ἢ πώλους ἐνεγκεῖν. τούτων οὐδεὶς εἰσῆλθεν εἰς οἰκίαν ἑτέραν,
εἰ μὴ πέμψαντος αὐτοῦ Κάτωνος ἢ τῆς γυναικός. ὁ δ' ἐρωτηθεὶς τί
2 πράττοι Κάτων, οὐδὲν ἀπεκρίνετο πλὴν ἀγνοεῖν. ἔδει δ' ἢ πράττειν τι
τῶν ἀναγκαίων οἴκοι τὸν δοῦλον ἢ καθεύδειν, καὶ σφόδρα τοῖς κοιμω-
μένοις ὁ Κάτων ἔχαιρε, πρᾳοτέρους τε τῶν ἐγρηγορότων νομίζων καὶ
πρὸς ὁτιοῦν βελτίονας χρῆσθαι τῶν δεομένων ὕπνου τοὺς ἀπολελαυ-
3 κότας. οἰόμενος δὲ τὰ μέγιστα ῥᾳδιουργεῖν ἀφροδισίων ἕνεκα τοὺς δούλους, ἔταξεν ὡρισμένου νομίσματος ὁμιλεῖν ταῖς θεραπαινίσιν, ἑτέρᾳ δὲ
γυναικὶ μηδένα πλησιάζειν. ἐν ἀρχῇ μὲν οὖν ἔτι πένης ὢν καὶ στρατευ-

47.10 πληγῆς ἢ S: πληγῆς καὶ UAl ἐξολισθόντος Reiske: ἐξολισθέντος SUA 47.12 ἐπι. τοῦ Κ. ἄξ. ἔσχε τέλ. S: τοῦ Κ. ἐπι. τέλ. ἄξ. ἔσχεν UA 48.1 ἀπεκρίνετο Koraes: ἀπεκρίνατο SUA

in the battle against Perseus. Then, however, when his
sword either was struck from his grasp by a blow or slipped
out of his hand, which was wet with perspiration, he turned
in his distress to some of his companions and, with them at
his side, he threw himself once again into the engagement
11 with the enemy. Then, with a great struggle against considerable opposition, he cleared away the area and at length recovered his sword in the midst of countless packs filled with
weapons and among the bodies of friend and foe piled on top
of one another indiscriminately. For this the young man was
accorded the admiration of his commander Paullus. In addition, there exists a letter by Cato himself addressed to his son
in which he praises in extravagant terms his initiative and
12 enterprise in the matter of his sword. Later on, the young
man actually married Paullus' daughter Tertia, the sister of
Scipio, thus doing more on his own to bring about a connection with that family of such great prominence than his father had until that point been able to do. So the care that
Cato lavished upon his son bore a result that was worthy of
Cato himself.

48(21). As far as slaves are concerned, he possessed
quite a few. He preferred to buy those prisoners of war who
were young and still susceptible, like puppies or colts, of
rearing and training. Not one of his slaves entered another
house unless he had been sent by Cato himself or his wife;
when asked what Cato was doing, none gave any response
2 other than, "Don't know." A slave was required either to be
busy with some essential task about the house or to be
sleeping. And Cato was quite pleased when he saw them
sleeping, for he considered that those who had taken advantage of the opportunity to rest were calmer than those who
were wide awake, and could be put to better use on any
3 project than those who were in need of sleep. And, since he
believed that, among slaves, sex was the greatest cause of
delinquency, he made it a rule that his male slaves could, for
a set fee, have intercourse with his female slaves, but no one
of them was allowed to consort with another woman. Now, at

όμενος πρὸς οὐδὲν ἐδυσκόλαινε τῶν περὶ δίαιταν, ἀλλ᾽ αἴσχιστον ἀπέ-
4 φαινε διὰ γαστέρα πρὸς οἰκέτην ζυγομαχεῖν. ὕστερον δὲ τῶν πραγμάτων ἐπιδιδόντων ποιούμενος ἑστιάσεις φίλων καὶ συναρχόντων, ἐκόλα-
ζεν εὐθὺς μετὰ τὸ δεῖπνον ἱμάντι τοὺς ἀμελέστερον ὑπουργήσαντας
ὁτιοῦν ἢ σκευάσαντας. ἀεὶ δέ τινα τοὺς δούλους ἐμηχανᾶτο στάσιν
ἔχειν καὶ διαφορὰν πρὸς ἀλλήλους, ὑπονοῶν τὴν ὁμόνοιαν αὐτῶν καὶ
δεδοικώς. τοὺς δ᾽ ἄξιον εἰργάσθαι τι θανάτου δόξαντας ἐδικαίου κρι-
5 θέντας ἐν τοῖς οἰκέταις πᾶσιν ἀποθνῄσκειν, εἰ καταγνωσθεῖεν. ἁπτόμε-
νος δὲ συντονώτερον πορισμοῦ τὴν μὲν γεωργίαν ἡγεῖτο μᾶλλον διαγωγὴν ἢ πρόσοδον, εἰς δ᾽ ἀσφαλῆ πράγματα καὶ βέβαια κατατιθέμενος τὰς
ἀφορμὰς ἐκτᾶτο λίμνας, ὕδατα θερμά, τόπους κναφεῦσιν ἀνειμένους,
†ἔργα πίσσια,† χώραν ἔχουσαν αὐτοφυεῖς νομὰς καὶ ὕλας, ἀφ᾽ ὧν αὐτῷ
χρήματα προσῄει πολλὰ μηδ᾽ ὑπὸ τοῦ Διός, ὥς φησιν αὐτός, βλαβῆναι
6 δυναμένων. ἐχρήσατο δὲ καὶ τῷ διαβεβλημένῳ μάλιστα τῶν δανεισμῶν
⟨τῷ⟩ ἐπὶ ναυτικοῖς τὸν τρόπον τοῦτον. ἐκέλευε τοὺς δανειζομένους ἐπὶ
κοινωνίᾳ πολλοὺς παρακαλεῖν· γενομένων δὲ πεντήκοντα καὶ πλοίων
τοσούτων, αὐτὸς εἶχε μίαν μερίδα διὰ Κουϊντίωνος ἀπελευθέρου, τοῖς
7 δανειζομένοις συμπραγματευομένου καὶ συμπλέοντος. ἦν δ᾽ οὖν οὐκ
εἰς ἅπαν ὁ κίνδυνος, ἀλλ᾽ εἰς μέρος μικρὸν ἐπὶ κέρδεσι μεγάλοις. ἐδίδου
δὲ καὶ τῶν οἰκετῶν τοῖς βουλομένοις ἀργύριον· οἱ δ᾽ ἐωνοῦντο παῖδας,
εἶτα τούτους ἀσκήσαντες καὶ διδάξαντες ἀναλώμασι τοῦ Κάτωνος μετ᾽
8 ἐνιαυτὸν ἀπεδίδοντο. πολλοὺς δὲ καὶ κατεῖχεν ὁ Κάτων, ὅσην ὁ πλεί-

48.5 ἔργα πίσσια S: ἐργατησίαν UA 48.6 τῷ add. Sintenis

first, when Cato was still poor and serving in the army, he
was not at all fastidious about his meals. Instead, he made it
clear that it was singularly reprehensible to bicker with a
4 slave for the sake of one's belly. Later, however, as his circumstances improved, when he entertained friends and col-
leagues, no sooner was dinner over than he would punish
those who had been the slightest bit negligent in any aspect
of the service or preparation of the feast by beating them
with a leather strap. And he was always devising ways of
insuring that there be some sort of dissension and dispute
among his slaves, since he viewed any harmonious feelings
among them with suspicion and apprehension. If any of his
slaves were suspected of having done something deserving of
capital punishment, he thought that they should be brought
to trial and, if condemned, executed in the presence of all the
5 slaves. When he began to apply himself more intensively to
the pursuit of profit, since he regarded farming more as an
avocation than as a source of income and since he was interested in investing his capital in safe and secure ventures, he
acquired fisheries, hot baths, areas set aside for fullers' establishments, (?) factories and land that was naturally provided with pasturage and timber. These investments produced a large return for him and were not, as he himself
6 says, subject to damage by Jupiter. In addition, he engaged
in the most disreputable branch of moneylending, namely
bottomry. This was how he operated: He would require
those who borrowed money from him to form a large corpo-
ration and, when the number of associates and the number of
ships reached fifty, he would himself retain one share in the
name of his freedman Quintio, who would sail with the bor-
7 rowers and serve as their business consultant. The point is
that the risk did not lie upon the entire operation but was
confined to a small share, and yet there was the prospect of
large profits. Cato would even lend money to those of his
slaves who wished to borrow. They would then purchase
boys and, after training them and giving them instruction at
8 Cato's expense, would sell them in a year's time. Cato would
actually retain a large number of them, and would credit to

στην διδοὺς ἐωνεῖτο τιμὴν ὑπολογιζόμενος. προτρέπων δὲ τὸν υἱὸν ἐπὶ ταῦτα, φησὶν οὐκ ἀνδρός, ἀλλὰ χήρας γυναικὸς εἶναι τὸ μειῶσαί τι τῶν ὑπαρχόντων. ἐκεῖνο δ' ἤδη σφοδρότερον τοῦ Κάτωνος, ὅτι θαυμαστὸν ἄνδρα καὶ θεῖον εἰπεῖν ἐτόλμησε πρὸς δόξαν, ὃς ἀπολείπει πλέον ἐν τοῖς λόγοις ὃ προσέθηκεν οὗ παρέλαβεν.

49(22). Ἤδη δὲ γέροντος αὐτοῦ γεγονότος, πρέσβεις Ἀθήνηθεν
ἧκον εἰς Ῥώμην οἱ περὶ Καρνεάδην τὸν Ἀκαδημαϊκὸν καὶ Διογένη τὸν
Στωικὸν φιλόσοφον καταδίκην τινὰ παραιτησόμενοι τοῦ δήμου τῶν
Ἀθηναίων, ἣν ἐρήμην ὦφλον Ὠρωπίων μὲν διωξάντων, Σικυωνίων δὲ
2 καταψηφισαμένων, τίμημα ταλάντων πεντακοσίων ἔχουσαν. εὐθὺς οὖν
οἱ φιλολογώτατοι τῶν νεανίσκων ἐπὶ τοὺς ἄνδρας ἵεντο καὶ συνῆσαν,
ἀκροώμενοι καὶ θαυμάζοντες αὐτούς. μάλιστα δ' ἡ Καρνεάδου χάρις,
ἧς ⟨ἦν⟩ δύναμίς τε πλείστη καὶ δόξα τῆς δυνάμεως οὐκ ἀποδέουσα,
μεγάλων ἐπιλαμβανομένη καὶ φιλανθρώπων ἀκροατηρίων ὡς πνεῦμα
3 τὴν πόλιν ἠχῆς ἐνέπλησε, καὶ λόγος κατεῖχεν, ὡς ἀνὴρ Ἕλλην εἰς ἔκ-
πληξιν ὑπερφυὴς πάντα κηλῶν καὶ χειρούμενος ἔρωτα δεινὸν ἐμβέβλη-
κε τοῖς νέοις, ὑφ' οὗ τῶν ἄλλων ἡδονῶν καὶ διατριβῶν ἐκπεσόντες ἐν-
4 θουσιῶσι περὶ φιλοσοφίαν. ταῦτα τοῖς μὲν ἄλλοις ἤρεσκε Ῥωμαίοις
γιγνόμενα, καὶ τὰ μειράκια παιδείας Ἑλληνικῆς μεταλαμβάνοντα καὶ
5 συνόντα θαυμαζομένοις ἀνδράσιν ἡδέως ἑώρων· ὁ δὲ Κάτων ἐξ ἀρχῆς
τε τοῦ ζήλου τῶν λόγων παραρρέοντος εἰς τὴν πόλιν ἤχθετο, φοβούμε-
νος μὴ τὸ φιλότιμον ἐνταῦθα τρέψαντες οἱ νέοι τὴν ἐπὶ τῷ λέγειν δόξαν
ἀγαπήσωσι μᾶλλον τῆς ἀπὸ τῶν ἔργων καὶ τῶν στρατειῶν· ἐπεὶ δὲ

49.1 ἧκον S: ἦλθον UA 49.2 ἧς A: ἣ SU| ἦν add. Madvig

the slave's account the amount offered by the highest bidder for the boy. He tried to persuade his son to take an interest in these practices, saying that it was a characteristic, not of a man, but of a widow to make some reduction in the value of the estate. But Cato has taken his enthusiasm too far when he has the audacity to say that the man who, when the final accounting is made, has added more to the estate that he leaves behind him than he had inherited is remarkable and deserves to be ranked with the gods in renown.

49(22). By now Cato had reached old age, when Carneades the Academic and Diogenes the Stoic philosopher arrived in Rome as ambassadors from Athens. They had come
seeking the abrogation of a judgment, involving a fine of five
hundred talents, that had been handed down by the Sicyonians against the people of Athens, who had lost their case by
default when an action was brought against them by the peo-
2 ple of Oropus. Immediately, those young men who had the
greatest interest in liberal pursuits flocked to the side of
these men, paying attention to their every word and idolizing
them. It was especially the appeal of Carneades, which was
exceptionally powerful and which had a reputation not at
all inferior to its power, that attracted large and sympathetic
audiences and, like a gale, filled the city with its resonant
3 presénce. Everyone was going around, saying that a man
from Greece, who had a remarkable ability to stun audiences, was putting everything under his magic spell and had
inspired in the young a fierce desire, which caused them to
forsake all other pleasures and pastimes and to pursue
4 learning with a passion. While this phenomenon met with
the approval of the other men of Rome, who were glad to see
their young men taking an interest in Greek culture and as-
5 sociating with men of repute, Cato from the very beginning
was disturbed by this passion for words which was infiltrat-
ing the city. He was afraid that the young men would turn
their ambition in that direction and would strive more for a
reputation that depended upon skill in speaking than for one
based upon actions and campaigns. So, when the reputation

προύβαινεν ἡ δόξα τῶν φιλοσόφων ἐν τῇ πόλει, καὶ τοὺς πρώτους
λόγους αὐτῶν πρὸς τὴν σύγκλητον ἀνὴρ ἐπιφανὴς σπουδάσας αὐτὸς
καὶ δεηθεὶς ἡρμήνευσε Γάιος Ἀκίλιος, ἔγνω μετ' εὐπρεπείας ἀποδιοπομ-
6 πήσασθαι τοὺς φιλοσόφους πάντας ἐκ τῆς πόλεως, καὶ παρελθὼν εἰς
τὴν σύγκλητον ἐμέμψατο τοῖς ἄρχουσιν, ὅτι πρεσβεία κάθηται πολὺν
χρόνον ἄπρακτος ἀνδρῶν, οἳ περὶ παντὸς οὗ βούλοιντο ῥᾳδίως πείθειν
7 δύνανται· δεῖν οὖν τὴν ταχίστην γνῶναί τι καὶ ψηφίσασθαι περὶ τῆς πρεσβείας, ὅπως οὗτοι μὲν ἐπὶ τὰς σχολὰς τραπόμενοι διαλέγωνται παισὶν
Ἑλλήνων, οἱ δὲ Ῥωμαίων νέοι τῶν νόμων καὶ τῶν ἀρχόντων ὡς πρότερον ἀκούωσι.

50(23). Ταῦτα δ' οὐχ, ὡς ἔνιοι νομίζουσι, Καρνεάδῃ δυσχεράνας
ἔπραξεν, ἀλλ' ὅλως φιλοσοφίᾳ προσκεκρουκώς, καὶ πᾶσαν Ἑλληνικὴν
μοῦσαν καὶ παιδείαν ὑπὸ φιλοτιμίας προπηλακίζων, ὅς γε καὶ Σωκράτη
φησὶ λάλον γενόμενον καὶ βίαιον ἐπιχειρεῖν, ᾧ τρόπῳ δυνατὸς ἦν, τυ-
ραννεῖν τῆς πατρίδος, καταλύοντα τὰ ἔθη καὶ πρὸς ἐναντίας τοῖς νό-
2 μοις δόξας ἕλκοντα καὶ μεθιστάντα τοὺς πολίτας. τὴν δ' Ἰσοκράτους
διατριβὴν ἐπισκώπτων, γηρᾶν φησι παρ' αὐτῷ τοὺς μαθητάς, ὡς ἐν
Ἅιδου παρὰ Μίνῳ χρησομένους ταῖς τέχναις καὶ δίκας ἐροῦντας. τὸν
δὲ παῖδα διαβάλλων πρὸς τὰ Ἑλληνικά, φωνῇ κέχρηται θρασυτέρᾳ τοῦ
γήρως, οἷον ἀποθεσπίζων καὶ προμαντεύων ὡς ἀπολοῦσι Ῥωμαῖοι τὰ
3 πράγματα, γραμμάτων Ἑλληνικῶν ἀναπλησθέντες. ἀλλὰ ταύτην μὲν
αὐτοῦ τὴν δυσφημίαν ὁ χρόνος ἀποδείκνυσι κενήν, ἐν ᾧ τοῖς τε πράγμασιν ἡ πόλις ἤρθη μεγίστη, καὶ πρὸς Ἑλληνικὰ μαθήματα καὶ παιδείαν ἅπασαν ἔσχεν οἰκείως. ὁ δ' οὐ μόνον ἀπηχθάνετο τοῖς φιλοσο-

50.1 δυνατὸς S: δυνατὸν UA

of these philosophers spread in the city and their opening
speeches before the senate were translated by Gaius Acilius,
a distinguished man who had himself eagerly requested the
honor, Cato resolved to exorcize all the philosophers from the
6 city without bringing discredit upon them. Coming forward
to address the senate, he reproached the authorities for allowing an embassy to remain so long unemployed which consisted of men who could easily make use of their persuasive
7 abilities in whatever endeavor they wished. What was needed, therefore, was for them to make up their minds regarding
the embassy and to call for a vote as soon as possible, so that
these men could go back to their schools and hold converse
with Greek boys, while the young men of Rome could return
to their earlier practice of heeding the laws and the authorities.

50(23). It was not, as some suppose, because he felt a
personal resentment toward Carneades that he did this.
Rather he had come to blows with philosophical pursuits in
general and was zealously trying to discredit Greek civilization and culture as a whole. After all, even Socrates was, according to him, a chatterbox and a fiend, whose intention it
was to lord it over his homeland by using whatever means
he could, namely by undermining traditional values and by
compelling his fellow citizens to modify their views so that
2 they were no longer in conformity with the laws. In addition, he heaped scorn upon Isocrates' method of teaching,
saying that his disciples reached old age while they were still
under his tutelage, so that they might use their skills to plead
cases before Minos in the underworld. And, in trying to
prejudice his son against Greek culture, he adopts a tone of
voice that is rather brash for an old man, playing the role of
soothsayer and prophet, predicting that Rome will fall when
3 it becomes infected with Greek literature. But this forebod-
ing of his is being shown by the passage of time to be
vacuous, now that the city's attainment of political supremacy has coincided with its appropriation of Greek learning and
culture in its entirety. Nor was it only the philosophers of

φοῦσιν Ἑλλήνων ἀλλὰ καὶ τοὺς ἰατρεύοντας ἐν Ῥώμῃ δι' ὑποψίας εἶχε,
4 καὶ τὸν Ἱπποκράτους ὡς ἔοικεν ἀκηκοὼς λόγον, ὃν εἶπε τοῦ μεγάλου
βασιλέως καλοῦντος αὐτὸν ἐπὶ πολλοῖς τισι ταλάντοις, οὐκ ἄν ποτε
βαρβάροις Ἑλλήνων πολεμίοις ἑαυτὸν παρασχεῖν, ἔλεγε κοινὸν ὅρκον
εἶναι τοῦτον ἰατρῶν ἁπάντων, καὶ παρεκελεύετο φυλάττεσθαι τῷ παιδὶ
5 πάντας. αὑτῷ δὲ γεγραμμένον ὑπόμνημα εἶναι, καὶ πρὸς τοῦτο θερα-
πεύειν καὶ διαιτᾶν τοὺς νοσοῦντας οἴκοι, νῆστιν μὲν οὐδέποτε διατηρῶν
6 οὐδένα, τρέφων δὲ λαχάνοις καὶ σαρκιδίοις νήσσης ἢ φαβὸς ἢ λαγῴ· καὶ
γὰρ τοῦτον κοῦφον εἶναι καὶ πρόσφορον ἀσθενοῦσι, πλὴν ὅτι πολλὰ
συμβαίνει τοῖς φαγοῦσιν ἐνυπνιάζεσθαι. τοιαύτῃ δὲ θεραπείᾳ καὶ διαίτῃ
χρώμενος ὑγιαίνειν μὲν αὐτός, ὑγιαίνοντας δὲ τοὺς αὑτοῦ διαφυλάττειν.

51(24). Καὶ περί γε τοῦτο φαίνεται γεγονὼς οὐκ ἀνεμέσητος· καὶ γὰρ
τὴν γυναῖκα καὶ τὸν υἱὸν ἀπέβαλεν. αὐτὸς δὲ τῷ σώματι πρὸς εὐεξίαν
καὶ ῥώμην ἀσφαλῶς πεπηγὼς ἐπὶ πλεῖστον ἀντεῖχεν, ὥστε καὶ γυναικὶ
πρεσβύτης ὢν σφόδρα πλησιάζειν, καὶ γῆμαι γάμον οὐ καθ' ἡλικίαν ἐκ
2 τοιαύτης προφάσεως· ἀποβαλὼν τὴν γυναῖκα τῷ μὲν υἱῷ Παύλου θυγατέρα, Σκιπίωνος δ' ἀδελφήν, ἠγάγετο πρὸς γάμον, αὐτὸς δὲ χηρεύων
ἐχρῆτο παιδίσκῃ, κρύφα φοιτώσῃ πρὸς αὐτόν. ἦν οὖν ἐν οἰκίᾳ μικρᾷ
νύμφην ἐχούσῃ τοῦ πράγματος αἴσθησις, καί ποτε τοῦ γυναίου θρασύ-

50.5 λαχάνοις καὶ UA: λαχάνοις ἢ Sl φαβοσηλάτω sic S: φάσσης ἢ λαγῴ UA 50.6 τοῦτον Hercher: τοῦτο SUA

Greece that earned his hatred; he regarded with suspicion
those Greeks who were practicing medicine in Rome as well.
4 It seems that he had heard the saying of Hippocrates, uttered
when the great king invited him to his court and offered him
some enormous figure as his fee, that he would never provide his services to barbarians, who were the enemies of the
Greeks. Cato was in the habit of saying that this was the
common pact that all physicians entered into, and he used to
5 caution his son against the lot of them. Also, he records that
there was a treatise that he himself had written, and he used
to prescribe treatments and diets for those in his household
who were ill by referring to it. He would never put anyone
on a starvation diet, but would build up his strength by
feeding him vegetables and small quantities of duck, pigeon
6 or hare. (For the latter, he said, was light and suited to those
in a weakened condition, except that it caused those who ate
it to have frequent dreams.) By making use of such treatment and diet he claims that he himself remained in good
health and he kept the members of his household in good
health as well.

51(24). I should add that, in regard to this claim, he appears to have been unable to avert the anger of the gods for,
as a matter of fact, he lost his wife and his son. As far as he
himself is concerned, since his sound bodily constitution en-
sured continuing good health and vigor, he resisted the on-
slaughts of old age for quite a long while, to the extent that
he still, even when he was quite an old man, was disposed to
pursue sexual activity, and he contracted a marriage that ill
2 became his years. He did this for the following reason: After
the death of his wife, he arranged for his son to take in marriage one of Paullus' daughters, a sister of Scipio's, while he
himself, now that he was a widower, had recourse to a prostitute, who would come to see him without anyone's knowing
of it. Well, this arrangement was eventually discovered,
there being a new bride in the house and the house itself
being a small one, and when, on one occasion, the woman
swept past the young Cato's bedroom rather more brazenly

τερον παρασοβῆσαι παρὰ τὸ δωμάτιον δόξαντος, ὁ νεανίας εἶπε μὲ
οὐδέν, ἐμβλέψας δέ πως πικρότερον καὶ διατραπεὶς οὐκ ἔλαθε τὸν πρε
3 σβύτην. ὡς οὖν ἔγνω τὸ πρᾶγμα δυσχεραινόμενον ὑπ᾽ αὐτῶν, οὐδὲ
ἐγκαλέσας οὐδὲ μεμψάμενος, ἀλλὰ καταβαίνων ὥσπερ εἰώθει μετ
φίλων εἰς ἀγοράν, Σαλώνιόν τινα τῶν ὑπογεγραμματευκότων αὐτῷ
παρόντα καὶ συμπροπέμποντα μεγάλῃ φωνῇ προσαγορεύσας ἠρώτη
4 σεν, εἰ τὸ θυγάτριον συνήρμοκε νυμφίῳ. τοῦ δ᾽ ἀνθρώπου φήσαντος ὡ
οὐδὲ μέλλει μὴ πρότερον ἐκείνῳ κοινωσάμενος, 'καὶ μὴν ἐγώ σοι,' φησίν
'εὕρηκα κηδεστὴν ἐπιτήδειον, εἰ μὴ νὴ Δία τὰ τῆς ἡλικίας δυσχεραίνοι-
5 το· τἆλλα γὰρ οὐ μεμπτός ἐστι, σφόδρα δὲ πρεσβύτης.' ὡς οὖν ὁ Σαλώνιος αὐτὸν ἐκέλευε ταῦτα φροντίζειν καὶ διδόναι τὴν κόρην ᾧ προαιρεῖ-
ται, πελάτιν τ᾽ οὖσαν αὐτοῦ καὶ δεομένην τῆς ἐκείνου κηδεμονίας, οὐδεμίαν ὁ Κάτων ἀναβολὴν ποιησάμενος αὐτὸς ἔφη τὴν παρθένον αἰτεῖν
6 αὐτῷ. καὶ τὸ μὲν πρῶτον ὡς εἰκὸς ὁ λόγος ἐξέπληξε τὸν ἄνθρωπον,
πόρρω μὲν γάμου τὸν Κάτωνα, πόρρω δ᾽ αὐτὸν οἰκίας ὑπατικῆς καὶ
θριαμβικῶν κηδευμάτων τιθέμενον· σπουδῇ δὲ χρώμενον ὁρῶν τὸν
Κάτωνα, ἄσμενος ἐδέξατο, καὶ καταβάντες εὐθὺς εἰς ἀγορὰν ἐποιοῦντο
7 τὴν ἐγγύην. πραττομένου δὲ τοῦ γάμου, παραλαβὼν τοὺς ἐπιτηδείους ὁ
υἱὸς τοῦ Κάτωνος ἠρώτησε τὸν πατέρα, μή τι μεμφόμενος ἢ λελυπημέ-
νος ὑπ᾽ αὐτοῦ μητρυιὰν ἐπάγεται. ὁ δὲ Κάτων ἀναβοήσας, 'εὐφήμησον,'
εἶπεν, 'ὦ παῖ· πάντα γὰρ ἀγαστά μοι τὰ παρὰ σοῦ καὶ μεμπτὸν οὐδέν·
ἐπιθυμῶ δὲ πλείονας ἐμαυτῷ τε παῖδας καὶ πολίτας τῇ πατρίδι τοιού-
8 τους ἀπολιπεῖν.' ταύτην δὲ τὴν γνώμην πρότερον εἰπεῖν φασι Πεισίστρα-
τον τὸν Ἀθηναίων τύραννον, ἐπιγήμαντα τοῖς ἐνηλίκοις παισὶ τὴν

51.6 θριαμβικῶν S: θριαμβευτικῶν UA| ἄσμενος S: ἀσμένως UA

than he thought appropriate, he made his feelings clear to the old man, without saying a word, by giving her a nasty sort of glance and then turning away from her in disgust.
3 When Cato realized that the affair was causing them offense, without making any complaints or recriminations he simply walked with his friends, as was his custom, down to the forum, where he met Salonius, one of his under-secretaries, who was there to join his retinue. Cato greeted him and asked in a loud voice if he had married off his young daugh-
4 ter yet. When the man replied that he would not even think of doing so without first consulting him, Cato said, "In that case, I have found a suitable son-in-law for you. That is, unless by some chance you should have an objection on the grounds of age. For, although there is otherwise nothing
5 wrong with him, he is quite elderly." So, when Salonius told him to take care of the matter and to give the girl to the man he had in mind, since she was his client and it was up to him to provide for her, Cato came straight to the point and said
6 that he was seeking the young lady's hand for himself. At first, of course, the man was completely stunned by what he heard, since he would have thought that the chances of Cato's taking a wife were as remote as the chances that he himself might join a family of consular rank and have relatives who had celebrated a triumph. But when he saw that Cato was in earnest, he welcomed the proposal gladly, and the two of them proceeded immediately to the forum to formalize the
7 betrothal. While arrangements for the marriage were being made, Cato's son, taking along his closest friends, went and asked his father if it was because he had some complaint against him or because he had suffered some injury at his hands that he was inflicting a stepmother upon the house. With a cry of protest Cato replied, "Bite your tongue, child! I have received nothing but wonderful treatment from you, nor is there any complaint that I have to make. It is my desire to leave behind more sons like you to benefit me and
8 more citizens like you to benefit the state." They say, however, that this sentiment was earlier expressed by Peisistratus, the tyrant of Athens, when he married Timonassa to be a

Ἀργολίδα Τιμώνασσαν, ἐξ ἧς Ἰοφῶντα καὶ Θεσσαλὸν αὐτῷ λέγουσι
9 γενέσθαι. γήμαντι δὲ τῷ Κάτωνι γίνεται παῖς, ᾧ παρωνύμιον ἀπὸ τῆς
μητρὸς ἔθετο Σαλώνιον. ὁ δὲ πρεσβύτερος υἱὸς ἐτελεύτησε στρατηγῶν,
10 καὶ μέμνηται μὲν αὐτοῦ πολλάκις ἐν τοῖς βιβλίοις ὁ Κάτων ὡς ἀνδρὸς
ἀγαθοῦ γεγονότος, πρᾴως δὲ καὶ φιλοσόφως λέγεται τὴν συμφορὰν
11 ἐνεγκεῖν, καὶ μηδὲν ἀμβλύτερος δι' αὐτὴν εἰς τὰ πολιτικὰ γενέσθαι. οὐ
γὰρ ὡς Λεύκιος Λεύκολλος ὕστερον καὶ Μέτελλος ὁ Πίος ἐξέκαμεν ὑπὸ
γήρως πρὸς τὰ δημόσια, λειτουργίαν τὴν πολιτείαν ἡγούμενος, οὐδ' ὡς
πρότερον Σκιπίων ὁ Ἀφρικανὸς διὰ τὸν ἀντικρούσαντα πρὸς τὴν δόξαν
αὐτοῦ φθόνον ἀποστραφεὶς τὸν δῆμον ἐκ μεταβολῆς ἐποιήσατο τοῦ
λοιποῦ βίου τέλος ἀπραγμοσύνην, ἀλλ' ὥσπερ Διονύσιόν τις ἔπεισε
κάλλιστον ἐντάφιον ἡγεῖσθαι τὴν τυραννίδα, κάλλιστον αὐτὸς ἐγγήραμα τὴν πολιτείαν ποιησάμενος, ἀναπαύσεσιν ἐχρῆτο καὶ παιδιαῖς,
ὁπότε σχολάζοι, τῷ συντάττεσθαι βιβλία καὶ τῷ γεωργεῖν.

52(25). Συνετάττετο μὲν οὖν λόγους τε παντοδαποὺς καὶ ἱστορίας·
γεωργίᾳ δὲ προσεῖχε νέος μὲν ὢν ἔτι καὶ διὰ τὴν χρείαν (φησὶ γὰρ δυσὶ
κεχρῆσθαι μόνοις πορισμοῖς, γεωργίᾳ καὶ φειδοῖ), τότε δὲ διαγωγὴν καὶ
2 θεωρίαν αὐτῷ τὰ γιγνόμενα κατ' ἀγρὸν παρεῖχε. καὶ συντέτακταί γε
βιβλίον γεωργικόν, ἐν ᾧ καὶ περὶ πλακούντων σκευασίας καὶ τηρήσεως
3 ὀπώρας γέγραφεν, ἐν παντὶ φιλοτιμούμενος περιττὸς εἶναι καὶ ἴδιος. ἦν
δὲ καὶ τὸ δεῖπνον ἐν ἀγρῷ δαψιλέστερον· ἐκάλει γὰρ ἑκάστοτε τῶν
ἀγρογειτόνων καὶ περιχώρων τοὺς συνήθεις καὶ συνδιῆγεν ἱλαρῶς, οὐ
τοῖς καθ' ἡλικίαν μόνον ἡδὺς ὢν συγγενέσθαι καὶ ποθεινός, ἀλλὰ καὶ

51.10 λέγεται τὴν UA: λέγεται καὶ τὴν S 52.2 σκευασίας UA: ἐργασίας S 52.3 μόνον S: μόνοις UA

stepmother to his adult sons. (She came from Argos and, so
they say, was the mother of his sons Iophon and Thessalus.)
9 After Cato's marriage, a son was born to him, to whom he
gave the agnomen Salonius, after his mother. The elder son,
10 however, died while holding office as praetor and, while Cato
frequently mentions him in his writings as having been a
fine and brave man, it is said that Cato bore his misfortune
with a philosophical self-control, nor did he become any the
less passionately committed to political life as a result of it.
11 For, unlike Lucius Lucullus and Metellus Pius afterwards, he
did not regard politics as a burdensome obligation and abandon public service because of the weariness brought on by
old age. Nor did he, like Scipio Africanus before him, turn his
back on the people and, because of the jealousy that had
buffeted his reputation, convert the pursuit of leisure into
the goal of his remaining years. Instead, just as someone
convinced Dionysius to consider tyranny to be the most attractive wrapping for a corpse, so he for his part looked upon
politics as the most attractive trappings for an old man.
When he did relax, his pastimes and diversions consisted of
writing books and farming.

52(25). He wrote, in addition to speeches on a variety of
topics, works of a historical nature. As far as farming is concerned, while he used to apply himself seriously to it when
he was still young—It was then an actual necessity, for he
says that there were only two sources of income available to
him, farming and thrift—at this time the affairs of his farm
merely served as an avocation and presented him with an
2 intellectual challenge. Indeed, he is the author of a book on
farming, in which he has even written about how to prepare
flat cakes and how to preserve fruit, seeking to prove himself
3 an expert in everything and striving after originality. He
tried to outdo himself also with the feasts that he provided
on his farm. He would always invite his friends from the
neighboring farms and the surrounding areas and would
have a delightful time with them. Nor was it only his contemporaries who found his company pleasant and who

τοῖς νέοις, ἅτε δὴ πολλῶν μὲν ἔμπειρος πραγμάτων γεγονώς, πολλοῖς δὲ
4 γράμμασι καὶ λόγοις ἀξίοις ἀκοῆς ἐντετυχηκώς. τὴν δὲ τράπεζαν ἐν
τοῖς μάλιστα φιλοποιὸν ἡγεῖτο, καὶ πολλὴ μὲν εὐφημία τῶν καλῶν καὶ
ἀγαθῶν πολιτῶν ἐπεισήγετο, πολλὴ δ' ἦν ἀμνηστία τῶν ἀχρήστων καὶ
πονηρῶν, μήτε ψόγῳ μήτ' ἐπαίνῳ πάροδον ὑπὲρ αὐτῶν τοῦ Κάτωνος εἰς
τὸ συμπόσιον διδόντος.

53(26). Ἔσχατον δὲ τῶν πολιτευμάτων αὐτοῦ τὴν Καρχηδόνος
ἀνάστασιν οἴονται γεγονέναι, τῷ μὲν ἔργῳ τέλος ἐπιθέντος τοῦ νέου
Σκιπίωνος, βουλῇ δὲ καὶ γνώμῃ μάλιστα τῇ Κάτωνος ἀραμένων τὸν
2 πόλεμον ἐξ αἰτίας τοιᾶσδε· Κάτων ἐπέμφθη πρὸς Καρχηδονίους καὶ
Μασσανάσσην τὸν Νομάδα πολεμοῦντας ἀλλήλοις, ἐπισκεψόμενος
τὰς προφάσεις τῆς διαφορᾶς. ὁ μὲν γὰρ ἦν τοῦ δήμου φίλος ἀπ' ἀρχῆς,
οἱ δ' ἐγεγόνεισαν ἔνσπονδοι μετὰ τὴν ὑπὸ Σκιπίωνος ἧτταν, ἀφαιρέσει τε
3 τῆς ἀρχῆς καὶ βαρεῖ δασμῷ χρημάτων κολουθέντες. εὑρὼν δὲ τὴν πόλιν οὐχ ὡς ᾤοντο Ῥωμαῖοι κεκακωμένην καὶ ταπεινὰ πράττουσαν, ἀλλὰ πολλῇ μὲν εὐανδροῦσαν ἡλικίᾳ, μεγάλων δὲ πλούτων γέμουσαν,
ὅπλων δὲ παντοδαπῶν καὶ παρασκευῆς πολεμιστηρίου μεστὴν καὶ
μικρὸν οὐδὲν ἐπὶ τούτοις φρονοῦσαν, οὐ τὰ Νομάδων ᾤετο καὶ Μασ-
σανάσσου πράγματα Ῥωμαίους ὥραν ἔχειν τίθεσθαι καὶ διαιτᾶν, ἀλλ'
εἰ μὴ καταλήψονται πόλιν ἄνωθεν ἐχθρὰν καὶ βαρύθυμον ηὐξημένην
4 ἀπίστως, πάλιν ἐν τοῖς ἴσοις κινδύνοις ἔσεσθαι. ταχέως οὖν ὑποστρέψας

52.3 γράμμασι Sintenis: πράγμασι SUA

sought him out. He appealed also to the young, since he had,
after all, undergone so many valuable experiences and since
he was familiar with so many writings and important
4 speeches. He regarded the table as the very best creator of
friendships and, while considerable praise of fine and up-
standing citizens was allowed, considerable neglect of those
who were worthless and wicked was the order of the day,
since Cato would permit neither censure nor commendation
of such men to gain admittance to the party.

53(26). The annihilation of Carthage is regarded as having been the last of his accomplishments in public life for,
while it was the younger Scipio who was actually responsible
for bringing the task to completion, it was primarily due to
the advice and counsel of Cato that the Romans had em-
2 barked upon the war. The cause of it was as follows: Cato
was dispatched to look into the reasons for the dispute between the Carthaginians and Massinissa the Numidian, who
were at war with one another. For the latter had been on
friendly terms with the Roman people from the very start,
and the former were subject to a treaty with the Romans,
dating from the time following their defeat at the hands of
Scipio, the terms of which imposed severe limitations upon
them by depriving them of their empire and subjecting them
3 to a heavy monetary tribute. But Cato learned that, contrary
to the impression that the Romans had formed, the city of
Carthage was not in a distressed and abased condition; rather
it was burgeoning with an abundance of young men, brim-
ming with copious wealth, teeming with weapons of every
description and with warlike preparations, and it gave indications that its morale was bolstered in no small way by this.
It occurred to Cato that now was not the time for the Romans
to be regulating and administering the affairs of Massinissa
and the Numidians. If they did not immediately take measures against a city that had always been hostile and resentful toward them and that had now grown to an incredible extent, they would find themselves back in a situation as
4 dangerous as before. So he returned hastily and instructed

ἐδίδασκε τὴν βουλὴν ὡς αἱ πρότερον ἧτται καὶ συμφοραὶ Καρχηδονίων οὐ τοσοῦτον τῆς δυνάμεως ὅσον τῆς ἀνοίας ἀπαρύσασαι, κινδυνεύουσιν αὐτοὺς οὐκ ἀσθενεστέρους, ἐμπειροτέρους δὲ πολέμων ἀπεργάσασθαι, ἤδη δὲ καὶ προανακινεῖσθαι τοῖς Νομαδικοῖς τοὺς πρὸς Ῥωμαίους ἀγῶνας, εἰρήνην δὲ καὶ σπονδὰς ὄνομα τοῦ πολέμου τῇ μελλήσει κεῖσθαι καιρὸν περιμένοντος.

54(27). Πρὸς τούτοις φασὶ τὸν Κάτωνα καὶ σῦκα τῶν Λιβυκῶν ἐπίτηδες ἐκβαλεῖν ἐν τῇ βουλῇ τὴν τήβεννον ἀναβαλλόμενον, εἶτα θαυμασάντων τὸ μέγεθος καὶ τὸ κάλλος, εἰπεῖν ὡς ἡ ταῦτα φέρουσα χώρα
2 τριῶν ἡμερῶν πλοῦν ἀπέχει τῆς Ῥώμης. ἐκεῖνο δ' ἤδη καὶ βιαιότερον, τὸ περὶ παντὸς οὗ δήποτε πράγματος γνώμην ἀποφαινόμενον προσεπιφωνεῖν οὕτως· 'δοκεῖ δέ μοι καὶ Καρχηδόνα μὴ εἶναι.' τοὐναντίον δὲ Πόπλιος Σκιπίων ὁ Νασικᾶς ἐπικαλούμενος ἀεὶ διετέλει λέγων καὶ ἀποφαι-
3 νόμενος· 'δοκεῖ μοι Καρχηδόνα εἶναι.' πολλὰ γὰρ ὡς ἔοικεν ὕβρει τὸν δῆμον ὁρῶν ἤδη πλημμελοῦντα, καὶ δι' εὐτυχίαν καὶ φρόνημα τῇ βουλῇ δυσκάθεκτον ὄντα, καὶ τὴν πόλιν ὅλην ὑπὸ δυνάμεως ὅπῃ ῥέψειε ταῖς ὁρμαῖς βίᾳ συνεφελκόμενον, ἐβούλετο τοῦτον γοῦν τὸν φόβον ὥσπερ χαλινὸν ἐπικεῖσθαι σωφρονιστῆρα τῇ θρασύτητι τῶν πολλῶν, ἔλαττον μὲν ἡγούμενος ἰσχύειν Καρχηδονίους τοῦ περιγενέσθαι Ῥω-
4 μαίων, μεῖζον δὲ τοῦ καταφρονεῖσθαι. τῷ δὲ Κάτωνι τοῦτ' αὐτὸ δεινὸν ἐφαίνετο, βακχεύοντι τῷ δήμῳ καὶ σφαλλομένῳ τὰ πολλὰ δι' ἐξουσίαν

53.4 περιμένοντος Reiske: περιμένοντας SUA

the senate that the previous defeats and misfortunes suffered by the Carthaginians had had the result more of relieving them of their folly than of sapping their strength and, rather than weakening them, seemed only to have given them greater experience of war. Furthermore, he was convinced that the conflict with the Numidians was serving as a warming-up exercise for the coming struggle with Rome, and that "peace" and "treaty" were merely the words used to refer to the period during which the war, which was simply waiting for the proper moment to break out, was being postponed.

54(27). In addition, so the story goes, while he was rearranging the folds of his toga in the senate Cato by design actually let fall some Libyan figs and then, after everyone had expressed admiration for their size and beauty, he said that the land that produced them was but three days' sail from
2 Rome. But Cato has carried things too far with that famous practice of his whereby he would add the words, "And I am of the opinion that Carthage should not be allowed to exist," whenever he was called upon to declare his position on any matter whatsoever. In opposition to this, Publius Scipio Nasica would always declare his position by saying, "I am of the
3 opinion that Carthage should be allowed to exist." For he seems to have become aware that the people were by this time being badly led astray by their sense of their own self-importance and that it was difficult, on account of the advances they had made and the presumption they exhibited, for the senate to keep them in check and, finally, that they were forcibly dragging the whole city with them under the weight of their influence, in whatever direction their passions inclined them. If nothing else, he wished to have at least this source of apprehension imposed, like a bridle, to serve as a corrective to the impudence of the masses, since he felt that Carthage was not so powerful that it could prevail over Rome, nor yet so weak that it could be treated with
4 contempt. But, as far as Cato was concerned, it was precisely this that seemed to be cause for alarm, that a city that had

πόλιν ἀεὶ μεγάλην, νῦν δὲ καὶ νήφουσαν ὑπὸ συμφορῶν καὶ κεκολα-
σμένην, ἐπικρέμασθαι, καὶ μὴ παντάπασι τοὺς ἔξωθεν ἀνελεῖν τῆς ἡγεμονίας φόβους, ἀναφορὰς αὐτοῖς πρὸς τὰς οἴκοθεν ἁμαρτίας ἀπολι-
5 πόντας. οὕτω μὲν ἐξεργάσασθαι λέγεται τὸν τρίτον καὶ τελευταῖον ὁ
Κάτων ἐπὶ Καρχηδονίους πόλεμον, ἀρξαμένων δὲ πολεμεῖν ἐτελεύτη-
σεν, ἀποθεσπίσας περὶ τοῦ μέλλοντος ἐπιθήσειν τῷ πολέμῳ τέλος ἀνδρός, ὃς ἦν μὲν τότε νεανίας, χιλίαρχος δὲ στρατευόμενος ἀπεδείκνυτο
6 καὶ γνώμης ἔργα καὶ τόλμης πρὸς τοὺς ἀγῶνας. ἀπαγγελλομένων δὲ
τούτων εἰς Ῥώμην πυνθανόμενον τὸν Κάτωνά φασιν εἰπεῖν·

οἶος πέπνυται, τοὶ δὲ σκιαὶ ἀίσσουσι.

7 ταύτην μὲν οὖν τὴν ἀπόφασιν ταχὺ δι' ἔργων ἐβεβαίωσεν ὁ Σκιπίων. ὁ
δὲ Κάτων ἀπέλιπε γενεὰν ἕνα μὲν υἱὸν ἐκ τῆς ἐπιγαμηθείσης, ᾧ παρωνύμιον ἔφαμεν γενέσθαι Σαλώνιον, ἕνα δ' υἱωνὸν ἐκ τοῦ τελευτήσαντος υἱοῦ. καὶ Σαλώνιος μὲν ἐτελεύτησε στρατηγῶν, ὁ δ' ἐξ αὐτοῦ γενόμενος
Μᾶρκος ὑπάτευσεν. ἦν δὲ πάππος οὗτος τοῦ φιλοσόφου Κάτωνος, ἀνδρὸς ἀρετῇ καὶ δόξῃ τῶν καθ' ἑαυτὸν ἐπιφανεστάτου γενομένου.

ΣΥΓΚΡΙΣΙΣ

55(28/1). Γεγραμμένων δὲ καὶ περὶ τούτου τῶν ἀξίων μνήμης, ὅλος
ὁ τούτου βίος ὅλῳ τῷ θατέρου παρατιθεὶς οὐκ εὐθεώρητον ἔχει τὴν
2 διαφοράν, ἐναφανιζομένην πολλαῖς καὶ μεγάλαις ὁμοιότησιν. εἰ δὲ δεῖ
κατὰ μέρος τῇ συγκρίσει διαλαβεῖν ὥσπερ ἔπος ἢ γραφὴν ἑκάτερον, τὸ
μὲν ἐξ οὐχ ὑπαρχούσης ἀφορμῆς εἰς πολιτείαν καὶ δόξαν ἀρετῇ καὶ

54.5 ἀπεδείκνυτο UA: ἐπεδείκνυτο S 55.1 περὶ τούτου Sansone: περὶ τούτων SUA

always been great and had now, in addition, been sobered and chastened by hardships was threatening the Roman people at a time when they were to a great extent intoxicated and staggering as a result of the authority that they now possessed. Rather, he felt, they should eliminate altogether the foreign threats to their supremacy and give themselves an
5 opportunity to mend their domestic faults. And thus Cato is said to have been responsible for bringing about the third and last war against the Carthaginians. He died, however, following the outbreak of war, having uttered a prophecy concerning the man who would bring the war to completion. He was then a young man, but his service on campaign as military tribune gave evidence of his good judgment and his
6 willingness to face the rigors of combat and, when Cato kept hearing the accounts of all this that were being brought back to Rome, he is said to have exclaimed:

Only he has sense; the rest are fluttering shades.

7 It was not long before Scipio justified this verdict with his accomplishments. Cato was survived by one son born to him by his second wife (who bore, as we said, the agnomen Salonius) and one grandson, whose father was that son of Cato's who had died. Salonius died while serving as praetor, and his son Marcus attained the consulship. This man was the grandfather of Cato the philosopher, a man of the utmost distinction among his contemporaries for virtue and nobility.

COMPARISON

55(28/1). Now that I have set down in writing the memorable achievements of this man also, we can see that, when one man's life is compared in its entirety with the other's, it is not easy to detect the difference between them, ob-
2 scured as it is by the many significant similarities. If we are obliged, however, to distinguish the one from the other by carrying out the comparison piecemeal, as is done in the case of a poem or a painting, we note first of all that both men had in common the fact that they made their way to an il-

δυνάμει προελθεῖν ἀμφοτέροις κοινόν ἐστι. φαίνεται δ' ὁ μὲν Ἀριστείδης
οὔπω τότε μεγάλων οὐσῶν τῶν Ἀθηνῶν καὶ ταῖς οὐσίαις ἔτι συμμέτροις
καὶ ὁμαλοῖς ἐπιβαλὼν δημαγωγοῖς καὶ στρατηγοῖς ἐπιφανὴς γενέσθαι.
3 (τὸ γὰρ μέγιστον ἦν τίμημα τότε πεντακοσίων μεδίμνων, τὸ δὲ δεύτερον
[ἱππεῖς] τριακοσίων, ἔσχατον δὲ καὶ τρίτον [οἱ ζευγῖται] διακοσίων.) ὁ
δὲ Κάτων ἐκ πολίχνης τε μικρᾶς καὶ διαίτης ἀγροίκου δοκούσης φέρων
ἀφῆκεν ἑαυτὸν ὥσπερ εἰς πέλαγος ἀχανὲς τὴν ἐν Ῥώμῃ πολιτείαν, οὐκέτι Κουρίων καὶ Φαβρικίων καὶ Ἀτιλίων ἔργον οὖσαν ἡγεμόνων, οὐδ'
ἀπ' ἀρότρου καὶ σκαφείου πένητας καὶ αὐτουργοὺς ἀναβαίνοντας ἐπὶ
τὸ βῆμα προσιεμένην ἄρχοντας καὶ δημαγωγούς, ἀλλὰ πρὸς γένη μεγάλα καὶ πλούτους καὶ νομὰς καὶ σπουδαρχίας ἀποβλέπειν εἰθισμέ-
νην, καὶ δι' ὄγκον ἤδη καὶ δύναμιν ἐντρυφῶσαν τοῖς ἄρχειν ἀξιοῦσιν.
4 οὐκ ἦν δ' ὅμοιον ἀντιπάλῳ χρῆσθαι Θεμιστοκλεῖ, μήτ' ἀπὸ γένους
λαμπρῷ καὶ κεκτημένῳ μέτρια (πέντε γὰρ ἢ τριῶν αὐτῷ ταλάντων
οὐσίαν γενέσθαι λέγουσιν ὅτε πρῶτον ἥπτετο τῆς πολιτείας) καὶ πρὸς
Σκιπίωνας Ἀφρικανοὺς καὶ Σερουίους Γάλβας καὶ Κουιντίους Φλαμι-
νίνους ἁμιλλᾶσθαι περὶ πρωτείων, μηδὲν ὁρμητήριον ἔχοντα πλὴν
φωνὴν παρρησιαζομένην ὑπὲρ τῶν δικαίων.

56(29/2). Ἔτι δ' Ἀριστείδης μὲν ἐν Μαραθῶνι καὶ πάλιν ἐν Πλαταιαῖς δέκατος ἦν στρατηγός, Κάτων δὲ δεύτερος μὲν ὕπατος ᾑρέθη
πολλῶν ἀντιμετιόντων, δεύτερος δὲ τιμητής, ἑπτὰ τοὺς ἐπιφανεστάτους
2 καὶ πρώτους ἁμιλλωμένους ὑπερβαλόμενος. καὶ μὴν Ἀριστείδης μὲν ἐν

55.2 προελθεῖν UA: παρελθεῖν S 55.3 ἱππεῖς et οἱ ζευγῖται del. Schaefer| Ἀτιλίων S: Ὀστιλίων UA

lustrious career in public life, not because they started out
from a privileged position, but on the basis of merit and effort. Yet it appears that Aristeides, for his part, rose to fame
at a time when Athens was not yet great and by competing
against popular leaders and generals who were still rela-
tively homogeneous and even from the point of view of
3 wealth. (At that time the highest income bracket was at the
level of five hundred bushels, the second at three hundred,
the third and last at two hundred.) On the other hand Cato,
though he came from a small village and from surroundings
that could be regarded as provincial, wasted no time in
launching himself, so to speak, upon the yawning billows of
the political life of Rome, which was no longer the handiwork
of leaders like Curius and Fabricius and Atilius, and which no
longer welcomed as officeholders and popular leaders poor
men who worked their fields with their own hands and who
mounted the speaker's platform straight from the plough and
the hoe. The state had instead become accustomed to con-
centrating upon prominent families, great fortunes, largesses
and ambitious election campaigns and, swollen by now with
pride and acting under the influence of its sense of its own
power, it was beginning to toy with those who made a bid for
4 public office. It was one thing to have as one's political op-
ponent Themistocles, who was not distinguished by birth and
whose wealth was modest. (They say that, when he first
entered public life, his assets amounted to three, or perhaps
five, talents.) It was something else to contend for supremacy with the likes of Scipio Africanus and Servius Galba and
Quinctius Flamininus, when one was starting out with no other advantage than a tongue that outspokenly championed the
cause of justice.

56(29/2). Furthermore, while Aristeides was one of ten
generals at Marathon and again at Plataea, Cato was elected,
out of a large number of men competing with him for the
post, one of two consuls, and he was elected one of two censors by prevailing over the seven most distinguished and in-
2 fluential opponents. And, indeed, in none of the victories in

οὐδενὶ τῶν κατορθωμάτων γέγονε πρῶτος, ἀλλὰ Μιλτιάδης ἔχει τοῦ Μαραθῶνος τὸ πρωτεῖον, Θεμιστοκλῆς δὲ τῆς Σαλαμῖνος, ἐν δὲ Πλαταιαῖς φησιν Ἡρόδοτος ἀνελέσθαι καλλίστην νίκην Παυσανίαν, Ἀριστείδῃ δὲ καὶ τῶν δευτερείων ἀμφισβητοῦσι Σωφάναι καὶ Ἀμεινίαι καὶ Καλλίμαχοι καὶ Κυνέγειροι διαπρεπῶς ἀριστεύσαντες ἐν ἐκείνοις τοῖς
3 ἀγῶσι· Κάτων δ' οὐ μόνον αὐτὸς ὑπατεύων ἐπρώτευσε καὶ χειρὶ καὶ γνώμῃ κατὰ τὸν Ἰβηρικὸν πόλεμον, ἀλλὰ καὶ χιλιαρχῶν περὶ Θερμοπύλας ὑπατεύοντος ἑτέρου τὴν δόξαν ἔσχε τῆς νίκης, μεγάλας ἐπ' Ἀντίοχον Ῥωμαίοις ἀναπετάσας κλισιάδας καὶ πρόσω μόνον ὁρῶντι τῷ βασιλεῖ περιστήσας κατὰ νώτου τὸν πόλεμον. ἐκείνη γὰρ ἡ νίκη, περιφανῶς ἔργον οὖσα Κάτωνος, ἐξήλασε τῆς Ἑλλάδος τὴν Ἀσίαν, παρ-
4 έσχε δ' ἐπιβατὴν αὖθις Σκιπίωνι. πολεμοῦντες μὲν οὖν ἀήττητοι γεγόνασιν ἀμφότεροι, τὰ δὲ περὶ τὴν πολιτείαν Ἀριστείδης μὲν ἔπταισεν ἐξοστρακισθεὶς καὶ καταστασιασθεὶς ὑπὸ Θεμιστοκλέους, Κάτων δ', οἵπερ ἦσαν ἐν Ῥώμῃ δυνατώτατοι καὶ μέγιστοι, πᾶσιν ὡς ἔπος εἰπεῖν ἀντιπάλοις χρώμενος καὶ μέχρι γήρως ὥσπερ ἀθλητὴς ἀγωνιζόμενος
5 ἄπτωτα διετήρησεν ἑαυτόν. πλείστας δὲ καὶ φυγὼν δημοσίας δίκας καὶ διώξας, πολλὰς μὲν εἷλε, πάσας δ' ἀπέφυγε, πρόβλημα τοῦ βίου καὶ δραστήριον ὄργανον ἔχων τὸν λόγον, ᾧ δικαιότερον ἄν τις ἢ τύχῃ καὶ δαίμονι τοῦ ἀνδρὸς τὸ μηδὲν παθεῖν παρ' ἀξίαν ἀνατιθείη. μέγα γὰρ καὶ Ἀριστοτέλει τῷ φιλοσόφῳ τοῦτο προσεμαρτύρησεν Ἀντίπατρος, γράφων περὶ αὐτοῦ μετὰ τὴν τελευτὴν ὅτι πρὸς τοῖς ἄλλοις ὁ ἀνὴρ καὶ τὸ πιθανὸν εἶχεν.

which Aristeides took part was he the hero. Miltiades is the
man who takes the prize for Marathon and Themistocles for
Salamis, and at Plataea Pausanias is the man, according to
Herodotus, who "won the most glorious victory," while Aristeides' claim even on second place was contested by men like
Sophanes, Ameinias, Callimachus and Cynegeirus, who fought
3 with conspicuous valor in those contests. On the other hand,
not only did Cato display his pre-eminence both in action and
in counsel during the Spanish war when he was himself serving as consul, but even as military tribune at Thermopylae,
when another man was consul, he captured the glory for the
victory, by throwing the doors wide open for the Romans to
enter against Antiochus and by enveloping the king and
bringing the war around to his back when he was looking
only to the front. For that victory, which was quite clearly
the result of Cato's action, drove Asia from Greece and, in
4 turn, paved the way for Scipio's victory. Now, neither man
was subjected to defeat on the field of battle but, when we
consider the fortunes of their political lives, we find that
Aristeides, for his part, suffered a fall when he was ostracized and overwhelmed by Themistocles as a result of fac-
tional strife. Cato, however, who had as his adversaries virtually without exception all of the most powerful and presti-
gious men in Rome and who, like some athlete, continued to
enter the ring until he was an old man, kept himself unde-
5 feated. And, although he was involved in a very large number of actions at law, both as defendant and plaintiff, he was
frequently successful in this latter capacity and always ac-
quitted in the former, since his skill in public speaking
served him as a vital shield and as a potent weapon. Indeed,
one could with greater justification ascribe to this skill the
fact that he suffered no undeserved reverses than to mere
chance and the man's good fortune. For this is a valuable as-
set, as Antipater attests in attributing it also to the philosopher Aristotle, when he writes about him after his death
that, in addition to his other qualities, the man had the ability to persuade.

57(30/3). Ὅτι μὲν δὴ τῆς πολιτικῆς ἄνθρωπος ἀρετῆς οὐ κτᾶται τελειοτέραν, ὁμολογούμενόν ἐστι· ταύτης δέ που μόριον οἱ πλεῖστοι τὴν οἰκονομικὴν οὐ σμικρὸν τίθενται· καὶ γὰρ ἡ πόλις, οἴκων τι σύστημα καὶ κεφάλαιον οὖσα, ῥώννυται πρὸς τὰ δημόσια τοῖς ἰδίοις βίοις τῶν πολιτῶν εὐθενούντων, ὅπου καὶ Λυκοῦργος, ἐξοικίσας μὲν ἄργυρον, ἐξοικίσας δὲ χρυσὸν τῆς Σπάρτης, νόμισμα δὲ διεφθαρμένου πυρὶ σιδήρου θέμενος αὐτοῖς, οἰκονομίας οὐκ ἀπήλλαξε τοὺς πολίτας, ἀλλὰ τὰ τρυφῶντα καὶ ὕπουλα καὶ φλεγμαίνοντα τοῦ πλούτου περιελών, ὅπως εὐπορήσωσι τῶν ἀναγκαίων καὶ χρησίμων ἅπαντες, ὡς ἄλλος οὐδεὶς νομοθέτης προενόησε, τὸν ἄπορον καὶ ἀνέστιον καὶ πένητα σύνοικον ἐπὶ κοινωνίᾳ πολιτείας μᾶλλον τοῦ πλουσίου καὶ ὑπερόγκου φοβηθείς.
2 φαίνεται τοίνυν ὁ μὲν Κάτων οὐδέν τι φαυλότερος οἴκου προστάτης ἢ πόλεως γενόμενος· καὶ γὰρ αὐτὸς ηὔξησε τὸν ἑαυτοῦ βίον καὶ κατέστη διδάσκαλος οἰκονομίας καὶ γεωργίας ἑτέροις, πολλὰ καὶ χρήσιμα περὶ τούτων συνταξάμενος· Ἀριστείδης δὲ τῇ πενίᾳ καὶ τὴν δικαιοσύνην συνδιέβαλεν ὡς οἰκοφθόρον καὶ πτωχοποιὸν καὶ πᾶσι μᾶλλον ἢ τοῖς
3 κεκτημένοις ὠφέλιμον. καίτοι πολλὰ μὲν Ἡσίοδος πρὸς δικαιοσύνην ἅμα καὶ πρὸς οἰκονομίαν παρακαλῶν ἡμᾶς εἴρηκε, καὶ τὴν ἀργίαν ὡς ἀδικίας ἀρχὴν λελοιδόρηκεν, εὖ δὲ καὶ Ὁμήρῳ πεποίηται,

ἔργον δέ μοι οὐ φίλον ἦεν
οὐδ' οἰκωφελίη, ἥ τε τρέφει ἀγλαὰ τέκνα,
ἀλλά μοι αἰεὶ νῆες ἐπήρετμοι φίλαι ἦσαν
καὶ πόλεμοι καὶ ἄκοντες ἐΰξεστοι καὶ ὀιστοί,

4 ὡς τοὺς αὐτοὺς ἀμελοῦντας οἰκίας καὶ ποριζομένους ἐξ ἀδικίας. οὐ

57.1 ἐπὶ κοινωνίᾳ UA: ἐν κοινωνίᾳ S 57.2 συνταξάμενος S: συλλεξάμενος UA

57(30/3). It is, of course, a matter of general agreement
that man possesses no virtue that is more comprehensive
than that exercised in civic life, and most people, I assume,
consider the management of a household as playing no small
role in it. For the state, inasmuch as it is, in effect, the sum
total of the community of households, enjoys health in its
public aspect to the extent that its citizens prosper in their
private lives. After all, even when Lycurgus evicted silver
and gold from Sparta and required by law that they use a
currency consisting of iron that had been made brittle by
fire, he did not free the citizens from the obligation of man-
aging their households well. Instead, with a degree of foresight that no other lawgiver has displayed, he trimmed off
the cancerous, ulcerated and inflamed elements of wealth so
that everyone might have abundant supplies of those things
that are essential and beneficial, for he was more apprehen-
sive of the needy, the homeless and the destitute having a
share in the rights of citizenship than he was of those who
2 possessed a surplus of riches. Now, as far as we can tell
about Cato, he was no less effective as a manager of the affairs of his household than he was as a manager of the affairs
of state, for not only did he bring about an increase in his
own personal means but he served as an instructor to others as well in matters of domestic economy and agriculture
by composing a number of valuable works on those subjects. Aristeides, on the other hand, through his poverty lent
support to those who denounce justice on the grounds that it
ruins households, breeds beggars and is of less value to the
3 man who possesses it than it is to everyone else. Yet Hesiod
has numerous passages in which he encourages us to pursue
household economy and justice at the same time, as well as
passages in which he condemns idleness as the author of injustice. Homer too has expressed it well when he says,

But I had no taste for the tilling of fields
or the care of the house, which nurses fine offspring,
but ever to my liking were oar-equipped ships
and battles and arrows and spears finely shaped,

as if to say that those who neglect their households and those

γάρ, ὡς τοὔλαιον οἱ ἰατροί φασι τοῦ σώματος εἶναι τοῖς μὲν ἐκτὸς ὠφελιμώτατον, τοῖς δ' ἐντὸς βλαβερώτατον, οὕτως ὁ δίκαιος ἑτέροις μέν ἐστι χρήσιμος, αὑτοῦ δὲ καὶ τῶν ἰδίων ἀκηδής, ἀλλ' ἔοικε ταύτῃ πεπηρῶσθαι τῷ Ἀριστείδῃ τὸ πολιτικόν, εἴπερ, ὡς οἱ πλεῖστοι λέγουσιν, οὐδὲ προῖκα τοῖς θυγατρίοις οὐδ' ἑαυτῷ ταφὴν καταλιπέσθαι προυνόησεν. ὅθεν ὁ μὲν Κάτωνος οἶκος ἄχρι γένους τετάρτου στρατηγοὺς καὶ ὑπάτους τῇ Ῥώμῃ παρεῖχε (καὶ γὰρ υἱωνοὶ καὶ τούτων ἔτι παῖδες ἦρξαν ἀρχὰς τὰς μεγίστας), τῆς δ' Ἀριστείδου τοῦ πρωτεύσαντος Ἑλλήνων γενεᾶς ἡ πολλὴ καὶ ἄπορος πενία τοὺς μὲν εἰς ἀγυρτικοὺς κατέβαλε πίνακας, τοὺς δὲ δημοσίῳ τὰς χεῖρας ἐράνῳ δι' ἔνδειαν ὑπέχειν ἠνάγκασεν, οὐδενὶ δὲ λαμπρὸν οὐδὲν οὐδ' ἄξιον ἐκείνου τοῦ ἀνδρὸς φρονῆσαι παρέσχεν.

58(31/4). Ἢ τοῦτο πρῶτον ἀμφιλογίαν ἔχει; πενία γὰρ αἰσχρὸν
μὲν οὐδαμοῦ δι' αὑτήν, ἀλλ' ὅπου δεῖγμα ῥαθυμίας ἐστίν, ἀκρασίας,
ἀλογιστίας, πολυτελείας· ἀνδρὶ δὲ σώφρονι καὶ φιλοπόνῳ καὶ δικαίῳ καὶ
ἀνδρείῳ καὶ δημοσιεύοντι ταῖς ἀρεταῖς ἁπάσαις συνοῦσα μεγαλοψυχί-
2 ας ἐστὶ καὶ μεγαλοφροσύνης σημεῖον. οὐ γὰρ ἔστι πράττειν μεγάλα
φροντίζοντα μικρῶν, οὐδὲ πολλοῖς δεομένοις βοηθεῖν πολλῶν αὐτὸν
δεόμενον. μέγα δ' εἰς πολιτείαν ἐφόδιον οὐχὶ πλοῦτος, ἀλλ' αὐτάρκεια,
τῷ μηδενὸς ἰδίᾳ τῶν περιττῶν δεῖσθαι πρὸς οὐδεμίαν ἀσχολίαν ἀπάγουσα τῶν δημοσίων. ἀπροσδεὴς μὲν γὰρ ἁπλῶς ὁ θεός, ἀνθρωπίνης δ' ἀρετῆς, ᾧ συνάγεται πρὸς τοὐλάχιστον ἡ χρεία, τοῦτο τελειότατον καὶ

57.4 καταλιπέσθαι UA: ὑπολιπέσθαι S

4 who live by injustice are one and the same. For it is not necessarily the case that the just man is valuable only to others and is neglectful of himself and his property, the way olive oil, so the physicians tell us, is most beneficial to the outside of the body but most deleterious to the inside. Rather, it is here that we can see a flaw in the civic aspect of Aristeides' career, if it is indeed the case, as most writers affirm, that he did not have the foresight to leave behind a dowry for his
5 little daughters or funeral expenses for himself. Thus, while Cato's family continued to provide Rome with praetors and consuls down through four generations, since grandsons and even great-grandsons held the highest offices, the serious and troublesome poverty that afflicted the descendants of Aristeides, foremost of the Greeks, degraded some of them to the point of resorting to mendicant tablets, while it compelled others to come, with outstretched hand, begging for public donations because of their need. Not one of them was inspired to perform a single deed that reflected well upon themselves or was worthy of that great man.

58(31/4). Or does this matter allow of debate beforehand? In no instance is poverty cause for shame in and of itself, but only where it is a mark of indolence, lack of self-control, imprudence or extravagance. Where, however, it is found in conjunction with a sensible man, a hard-working man, a just man, a courageous man, a man who displays all the virtues in his exercise of public service, it is a mark of
2 magnanimity and unselfishness. For it is not possible to accomplish great things when one's mind is filled with trivialities, nor can one come to the aid of many needy people when one has many needs oneself. It is not wealth, it is self-sufficiency that provides great assistance on the road to success in political life; for self-sufficiency, by permitting a man to dispense with the need for luxuries in private life, provides no distractions to interfere with his involvement in public affairs. God has absolutely no needs at all but, as far as human virtue is concerned, the aspect of it that is most sublime and most nearly god-like is that which reduces one's wants

3 θειότατον. ὡς γὰρ σῶμα τὸ καλῶς πρὸς εὐεξίαν κεκραμένον οὔτ'
ἐσθῆτος οὔτε τροφῆς δεῖται περιττῆς, οὕτω καὶ οἶκος καὶ βίος ὑγιαίνων
ἀπὸ τῶν τυχόντων διοικεῖται. δεῖ δὲ τῇ χρείᾳ σύμμετρον ἔχειν τὴν κτῆ-
σιν· ὡς ὅ γε πολλὰ συνάγων, ὀλίγοις δὲ χρώμενος, οὐκ ἔστιν αὐτάρκης,
ἀλλ' εἴτε μὴ δεῖται, τῆς παρασκευῆς ὧν οὐκ ὀρέγεται μάταιος, εἴτ' ὀρέ-
4 γεται, μικρολογίᾳ κολούων τὴν ἀπόλαυσιν ἄθλιος. αὐτοῦ γέ τοι Κάτωνος ἡδέως ἂν πυθοίμην· εἰ μὲν ἀπολαυστὸν ὁ πλοῦτός ἐστι, τί σεμνύ-
νῃ τῷ πολλὰ κεκτημένος ἀρκεῖσθαι μετρίοις; εἰ δὲ λαμπρόν ἐστιν, ὥσπερ ἐστίν, ἄρτῳ τε χρῆσθαι τῷ προστυχόντι, καὶ πιεῖν οἷον ἐρέται πί-
νουσι καὶ θεράποντες οἶνον, καὶ πορφύρας μὴ δεηθῆναι μηδ' οἰκίας
κεκονιαμένης, οὐδὲν οὔτ' Ἀριστείδης οὔτ' Ἐπαμεινώνδας οὔτε Μάνιος
Κούριος οὔτε Γάιος Φαβρίκιος ἐνέλιπον τοῦ προσήκοντος, χαίρειν
5 ἐάσαντες τὴν κτῆσιν ὧν τὴν χρῆσιν ἀπεδοκίμαζον. οὐ γὰρ ἦν ἀναγκαῖον ἀνθρώπῳ γογγυλίδας ἥδιστον ὄψον πεποιημένῳ καὶ δι' αὑτοῦ ταύτας
ἕψοντι, ματτούσης ἅμα τῆς γυναικὸς ἄλφιτα, τοσαυτάκις περὶ ἀσσαρίου θρυλεῖν καὶ γράφειν ἀφ' ἧς ἄν τις ἐργασίας τάχιστα πλούσιος γένοιτο. μέγα γὰρ τὸ εὐτελὲς καὶ αὔταρκες, ὅτι τῆς ἐπιθυμίας ἅμα καὶ τῆς
6 φροντίδος ἀπαλλάττει τῶν περιττῶν. διὸ καὶ τοῦτό φασιν ἐν τῇ Καλλίου
δίκῃ τὸν Ἀριστείδην εἰπεῖν ὡς αἰσχύνεσθαι πενίαν προσήκει τοῖς ἀκου-
7 σίως πενομένοις, τοῖς δ' ὥσπερ αὐτὸς ἑκουσίως ἐγκαλλωπίζεσθαι. γε-
λοῖον γὰρ οἴεσθαι ῥαθυμίας εἶναι τὴν Ἀριστείδου πενίαν, ᾧ παρῆν
αἰσχρὸν ἐργασαμένῳ μηδέν, ἀλλ' ἕνα σκυλεύσαντι βάρβαρον ἢ μίαν

58.4 οἷον S: ὃν UAl ἐρέται Sansone: ἐργάται SUA 58.5 δι' αὑτοῦ UA: ὕδατι S

3 to the lowest possible degree. For, just as the body that is
perfectly tempered to produce top condition does not need
excessive clothing or nourishment, in the same manner a
healthy household or individual is able to support itself on
the basis of what is available. One's possessions ought to be
commensurate with one's needs. The man who, while amassing much, uses little is not self-sufficient. Rather, if he does
not need what he has amassed, he is a fool for amassing what
he does not crave; if he does crave it, he makes himself mis-
4 erable by curbing his enjoyment out of parsimoniousness. To
tell the truth, I would be happy to hear how Cato himself
would respond to this question: "If wealth is something that
is to be put to good use, why do you pride yourself on having
acquired much and, at the same time, on being satisfied with
little?" If, on the other hand, it is the case (as I am sure it is)
that it confers distinction on a man to consume whatever
bread is available, to drink the same sort of wine that rowers
and servants drink, to feel no need for a purple garment or
for a dwelling with plastered walls, then in no sense did either Aristeides or Epameinondas or Manius Curius or Gaius
Fabricius lack propriety by spurning the acquisition of things
5 that they did not see fit to use. For there was no need for a
man who had formed the opinion that turnips are the finest
delicacy and who boils them himself while his wife makes
barley-cakes to chatter on with such insistence about an as
and to write about the kind of business that a man should
enter in order to become rich most quickly. The reason the
simple, self-sufficient life is noble is that it releases a man at
one and the same time from desire for and concern about
6 luxuries. And it is for this reason, they say, that Aristeides
included in his speech at Callias' trial the statement that
those who cannot help being poor ought to feel shame over
poverty, while those who, like himself, were poor by choice
7 ought to pride themselves on it. For it is absurd to imagine
that Aristeides' poverty was born of indolence, seeing that he
had the opportunity to become wealthy, without doing anything shameful, merely by plundering a single barbarian or
expropriating a single tent. Well, that is enough said about

σκηνὴν καταλαβόντι πλουσίῳ γενέσθαι. ταῦτα μὲν οὖν περὶ τούτων.

59(32/5). Στρατηγίαι δ' αἱ μὲν Κάτωνος οὐδὲν ὡς μεγάλοις πράγμασι μέγα προσέθηκαν, ἐν δὲ ταῖς Ἀριστείδου τὰ κάλλιστα καὶ λαμ-
πρότατα καὶ πρῶτα τῶν Ἑλληνικῶν ἔργων ἐστίν, ὁ Μαραθών, ἡ Σαλα-
2 μίς, αἱ Πλαταιαί, καὶ οὐκ ἄξιον δήπου παραβαλεῖν τῷ Ξέρξῃ τὸν Ἀντίοχον καὶ τὰ περιαιρεθέντα τῶν Ἰβηρικῶν πόλεων τείχη ταῖς τοσαύταις
μὲν ἐν γῇ, τοσαύταις δ' ἐν θαλάσσῃ πεσούσαις μυριάσιν· ἐν οἷς Ἀριστείδης ἔργῳ μὲν οὐδενὸς ἐλείπετο, δόξης δὲ καὶ στεφάνων, ὥσπερ ἀμέλει
πλούτου καὶ χρημάτων, ὑφήκατο τοῖς μᾶλλον δεομένοις, ὅτι καὶ τού-
3 των πάντων διέφερεν. ἐγὼ δ' οὐ μέμφομαι μὲν Κάτωνος τὸ μεγαλύνειν
ἀεὶ καὶ πρῶτον ἁπάντων ἑαυτὸν τίθεσθαι (καίτοι φησὶν ἔν τινι λόγῳ τὸ
ἐπαινεῖν αὑτὸν ὥσπερ τὸ λοιδορεῖν ἄτοπον εἶναι), τελειότερος δέ μοι
δοκεῖ πρὸς ἀρετὴν τοῦ πολλάκις ἑαυτὸν ἐγκωμιάζοντος ὁ μηδ' ἑτέρων
4 τοῦτο ποιούντων δεόμενος. τὸ γὰρ ἀφιλότιμον οὐ μικρὸν εἰς πρᾳότητα
πολιτικὴν ἐφόδιον, καὶ τοὐναντίον ἡ φιλοτιμία χαλεπὸν καὶ φθόνου γο-
νιμώτατον· ἧς ὁ μὲν ἀπήλλακτο παντάπασιν, ὁ δὲ καὶ πάνυ πολλῆς
μετεῖχεν. Ἀριστείδης μὲν γὰρ Θεμιστοκλεῖ τὰ μέγιστα συμπράττων, καὶ
τρόπον τινὰ καὶ τὴν στρατηγίαν αὐτοῦ δορυφορῶν, ὤρθωσε τὰς Ἀθήνας, Κάτων δ' ἀντιπράττων Σκιπίωνι μικροῦ μὲν ἀνέτρεψε καὶ διελυμή-
νατο τὴν ἐπὶ Καρχηδονίους αὐτοῦ στρατηγίαν ἐν ᾗ τὸν ἀήττητον Ἀννίβαν καθεῖλε, τέλος δὲ μηχανώμενος ἀεί τινας ὑποψίας καὶ διαβολάς,
αὐτὸν μὲν ἐξήλασε τῆς πόλεως, τὸν δ' ἀδελφὸν αἰσχίστῃ κλοπῆς καταδίκῃ περιέβαλεν.

59.4 μὲν γὰρ Ziegler: μέν γε SUA

that.

59(32/5). As far as their military commands are concerned, Cato's made no great addition to Roman power, which was already great, whereas those of Aristeides included the finest, most glorious and most significant of the Greeks' accomplishments, namely Marathon, Salamis and Plataea. And Antiochus surely does not merit comparison with Xerxes, nor is the tearing down of the fortifications of the Spanish cities comparable to those tens of thousands who died on land and those tens of thousands who died at sea. When it came to actions, Aristeides was second to none in these engagements; as to honors and distinctions, as indeed was the case with wealth and riches, he surrendered them to those who felt a greater need for them, because he was above all of these things as well. Now I do not find fault with Cato's practice of constantly glorifying himself and rating himself ahead of everyone else (although, to be sure, in one of his speeches he says that praising oneself makes as little sense as reviling oneself), but I do think that the man who frequently sings his own praises has not attained the same sufficiency of virtue as the man who does not even feel the need for others to praise him. For freedom from ambition provides considerable assistance on the road to forbearance in political life while, on the other hand, ambition is a nasty thing and is a fruitful source of resentment. While the one man was entirely free from ambition, the other possessed it in quite a large measure. For Aristeides proved to be the salvation of Athens when he cooperated with Themistocles on matters of the utmost importance and even, so to speak, stood guard over him when he was serving as general. But Cato, by his opposition to Scipio, very nearly sabotaged and undermined that man's command against the Carthaginians, in the course of which he defeated the invincible Hannibal, and ultimately, by persisting in devising grounds for suspicion and malicious charges, hounded him out of the city and caused a particularly disgraceful condemnation for embezzlement to be imposed upon his brother.

60(33/6). Ἦν τοίνυν πλείστοις ὁ Κάτων κεκόσμηκε καὶ καλλίστοι
ἐπαίνοις ἀεὶ σωφροσύνην, Ἀριστείδης μὲν ἄθικτον ὡς ἀληθῶς καὶ κα
θαρὰν ἐτήρησεν, αὐτοῦ δὲ τοῦ Κάτωνος ὁ παρ' ἀξίαν ἅμα καὶ παρ
ὥραν γάμος οὐ μικρὰν οὐδὲ φαύλην εἰς τοῦτο διαβολὴν κατεσκέδασε
2 πρεσβύτην γὰρ ἤδη τοσοῦτον ἐνηλίκῳ παιδὶ καὶ γυναικὶ νύμφῃ παιδὸ
ἐπιγῆμαι κόρην ὑπηρέτου καὶ δημοσιεύοντος ἐπὶ μισθῷ πατρὸς οὐδαμ
καλόν, ἀλλ' εἴτε πρὸς ἡδονὴν ταῦτ' ἔπραξεν, εἴτ' ὀργῇ διὰ τὴν ἑταίρα
ἀμυνόμενος τὸν υἱόν, αἰσχύνην ἔχει καὶ τὸ ἔργον καὶ ἡ πρόφασις. ᾧ δ
αὐτὸς ἐχρήσατο λόγῳ κατειρωνευόμενος τὸ μειράκιον, οὐκ ἦν ἀληθής
3 εἰ γὰρ ἐβούλετο παῖδας ἀγαθοὺς ὁμοίως τεκνῶσαι, γάμον ἔδει λαβεῖ
γενναῖον ἐξ ἀρχῆς σκεψάμενον, οὐχ ἕως μὲν ἐλάνθανεν ἀνεγγύῳ γυναι
κὶ καὶ κοινῇ συγκοιμώμενος ἀγαπᾶν, ἐπεὶ δ' ἐφωράθη, ποιήσασθαι πεν
θερὸν ὃν ῥᾷστα πείσειν, οὐχ ᾧ κάλλιστα κηδεύσειν ἔμελλεν.

60.2 οὐδαμῇ S: οὐδαμοῦ UA 60.3 συγκοιμώμενος UA: συγκοιμώμενον S

60(33/6). Indeed, the self-control that Cato was constantly glorifying with so many fine encomiums Aristeides
maintained in a truly pure and unsullied condition but, as far
as Cato himself is concerned, his marriage, which was unworthy both of his status and of his years, cast grave and not
2 inconsiderable infamy upon him in just this regard. Under
no circumstances is it admirable for a man who has attained
such advanced years to bring in as a stepmother to an adult
son and to the son's bride the daughter of a mere retainer
who serves for hire as a public official; in this case, regardless of whether it was done for reasons of personal gratification or out of anger, in order to get back at his son in the
matter of the prostitute, both the act and its motivation create opprobrium. Furthermore, the explanation that he himself condescendingly gave to the young man was not true.
3 For, if he wished to sire children of comparable quality, he
ought to have contracted a noble marriage and to have made
this his prime consideration from the start, rather than
contenting himself, for as long as he could get away with it,
with the bed of a woman whom he had no intention of making his legal wife and who was of no particular distinction
and then, when he was detected, taking as his father-in-
law, not the man whose alliance was likely to confer the
greatest distinction on him, but the man whom he was most
likely to persuade.

[illegible] Indeed, the settlement that Cato was constantly glorifying with so many fine encomiums [illegible] maintained to a truly pure and unsullied condition, so far as Cato himself is concerned, his marriage [illegible] was unworthy both of his name and of his years, [illegible] upon him in [illegible] this regard. Under no circumstances is it admirable for a man who has attained such advanced years to bring in a stepmother to his adult son and to [illegible] the daughter of [illegible] who works for hire as a public official [illegible] regardless of whether it was done for reasons of personal gratification or out of anger, in order to get back at his son [illegible] the [illegible] of the prostitute, both the act and its motivation are reprehensible. [illegible] the explanation that he himself condescendingly gave to the young man was not true. For, if he wished to see children of comparable quality, he ought to have considered a noble marriage and to have made this his prime consideration from the start, rather than compounding himself, for as long as he could get away with it, with the bed of a woman whom he had no intention of making his legal wife and who was of no particular distinction and then, when he was detected, taking as his father-in-law not the man whose alliance was likely to confer the greatest distinction on him, but the man whom he was most likely to persuade.

COMMENTARY

1: Plutarch often begins a pair of Lives with some general reflections and with a consideration of his reasons for comparing the two men he has chosen (see, for example, *Pel.* 1-2, *Per.* 1-2, *Sert.* 1, *Thes.* 1-2). Here, however, as at the beginning of *Lys.*, *Ages.* and *Cor.*, there is no such long introduction. Plutarch begins immediately with a discussion of Aristeides' wealth and, as we shall see, it is on their attitudes toward wealth that Plutarch focuses his comparison of Aristeides and Cato. These two men have little enough in common, and it is only after Plutarch's day that we see their names joined (Aus. *Mos.* 386-88, *Parent.* 22.3-4, Amm. Marc. 30.4.21), presumably as a result of the influence of Plutarch.

1.2: Demetrius (born c. 350 BC) came from **Phalerum**, the deme that neighbors Alopece, and was a student of Aristotle and Theophrastus. For the fragments of his *Socrates* (or *Apology of Socrates*) see frr. 91-98 Wehrli. Demetrius seems to have taken a perverse pleasure in showing that such figures as Aristeides and Socrates (whom he represents as a bigamist; see also 1.9) were less admirable than they were reputed to be.

1.2: The **archon eponymous** held office at Athens for one year, which year was named after him. Aristeides in fact held the office for the year beginning in summer 489, although Demetrius believed that he was appointed after the battle of Plataea (see 1.8). We cannot be certain whether the Archon at this time was elected or appointed (see Rhodes 273), but in any case the office had ceased being restricted to the **Pentacosiomedimnoi**, or those whose annual income was equivalent to at least 500 bushels of grain, already in the time of Solon. For a good account of Plutarch's arguments and methods in this opening section, see Russell 55-57.

1.2 ostracized: This was in 482. See 1.7 and 7.2-8.

1.3 choregic tripods: There being no personal income tax in ancient Greece, wealthy individuals were asked to subsidize specific expenditures by the state, for example the outfitting of a warship or the production of a dramatic or musical performance. The citizen who bore the expense of training a chorus for one of the musical competitons was called a *choregus* and, if his production won first prize, he would advertise his (and his tribe's) victory by erecting a monument consisting of an inscribed base surmounted by the tripod that served as the prize (see A. Pickard-Cambridge, *The Dramatic Festivals of Athens* [1968] 77-78, with figs. 30-31). For the interesting history of the inscription that Demetrius mentions, see A. N. Oikonomides, *The Ancient World* 3 (1980) 17-19.

1.4 Epameinondas . . . Plato: Here Plutarch employs an argument of his own to show that Demetrius was wrong to use the inscription as evidence of Aristeides' affluence. Plutarch's biography of Epameinondas, the Theban general of the early 4th century, is now lost, but he refers at *Pel.* 3.6 to Epameinondas' poverty, which he here exaggerates as **dire poverty**. (The **lavish scale** of the production is also likely to be an exaggeration.) While the (relative) poverty of Epameinondas was, as Plutarch suggests, well known (Paus. 9.13.1, Nepos *Epam.* 2.1), the reference to **the philosopher Plato** is specious. For he belonged to an illustrious and probably fairly wealthy family (see Davies 322-35). Epameinondas' choregia is not otherwise attested (but Plutarch's information regarding him is usually reliable); for Plato's see *Dion* 17.5, D.L. 3.3.

1.4 chorus of men with flute accompaniment: The Greek *aulos* was a reed instrument more like an oboe than a flute. The phrase αὐληταῖς ἀνδράσιν means literally "for male *aulos*-players," and all translators and commentators take it to refer to a performance by a group of pipers. But the *aulos* is a solo instrument, and there is no evidence for such an ensemble (which would be suitable, in any case, only for Caledonian ears). Demosthenes uses the same phrase (21.156) and it is clear from the context that the reference is to a dithyrambic chorus of men accompanied by a single flute-player which, according to Demosthenes, is far more expensive than a tragic chorus. See E. Reisch, *De musicis Graecorum certaminibus* (1885) 59.

1.6: Panaetius of Rhodes was a Stoic philosopher of the 2nd century BC. He tried to show (fr. 131 van Straaten), using an argument of the sort that modern scholars approve, that the Aristeides named in Demetrius' inscription is not the son of Lysimachus. Panaetius, who lived in Athens for at least 20 years, must have consulted either the official *Fasti*, which gave complete lists of victorious tribes and choregi at the festival of Dionysus, or the work of Aristotle (now lost) called *Didaskaliai* (see Pickard-Cambridge, *Dramatic Festivals*, 70-72).

1.6 the tripod: Earlier (1.3) the reference had been to "tripods." Whether that was an error on the part of Plutarch or Demetrius is unclear. Only one tripod was given to the winning tribe.

1.6 Xenophilus: Aristeides, son of Xenophilus, also of the tribe Antiochis, was the victorious choregus for a men's dithyrambic chorus in 477/6; see Simonides XXVIII Page.

1.6 style of writing: In the archonship of **Eucleides** (403/2 BC) Athens officially adopted the Ionic alphabet; L. Threatte, *The Grammar of Attic Inscriptions* I (1980) 26-27. But something has gone wrong either with Panaetius' scholarship or with Plutarch's account, for **the period after Eucleides** is incompatible with the period **from the time of the Persian Wars down to the end** (one manuscript even reads "beginning") **of the Peloponnesian War**.

1.7 Pericles' teacher Damon: Plutarch's argument is specious. He does not know, nor is there any evidence, that Damon was poor. In fact, Damon may have married into a branch of the influential Alcmaeonid family (Davies 383). At *Per.* 4.3 Plutarch gives a more clearly political motive for Damon's ostracism (for which see Rhodes 341-42).

1.8: Idomeneus of Lampsacus, born c. 325 BC, was a student of Epicurus. He appears to have written a work on the Athenian demagogues (*FGrH* 338 F 1-15) in which Aristeides was glorified, perhaps at the expense of Themistocles. Here he argues against Demetrius (see 1.2). Both must have taken Arist. *Ath. Pol.* 22.5 to mean that Athenian archons were elected before 487/6, and appointed by lot thereafter. Demetrius put Aristeides' archonship **after the battle of Plataea** (479 BC), apparently confusing it with the battle of Marathon (490 BC), after which Aristeides in fact held the archonship. (See, however, L. Piccirilli, "Demetrio Falereo e l'arcontato di Aristide," *Annali d. Scuola Norm. Sup. di Pisa, Cl. di lett. e fil.* 13 [1983] 659-72, for a defense of Demetrius' view.) Idomeneus had only to consult the official record of archons to learn the truth (see 5.9-10, for which Idomeneus was perhaps the source). Plutarch's logic leaves something to be desired for, if the archonship followed Plataea (which, in any case, Plutarch knows to be false), it was, as far as Plutarch is aware, by appointment rather than by election.

.9: Socrates claims at his trial (Pl. *Ap.* 38b) that he can afford to pay a fine of no more than one mina, yet Demetrius (in his *Socrates*, see 1.2) was determined to show that he was well-off. When he asserts that Socrates had **the estate which he had inherited** (or "his ancestral estate;" the Greek says only τὴν οἰκίαν, but this must be what the article implies), he is apparently rejecting the tradition, preserved only in Liban. *Apol. Socr.* 17, that Socrates inherited 80 minas, but lost the sum on a business venture. Demetrius is clearly fabricating (unless he has gotten this, like the next, from Aristoxenus).

.9 seventy minas: According to the manuscript reading, the 70 minas were τοκιζομένας ὑπὸ Κρίτωνος, which is regularly taken to mean that the money was lent by Socrates to Crito. The absurdity of this (at Pl. *Ap.* 38b and *Crit.* 45b Crito offers to give Socrates money) may be accounted for by reference to the obvious lunacy of Demetrius, but in fact the Greek cannot mean this. Given the way in which τοκίζεσθαι is used elsewhere, the phrase can only mean "lent (to Socrates) at interest by Crito," which is not a good illustration of the affluence of Socrates. I have ventured to change to ἀπὸ Κρίτωνος, taking the phrase with ὑπάρχειν (cf. *Alex.* 20.7, Thuc. 6.86.5). That Socrates *lent* money on interest was asserted by Aristoxenus (fr. 59 Wehrli). Demetrius went even farther, apparently, and alleged that it was his friend Crito's money that he used for this purpose. Plutarch rightly treats all this as nonsense for, as Xenophon records (*Oec.* 2.3), Socrates' net worth, including his house, was only about five minas.

.1: Cleisthenes, the leader of the "democratic" faction, came, like Aristeides, from the deme Alopece. His reform of the Athenian constitution is dated to 508/7 BC, following the expulsion of the Peisistratids. Plutarch refers to Aristeides as a disciple of Cleisthenes also at *mor.* 791a and 805f.

.1 Lycurgus: Plutarch (who wrote a Life of Lycurgus) and the Greeks generally liked to attribute personal motives to political decisions. So Aristeides joins the "aristocratic" faction because of his admiration for

Lycurgus. In fact, however, aristocratic admiration for the Spartan lawgiver is characteristic rather of a later period, and the connection between Aristeides and Lycurgus is likely to be an invention of the 4th century; cf. E. Rawson, *The Spartan Tradition in European Thought* (1969) 18 n. 2.

2.1 the opposition of Themistocles: From the time of the Aristotelian *Constitution of Athens* Athenian politics is conceived of as being determined by two rival factions led by two personal antagonists. We find similar language, for example, at *Per.* 9.2 and 11.1, of the opposition between Pericles and Cimon and that between Pericles and Thucydides.

2.2 some say: Cf. Ael. *VH* 13.44.

2.3: Ariston was a Peripatetic philosopher of the 3rd century BC. This anecdote, repeated by Plutarch at *Them.* 3.2, seems to be pure fabrication on the part of Ariston; cf. Frost 72.

2.4 the boy's appeal began to fade: That is, when he began to reach the age at which he ceased being an appropriate object of homosexual attention. Cf. K. J. Dover, *Greek Homosexuality* (1978) 85-86; S. Lida Tarán, *JHS* 105 (1985) 90-107.

2.5 when someone said: This anecdote appears again at *mor.* 807a- (also Synesius, *Epist.* 93) but not, significantly, in the Life of Themistocles. It is common for Plutarch to minimize or explain away or even suppress entirely material that is prejudicial to the subject of the Life that he is engaged in writing. At *Them.* 5.6, in fact, Plutarch recounts an incident indicative of Themistocles' impartiality.

2.6 He kept aloof from political alliances: Cf. *mor.* 186a. For these political "clubs," see W. R. Connor, *The New Politicians of Fifth-Century Athens* (1971) 25-29. According to Connor (55), Plutarch's account "is suspect; its presumption that the *hetaireiai* were inevitably engaged in wrongdoing seems to point to an origin in the late fifth century, after the gradual conversion of these clubs to revolutionary cells."

2.6 derive satisfaction: The manuscripts are divided between χαίρει and θαρρεῖν, which editors generally adopt. But θαρρεῖν + dat. means "to be emboldened by X," where X provides the stimulus to action. Here, however, X would itself refer to the action in question.

3.1 compelled against his better judgment: Compare *Per.* 7.3-4 where Pericles attaches himself to the democratic cause "contrary to his own nature," out of opposition to the aristocratic Cimon. See on 2.

3.1 agitating . . . on his own behalf: The translation follows the suggestion of Sintenis and Hercher regarding the force of the middle voice (the active is used in the parallel passage at *Them.* 3.3). This is appropriate to the context (**agitating** and **trying to oppose** correspond to **check his power** and **protect himself**), but I can find no other instance of κινεῖν in the middle.

3.2 the pit: The *barathron*, a ravine into which the bodies of executed criminals were thrown (Xen. *Hell.* 1.7.20, Pl. *Rep.* 439e), was situated not far from Themistocles' house; J. Travlos, *Pictorial Dictionary of*

Ancient Athens (1971) 121. This anecdote recurs in Cyril *Contra Jul.* 6.188 (PG 76.788A Migne), perhaps from Theopompus, whom Cyril cites just before.

3.4 θαυμαστὴ . . . ἡ εὐστάθεια: Cf. *Publ.* 14.8.

3.4 προῖκα καὶ ἀμισθὶ: Cf. *mor.* 349e, 706c.

3.4 his calm self-control: See on 23.1.

3.5 the famous verses: These are lines 592-94 (given in Gilbert Murray's translation) of Aeschylus' *Seven Against Thebes*, first performed in spring 467. This anecdote provides the only evidence that Aristeides was alive as late as 467, but it is not reliable evidence. For the anecdote depends upon the identification of Aristeides the Just (see 6.1-2) with Amphiaraus, who sought **not to seem just**. But in fact Aeschylus wrote not δίκαιος but ἄριστος, as the manuscript tradition unanimously attests and as Plutarch is himself aware (*mor.* 32d, 186b, *Phil.* 15.7). The anecdote arose after the time of Plato, who quotes these lines of Aeschylus (*Rep.* 361b-62b) in the course of a discussion of the just man and the unjust man; Wilamowitz, *Aristoteles und Athen* I (1893) 160. Shackleton Bailey (on Cic. *Att.* 2.19.3) notes, "Roman audiences seem to have been quick to take such cues: cf. similar incidents in *Sest.* 118ff.; Suet. *Aug.* 53, 68, *Tib.* 45, *Galb.* 13." See also Plut. *Phil.* 11.3-4.

4.1 πρὸς εὔνοιαν . . . . ἀντιβῆναι: The phrasing is similar to that at Pl. *Laws* 634a πρὸς τὰ ἀριστερὰ μόνον δυναμένην ἀντιβαίνειν, πρὸς δὲ τὰ δεξιὰ καὶ κομψὰ καὶ θωπευτικὰ ἀδυνατοῦσαν.

4.3 supervisor of public revenues: There is no evidence for the existence of such a magistrate at Athens or, indeed, of any elected financial officer before the 4th century BC; cf. P. J. Rhodes, *The Athenian Boule* (1972) 104-7. The remainder of chapter 4, therefore, is likely to be (anachronistic) fabrication inspired by Aristeides' fame as the assessor of tributes of the Delian League (see chapter 24).

4.3 There's nothing wrong . . . : Wilamowitz (*Hermes* 14 [1879] 183) recognized that this was a line from Eupolis' (lost) comedy *The Demes*. This play seems to have been one of the models for Aristophanes' *Frogs*, in which Dionysus traveled to the underworld to bring back a much-needed poet. But in Eupolis' play (produced in 412 BC) it was deceased political leaders who were restored to life. These included Aristeides, who perhaps beat out Themistocles for the honor in a scene that contained this line, and Pericles, who perhaps beat out Cimon. A scene between Aristeides and Themistocles is perhaps the source of the anecdote in 24.6-7, while the anachronism in 25.3, where Aristeides comments on an event that took place after his death, is reminiscent of Aristophanes' "Aeschylus" passing judgment on Alcibiades (*Frogs* 1431-32). For comedy as a source for later biographers see J. A. Fairweather, *Ancient Society* 5 (1974) 244-45, M. R. Lefkowitz, *The Lives of the Greek Poets* (1981).

4.4 Idomeneus: See on 1.8. Here (= *FGrH* 338 F 7) Idomeneus has manufactured "history" out of the plot of Eupolis' *Demes*. It is difficult to tell what the relationship is between this incident and the conviction referred to below (chapter 26) on the authority of Craterus. That story is incompatible with this, as there 1) Aristeides leaves Athens permanently following his conviction and 2) Themistocles has already gone into exile. Plutarch, although he has no means of determining the historicity of either account, transmits unquestioningly Idomeneus' anecdote, which reflects favorably on Aristeides, while he raises doubts about the validity of that of Craterus, which shows his hero in a less pleasing light.

4.6: For γάρ at the start of a quotation, giving the connection between the quotation and the context, see 35.3-11, Hillyard 126. The word is not to be translated.

5.1 Marathon: N. G. L. Hammond (*Studies in Greek History* [1973] 239-42) has shown that Plutarch's account derives not from Herodotus but from an Atthidographer, perhaps Demon, who is also the source of Nepos *Milt.* 4-6.

5.1 the burning of Sardis: In 498 BC, during the Ionian revolt; cf. Hdt. 5.101-2.

5.2 played no small role: Herodotus does not mention Aristeides at all in connection with the battle of Marathon. E. Meinhardt (*Perikles bei Plutarch* [1957] 39) notes as characteristic of Plutarch's method that he assigns to his hero actions that are not attributed in his sources to a particular individual. For the expression ῥοπὴν ἐποίησε see *Alc.* 40.1, *Marc.* 31.9, *Per.* 11.2, *Phoc.* 14.6.

5.2 διδάσκων τοὺς συνάρχοντας: Compare 20.1 διδάσκων τοὺς συστρατήγους. Plutarch likes to emphasize his heroes' role as instructors, e.g. 8.5, 23.3, 28.8, 53.4, 57.2, *Per.* 12.3, 15.1, *Fab.* 4.4, 14.5.

5.2 it is no disgrace: As Calabi Limentani notes, the sentiment is similar to that at Arist. *Pol.* 1325b12.

5.3: For the spelling φιλονεικίαν in the manuscripts, see Hillyard 74-75.

5.4 the center of the Athenian line: According to Herodotus (6.111.3, 113.1) the center of the line was weak and gave way before the enemy onslaught, while the wings, manned by the Plataeans and by the polemarch Callimachus (not mentioned here by Plutarch, but cf. 56.2, *mor.* 628e) carried the day. Plutarch suppresses this and tries to give the impression that Aristeides and Themistocles were somehow responsible for the victory. He does this by omitting the proper subject ("the Athenians") of the verbs in 5.5, leading the reader to assume that Aristeides and Themistocles continue as subjects.

5.4 Λεοντίδα: For the spelling (so the manuscripts, twice) see F. J. Frost, *Classical Philology* 61 (1966) 216-17.

5.4 Themistocles: At *Them.* 3.4 he is still young at the time of the battle of Marathon and is terribly jealous of the success of Miltiades. The impression given there is that he did not participate in the battle. Themistocles is, for Plutarch, the type of the contentious and ambitious man, while Aristeides is the paragon of cooperation. So, despite their incompatibility, the anecdotes that reflect these qualities are both given.

5.5 forced off course: As Plutarch is well aware (*mor.* 862c), Herodotus represents the Persians as *intending* to sail for Athens (6.115). But, since Herodotus' account brings discredit upon the Alcmaeonids, who intended to betray the city into the hands of the enemy, Plutarch ascribes the Persians' course to the forces of nature and emphasizes the haste of the Athenians. For the time actually required to sail from Marathon to Athens (at the very least 24 hours), see A. Trevor Hodge, *TAPA* 105 (1975) 155-73.

5.7: For **Callias** see 25.4-8 and Davies 254-61. He held the hereditary title of **Torchbearer** at the Eleusinian Mysteries, among the symbols of which office were a special knot of hair and a headband; G. E. Mylonas, *Eleusis and the Eleusinian Mysteries* (1961) 232-35.

5.8 "Pitriches": Callias' family in fact made a fortune from mining, thus accounting for the epithet which was applied to him by some comic poet. This anecdote (given also in a late scholion to Ar. *Nub*. 63a and by Photius and the Suda s.v. λακκόπλουτον; cf. Heraclid. Pont. fr. 58 Wehrli, Hesych. s.v. λακκ.) was evidently fabricated to give a more discreditable explanation for the epithet, which occurs elsewhere, apart from the lexicographers, only in the Suda s.v. Καλλίας and, not in connection with Callias, in Alciphron (1.9.2, 3.4.3), whose language is heavily indebted to the writers of comedy. Callias was referred to in Cratinus' comedy *Archilochi* (fr. 12 K-A).

5.9 Demetrius: See on 1.2 and 1.8. According to epigraphic evidence, Phaenippus was archon in 490/89, Aristeides in 489/8 and Xanthippus (*sic*) in 479/8; A. E. Samuel, *Greek and Roman Chronology* (1972) 205-6.

6.1: For περὶ + acc. "as a periphrasis for the simple genitive," see Holden's commentary on *Per*., Index s.v. Cf. 10.1.

6.1 αἴσθησιν παρεῖχε: Cf. *Arat*. 19.2, *Galba* 11.4, *Marc*. 6.7, *Otho* 17.5, *mor*. 92f, 161e.

6.1 that virtue's exercise . . . general: Apparently a reference to the Platonic doctrine (*Rep*. 443e) that justice is the virtue of widest application.

6.2 The Just: The epithet is first attested in the orator Aeschines (3.181; cf. 1.25), but his reputation for justice was established already in the fifth century, as is clear from Herodotus (8.79.1) and Eupolis (fr. 99 K-A).

6.2 a title which: For Plutarch's interest in names, see 28.3, *Cor*. 11, *Dem*. 42.10-11, *Mar*. 1 and the lost work (Lamprias cat. 100) Concerning Which of the Three is the Proper Name. His argument here is tendentious for, although he knows of appellations based upon virtue (*Cor*. 11.2), he suppresses mention of them. His point here is merely that, if rulers wish to identify themselves with divinity, they must do so by exhibiting virtue; see especially G. W. Bowersock in *Entretiens sur l'antiquité classique* 19 (1973) 187-90. The epithets given here are all attested for kings of the Hellenistic period; see Calabi Limentani. Nepos (*Arist*. 1.2) agrees that Aristeides alone had this epithet.

6.3 συνοικειοῦν καὶ συναφομοιοῦν ἑαυτούς: The same phrase at *mor*. 52e.

6.3 space and the elements: Calabi Limentani claims that it is not difficult to find Stoic features in this passage, though she gives no specifics. In fact, for the Stoics, the elements are *not* everlasting, but are destroyed in the final conflagration (SVF II fr. 299). But by the same token, this is not, as Perrin has it, "a choice specimen of the phraseology of the Epicurean school." For the standard Epicurean terminology is τὸ κενὸν καὶ αἱ ἄτομοι (or τὰ ἄτομα); cf. e.g. *mor.* 720f, 1112c. Plutarch speaks of στοιχεῖα precisely because he wishes to use terms of general application and is not here adhering to the tenets of a particular school. In fact, Plutarch was a Platonist, and there is nothing here that is incompatible with the doctrines of the late Academy.

6.3 justice and right: The word θέμις is quite rare in Greek prose except in the expression (οὐ) θέμις ἐστί and when used as a proper name. (For Themis and Dike personified see *Alex.* 52.6, *mor.* 781b, 819e.) For Plutarch it has poetic and archaic associations. When the pair θέμις and δίκη are found, the reference is normally to divine justice: Pind. *Isthm.* 9.5, Parm. 28 B 1.28 D-K, Max. Tyr. 35.2, Ant. Liber. *Met.* 4.4, Himer. *Or.* 14.10 (= Alcaeus fr. 307 L-P), Themist. *Or.* 9.122d (almost personified; cf. 123a). But cf. Julian *Or.* 2.88d. In general see R. Hirzel, *Themis, Dike und Verwandtes* (1907), H. Vos, ΘΕΜΙΣ (1956).

6.3 τῷ φρονεῖν . . . θεῖόν ἐστι: For the text, see G. N. Bernardakis, *Symbolae criticae et palaeographicae in Plutarchi Vitas Parallelas et Moralia* (1879) 20-21.

6.4 envy . . . fear . . . affection: These three responses to the divine are pointedly repeated in the following section (7.1-2), where we are told that Aristeides was first loved (ἀγαπωμένῳ), then envied (φθονεῖσθαι) and finally ostracized, allegedly because the people were afraid (φόβον) that he was aiming at tyranny.

6.5 virtue: Plutarch's language appears to be very loose throughout this section. At times he speaks in terms of justice (δικαιοσύνη . . . Δίκαιον . . . δίκης . . . τὴν δικαιοσύνην . . . ἡ μὲν δικαιοσύνη . . . ἡ δ' ἀδικία) and at times in terms of virtue (τῆς ἀρετῆς . . . ἀρετῇ . . . ἡ ἀρετὴ . . . τὴν δ' ἀρετὴν). Either Plutarch is being careless or, more likely, he is assuming the Platonic doctrine (*Gorg.* 507c) that the possession of one of the virtues implies the possession of all.

6.5 κακῶς φρονοῦντες, ὡς: Like much in this section, this expression has a poetic flavor; cf. Eur. *Med.* 250.

6.5 brutish: Cf. *mor.* 1125a, where it is said that the beasts live the kind of life they do because they have no knowledge of the justice of the gods. The opposition between the divine and the brutish is taken from the discussion of the profitability of justice in Plato's *Republic* (589d).

7.1 affection . . . jealousy: See 6.4. For the powerful role played by envy in Greek life and politics, see P. Walcot, *Envy and the Greeks* (1978).

7.1 Themistocles: Plutarch is convinced of Themistocles' responsibility for Aristeides' ostracism; cf. 25.10, 56.4, *Them.* 5.7, 11.1. He introduces it here even though it is somewhat out of place, since the previous section was designed to explain Aristeides' ostracism in terms of the people's fear and envy. Therefore we can be sure that he did not invent it (cf. Nepos *Arist.* 1.2), but found it in a source, now lost, in which he had some confidence.

7.1 pronouncing judgment: See 4.2 for an instance of this. But the claim that Aristeides was arrogating the authority of the courts of law is, according to Frost 91, anachronistic.

7.1 their victory: That is, in the battle of Marathon, 490 BC. Aristotle (*Ath. Pol.* 22.3) had given Athenian self-confidence following the battle of Marathon as a motive for the first ostracism, that of Hipparchus in 487. Aristeides was not ostracized until 482.

7.2 ostracism was not a punishment . . . assuaging envy: Very similar phrasing in *Them.* 22.4-5, *Alc.* 13.6, *Nic.* 11.6. The source is likely to be Ephorus, who is presumably the source of the similar sentiment in Diodorus 11.55.3. But the sentiment is implicit already in Thucydides, who says (8.73.3) that Hyperbolus (see below) was ostracized, not out of fear of his power and prestige, but because of his wickedness.

7.3 Hyperbolus: His ostracism, the last imposed by the Athenians, occurred in or shortly after 417 BC. It is described also at *Alc.* 13.4-9, *Nic.* 11.3-9.

7.4 ἐπιφέρειν τὸ ὄστρακον: For the idiom, see 1.2 ὄστρακον ἐπιφέρεσθαι, *Alc.* 13.6 τὸ ὄστρακον ἐπιφέρειν, 13.7 τὸ ὄστρακον ἐποίσουσι, and compare Diodorus 11.55.1 τὸν ὀστρακισμὸν ἐπαγαγόντες.

7.5 the procedure: Plutarch is drawing on, among others, the Athenian writer Philochorus (*FGrH* 328 F 30), who lived c. 340-265 BC. For Athenian ostracism, see Rhodes 267-71 (with recent bibliography) and E. Vanderpool, "Ostracism at Athens," in *Lectures in Memory of Louise Taft Semple*, second series, 1966-1970 (1973) 217-50. The latter illustrates several of the potsherds (*ostraka*), thousands of which have been found by archaeologists in Athens, including some bearing Aristeides' name.

7.5 particular spot: The *perischoinisma* (*mor.* 847a), near the Altar of the Twelve Gods; R. Martin, *Recherches sur l'agora grecque* (1951) 325-27, but see also Wycherley, *JHS* 75 (1955) 117-18.

7.7 we are told: The same anecdote at *mor.* 186a and the Suda s.v. Ἀριστείδης. At Nepos *Arist.* 1.3-4 there is a less developed version, in which Aristeides does not help the man write his own name, but merely notices him writing. He asks the same question and receives the same reply as in Plutarch's version. That some citizens needed help recording their votes is shown by a group of 190 potsherds having Themistocles' name written on them by fewer than 20 hands, and by one potsherd on which someone's efforts to write Aristeides' name were consummated by a second hand (see Vanderpool 225, 230).

7.8: Achilles swore (*Il.* 1.240) that a time would come when longing for Achilles would afflict all the sons of the Achaeans.

8.1 within three years: Aristeides was ostracized early in the spring of 482; the decree recalling those who had been ostracized (proposed, according to *Them.* 11.1, by Themistocles) was passed probably late in the spring of 480. The text of Aristotle *Ath. Pol.* 22.8 reads "in the fourth year;" that of Nepos *Arist.* 1.5 "in the sixth year." The battle of

Salamis took place late in September, 480. For the chronology, see Rhodes 281, Frost 123-28.

8.1 οὐκ ὀρθῶς στοχαζόμενοι τοῦ ἀνδρός: Exactly the same expression at *Fab.* 10.1; cf. also *Cor.* 18.2.

8.1 commander in chief: In fact, there was no such office at this time. Rather, as Plutarch was aware (see 5.1-2), the Athenians elected a board of ten generals having equal authority. But Plutarch often speaks in terms appropriate to his own day; cf. 11.1, *Them.* 6.1-2 and K. J. Dover, *JHS* 80 (1960) 72-73.

8.1 ἐνδοξότατον ἐπὶ σωτηρίᾳ: These words are to be taken together; cf. *mor.* 1036f ἐπὶ σοφίᾳ γενομένων αὐτῶν ἐνδόξων.

8.2: Eurybiades was the commander of the Peloponnesian forces, who preferred to abandon the allied position at Salamis and defend the Peloponnese at the Isthmus.

8.2 the straits . . . the islands: The Greek fleet was stationed at the island of Salamis, in the straits between Salamis and the mainland of Attica. At night the Persians blocked both entrances to the straits and landed troops on Psyttaleia and some other very small islands in and near the straits. See Aeschylus *Persae* 364-68, 447-53, Herodotus 8.76.1.

8.2 returned from Aegina: See Herodotus 8.79.1. Plutarch is not concerned to tell us (indeed, he probably does not know) whether Aristeides was returning from exile in Aegina or had earlier returned to Athens, whence he had been sent on a mission to Aegina.

8.3 salutary competition: Compare Aristeides' behavior before Marathon (5.2-3), where his allaying of rivalry among the Athenian generals had a salutary result. Cooperation is Aristeides' most conspicuous virtue. Needless to say, this entire speech is purely Plutarch's invention.

8.3 commanding . . . advising: Aristotle (*Ath. Pol.* 23.3) says that the Athenians regarded Themistocles as a commander and Aristeides as an adviser: ἐχρῶντο τῷ μὲν στρατηγῷ, τῷ δὲ συμβούλῳ.

8.3 ἅπτεσθαι τῶν ἀρίστων λογισμῶν: Cf. Sophocles *Ant.* 179 τῶν ἀρίστων ἅπτεται βουλευμάτων. For Plutarch's familiarity with this passage from tragedy, see *Cic.* 52.2, *Fab.* 27.1.

8.5 the plan . . . to deceive the Persians: Themistocles had sent one of his slaves with a message to Xerxes, to the effect that the Greeks were planning to withdraw from Salamis. The message encouraged the Persians to surround the Greeks and attack at once (*Them.* 12.3-4, Hdt. 8.75). The intention was to lure the Persians into giving battle in the straits, a location that favored the smaller Greek fleet.

8.6 Cleocritus the Corinthian: Mentioned only here and 20.2. In Herodotus (8.59-61), Themistocles is in conflict with a Corinthian named Adeimantus. But this story is not given by Herodotus, and it is clear that he was not Plutarch's only source.

8.6 Aristeides contradicted him: Plutarch seeks to give the impression that Aristeides' approval of Themistocles' strategy was decisive. He omits to mention what he says at *Them.* 12.8 (from Hdt. 8.81-82), that the Greeks still did not believe Aristeides' report of the encirclement.

9.1 while the commanders . . . were thus occupied: Plutarch gives the impression that, while the other commanders were engaged in disputes among themselves, Aristeides was acting. But according to Herodotus (8.95) and Aeschylus (*Pers.* 454-59), the Athenians did not occupy Psyttaleia until after the battle had begun. In any case, there are enough discrepancies between the accounts of Herodotus and Aeschylus (who does not mention Aristeides) to lead one to believe that Aristeides' contribution to the battle of Salamis may have been a fiction to begin with; cf. C. W. Fornara, "The Hoplite Achievement at Psyttaleia," *JHS* 86 (1966) 51-54.

9.1: For **Psyttaleia** and the battle of Salamis in general, see Frost 133-69, N. G. L. Hammond, "The Battle of Salamis," *JHS* 76 (1956) 32-54, G. Roux, "Eschyle, Hérodote, Diodore, Plutarque racontent la bataille de Salamine," *BCH* 98 (1974) 51-94.

9.1 the citizens: These men were hoplites, or heavily armed infantrymen, according to Herodotus (8.95; cf. τοῖς ὅπλοις below), and it has been suggested that we read "the hoplites" here (i.e ὁπλιτῶν for πολιτῶν). But Herodotus also asserts that these men were Athenians, and there seems to be no good reason to change the manuscript reading.

9.1 except those men of rank: According to Aeschylus (*Pers.* 464), Herodotus (8.95) and Aristodemus (*FGrH* 104 F 1.4), all the Persians on the island were killed. The story that follows is referred to only here, *Them.* 13.2-5 (where it is attributed to Phaenias) and *Pel.* 21.3. That it is fictitious is clear from the fact that, contrary to the testimony of Aeschylus and Herodotus, it requires the occupation of Psyttaleia to take place before the battle; that it is the invention of Phaenias is shown by the fact that the cult of **Dionysus Omestes** ("D. who eats raw meat") is confined to Phaenias' native Lesbos and the surrounding islands. See A. Henrichs, "Human Sacrifice in Greek Religion: Three Case Studies," *Entretiens sur l'antiquité classique* 27 (1980) 195-235, esp. 208-24.

9.3 ὡς μήτε . . . διαφυγεῖν: Plutarch occasionally uses ὡς + infin. for the usual ὥστε; e.g. 47.4, *Lyc.* 28.6, *Marc.* 13.4, *Tim.* 8.3. While it is normally purely consecutive in sense, here, as at *Pel.* 29.5 and *Tim.* 10.4, it almost has final force. In Plutarch's sources it is the *Persians* who occupy the island in order to save friends and kill enemies: Herodotus 8.76.2 ἵνα τοὺς μὲν περιποιῶσι, τοὺς δὲ διαφθείρωσι, Aesch. *Pers.* 450-53 ὅπως . . . κτείνοιεν . . . Ἑλλήνων στρατόν, φίλους δ' ὑπεκσῴζοιεν.

9.4 a trophy . . . on Psyttaleia: According to Pausanias (1.36.1-2), the trophy was erected on Salamis, while on Psyttaleia there was nothing but some crude wooden images of Pan.

9.5-6: In Herodotus (8.108-10), Themistocles recommends that the Greeks sail to the Hellespont and destroy the bridges that Xerxes had built there, but the Spartan Eurybiades argues that trapping the Persians in Europe would make them desperate and all the more dangerous. Themistocles is persuaded by this reasoning and sends his slave Sicinnus to tell Xerxes that Themistocles restrained the Greeks when they wanted to destroy the bridges (cf. Thuc. 1.137.4). Plutarch, both here and at *Them.* 16, is either inventing or following an alternate tradition. Themistocles is now merely *pretending* to favor the destruction of the bridges; it is the Athenian Aristeides who sensibly argues against the venture; the messenger is Arnaces (similarly Polyaenus 1.30.4); the purpose of the message is to hasten Xerxes' departure from Greece (similarly Diodorus 11.19.5-6, Nepos *Them.* 5.1-2, Frontin. *Strat.* 2.6.8, Justin. 2.13.5-7), rather than, as in Herodotus, to provide for Themistocles' future security by ingratiating himself with the Persian king.

10.1 approximately 300,000 men: This greatly exaggerated figure is from Herodotus (8.100.5, 8.113.3, 9.32.2). Diodorus has now 400,000 (11. 19.6), now 500,000 (11.30.1).

10.1 bits of lumber on the seas: The substance of Mardonius' letter, which is not mentioned elsewhere and is surely fictitious, derives from a speech in Herodotus (8.100.2-5) in which Mardonius tries to cheer up Xerxes after the defeat at Salamis. He says that the decisive contest is not one of "bits of lumber, but of men and horses."

10.2 to the Athenians he sent a separate letter: In Herodotus 8. 140, Mardonius sends the Macedonian king Alexander (see 15.3 below) to convey Xerxes' terms. The terms differ slightly in Herodotus, Plutarch and Diodorus who, like Plutarch, does not mention Alexander (11. 28.1).

10.4 decree that Aristeides had proposed: Herodotus, of whose account 10.2-6 is a summary, mentions neither Aristeides nor a formal decree (8.140-44). Blass (Introduction, p. 3) suggested that these derive from Craterus, whose compilation of Athenian decrees Plutarch is known to have used (26.1, *Cim.* 13.5). This suggestion is confirmed by a consideration that is mentioned neither by Blass nor by P. Krech (*De Crateri* Ψηφισμάτων Συναγωγῇ *et de locis aliquot Plutarchi ex ea petitis* [1888] 56-61), namely that, as a Macedonian, Craterus would likely have suppressed the traitorous role of Alexander (10.2).

10.5 Aristeides brought the delegation: The only delegation that Plutarch has mentioned is that of the Lacedaemonians, but Aristeides will shortly address also a delegation from the Persians. This awkwardness results from Plutarch's use of two sources, Herodotus and Craterus.

10.6 ἄχρι ἄν: Plutarch regularly allows this hiatus; cf. e.g. ἄχρι οὗ *Aem.* 17.9, *Fab.* 11.5, 14.2, 22.4, *Phil.* 21.1, μέχρι ἄν *Flam.* 20.9, *Phil.* 20.1.

10.9: Oresteium is a town in Arcadia, perhaps one fourth of the way from Sparta to Athens.

10.9 This is the account that Idomeneus gives: For Idomeneus, see 1.8. In fact, everything in 10.7-9 is taken from Herodotus 9.6-11 (including some direct quotations), with the exception of Aristeides' name—Herodotus speaks only of "Athenian messengers"—and the concluding *mot* (**it was an inopportune pleasantry . . .**). Idomeneus' contribution, then, was to add these two details to Herodotus' account, his purpose being to contrast the straightforward character of Aristeides with that of the devious Themistocles. For this story now becomes the converse of the famous account given in *Them.* 19.2-3, according to which Themistocles went as ambassador to Sparta in the following year and caused delays during which the fortifications of Athens could be built. (Plutarch, in the Lives of both Aristeides and Themistocles, suppresses mention of Aristeides' complicity in the plot, which was familiar from Thuc. 1.91.3 and Arist. *Ath. Pol.* 23.4; likewise, here he ignores Herodotus' allegation that the Spartans delayed because their wall at the Isthmus was not yet complete, an allegation that he denies at *mor.* 871e.) See on 22.1.

0.10 in Aristeides' proposal: Again Plutarch cites an official decree, again surely from Craterus' compilation (10.4). Here Craterus contradicts Idomeneus. At 4.4 Plutarch cites Idomeneus and at 26.1-3 Craterus for details of what seems to be the same incident. Thus it seems that these two men, the one a follower of Epicurus, the other of Aristotle, were engaged in polemics. (We do not know which of them wrote earlier.)

1.1 commander in chief: Cf. 8.1. Here Plutarch is concerned to stress Aristeides' role (cf. Hdt. 9.28.6). Later, however, when he compares Aristeides and Cato, he indicates that Aristeides was only one of ten generals (56.1-2).

1.2 He was joined there by Pausanias: In fact, the Spartan general Pausanias was joined by Aristeides and the Athenians (Hdt. 9.19.2), and it was not at Plataea but at Eleusis (cf. below 11.5). Plutarch's version magnifies Aristeides' importance.

1.2 περιεφράξαντο: The general meaning of this sentence is clear, as it derives from Hdt. 9.15.3. But the verb is used in a most unusual, if not unique, way. (It never has a word meaning "wall" as its object; it is very rarely found in the middle voice.) It appears to be a reminiscence of Hdt. 9.70.1, where the meaning of ἐφράξαντο . . . τὸ τεῖχος (this is the very wall referred to) is not entirely clear.

1.2 ten stades: Slightly more than a mile. The figure is from Herodotus.

1.3 Teisamenus of Elis: See Hdt. 9.33-36 for his life story and for his prophecy that the Greeks will be successful "if they remain on the defensive, but not if they cross the Asopus and initiate the fighting." For the importance of seers in Greek warfare, see Pritchett III 47-90.

1.3 Aristeides, when he sent to Delphi: This account is not found elsewhere (but cf. Clem. Alex. *Protr.* 2.40.2), and everything from here to 11.9 probably depends on local tradition. Plutarch was himself Boeotian and had surely visited Plataea, and he spent a good deal of his time in Delphi, where he was a priest in the temple of Apollo (Jones 26). The oracular response is quoted at least partly in the Phocian dialect, and therefore perhaps from an official document. Cf. H. W. Parke and D. E. W. Wormell, *The Delphic Oracle* I (1956) 174-76.

1.4 northwesterly: The Greek says, "the summertime setting of the sun." For the meaning of this expression, see Aristotle *Meteorologica* 2.6.

1.4 nympholepsy: Cf. Pl. *Phdr.* 238d. Popular belief in the power of the nymphs to possess continued in Greece until recent times: G. F. Abbott, *Macedonian Folklore* (1903) 242-49, J. C. Lawson, *Modern Greek Folklore and Ancient Greek Religion* (1910) 130-62.

11.5 back to Athenian soil: The Greek forces had joined at Eleusis, in Athenian territory (cf. 11.2), before moving to Plataea. But Plutarch had not mentioned this.

11.7 an army deficient in cavalry: The only Greeks who possessed effective cavalry forces at this time were the Boeotians and the Thessalians, both of whom had joined with the Persians.

11.9 at a much later date: According to *Alex.* 34.2 (the only other reference to this incident), this was at the end of 331, immediately after Alexander's victory at the battle of Gaugamela. The Olympic Games would not be held until the summer of 328, two and a half years later. This, along with the fact that the Plataeans had already "given themselves" to the Athenians in 519 BC (Hdt. 6.108.1, Thuc. 3.68.5), raises suspicions as to the historicity of this account.

12.1 The Tegeans began a quarrel: This is a condensed version of an account in Herodotus (9.26-28.1), who gives in detail the speeches of "the Tegeans" and "the Athenians," with no mention of Aristeides.

12.2 does not allow us to debate: In fact, "the Athenians" in Herodotus recount at length the accomplishments of their ancestors. But cf. *mor.* 872a, and the entire essay On the Maliciousness of Herodotus, for Plutarch's view of Herodotus' reliability.

12.3 not to vie with our allies: Similarly Aristeides had reproached the Spartans (10.9) with deceiving their allies, rather than the enemy, and had shown the Athenians (5.2-3) that cooperation, rather than rivalry, was the most effective means of defeating the common enemy. This is the essence of Aristeides' character as Plutarch conceives it. Whether it is Plutarch's own formulation or is derived from one of Plutarch's sources, it is simply a generalization based upon the account in Herodotus (8.79.2-3; cf. 8.3 above) of Aristeides' cooperation with his rival Themistocles.

13.3 οἵ: This has been deleted because it produces hiatus. It is normal for the pronoun to be omitted in the second of two relative clauses: e.g. 46.3, *Nic.* 5.3, Eur. *Suppl.* 861-62, oracle in Hdt. 1.47.3, Hdt. 8.106.1, Xen. *An.* 3.2.5, Thuc. 1.36.1, 2.84.2, 6.64.2, 7.29.5, Pl. *Crito* 47e, *Phd.* 65a, 81b, 82d, *Prot.* 313b, *Rep.* 533d, D.S. 1.34.2, Paus. 10.4.1.

13.3: Aeschines of Lamptrae and Agasias of Acharnae were not previously known from any other source. For this reason, and because the account of the conspiracy is found only here, scholars have been inclined to doubt the historicity of all of chapter 13. But recently a number of ostraka, dating to the 480s, have been discovered in Athens bearing the name of Agasias of Lamptrae (*sic*). It therefore may be the case that Plutarch's account has some historical basis and that he (or his source) has confused the demotics of the two conspirators. So F. D. Harvey, "The Conspiracy of Agasias and Aischines," *Klio* 66 (1984) 58-73. The conspicuous willingness of Aristeides the Just to sacrifice **justice** to **expediency** when the security of the state is con cerned has a parallel in 25.1-2 (contrast 22.2-4). Since Theophrastus is named as the source for that passage, he is perhaps the most likely source here as well.

13.3 βουλευόμενοι: Recent editors have adopted Sauppe's conjecture (*Göttingische Gelehrte Anzeigen* [1870] 1008) βουλόμενοι. But this gives no construction to τῇ πατρίδι. For the dative, cf. Joseph. *BJ* 2.607 εἰ μὴ καλῶς ὑμῖν ἐβουλευσάμην, Thuc. 1.43.4 τὰ ἄριστα βουλεύσεσθε ὑμῖν αὐτοῖς, 4.74.2 βουλεύσειν δὲ τῇ πόλει τὰ ἄριστα.

14.1 After this: Plutarch often uses this sort of transitional formula to give the impression that his account is chronologically arranged. In fact, however, the battle here described preceded the discussion recorded in chapter 12. See Hdt. 9.20-28.

14.5 Aristeides undertook the mission: Herodotus, whom Plutarch is here following quite closely, does not mention Aristeides (9.21.3). But Plutarch is apparently using a second source, in addition to Herodotus, namely the same source (Ephorus?) used by Diodorus, who does name Aristeides (11.30.4).

14.6 treating this as the decisive encounter: This is Plutarch's addition, designed to magnify this preliminary skirmish which, according to Herodotus (9.25.1) and Diodorus (11.30.4), was of importance primarily for raising the morale of the Greeks.

14.6 abandoned his body and fled: Herodotus' account is less flattering to the Athenians. According to him (9.23), the Persians fought fiercely with the Athenians over Masistius' body and actually recovered it briefly, before the other Greeks answered the Athenians' call for help.

14.8 horses and mules: For this extravagant form of mourning (also in Herodotus: 9.24), cf. *Pel.* 33.3, 34.2, *Alex.* 72.3, Eur. *Alc.* 428-29 and (perhaps) Propertius 4.8.15.

15.1 victorious if they remained on the defensive: Cf. 11.3. Mardonius also had a Greek prophet in his employ, who predicted success if he did not attack (Hdt. 9.37.1).

15.3 requested that Aristeides . . . come: According to Herodotus' account (9.44), the horseman asked to see "the Athenian generals," whom Herodotus does not name.

15.3 Alexander, king of the Macedonians: This is Alexander I, son of Amyntas, called "the Philhellene." As Macedonian king (from 494-454 BC) he was Xerxes' vassal, but he favored (or, once the war was over, pretended that he had favored) the Greek cause. Cf. 10.2.

15.5 it was not right to keep this from Pausanias: In Herodotus (9.45.1) Alexander begs the Athenian generals to tell no one but Pausanias. Further, it is Alexander himself (9.45.3) who asks that the Greeks recall his services if the Greeks should be victorious. Again, by the slightest of changes, Plutarch enhances the character of his hero. And again, what is emphasized in Aristeides' character is his willingness to cooperate with and defer to those with whom he shares power.

6.1 according to Herodotus: The reason Plutarch names his source here (Hdt. 9.46.2) is that he will not himself vouch for the truth of the account. Indeed, he does not believe it for, at *mor.* 872b, he says, "It is ridiculous that [the Spartans] should be unwilling to fight unless they were familiar with the enemy." (Plutarch is of course tendentious. That is not the point. The point is that the Athenians *were* familiar with the enemy.) Why, then, does he include the account? Because it gives him an opportunity to display Aristeides' willingness to co-operate and his lack of rancor.

16.1 their earlier success: For Athenian confidence following their victory in the battle of Marathon, cf. 7.1.

16.2 the other Athenian generals: In fact, according to Herodotus (9.46.3), the Athenians agreed immediately to Pausanias' proposal, even saying that they had had the same idea themselves. Herodotus does not mention Aristeides, whose role has perhaps been invented by Ephorus. Cf. 14.5, where again Aristeides does the right thing while others balk.

16.3 μὴ πρὸς ὁμοφύλους καὶ συγγενεῖς: Cf. *Arat.* 45.7 δεινὸν ἄνδρας ὁμοφύλους καὶ συγγενεῖς οὕτω μεταχειρίσασθαι, *Tim.* 29.6 οὐδ' ἀπὸ συγγενῶν φόνου καὶ ὁμοφύλων . . . ἀλλὰ βαρβαρικά. For the natural enmity between Greeks and barbarians, cf. 50.4, Hdt. 1.4.4.

16.4 bows and arrows: Traditionally regarded as cowardly weapons; cf. Eur. *HF* 161, with the commentary of G. W. Bond (1981).

16.6 some deserters: This detail is not in Herodotus, but is a conventional feature of descriptions of battles in Diodorus and, presumably, in Diodorus' source Ephorus: *Hermes* 115 (1987) 77-82.

16.8 καθύβριστο: For the language, compare *Rom.* 23.6 καθυβρίσαι πολλὰ τὴν χώραν, *Cam.* 2.10 πολλὰ τὴν χώραν καθυβρίσαντες. Herodotus merely says (9.49.2, cf. Paus. 9.4.3) that the Persian cavalry "choked the fountain of Gargaphia, from which the entire Greek army was supplied with water." (For the location of the fountain, and for the topography of Plataea in general, see W. K. Pritchett, *Studies in Ancient Greek Topography* I [1965] 103-21, esp. 113-15.)

17.1 rushed off toward . . . Plataea: Plutarch repeats a statemen from Herodotus (9.52) of which he elsewhere (*mor.* 872b-c) strongl disapproves. Cf. on 16.1.

17.3 Here . . . is my ballot: According to Herodotus, from whom thi story is taken (9.53.2-55.2), Amompharetus had not been present at th conference at which it was decided to move camp. The Athenians use pebbles (ψῆφοι) as ballots, but the Spartans actually voted by acclama tion, as Plutarch was aware (*Lyc.* 26.4).

17.4 the Athenians, who were already moving off: According t Herodotus (9.54), the Athenians did not move, because they distruste the Spartans. Further, it was they who sent to Pausanias, to ask for in structions.

17.4 cause Amompharetus to move: Amompharetus did, in fact move (Hdt. 9.56.1-57.1). But if Plutarch were to mention the fact h would deprive his anecdote of much of its force. So we are left wit the impression that Amompharetus remained where he was.

17.5 βοῇ . . . τοὺς Ἕλληνας: Cf. Hdt. 9.59.2 βοῇ τε καὶ ὁμίλῳ ἐπήισαν ὡς ἀνα ταсσόμενοι τοὺς Ἕλληνας.

7.6 **μικρᾶς ῥοπῆς ἐδέησε:** The metaphor is of a scale that requires but little impetus to tip the balance. Cf. *Cic.* 10.5, *Dion* 33.3, *Pel.* 29.2, *mor.* 650e, Pl. *Rep.* 556e, [Arist.] *Probl.* 1.17, Aretaeus 3.12.1.

7.6 **forgot . . . battle-signal:** This detail is found only here and was likely invented by Plutarch or his source. Cf. *mor.* 872c, where Plutarch challenges Herodotus' assertion that only the Spartans and Tegeans engaged the Persians. For the expression **ἔλαθε δ' αὐτόν . . . σύνθημα δοῦναι**, cf. *Pel.* 11.7, *Pomp.* 42.3, Paus. 9.41.1, P.Oxy. 530.5. The insertion of μὴ by one manuscript seems to be a mere slip.

7.7 **not to retaliate:** Cf. 11.3.

7.8 **Callicrates:** Plutarch takes this anecdote from Herodotus, who gives it (9.72) after his description of the battle. But Plutarch more effectively recounts it in its proper place (cf. Hdt. 9.61.3).

7.10 **According to some authorities:** It is not clear to whom Plutarch is referring. Again (cf. 16.1) he distances himself from the account by giving it on someone else's authority. He is right to do so, as the aetiology is certainly false. In the first place, the Spartan ritual in honor of Ortheia (for which see W. den Boer, *Laconian Studies* [1954] 261-74) surely antedates the Persian Wars. In the second place, the ritual requires the **ephebes** (young men undergoing initiation) to steal cheeses from the altar, which have no place in the sacrifices preliminary to a battle. (These were rather sacrifices of animals, the **rods and whips** being used to drive the victims to the altar.)

7.10: The **procession of Lydians** is not elsewhere referred to, but Plutarch presumably knows of it from personal experience, as he says that he has himself witnessed the rite (*Lyc.* 18.2; cf. also *mor.* 239c-d).

8.1: To Herodotus' account (9.61.3) Plutarch has added Pausanias' **tears**, the **other gods who watch over the Plataean land** (cf. 11.3 and Thuc. 2.74.3) and the inspiring speech.

8.1 **δράσαντάς γέ τι παθεῖν:** For this opposition (which is proverbial: Aesch. *Choe.* 313), cf. *Ant.* 42.1, *Cam.* 20.4, *Eum.* 7.13, *Marc.* 31.5, *Otho* 9.5, *Per.* 34.4, *Publ.* 9.4, *Pyr.* 14.13, *mor.* 727d.

8.2 **ἐφάνη τὰ ἱερὰ:** Apparently like e.g. Hdt. 9.61.3 τῶν σφαγίων οὐ γινομένων, Xen. *An.* 2.2.3 οὐκ ἐγίγνετο τὰ ἱερά, 6.4.9 τὰ ἱερὰ ἐγένετο.

8.2 **a single, spirited creature:** Compare *Flam.* 8.6: the Macedonian phalanx "resembles in its strength an indomitable creature so long as it remains a single body and keeps its shields locked" (cf. 18.3 below). The image here is probably of a wild boar, which is conspicuous for its **bristling** and its ferocity in defending itself (cf. J. K. Anderson, *Hunting in the Ancient World* [1985] 51-55).

8.3 **set up . . . wicker-work shields:** Cf. Hdt. 9.61.3. For the Persian shield (and the **scimitars and short swords** below), see the text and illustration in J. Warry, *Warfare in the Classical World* (1980) 38-39.

8.5 **as is alleged:** Namely by Herodotus (9.60.1), nor is there any reason to doubt that Pausanias sent a message. But Plutarch refuses to believe that the Athenians needed anything more than the sounds of battle to inspire them to come to the aid of the Spartans.

18.6: Aristeides is not named by Herodotus, who mentions only "th Athenians" (9.61.1). The sentiments that Plutarch puts into Aristeide mouth are consistent with the character of the man who elsewher (e.g. 10.9, 16.3) insists that "friends" should not fight with one anothe and allow "the enemy" an advantage.

18.6 Ἑλληνίους θεούς: This expression occurs only here in the Lives an is very rare in prose (Hdt. 5.49.3, 92η.5, Lucian *Herc.* 2, Aelian *VH* 12.1 Heliodorus *Aeth.* 2.23.1). The solemnity of the expression, which is du to its archaic and poetic flavor, is enhanced by Plutarch's omission o the definite article (cf. 18.1 θεοῖς ἄλλοις . . . Πλαταιίδα γῆν).

18.6 approximately fifty thousand: This figure reproduces Herodo tus' estimate (9.32.2) of the number of Greeks serving in Mardonius army. Of them, only the Boeotians opposed the Athenians (9.67).

18.7 followed along: Plutarch wishes to exculpate his fellow Boeo tians and uses the same argument found in Thucydides (3.62.4) an Pausanias (9.6.2).

19.1 Arimnestus: His name is given as Aeimnestus by Aristodemu (*FGrH* 104 F 2.5). The manuscripts at Hdt. 9.64.2 are divided betwee these two forms. The detail of the blow to the head with a stone is nc found in Herodotus, but was perhaps in the source of Aristodemus, wh records that Mardonius fell "fighting with his head bare." G. L. Hux ley (*GRBS* 4 [1963] 5-7) identifies this man with the Plataean general o the same name mentioned in 11.5, saying that Plutarch is mistaken i calling him a Spartan. But the Plataeans fought by the side of th Athenians, not by the side of the Spartans; cf. Hdt. 9.28.

19.1: The **oracle of Amphiaraus** was at Oropus, a town on the borde between Boeotian and Athenian territory. Those who wished to con sult the oracle slept in the precinct and received prophecies in thei dreams; E. R. Dodds, *The Greeks and the Irrational* (1951) 110. At *mor* 412a-b Plutarch repeats this account, which is found nowhere else.

19.2 the Ptoon sanctuary: The oracle of Ptoan Apollo near Acrae phia in Boeotia. For its history, see J. Ducat, *Les kouroi du Ptoion* (1971) 439-50. According to Herodotus (8.133-35), Mardonius sent Carian man named Mys to consult a number of Boeotian oracles, in cluding those of Amphiaraus, Trophonius (whence, apparently, th curious variation in the manuscripts here) and Ptoan Apollo. Herod otus' account is referred to also at *mor.* 411f-12a and Paus. 9.23.6.

19.2 the god's: Amphiaraus was a hero, but was honored as a god Paus. 1.34.2.

19.2 within their wooden walls: That is, the fortifications men tioned in 11.2.

19.3 three hundred of the foremost citizens: Cf. Hdt. 9.67.

19.3 the engagement itself: As distinct from a subsequent pursui (which, in this case, did not occur). Normally, in ancient warfare there were many fewer casualties during the actual battle than during the rout that followed.

19.3: ἧκεν αὐτοῖς ἄγγελος = ἤγγελται, and so can introduce indirect dis course. Cf. Hom. *Il.* 11.715 (= 18.167) ἄγγελος ἦλθε . . . θωρήσσεσθαι, Thuc. 1. 27.1 ἦλθον ἄγγελοι ὅτι πολιορκοῦνται, Xen. *Cyr.* 5.3.26 ἤκουσιν αὐτῷ ἄγγελοι ὡς ὁ Ἀσσύριος . . . ἐνέγκοι.

19.4: That the **Lacedaemonians were inexperienced in conducting siege operations** is mentioned by Herodotus (9.70.2). Cf. also Thuc. 1.102.2, Plut. *Sulla* 42.5, *mor.* 228d. According to Herodotus, even after the Athenians arrived, the battle raged for a long time. But Plutarch's wording gives the impression that the Athenians (under the command of Aristeides, who is nowhere mentioned in this section) made short work of it.

19.5: The number **1,360** is not in Herodotus, whose causalty-list is: Megarians and Phliasians 600 (9.69.2), Athenians 52, Tegeans 16, Lacedaemonians *from Sparta* 91 (9.70.5). This might mean that 601 non-Spartan Lacedaemonians were killed, but we have no way of knowing where Plutarch's total comes from. Perhaps Cleidemus?

19.6: For **Cleidemus**, the fourth-century writer on Athenian affairs, see Jacoby, *FGrH* 323; for the **Sphragitic Nymphs**, 11.3-4, *mor.* 628e-f, Paus. 9.3.9.

19.7 Herodotus: Cf. Hdt. 9.69.1 and 9.85.3. Plutarch criticizes this statement also at *mor.* 872c-73e. His point here is that, since the total of the Greek dead was 1,360 and the total of the Athenian, Tegean and Lacedaemonian dead was 159, these three cannot have been the only Greek cities to have seen action. This is a sensible argument if the two figures are correct (but see note on 19.5).

19.7 inscription on the altar: Quoted also at *mor.* 873b, this poem is found in the Palatine Anthology (6.50), where it is attributed to Simonides and where an additional line appears between lines 1 and 2. The additional line may not be original, however, and Plutarch is probably quoting accurately an inscription which he has himself seen. For the unusual metrical form ("one pentameter after more than one hexameter"), see M. L. West, *Greek Metre* (1982) 45. The altar is that of Zeus Eleutherius (cf. Paus. 9.2.5), or **Liberator Zeus**.

19.8 the third day of Boedromion: The manuscripts read "the fourth day," but at *Cam.* 19.5 and *mor.* 349f Plutarch says "the third." Plutarch wrote a work On Days (now lost) and was very much interested in the calendar (for his accuracy and consistency in these matters, see *Rheinisches Museum* 118 [1975] 238-39). It is less likely that he has made a mistake (especially in a passage where he praises the accuracy of modern-day astronomy) than that the manuscripts are in error. The error was caused by what follows, where the Greek reads literally "the fourth day from the end of Panemus."

19.9 astronomy has advanced: There is a similar confident assertion of modern excellence at *mor.* 269d.

19.9 people cannot agree: Each Greek city had its own calendar. Not only did the names of the months differ from one city to another but, because of the juggling necessary to reconcile a system based upon twelve 30-day months with the solar year, the months began and ended at different times in different cities. Thus, in a given year, 3 Boedromion at Athens might or might not coincide with 27 Panemus at Thebes.

20: The material in this section is not found in any other author (cf. also *mor.* 873a-b). Herodotus says nothing of an **award of valor**; according to Diodorus (11.33.1), it was given to Pausanias and the Spartans. Plutarch's source is presumably local tradition, in which case it is likely that he is himself responsible for adding Aristeides' name. For such awards of valor, see Pritchett II 276-90, esp. 283-86.

20.1 παρ' οὐδὲν ἂν ἦλθεν . . . ἀπολέσθαι: For this idiom, frequent in the Lives, see *Ant.* 63.11, *Brut.* 15.3, *Caes.* 39.6, *Cam.* 8.6, *Cato min.* 11.3, 23.2 *Cic.* 39.2, *Gracch.* 21.7, *Pel.* 8.9, *Per.* 28.8, *Pyr.* 10.2, 14.10.

20.1 teach them a lesson: Cf. 5.2.

20.2: Theogeiton is not mentioned elsewhere, **Cleocritus** only here and 8.6.

20.3 set aside the sum of eighty talents: That is, from the booty taken from the Persians. It was conventional to dedicate a tenth part of the booty to the gods; cf. Pritchett I 53-100.

20.3: According to Pausanias (9.4.1-2), the **sanctuary of Athena** the Warlike was financed from the spoils of the battle of *Marathon*. Clearly the local guides were inconsistent in their accounts. Pausanias also describes the acrolithic **statue**, which he says was the work of Phidias, and the **paintings** in the temple, which he says were the work of Polygnotus and Onasias. (He also mentions a portrait of Arimnestus, for whom see 11.5-8.)

20.3 to this very day retain their freshness: This is not a comment on their state of preservation (so translators since Amyot), but is a critical statement. Compare what Plutarch says about the works of art created during Pericles' administration at *Per.* 13.1-5, esp. 13.5: "As far as beauty is concerned, each one was immediately a classic (ἀρχαῖον) at the time of its creation; as far as freshness (ἀκμῇ) is concerned, each is to this very day (μέχρι νῦν) modern and newly wrought." See also *mor.* 504d, where the same word (ἀκμάζων) is used to refer, not to works of art, but to the poetry of Homer.

20.4: The **common hearth at Delphi** contained an eternal flame, for which see *Numa* 9.11, *mor.* 385c, Aesch. *Choe.* 1037. According to R. Parker (*Miasma* [1983] 23), the re-purification here described "was the most potent renewal a Greek community could undergo, since, lodged in the individual hearths of houses and the collective hearth of the city, fire was the symbolic middle point around which the life of the group revolved."

20.5: Euchidas is named only here and in the Suda s.v., where he is simply mentioned along with some others as having been a very fast runner. This anecdote is found, without Euchidas' name, in the scholia to Ael. Arist. *Panath.* 190 Lenz-Behr (III 199-200 Dindorf), where it probably derives from Plutarch.

20.5 one thousand stades: About 110 miles. It is by no means impossible to run this distance in one day: V. J. Matthews, "The *Hemerodromoi*: Ultra Long-Distance Running in Antiquity," *The Classical World*

68 (1974) 161-69, H. M. Lee, "Modern Ultra-long Distance Running and Philippides' Run from Athens to Sparta," *The Ancient World* 9 (1984) 107-13. In all likelihood Euchidas was a *hemerodromos*, or a man employed to carry messages over long distances on foot.

20.6 Thereupon he . . . expired: Compare the story (*mor*. 347c) of Eucles who, after fighting in the battle of *Marathon*, ran back to Athens to announce the victory, and thereupon expired (εὐθὺς ἐκπνεῦσαι).

20.6: For **Artemis Eucleia**, see A. Schachter, *Cults of Boiotia* I (1981) 102, 106. Burial within the sanctuary (cf. e.g. Eur. *Med*. 1378-79) indicates that Euchidas became a "hero."

21.1 general assembly: What Plutarch says here is not found in Herodotus, who says only (9.86.1) that the Greeks met and decided to march against Thebes. But according to Diodorus (11.29.1), before the battle began the Greeks swore that if they defeated the Persians they would celebrate the Eleutheria and hold contests at Plataea. Therefore this material appears to derive from Diodorus' fourth-century source, presumably Ephorus. (Most scholars doubt, however, that it is historical and goes back to the fifth century; supporters of its historicity include A. E. Raubitschek, *TAPA* 91 [1960] 178-83 and P. Siewert, *Der Eid von Plataiai* [1972] 89-90.) In any case, the role ascribed here to Aristeides is certainly a fabrication, whether Plutarch's or his source's. Cf. Thuc. 2.71.2-4 and 3.58.4-5, where Pausanias, not Aristeides, is prominently named.

21.1: For the **Eleutheria**, held **every fourth year** like the Olympic, Pythian and Panathenaic Games, see Pausanias 9.2.5-6, Strabo 9.2.31, Philostratus *Gymn*. 8, 24, L. Robert in *Entretiens sur l'antiquité classique* 14 (1968) 187-90.

21.2 sacrifices to the god: That is, to Zeus Eleutherius (19.8), the definitive treatment of whose cult will be found in the forthcoming third volume of A. Schachter's *Cults of Boiotia*.

21.3 They continue . . . as follows: Plutarch has undoubtedly witnessed the rite himself. His detailed description therefore possesses a special value. See W. Burkert, *Homo Necans* (1983) 56-58.

21.3 On the sixteenth of Maemacterion: The battle itself had taken place on the third of Boedromion (see 19.8), more than two months earlier. The discrepancy in the date is perhaps to be accounted for by assuming that a pre-existing (and quite ancient) ritual has been adapted to the celebration of the victory in battle. See D. Sansone, *Greek Athletics and the Genesis of Sport* (1988) 115-17.

21.3 one black bull: Black victims were traditionally offered to the dead; cf. Homer *Od*. 10.527.

21.3 wine . . . milk . . . olive oil: Cf. Hom. *Od*. 11.27-28 (honey, milk, wine, water), Aesch. *Pers*. 611-17 (milk, honey, water, wine, olive oil), Eur. *IT* 162-65 and *Or*. 115 (milk, wine, honey).

21.4 it is not proper for a slave: This appears to be a rationalization. Slaves were not permitted to participate in, for example, the Olympic Games either.

21.4 a purple tunic: This is either, like the sword and the trumpet, a military feature (cf. Xen. *Lac.* 11.3) or reflects the fact that this is the color appropriate to the dead and the chthonic powers (Aesch. *Eum.* 1028, Lysias 6.51, E. Wunderlich, *Die Bedeutung der roten Farbe im Kultus der Griechen und Römer* [1925] 46-51).

21.4 water pitcher: In addition to funerary associations (e.g. *Marc.* 30.5, *Phil.* 21.3; cf. Thomas Browne's *Hydriotaphia*), such vessels also have associations with voting and lotteries (Arist. *Ath. Pol.* 63.2, 64.4, Xen. *Hell.* 1.7.9), which perhaps accounts for the fact that this one is kept in **the records office**.

21.5 washes . . . anoints: For the significance of this ritual, see W. Burkert, *Structure and History in Greek Mythology and Religion* (1979) 41-43.

21.5 αἱμακουρίαν: This word occurs elsewhere only at Pind. *Ol.* 1.90, where the scholiast tells us that it is Boeotian. Other Boeotian words in Plutarch are κοίρανος (*Alex.* 71.7, nowhere else in Greek prose) and uncompounded ἀγορεύω (*Sol.* 12.6, 21.1, *mor.* 874b).

22.1 democratic form of government: Plutarch attributes Aristeides' "departure" from his earlier aristocratic allegiance (2.1) to a perceptive grasp of the Zeitgeist. All of this is naive fabrication based solely upon Aristotle's comment (*Ath. Pol.* 23.3; cf. also 41.2) that the "champions of the people" after the Persian Wars were Aristeides and Themistocles.

22.1 drafted a motion: This, too, appears to be fictional. According to Aristotle (*Ath. Pol.* 26.2), the archons were still chosen only from among the Pentacosiomedimnoi (cf. 1.2 above) and the Knights down to the year 457.

22.1: Given the dearth of genuine ancient evidence concerning the career of Aristeides, it is surprising to find no mention at this point of Aristeides' participation, attested by Thucydides and Aristotle, in the building of the walls of Athens. Plutarch has suppressed this story because he wishes to eliminate any hint of deviousness on the part of his hero (cf. on 10.9). Likewise Plutarch suppresses (if indeed he knew it) the punning comment by Aristeides' younger contemporary Callaeschrus, that Aristeides was "more foxy in character than in deme" (μᾶλλον τῷ τρόπῳ Ἀλωπέκηθεν ἢ τῷ δήμῳ, "Themistocles" *Epist.* 4.12).

22.2-4: This anecdote is found also at *Them.* 20.1-2 (where the target is Pagasae, the otherwise unattested winter quarters of the Greek fleet) and at Cic. *de off.* 3.11.49 and Val. Max. 6.5 ext. 2 (where the target is the dockyards of the *Spartan* fleet at Gytheium). In 456 or 455 the Spartan dockyards (τὸ νεώριον Thuc. 1.108.5, τὰ νεώρια D.S. 11.84.6; cf. τὸ νεώριον *Them.* 20.2) were in fact fired by the Athenians under Tolmides. Our anecdote appears to be a conflation of this incident with the account found in Diodorus (11.42) in which Themistocles has a secret plan that is advantageous to Athens and that he confides to Aristeides and Xanthippus. The conflation "is probably an invention of the rhetorical schools to illustrate the contrast between justice and expediency, two qualities of which Aristeides and Themistocles came to be personal types" (Perrin on *Them.* 20.1).

22.3 τὸ ναύσταθμον: It is impossible to determine whether this word is neuter or masculine in Plutarch (cf. *Lys.* 11.10, *Pomp.* 24.4, *Nic.* 16.2, etc.). Nor is it clear whether Plutarch intends it to mean "dockyard" (cf. τὸ νεώριον *Them.* 20.2) or "fleet" (cf. *classem* Cic. *de off.* 3.11.49 and Val. Max. 6.5 ext. 2).

22.3 advantageous . . . wicked: Compare *Tim.* 5.1, where Timoleon is praised by Plutarch for preferring justice to expediency. On occasion, however, Aristeides is willing to sacrifice the claims of justice to those of expediency (13.2, 25.2-3).

23.1 When, during his generalship, he was dispatched along with Cimon: Aristeides and Cimon, as two members of the Athenian board of ten generals, participated in the Greek expedition against Cyprus and Byzantium in 478-77. The account in Plutarch's Life of Cimon, which begins, "When, during his generalship, [Cimon] was dispatched" (6.1), is similar, but there the emphasis is on Cimon's role. For example, at *Cim.* 6.2 we learn that Cimon "treated with forbearance and compassion (πρᾴως . . . καὶ φιλανθρώπως ἐξομιλῶν) those who had grievances and he deprived [the Spartans], without their knowing it (ἔλαθεν . . . παρελόμενος), of the leadership of Greece, not by means of arms, but by his words and character."

23.1 forbearance and compassion: These two qualities, which are of considerable importance to Plutarch and are found together also at *Cim.* 6.2 and *Pyr.* 11.8, are studied in two articles by Hubert Martin, Jr., "The Concept of Prâotês in Plutarch's *Lives*," *GRBS* 3 (1960) 65-73 and "The Concept of *Philanthropia* in Plutarch's *Lives*," *AJP* 82 (1961) 164-75. The former (πρᾳότης) is to be found in both Aristeides (3.4, *Them.* 3.3) and Cato (51.10), but in Cato to a lesser degree (32.5, 59.4).

23.2: The Greeks' abandonment of the Spartans and adoption of the Athenians as their leaders is attributed to the justice of Aristeides and the excesses of Pausanias also at Arist. *Ath. Pol.* 23.4, Nepos *Arist.* 2.2-3 and D.S. 11.46.4-5. Thucydides (1.95, 1.130.2) refers to Pausanias' excesses, but does not mention Aristeides.

23.3 show him the error of his ways: Cf. on 5.2. This incident is no doubt a fabrication based upon the general accounts of Pausanias' inaccessibility (Thuc. 1.130.2, Nepos *Paus.* 3.3).

23.4 Chios, Samos and Lesbos: According to Aristotle, these three islands were the only members of their empire that the Athenians did not treat "despotically" (*Ath. Pol.* 24.2). It may, therefore, in fact be the case that they "played a prominent role in the transfer of leadership" from Sparta to Athens (T. J. Quinn, *Athens and Samos, Lesbos and Chios: 478-404 B.C.* [1981] 9).

23.4 μετατάξασθαι πρὸς τοὺς Ἀθηναίους: This phrase is Plutarch's adaptation of Thuc. 1.95.4 τοὺς ξυμμάχους . . . παρ' Ἀθηναίους μετατάξασθαι (Plutarch prefers πρός: *Them* 9.2, *mor.* 396e).

23.5 Ouliades and Antagoras: These men are not otherwise attested (neither is this incident), but the former name is unusual and has Samian associations (G. Shipley, *A History of Samos, 800-188 BC* [1987]

110), so there is likely to be some historical basis to this account.

23.7: This section is an expansion of Thucydides' statement at 1.95.7 that "the Spartans no longer sent out any commanders, fearing that those who left the country might be corrupted, as they saw had been the case with Pausanias." Other sources, however, indicate that the Spartans were unwilling (Arist. *Ath. Pol.* 23.2) to relinquish the leadership and were resentful (D.S. 1.50.1) of the Athenians. For Plutarch's attitude toward Sparta, see F. Ollier, *Le mirage spartiate* II (1943) 187-215.

24.2 master of such vast resources: A reminiscence of Demosth. 23. 209, where we read that, despite his position of authority, Aristeides did not enrich himself by as much as a single drachma, but was in fact buried at public expense (cf. on 27.1 below). This had become a commonplace by Plutarch's time; cf. Philostr. *VA* 6.21.

24.2 ἁρμοδίως: Plutarch elsewhere (*mor.* 264a, 285b, 793a) uses the adjective ἁρμόδιος, but never the adjective ἁρμόνιος or the adverb derived from it. For the corruption in the manuscript S (see apparatus), see *Sol.* 2.3.

24.3 Era of Cronus: The "Golden Age" of Greek legend, for which see H. C. Baldry, "Who Invented the Golden Age?" *Classical Quarterly* 2 (1952) 83-92. At *Cim.* 10.7 Plutarch speaks of the generosity of Cimon as recalling the Era of Cronus.

24.4 460 talents: The same figure in Thucydides (1.96.2) and Nepos (*Arist.* 3.1). Diodorus (11.47.1) gives the figure as 560 (but cf. 12.40.2, where the figure for the year 431 BC is given as 460 talents). See M. Chambers, "Four Hundred Sixty Talents," *Classical Philology* 53 (1958) 26-32 and, in general, B. D. Meritt et al., *The Athenian Tribute Lists* I-IV (1939-53).

24.4 Thucydides says . . . six hundred talents: Thuc. 2.13.3. The **beginning of the war** is 431 BC (see previous note).

24.5 1,300 talents: According to the orators Aeschines (2.175) and Andocides (3.9), the tribute at or shortly after the Peace of Nicias (421 BC) amounted to "more than 1,200 talents per annum." The latter (And. 4. 11) also castigates Alcibiades for making the tribute nearly double what it had been in the time of Aristeides.

24.5 down the path . . . statues and temples: What is here held against the popular leaders is elsewhere, by a characteristic act of Plutarchean sleight of hand, credited to the genius of Pericles (*Per.* 9.2-3, 12, *Fab.* 30.7). For the theoric fund (**subsidies of festival performances**), see A. Pickard-Cambridge, *The Dramatic Festivals of Athens* (1968) 266-68, Rhodes 514-16.

24.6: This anecdote does not occur elsewhere. Its ultimate source is likely to be Old Comedy (see next note), to which the word **bag** (perhaps with an obscene connotation) is appropriate.

24.7 the ability to restrain his fingers: This may be no more than a paraphrase of the line from Eupolis' *Demes* quoted in 4.3. The anecdote is reminiscent of that told at *Per.* 8.8 (perhaps from Ion of Chios; cf. Athenaeus 603e-4d) about Pericles and Sophocles.

25.1 oath of allegiance: See Arist. *Ath. Pol.* 23.5, H. Jacobson, "The

Oath of the Delian League," *Philologus* 119 (1975) 256-58. The **pieces of metal** symbolized the fate of those who would break the oath, against whom **the curses** were directed. For the foundation of the Delian League and its history, see R. Meiggs, *The Athenian Empire* (1972) and, most recently, M. F. McGregor, *The Athenians and their Empire* (1987).

25.1 he would tell the Athenians: It is not known to what incident this refers or what historical basis, if any, it has. For the expression τὴν ἐπιορκίαν τρέψαντας εἰς αὐτὸν, compare Aristophanes *Lys*. 914-15.

25.2 Theophrastus: Fr. 136 Wimmer. Compare 13.2 above, where Aristeides sacrifices justice to expediency in the interests of the state.

25.3: The manuscripts are divided between **they say** and "he (i.e. Theophrastus) says." It is impossible to determine which is correct. The treasury of the league was in fact moved **from Delos to Athens** in 454 BC, after the death of Aristeides. What we may see here is a reference to a fictional debate between "Aristeides" and "Pericles," both of whom were characters in Eupolis' *Demes* (see on 4.3 and 24.7).

25.4 the following account: This is attributed below (25.9) to **Aeschines, the follower of Socrates**, presumably coming from his dialogue entitled *Callias*. See H. Dittmar, *Aischines von Sphettos* (1912) 186-210.

25.4: Callias the Torchbearer was mentioned earlier (5.7-8), and the implications of these two anecdotes for the character of Aristeides are spelled out below (chapter 58). The relationship between the fabulously wealthy Callias and the "poor" Aristeides the Just was a congenial subject for moralizing storytellers.

25.9 Plato: At *Gorg*. 519a Socrates says that men like Themistocles, Cimon and Pericles "unrestrainedly and unjustly filled the city with harbors, dockyards, fortifications, revenues and similar nonsense," and he later (526b) claims that only Aristeides was truly praiseworthy.

25.10 Themistocles was publicly prosecuted: See J. F. Barrett, "The Downfall of Themistocles," *GRBS* 18 (1977) 291-305. It appears from Ephorus, the source of D.S. 11.54-55, that there may have been two attempts to prosecute Themistocles for treason. This would account for the fact that **Alcmaeon** is named here (and at *mor*. 805c), whereas Leobotes, son of Alcmaeon, is named as the prosecutor at *Them*. 23.1 and *mor*. 605e.

25.10 τὴν αὐτὴν λαβὴν παρέσχεν: Cf. 42.4, *Sulla* 10.3 τὴν αὐτὴν λαβὴν παρασχών. The image is drawn from the realm of wrestling: *Ages*. 38.4, *Alc*. 2.3, *Fab*. 5.4.

26.1 Craterus the Macedonian: *FGrH* 342 F 12. For Craterus, see on 4. 4, 10.4 and 10.10.

26.2 informers: For these, see *Sol*. 24.1-2 and J. O. Lofberg, *Sycophancy in Athens* (1917). Calabi Limentani well points out that there was a scene (fr. 99 K-A) between Aristeides and a sycophant in Eupolis' *Demes* (see on 4.3-4, 24.7, 25.3).

26.3 collecting the tribute: Many editors follow Westermann in changing the manuscript reading (ἔπραττε) so that Plutarch says, "assigning (ἔταττε) the tribute," since Aristeides is elsewhere (Dem. 23.209, Aeschin. 2.23, 3.258, Ael. *VH* 11.9, Philostr. *VA* 6.21) "the man who assigned the tribute."

26.3 not afford to pay: Another indication of Aristeides' "poverty." For, while **the fine of fifty minas** is much greater than the one mina that Socrates could afford (see on 1.9), it is much less than the 50-talent fine (*Cim.* 4.4) imposed on Miltiades or the 15- or 50-talent fine (*Per.* 35.4) imposed on Pericles. (1 talent = 60 minas.)

26.5: Cf. *Nic.* 6.1, where Plutarch says that the Athenians' suspicion of their leaders "was evident from the fine imposed on Pericles, from the ostracism of Damon, from the distrust that the masses felt toward Antiphon of Rhamnus and especially from the fate of Paches, the conqueror of Lesbos, who snatched up a sword while the accounts of his command were being questioned and committed suicide right in the courtroom."

26.5 nowhere make mention: A good illustration of the lengths Plutarch will go to in order to protect the good name of Aristeides. Even if this anecdote were true, it would not reflect discredit upon Plutarch's hero, but would merely illustrate, like the other instances given, the Athenians' maltreatment of their famous men. But not satisfied with that, Plutarch must go on to assert, using an argumentum ex silentio, that the anecdote is not true. On top of that, he expects us to have forgotten the conviction that he told us about in 4.4-7.

27.1: The **tomb of Aristeides** (cf. 1.2) serves as an additional argument against Craterus' assertion that Aristeides died in exile.

27.1 by the city: Burial at public expense is recorded for Aristeides by Demosthenes (23.209).

27.1 μηδ' ἐντάφια καταλιπόντι: Cf. Plut. fr. 140 Sandbach οὐδ' ἐντάφια καταλιπών, Ael. *VH* 11.9 οὐδὲ ἐντάφια ἑαυτῷ κατέλιπεν ἱκανά, Nepos *Arist.* 3.3 *in tanta paupertate decessit ut qui efferretur vix reliquerit.* It is, however, impossible to believe that Aristeides' estate was smaller than the ten (Dem. 40.52) or even three (Lys. 31.21) minas that sufficed for burial costs.

27.2 from the town hall: Rather than from the house of their father or legal guardian; in other words, at public expense. Cf. Aeschin. 3. 258, Nepos *Arist.* 3.3, Frontin. *Strat.* 4.3.5.

27.2: Demosthenes (20.115) relates that **Aristeides' son Lysimachus** received "100 acres of cultivated land in Euboea and 100 of arable, as well as 100 minas in silver and four drachmas per day, on a proposal of Alcibiades." Davies (51-52) regards this decree as a fabrication.

27.3 Callisthenes: *FGrH* 124 F 48.

27.3 victors in the Olympic Games: According to an Athenian inscription from the 5th century BC, "Those citizens who have won the athletic competitions at Olympia . . . shall have a free meal every day for the rest of their lives in the *prytaneion* and other honors as well" (IG I^2 77.11; translation from S. G. Miller, *Arete* [1979] 94). The other honors included (*Sol.* 23.3) a grant of 500 drachmas (= 5 minas). But

Calabi Limentani well points out that it is unlikely that women were allowed to dine alongside men.

27.3: For **Demetrius of Phalerum** see on 1.2-9, 5.9. Plutarch is probably referring here (= fr. 96 Wehrli), as in 1.2 and 27.4, to the work on Socrates. Demetrius also wrote a work entitled "Aristeides."

27.3: Hieronymus of Rhodes (fr. 43 Wehrli) and **Aristoxenus** (fr. 58 Wehrli) were, like Demetrius, associated with the school founded by **Aristotle.** Apparently something in Aristotle's (unfortunately lost) **On Nobility** (fr. 93 Rose) provoked a longstanding dispute among his followers. See Athenaeus 555d-56b, D.L. 2.26. For a detailed attempt to make sense of this dispute, see L. Woodbury, "Socrates and the Daughter of Aristides," *Phoenix* 27 (1973) 7-25 and, for a different and less satisfying view, P. J. Bicknell, "Sokrates' Mistress Xanthippe," *Apeiron* 8 (1974) 1-5.

27.4: For **Panaetius,** see on 1.6. There he was cited to refute Demetrius' assertion that Aristeides was affluent; here (= fr. 132 van Straaten) he refutes Demetrius and the others who wrote about Socrates' two wives.

27.4 descendant: The Greek word actually means "daughter's son," which is impossible on chronological grounds. Either, therefore, the word can in fact bear this less restricted meaning or Plutarch has misrepresented Demetrius.

27.4 tablet that interpreted dreams: Cf. Alciphron *Ep.* 3.23.1, "I want to go to one of those who set out their tablets beside the Iaccheium and who claim that they can interpret dreams, and I want to pay my two drachmas . . ." (The fee seems to have been one sixth that amount in the fifth century BC; cf. Aristoph. *Wasps* 52-53.)

27.5 in charge of the government: Demetrius governed Athens in Cassander's name from 317 to 307 BC.

27.6: Aristogeiton, with Harmodius, assassinated the Athenian tyrant Hipparchus in 514 BC. He was celebrated as a liberator, becoming the subject of popular songs and having his statue erected in the marketplace of Athens.

27.7 nobility and compassion: For the latter, see on 23.1. For the combination, cf. *Cic.* 52.3, *Demetr.* 50.1, *mor.* 88b, 1038e. For the combination **admired and stands as a model,** cf. 2.1, *Luc.* 21.3, *Mar.* 35.1, *Per.* 2.2, *mor.* 40b, 84b, 85a, 471a, 476c. Plutarch is very fond of using pairs of synonyms or near-synonyms. These two pairs close this Life with a rhetorical flourish, and emphasize the moral qualities and exemplary status of Athens (cf. also 22.4, 32.3) and, by extension, of Aristeides. (Note that the last word in the Greek is a form of the word **justice,** the especial virtue of Aristeides.) Plutarch views his mission in writing biographies as one of setting before his reader paradigms of virtue.

28.1: As often, the second Life of a pair begins with the connective word δὲ (not translated here): *Brut.*, *Cat. min.*, *Cic.*, *Crass.*, *Eum.*, *Fab.*, *Flam.*, *Gracch.*, *Luc.*, *Marc.*, *Numa*, *Pomp.*, *Publ.*, *Sulla.* The opening sentence is a close paraphrase of Nepos *Cat.* 1.1 *M. Cato, ortus municipio Tusculo, adulescentulus priusquam honoribus operam daret versa-*

tus est in Sabinis, quod ibi heredium a patre relictum habebat. For the importance of Nepos as a source for Plutarch, see J. Geiger, "Nepos and Plutarch: From Latin to Greek Political Biography," *Illinois Classical Studies* 13 (1988).

28.3: Despite his study of proper names (see on 6.2), Plutarch is here mistaken. Cato's **third name** (cognomen) never changed; even according to Plutarch (28.1) the name of his **paternal great-grandfather** was "Cato." **Priscus** (= "elder") was, indeed, a Roman cognomen, but is not attested in Cato's family, the gens Porcia. Perhaps Plutarch saw somewhere a reference to "Cato priscus" (cf. Hor. *Carm.* 3.21. 11), a reference intended to differentiate our Cato from the younger Cato.

28.4 Cato's quite snappish . . . : This epigram is not known from any other source. Its author seems to suggest that Cato's appearance and character were those of an animal. (Cf. Livy 38.54.1, where it is said that Cato was in the habit of "barking at" (*adlatrare*) Scipio because of his eminence.) According to the physiognomonical writers, **grey eyes** are indicative of a savage character, "since most wild animals are grey-eyed;" see R. Foerster (ed.), *Scriptores Physiognomonici Graeci et Latini* I (1893) 390. Plutarch's interest in his heroes' personal appearance is examined by Wardman (140-44).

28.5 solid: Cf. 51.1 and Livy 39.40.11 *in patientia laboris periculique ferrei prope corporis animique.*

28.5 from the start: Cf. fr. 128 Malcovati, from Cato's speech On his own Virtues: *a principio in parsimonia atque in duritia atque industria omnem adulescentiam meam abstinui agro colendo.*

28.5: For speech as an **instrument**, cf. 56.5, *Ant.* 27.4, *Cic.* 4.4, *Fab.* 1.7, *Per.* 8.1, *Phoc.* 3.9, *mor.* 33f, 802b. On this passage in general, see R. Till, *Hermes* 81 (1953) 445-46.

28.7 mercenary tendencies . . . reputation: Aristeides displayed the same virtue (3.4).

28.8 seventeen years old: Cf. Nepos *Cat.* 1.2 *primum stipendium meruit annorum decem septemque.* (Cato was born in 234 BC.) The source for this information is Cato's speech On the Achaeans, in which he said (fr. 187 Malcovati) *cumque Hannibal terram Italiam laceraret atque vexaret.*

28.8 In battle . . . aggressive hand: Cf. Livy 39.40.6 *in bello manu fortissimus.*

28.8 instructing: See on 5.2. This saying of Cato's is found also at *Cor.* 8.3 and *mor.* 199b.

28.9 never even became annoyed or found fault: Cf. 48.3. For the expression, compare *mor.* 37e.

28.10 vinegar-water: This was the standard drink (Lat. *posca*) of the common Roman soldier, offered to Jesus on the cross (Luke 23.36).

29.1: Manius Curius Dentatus, consul in 290, 275 and 274, celebrated a triumph over the Sabines and one (in 275) over the Samnites and Pyrrhus. For the proximity of Cato's farm to that of Curius, cf. Cic. *de Sen.* 16.55 *cuius quidem ego* (Cato is speaking) *villam contemplans (abest*

enim non longe a me) admirari satis non possum vel hominis ipsius continentiam vel temporum disciplinam; Astin 1-2. Cato lauds Curius again at 35.14 below; cf. 55.3, 58.4.

29.1 driving Pyrrhus from Italy: Cf. *Pyr.* 25.2-9.

29.1 after three triumphs: Cf. Cic. *de Sen.* 16.55 *in hac vita M'. Curius, cum de Samnitibus, de Sabinis, de Pyrrho triumphavisset, consumpsit extremum tempus aetatis.*

29.2: Ziegler inserted καὶ before **ἐνταῦθα** unnecessarily; for the asyndeton, compare 20.2, *mor.* 149c, 968f.

29.2 engaged in boiling turnips: Not only are turnips inappropriate fare for so great a man, but Curius was cooking them himself (αὐτόν; cf. 58.5). This anecdote occurs frequently elsewhere: *mor.* 194e-f, Cic. *de Sen.* 16.56, *Rep.* 3.28.40 (cf. *Parad. Stoic.* 48), Val. Max. 4.3.5, Pliny *NH* 19.87, Frontin. 4.3.2, Florus 1.13.22, Ampel. 18.8, Athen. 419a, *DVI* 33. 7, Schol. Bob. 13.12-16 Hildebrandt. Plutarch's source is neither Cicero nor Valerius (who do not mention turnips) nor Frontinus (who names Fabricius, not Curius). F. Münzer (*Beiträge zur Quellenkritik der Naturgeschichte des Plinius* [1897] 194 n. 1) suggested Calpurnius Piso, while F. Leo (*Die griechisch-römische Biographie* [1901] 167) thought of Megacles, whom Athenaeus cites as his source. Leo further thought that the anecdote occurred in Livy, on the grounds that Pliny refers to *annales nostri.* But elsewhere (*NH* 8.11) Pliny says *imperatorum nomina annalibus detraxerit* (sc. *Cato*), which is certainly a reference to Cato's *Origines* (= Bk. 4, fr. 9 Jordan; cf. Nepos *Cat.* 3.4 *duces non nominavit*) and the Perioche of Livy 49 says that Cato's speech against Servius Galba (= Bk. 7, frr. 1-3 Jordan) was included by Cato *in annalibus ipsius.* F. Padberg (*Cicero und Cato Censorius* [1933] 57) suggested that this anecdote occurred in the *Origines*, and this is surely where Plutarch found it. If Cato did not name names in his *Origines*—Perhaps here he simply referred to "the man who triumphed over the Samnites"?—that would account for the confusion in Frontinus (and perhaps in Gellius 1.14). For the association of Curius and Fabricius cf. 55.3, 58.4 below and Cic. *de Amic.* 5.18, 8.28, *de Sen.* 6.15, 13.43, *Sest.* 68. 143, *Piso.* 24.58, Hor. *Carm.* 1.12.40-41, Sen. *Ep.* 120.19, Colum. *praef.* 14, Lucan 10.151, Mart. 7.58.7, 9.28.4, 11.16.6, Apul. *Ap.* 10, 18, as well as the juxtaposition of anecdotes about the two in the passages referred to above from *mor.*, Valerius, Florus and Ampelius.

29.2 sum of money: Curius' immunity from bribery was celebrated in Ennius' memorable line (*Ann.* 456 Skutsch) *quem nemo ferro potuit superare nec auro.*

29.2 ἀπεπέμψατο: For the middle (which deserves consideration as the lectio difficilior), cf. Hdt. 1.33, Pl. *Epist.* 2.312a, Cassius Dio 1.291.11 Boissevain (= Zonar. 9.21.1), 59.23.5.

29.3: For περικόπτω, a metaphor from pruning olive trees (Theophr. *HP* 4.16.1, *Tab. Heracl.* 1.173), cf. *Agis* 7.6, *Per.* 21.1. At *mor.* 752f it is rather a metaphor from clipping the wings of a bird. During his censorship, Cato would attempt to cut back the luxurious living of others; cf. 45.2 περικοπῇ τῆς πολυτελείας.

29.3: Fabius recovered **Tarentum** from Hannibal in 209, when Cat was 25 years old. Cf. *Fab.* 21-22; J. F. Lazenby, *Hannibal's War* (1978 175-76. Cato's service with Fabius at Tarentum was probably invente by Cicero (*de Sen.* 4.10, 12.39) to motivate the encounter with Near chus; F. Münzer, *Hermes* 40 (1905) 53, 64-65.

29.3: Nearchus the **Pythagorean** is attested only here and in Plu tarch's source, Cic. *de Sen.* 12.41, where the encounter is likely to b Cicero's invention.

29.4 Plato: *Tim.* 69d; cf. Cic. *de Sen.* 13.44 *Plato escam malorum appella voluptatem.* Plutarch alludes to this passage also at *mor.* 13a, 554f an 1107a.

29.5-6: Plutarch perceptively notes the discrepancy between the gen eral view (Cic. *Acad.* 2.2.5, *Rep.* 5.1.2 Ziegler, *de Sen.* 8.26, Nepos *Cat.* 3.2, Val. Max. 8.7.1, Quint. 12.11.23) that Cato read Greek extensively only i his old age and the observation (based upon his own reading?) tha Greek influence is to be found throughout his writings. For the ques tion of Cato's indebtedness to Greek literature, see Astin 148-49, 157-81.

29.5: For βραχέα = ὀλίγα cf. 34.3, *Lys.* 23.5, *Per.* 33.6, *Pomp.* 75.4, *Tim.* 11.5, *mor.* 14a, 983a.

29.6 sayings and aphorisms: Cf. Phot. *Bibl.* 495a12 ἀποφθέγματα κα γνωμολογίαι (of Demosthenes). Cato is credited with compiling a collec tion of apophthegmata (Cic. *de Off.* 1.104; cf. *de Or.* 2.271, Astin 186-88) which is perhaps the source of much of chapters 35-36 below, but th word γνωμολογίαις (for which cf. *Fab.* 1.8, *mor.* 712b) shows that Plu tarch is also referring to aphorisms contained in other writings. A 35.4-5 and 51.7-8 Plutarch identifies two of the apophthegmata trans lated from the Greek.

30.1 Valerius Flaccus: Cf. Nepos *Cat.* 1.1 *hortatu L. Valerii Flacci . . Romam demigravit in foroque esse coepit.* Nepos tells us that his (oral source for this information was M. Perperna, consul in 92 BC.

30.2 from his servants: That is, Valerius' own servants, for Cato' were not so communicative (48.1).

30.2 stripped: The Greek can mean either "naked" or "lightly clad." At any rate, this is the proper attire for agricultural work according t ancient authorities; see M. L. West (ed.), *Hesiod. Works and Days* (1978 257-58.

30.3 military tribuneship . . . quaestor: Nepos (*Cat.* 1.2-3) give the dates as 214 and 204 BC, respectively.

30.4 consulship . . . censorship: In 195 and 184 BC.

30.4 Fabius Maximus: Cf. Cicero *de Sen.* 4.10 *ego* (Cato is speaking) *Q. Maximum . . . senem adulescens ita dilexi ut aequalem.*

30.5 Fabius was thought to be jealous: Fabius' apparent jealous of Scipio is referred to also in Plutarch's Life of Fabius (25.2-3).

30.5 outspoken in his criticism: This account is not recorded else where. But there are such striking similarities between it and the ac count of the affair of Pleminius (Livy 29.8-22 and elsewhere), i which Cato is not named and which Plutarch does not mention, that i appears to be a fictitious doublet of that well-attested affair; Astin 13

15.

30.6 sailing . . . at full speed: The same metaphor at *mor.* 446b, Philo *Mut.* 215, *Legat.* 177, Lucian *J. Trag.* 50.

30.6 Cato left Sicily: According to Livy (29.25.10), Cato was with the fleet when it sailed for Africa. Either, therefore, Cato returned to Sicily and resumed his duties as quaestor after denouncing his commander, or Plutarch's account is inaccurate.

30.6 palaestras and theaters: Cf. Livy 29.19.12 *cum pallio crepidisque inambulare in gymnasio, libellis eum palaestraeque operam dare.* Athletics and literature are conspicuous features of Greek culture, Scipio's enthusiasm for which was not entirely shared by Cato.

30.7: The impressive display that Scipio mounted to maintain his command is recounted in greater detail at Livy 29.22.1-6.

31.1 Demosthenes: Cf. Appian *Iber.* 39.160 = Suda s.v. Κάτων, "the Romans, when they learned that the finest orator among the Greeks had been Demosthenes, used to call him 'Demosthenes' for his eloquence." Likewise Diodorus (34/35.33.3) refers to "Marcus Cato, nicknamed Demosthenes."

31.3 γέροντα πολὺν: There seems to be no parallel to this expression. Manuscript Z, a copy of S, reads πολιὸν. Sintenis proposed παλαιὸν, comparing *mor.* 795c and Paus. 8.11.2.

31.3 like some champion athlete: Plutarch is comparing Cato to a wrestler, as is clear from 56.4. Comparison with an athlete is frequent in Plutarch: *Fab.* 5.4, 19.3, 23.2, *Per.* 4.2, 28.5, *Phil.* 18.3, *Sulla* 29.1.

31.4 He claims: This statement appears to come from Cato's speech On his own Expenditures (frr. 173-75 Malcovati). Some, but not all, of what follows may derive from the same source.

31.4 one hundred drachmas: This was the cost (= 100 denarii) of an ordinary soldier's outfit; see E. Badian, *Publicans and Sinners* (1972) 21-22. During his censorship, Cato imposed a fine on all garments worth more than 1,500 drachmas (see 45.2).

31.4 rowers: Two manuscripts read "workmen," which is inappropriate to the context. (The corruption recurs in 58.4.) In any case, three Latin authors who preserve this saying confirm that "rowers" is correct: Pliny *NH* 14.91, Val. Max. 4.3.11, Frontin. 4.3.1. On his farm, Cato drank the same wine as his servants (30.2).

31.4 thirty asses: The as was the smallest Roman coin (cf. 31.6). To have done without the **meat or fish** would have meant to be content merely with bread.

31.5 fancy Babylonian rug: From whom might Cato have inherited such an object? In fact, this saying probably belongs rather to Cato the Younger, who was brought up in the affluent family of the Livii Drusi. For Pliny, when he tells us (*NH* 8.196) that Babylon was especially famous for such tapestries, also mentions the fact that Metellus Scipio reproached Cato the Younger with the sale of one of them for 800,000 sesterces.

31.5 plastered walls: Cf. Gellius 13.24.1 *M. Cato . . . villas suas inexcultas et rudes ne tectorio quidem praelitas fuisse dicit ad annum usque* *aetatis suae septuagesimum* (there follows a direct quotation, = fr. 174 Malcovati). Pinnius, for example, the dedicatee of Book 3 of Varro's *de Re Rustica* (3.1.10), had a villa with impressive plastered walls. Such plaster-work made possible the remarkable wall paintings that can be seen in the villas at Pompeii.

31.5 sell off even these: In *de Agr.* 2.7 Cato says that the paterfamilias should sell slaves when they are old or sick and that, in general, he should be eager to sell rather than to buy. Astin (349-50) takes a more kindly view of this advice than does Plutarch (32).

31.6 even an as: Cf. 58.5 and Seneca *Epist.* 94.27, where Cato is quoted as saying *quod non opus est asse carum est.*

32.2 humane behavior . . . justice: According to the Stoic philosopher Chrysippus, on the contrary, humane behavior is a species of justice (fr. 264 von Arnim). For Plutarch's complex relationship with Stoic philosophy, see D. Babut, *Plutarque et le stoïcisme* (1969). At any rate, Plutarch's purpose here is to suggest subtly the inferiority of Cato to Aristeides. For justice is quite irrelevant to the argument here, but we are reminded that Aristeides is the paragon of justice, and we recall the passage in the corresponding position in his Life (chapter 6) in which justice is lauded as divine.

32.2 even to the creatures that are deprived of reason: One of the most attractive features of Plutarch's personality is his sympathetic view of animals. See Barrow 112-17.

32.3 The story goes: Plutarch's source (also the source of Pliny *NH* 8. 175 and Aelian *NA* 6.49) is Aristotle *HA* 6.24, where we are told that this mule lived to the age of eighty. Both here and at *mor.* 970a-b Plutarch has embellished slightly in order to enhance the humaneness of the Athenians.

32.4: Cimon was the father of the Athenian general Miltiades. Herodotus (6.103.2-3) mentions his three victories in the four-horse chariot race and preserves the information that the horses were buried near Cimon's tomb. Aelian (*VH* 9.32) adds the information that bronze statues of these horses were made and that they stood in Athens.

32.4: Xanthippus was the father of Pericles. The anecdote is given at greater length at *Them.* 10.10, where we are told that the dog died immediately after its exertions, and at Aelian *NA* 12.35, where Aristotle and Philochorus are named as sources. Aelian speaks of more than one dog, which is inconsistent with the toponym (not given by Aelian), literally "grave of the dog."

32.5 forbearing: See on 23.1.

32.6 After all: The point seems to be that by selling a useless slave one is wronging two people, the slave and the purchaser, rather than, as Blass explains, that the uselessness of the slave is emphasized to account for the small price that one receives.

32.7 Cato . . . says: Again, Plutarch quotes from one of Cato's lost speeches, probably the one entitled On his Consulship (frr. 21-55 Malcovati).

32.7 magnanimity or . . . parsimony: While formally Plutarch leaves it to his reader to judge for himself, there can be little doubt of his own disapproval. From 48.8 and 58.5 it is clear that Plutarch regards Cato's obsession with economy as excessive. This obsession is aptly described by the term parsimony (μικρολογία, lit. "keeping an account of trifles") and is exemplified in Theophrastus' portrait of the parsimonious man (*Char.* 10). The contrast with magnanimity (μεγαλοψυχία, lit. "having a lofty spirit"), which is not a natural contrast and is unparalleled in Plutarch's writings, is deliberate and tendentious. For, while Cato's treatment of his slaves could perhaps be ascribed to worthy motives (so 32.1), it could not be characterized as magnanimity. Plutarch later (58.1-2) makes it clear that a concern with trifles is incompatible with magnanimity.

33.1: The **Attic bushel** = approximately 40 liters. According to Polybius (6.39.13), the usual ration for a Roman infantryman was two thirds of an Attic bushel of wheat per month, for a cavalryman 2 bushels per month. Each cavalryman also received 7 bushels of barley per month for his horse.

33.2: Cato went to **Sardinia** as praetor in 198 BC, according to Livy 32.8.5. Of Cato as governor Livy says (32.27.3-4), "he was honest and upright, but in his curtailment of usury he was considered a bit too severe; the usurers were expelled from the island and the expenditures that the allies were ordinarily expected to undertake for the upkeep of the praetors were reduced or eliminated."

33.3: "No Roman praetor will have walked about Sardinia without a military escort, without lictors, and without at least a few personal servants of his own" (Astin 21). The point, as Astin makes clear, is that Cato did not cause the *state* to incur any additional expenditure beyond that for the single servant.

33.4 congenial and unpretentious: Cf. *Phil.* 2.1-3, where Plutarch refers to Philopoemen's congeniality and unpretentiousness to account for his hostess' mistaking him for an attendant.

34.1: In **Plato**'s *Symposium* (215a-e), Alcibiades compares Socrates to a figurine representing an ugly satyr that opens up to reveal a lovely image of a god. But Plutarch is also thinking of the later passage (221d-22a) in which Alcibiades says that **Socrates' speech** is cloaked in the hide of an aggressive satyr but that, underneath the surface that consists of apparently ridiculous discourse on everyday items, there is a core of weighty and serious substance.

34.2: Lysias was an Attic orator with a smooth and direct style very different from the rugged terseness of Cato. Plutarch is here criticizing Cicero, who compares Cato with Lysias at *Brut.* 16.63-64 (but who later, at 85.293-94, undermines the comparison). Despite his disclaimer at *Demosth.* 2.2-4 that he did not begin the study of Latin literature until late in life and that he is not competent to evaluate the products of Roman oratory, it is clear that Plutarch's knowledge of Cicero and Cato rests upon first-hand familiarity with at least some of their works. On the question of Plutarch's Latin sources, see Jones 81-87.

34.3 some people believe: For example, Polemo of Laodicea, a younger contemporary of Plutarch's, wrote an influential physiognomonical treatise (in which, incidentally, Polemo gave a scurrilous description of Plutarch's good friend Favorinus of Arelate). At *Alex.* 1.2-3 Plutarch compares the biographer to the painter: just as the latter pays particular attention to the facial features in which character is reflected, so the former often concerns himself with sayings and jests. (But Plutarch does not disregard his subject's appearance entirely; see on 28.4.)

35.2: This seems to be Plutarch's own neat formulation (cf. also *mor.* 198d, 668b) of Cato's saying, which is recorded elsewhere (Polyb. 31.25. 5, D.S. 31.24, 37.3.6, Athen. 274f-75a) as taking something like the following form: "One can see how low we have sunk when a jar of smoked fish sells for more than an ox" (or, "for more than 300 drachmas"). Cato again expressed a similar sentiment in his *Carmen de Moribus* (fr. 2 Jordan; cf. Pliny *NH* 9.67) when, in praising the good old days, he said, "In those days horses cost more than cooks."

35.3 men whose advice: Cato (or Plutarch?) is here influenced by Isocrates, who says (8.52) of the Athenians, "We follow the advice of such men as no one could fail to despise, and we appoint those very men as masters of all the affairs of state to whom no one would entrust any of his private affairs."

35.4 "All men . . . us.": For the possible background to this saying (which appears also at *mor.* 198d), see Livy 34.1-4 and P. Desideri, "Catone e le donne," *Opus* 3 (1984) 63-74.

35.4 Themistocles': Cf. *Them.* 18.7, *mor.* 1c, 185d. See on 29.6.

35.5 φειδέσθω τῆς ἐξουσίας: Cf. *mor.* 198f φείδεσθαι δὲ τῆς ἐξουσίας παρεκάλει (sc. Cato!) τοὺς δυναμένους. This passage is from the work entitled "Sayings of Kings and Generals," which represents Plutarch's own preliminary collection of sayings to be used as raw materials in his writing and which has here subtly influenced his choice of expression.

35.6: Later, during the period of the Roman Empire, the central government regulated the price of **purple fabric** by law. In Cato's day (when, in any case, the centers of production of purple dye lay outside the jurisdiction of Rome) Roman demand for the stuff determined its price on the open market. See in general M. Reinhold, *History of Purple as a Status Symbol in Antiquity* (1970).

35.8-9: One of Cato's speeches (frr. 185-86 Malcovati) argued in favor of the proposition that no one be elected consul more than once. These two sayings are perhaps to be connected with that speech; Astin 120.

35.8 lictors: These were attendants who walked before certain Roman magistrates (the number of lictors attending each magistrate depending upon the importance of his office) carrying the *fasces*, bundles of rods that were the traditional symbols of Roman authority.

35.10 cursed, not blessed: It is normally parents' fondest wish to be survived by their offspring; R. Lattimore, *Themes in Greek and Latin Epitaphs* (1942) 187-91.

35.12: Eumenes II, King of Pergamum, visited Rome in 189 and again in 172 BC, when he warned of the threat posed by the Macedonian

King Perseus. For the latter visit, which is presumably the one referred to here, see E. V. Hansen, *The Attalids of Pergamon*[2] (1971) 109-10. Cato's coldness toward Eumenes may be a reflection of his attachment to the king's adversaries, the Rhodians, whom Cato defended in a speech delivered in 167 BC (frr. 163-71 Malcovati).

35.13 ὁ βασιλεὺς: Most editors follow Koraes in deleting these words as a gloss, but this sort of apposition is not uncommon. Sintenis well compares Athen. 606d φιλανθρωπότατον δέ ἐστι καὶ συνετώτατον τὸ ζῷον ὁ δελφίς. For the thought, cf. Hom. *Il.* 1.231 "community-devouring king," Hes. *Op.* 39-39 and 263-64 "gift-devouring kings."

35.15: Cf. *mor.* 544c.

35.16: Cf. *mor.* 198d. The sentiment is reminiscent of the second book of Plato's *Republic*, in which Socrates meets the challenge of demonstrating that acting justly, even if one receives no rewards for doing so, is preferable to acting unjustly, even if one escapes detection. Platonic influence may account for the choice of the expression εὖ πράξας, which normally means "fare well" rather than **act honorably**. For the point of the *Republic*, which concludes with this expression, is that acting honorably entails faring well.

35.17: Cf. *mor.* 198e, Caec. Balb. *Sent.* 84 = [Sen.] *de Moribus* 111 *Ignoscas semper alteri, numquam tibi.* According to Velleius Paterculus (2.30. 3), the opposite is what is in reality more commonly encountered: *familiare est hominibus omnia sibi ignoscere, nihil aliis remittere.*

36.1: The embassy described here took place in 149 BC, the year of Cato's death. The Romans were trying to mediate between Prusias II of Bithynia and his son Nicomedes, who was receiving support from Attalus II of Pergamum in his attempt to depose his father. Cato's saying is found also at D.S. 32.20, Polyb. 36.14, App. *Mithr.* 6.20, Livy *Per.* 50, *Oxy. Epit.* 50. Diodorus, Polybius and Livy name the ambassadors, the second of whom was apparently the A. Hostilius Mancinus of whom Gellius informs us (4.14) that he was wounded in the head when a prostitute threw a stone down at him (according to others it was a roofing tile).

36.1: Plutarch does not consider the **heart** the seat of intelligence, but Cato and his contemporaries did (cf. 36.7, 39.7). The Latin for "insane" is *vecors*, for "remember" is *recordari* and, in fact, the Perioche of Livy, Book 50, says of the third ambassador, *ingenio socors haberetur.*

36.2: In 167 BC the Romans deported to Italy some 1,000 prominent members of the Achaean League, among whom was the historian **Polybius**. In late 150 or early 149 their return to Greece was finally brought about through the agency of Polybius' friend **Scipio** Aemilianus with, apparently, the help of Cato. This anecdote (but not the sequel in 36.3) is also found at *mor.* 199e.

36.2 grandfathers: They had been in Italy for 17 years (and in fact, according to Paus. 7.10.12, only about 300 of the 1,000 remained). The Greek word used by Plutarch is a diminutive, expressive of contempt.

36.3 Odysseus: For Cato's familiarity with Homer, see 54.6. Cato may here be teasing Polybius for his tendency to view himself as another

Odysseus (see F. W. Walbank, *C&M* 9 [1948] 171-72 and *JRS* 52 [1962] 10-11). For Odysseus' **cap** (πιλίον), which is a regular feature of the representation of this hero in Greek, Roman and Etruscan art from the end of the 5th century BC, see F. Brommer, *Odysseus* (1983) 110-11. Odysseus is also frequently shown wearing a baldric, which is perhaps what the word translated **belt** (ζώνη) was intended to mean. In other words, Plutarch has translated back into Greek Cato's Latin, *pileum* and *zona*.

36.4 wise men . . . fools: This is more concisely formulated by Poor Richard as "Fools make feasts, and wise men eat them."

36.5 blushed . . . blanched: The former is a sign of modesty, the latter of fear: Aristotle *Eth. Nic.* 1128b13-15, *Categ.* 9b31-32. This saying appears also at *mor.* 29e, 198e and 528f. Cf. also Caec. Balb. *Sent.* 61 *erubescere est utilius iuvenem quam pallescere.*

36.5 hands . . . feet: The former for plundering, the latter for running away. The true soldier, of course, like Cato, exercises his feet (cf. 28.9) **on the march** and his hands (cf. 28.8) **on the battlefield.** This saying appears also at *mor.* 198e.

36.6: This saying is presumably to be connected with the speech that Cato delivered during his censorship in 184 BC (frr. 72-82 Malcovati). As censor Cato had the authority to deprive a knight of his horse, and he did this in the case of a certain Lucius Veturius, whose morals were found to be wanting and whose obesity rendered him unfit for military service.

36.7: The same saying appears also at *mor.* 14d. The word translated **intellect** means literally "heart." As at 36.1 and 39.7, Plutarch is giving a literal translation of Cato's Latin.

36.8: This saying, which is found also at *mor.* 759c, seemed to P. Boyancé to be inappropriate in the mouth of Cato, and he suggested (*REG* 68 [1955] 324-25) that it was in fact a reference to the epigram of (Q. Lutatius) Catulus preserved in Gell. 19.9.14. But Cato's point appears to be that the lover is worthless as a soldier, since his **soul** (ψυχή, like Latin *animus*, can also mean "courage, martial spirit") has its abode elsewhere.

36.9 intestate: Despite recent criticism (by T. Tzannetatos in *Geras Antoniou Keramopoullou* [1953] 533-39 and R. Flacelière in *REG* 80 [1967] 195-97), the standard view of the meaning of the word **ἀδιάθετος** here is correct. That view goes back to Daniel Wyttenbach, since whose time dozens of papyri have been discovered that exhibit this word in just this meaning. Cato's regrets seem not to have been momentous: he did not die on that day; he appears to have made his journey safely; if the woman divulged the secret, it was not vital.

36.10: This saying is found also at *mor.* 199a, 784a, 829f, Stob. 4.50.82. In recounting Cato's sayings Plutarch has not been as careful to avoid hiatus as he usually is: ἄνθρωπε, εἶπε and πολλὰ ἔχοντι here, μάχη ἐστί in 36.12 and, if the manuscripts are correct, ὦτα οὐκ in 35.1.

36.12 This gives some idea: A formal conclusion to the sections (35-36) containing Cato's sayings, which had been formally introduced in

34.3 (cf. 42.1). For the importance of this "characterological" (as opposed to chronological) element in Plutarch's Lives, see Gossage 57-60.

37.1: Cato was elected consul along with . . . Valerius Flaccus (see 30.1-4) for the year 195 BC. According to Livy (33.43.1-4), the senate decided that, because of the magnitude of the war in Spain, one of the consuls should have charge of Hispania Citerior (**the province that the Romans call "Inner Spain"**), and that he should take with him two legions, 15,000 allies, 800 cavalry and 20 ships. Cato and Valerius drew lots, the former receiving Spain and the latter Italy as his province.

37.1 he was engaged: At the beginning of his Life of Alexander, Plutarch tells us that, since he is writing biography rather than history, he is less concerned with battles and campaigns than with anecdotes that reveal the character of his subject. So here he declines to recount Cato's Spanish campaigns, although they were described at length in sources available to him, namely Livy (34.8-21), Polybius and Cato himself (see 37.3). For these campaigns, see Astin 28-50, 302-18 and J. S. Richardson, *Hispaniae* (1986) 80-94.

37.1: The **Celtiberi** were a tribe of Celtic origin serving as mercenaries in the war against the Romans. According to Livy (34.19.4; cf. Zonar. 9.17), Cato offered to pay them twice what they were receiving from the enemy if they came over to the Roman side.

37.2: The same anecdote at *mor.* 199c and Frontin. 4.7.35.

37.3 Polybius: The historian's nineteenth book, which dealt with events in the years 196-192 BC, is now lost. This anecdote survives, however, also at Livy 34.17.11, App. *Iber.* 41, Frontin. 1.1.1, Polyaen. 8. 17, *DVI* 47.2 and Zonar. 9.17. Cato sent letters that arrived in the various cities on the same day, instructing them to tear down their fortifications immediately.

37.3: Since the **Baetis River** (= the Guadalquivir) runs from NE to SW, it is impossible to tell what **this side of** (from the Roman point of view) means. In any case, Plutarch (or his source) is in error, as Appian (*Iber.* 41) and Livy (34.17.5) speak rather of the Ebro.

37.3 Cato himself claims: This was either in his speech On his Consulship (frr. 21-55 Malcovati) or in the seventh book of his *Origines*. The claim that he **captured more cities in Spain than he spent days there** is found also at *mor.* 199c. Cato spent one year in Spain, but he cannot have found, let alone captured, **four hundred** cities there.

37.4-5: All of these sayings are found also at *mor.* 199d.

37.4 pound of silver: According to Livy, Cato gave to each soldier 270 asses. The Roman historian's "precise figures, probably based on official records, are to be preferred to Plutarch's rather vague statement" (J. Briscoe on Livy 34.46.3).

37.6 ἐφύλαττε καθαροὺς παντὸς λήμματος: Cf. *Arat.* 9.3 καθαρὰν καὶ ἄθικτον αἵματος ἐμφυλίου τὴν πρᾶξιν ἡ τύχη διεφύλαξε, *Fab.* 30.6 ἀδωρότατον ἑαυτὸν καὶ καθαρώτατον ἐφύλαξεν, *Gracch.* 41.6 λημμάτων ἀδίκων καθαροὺς . . . διεφύλαξαν ἑαυτούς, *Numa* 20.8 πάσης κακίας ἄθικτον ἐπ' ἐκείνου καὶ καθαρὸν διαφυλάττουσα τὸν βίον. Compare also 60.1. Both Aristeides (5.6, 24.2) and Cato (28.7, here) are remarkable for their refusal to take advantage of their positions of authority in order to enrich themselves.

37.6 five attendants: Apuleius (*Apol.* 17) refers to a speech of Cato's in which he said that he set out as consul for Spain with three servants (cf. Val. Max. 4.3.11) but, when he reached the Villa Publica in the Campus Martius, he realized that they were too few, so he purchased two slaves in the forum.

37.6 Paccius: This anecdote is found only here and at *mor.* 199d (without Paccius' name). Captives are the property of the state, and their purchase price ought to go to the public **treasury** (hence Cato's action). Apparently Paccius had bought the captives from an individual soldier on the black market, rather than at public auction.

38.1 Scipio: According to Nepos (*Cat.* 2.2), Scipio Africanus, in his second consulship (194 BC), wished to succeed Cato in Spain, but was unable to persuade the senate to let him do this. But Astin (51-52) has shown that both Plutarch and Nepos are in error, and that Scipio neither went, nor sought to go, to Spain in that year. Rather this story is a result of the known hostility between Scipio and Cato (30.5) and of the fact that a man named P. Cornelius Scipio Nasica served in Spain as praetor in that year.

38.3 Scipio bitterly protested: Cato's retention of military command after his term of office had expired would have been illegal. Also, his treatment of deserters, although lawful, might be regarded as excessive: "Desertion, mutiny and insubordination made the individual soldier liable to the death penalty. In practice, however, this sentence was commonly avoided." (G. R. Watson, *The Roman Soldier* [1969] 120-21)

38.3 common men like himself: Cato belonged to a plebeian *gens* and was himself a "new man" (28.2), whereas Scipio was a member of the most distinguished patrician *gens*, the Cornelii.

38.3 δόξῃ προήκοντας: Cf. *Cat. min.* 14.2 δόξῃ πολὺ προήκοντα, *Sert.* 4.5 προήκουσιν ἡλικίᾳ τε καὶ δόξῃ. For this usage, see also Eur. fr. 1109.8 Nauck, Thuc. 2.34.6, Xen. *Hell.* 7.1.23, Cassius Dio 42.57.2, 45.16.1, 57.3.3, 58.27.4.

38.4 μηδὲν ἀλλάττειν μηδὲ κινεῖν: According to R. Till (*Hermes* 81 [1953] 444-45), this expression is unique in Greek, and represents a translation of the Latin formula *neque mutare neque movere.*

38.4: Cato's **triumph** in 194, following his Spanish campaign, is described by Livy (34.46.2-3).

38.4 On the contrary: Cato's continued activity even into old age is frequently repeated: 31.3, 42.4-5, 56.4, Cic. *Rep.* 1.1.1, *de Sen.* passim.

38.4 ἀπτομένοις πολιτείας: Cf. *Cat. min.* 42.6, *Cic.* 7.1, *Them.* 25.3, *mor.* 785d, 800b, 806f.

38.4 thirst for esteem: This image is not as common in Greek as one might expect, but cf. *Cor.* 4.1, *mor.* 790d and Philo *Spec.* 4.82.

39.1: Tiberius Sempronius Longus was consul in 194 BC, having Italy as his province (Livy 34.43). It is not clear what lies behind Plutarch's reference to **Thrace and the region near the Danube**. There appears to have been some geographical confusion on the part of Plutarch or his source. During his consulship, Sempronius was engaged in military action in Italy against the Boii (Livy 34.46-47), a Celtic people that later settled on the Danube in Pannonia and Noricum (but not in Thrace). In the second book of his *Origines* (fr. 8 Jordan), Cato said that the Boii consisted of 112 tribes, information that Cato probably learned while serving with Sempronius.

39.1: Manius Acilius Glabrio was consul in 191 BC. Cf. Cic. *de Sen.* 10. 32 *quadriennio post* (i.e. after his consulship) *cum tribunus militaris depugnavi apud Thermopylas M'. Acilio Glabrione consule.* It was unusual for a man who had been consul to serve as **military tribune** (Astin 56); Plutarch notes the same eagerness to serve in the case of Flamininus, *Flam.* 20.1.

39.1: Antiochus III ("**the Great**") ruled the Seleucid kingdom in Asia from 223 BC to his death in 187. Cato's role in the war against Antiochus is described below (chapters 40-41).

39.2: Seleucus I ("**the Conqueror**;" for his nickname, see 6.2) was one of the successors of Alexander the Great. He founded the Seleucid dynasty and died in 281 BC. He was great-great-grandfather of Antiochus III. The Seleucid kingdom had been divided between Antiochus' father, Seleucus II, and his uncle Antiochus "the Hawk" (cf. 6.2), but Antiochus III and his brother, Seleucus III, re-established the unity of the kingdom.

39.2 ἐξ ὑπαρχῆς: For this expression, see Holden on *Tim.* 23.1 and add *Cic.* 17.1, *Rom.* 19.1, *mor.* 40e, 557e, 586a, 655d, 677c, 704a, 951d.

39.3 liberated . . . autonomous: At the Isthmian festival in 196 BC Flamininus announced the "liberation" of Greece. This announcement was greeted by the Greeks with the same delirious joy with which they greeted the same announcement made in the same place during Plutarch's lifetime, by Nero in AD 67 (*Flam.* 10-12). For the value of the "liberation of Greece" as propaganda, see E. S. Gruen, *The Hellenistic World and the Coming of Rome* (1984) 132-57.

39.4 as has been described: See *Flam.* 15.3-4. This statement does not necessarily mean that the Lives of Philopoemen and Flamininus were written and published before those of Aristeides and Cato. It is possible, for instance, that Plutarch worked on the two pairs of Lives concurrently or that this statement (like some of the other cross-references in the Lives) was added, either by Plutarch himself or by someone else, after the time of original publication. See C. P. Jones, *JRS* 56 (1966) 66-67.

39.5 a speech of his exists: Apparently some Greek thought it would be a pleasant challenge to compose a speech in which Cato, the outspoken denouncer of Greek culture, praised Athens in elegant Greek. By Plutarch's day this rhetorical exercise was thought by some to be a genuine speech. But Plutarch, in scholarly fashion, uses reliable evidence, namely the explicit testimony of one of Cato's authentic speeches (see 39.7), to show that Cato spoke through an interpreter. Flamininus (*Flam.* 10.5) made his proclamation through a herald who presumably spoke in Greek and, according to Val. Max. 2.2.2, it was the normal procedure for Roman officials at this time to use interpreters. Livy explicitly mentions that Aemilius Paullus spoke in Greek to Perseus (45.8. 6) precisely because it was so unusual.

39.5 τὸ δ' οὐκ ἀληθές ἐστιν, ἀλλὰ: Cf. Pl. *Apol.* 37a τὸ δὲ οὐκ ἔστιν . . . τοιοῦτον ἀλλὰ, 38a τὰ δὲ ἔχει μὲν οὕτως, *Crat.* 439c τὸ δ' . . . οὐχ οὕτως ἔχει ἀλλ', *Phd.* 87c τὸ δ' . . . οὐχ οὕτως ἔχει, *Symp.* 183d τὸ δὲ οἶμαι ὧδ' ἔχει, 198d τὸ δὲ . . . οὐ τοῦτο ἦν . . . ἀλλὰ, *Tht.* 166a τὸ δέ . . . τῇδ' ἔχει, Isocr. 15.134 τὸ δ' οὐχ οὕτως ἀλλὰ, Demosth. 10.22 τὸ δ' οὐχ οὕτως ἔχει, 18.140 τὸ δ' οὐ τοιοῦτόν ἐστι, Luc. *Anach.* 35 τὸ δὲ οὐχ οὕτως ἔχει σοι ἀλλ', *Pro Imag.* 3 τὸ δὲ οὐχ οὕτως ἔχει.

39.6 Postumius Albinus: The same anecdote is found at *mor.* 199e, Polyb. 39.1, Nepos fr. 56 Marshall and Macrob. *Sat.* praef. 13-15. The **Amphictyons** were the members of the Dephic Amphictyony, a loosely-organized council that sought to represent the interests of Greece as a whole. It is "mentioned simply as a body of great authority; it had no connection with literature" (Walbank on Polyb. 39.1.6). On another occasion, Cato ridiculed the tribune M. Caelius for dabbling in Greek poetry (fr. 115 Malcovati).

39.7 the Athenians were impressed: For Cato's fondness for praising himself, see 41.2, 46.7, 59.3. A brief quotation (fr. 20 Malcovati) survives from the Latin speech that Cato delivered in Athens: *Antiochus epistulis bellum gerit, calamo et atramento militat.*

39.7 τάχος . . . ὀξύτητα: Cf. *Caes.* 50.3, *Cor.* 11.4, *Pomp.* 17.2, 76.5, *mor.* 392b, 447a, 588a.

39.7: The word translated **minds** means literally "hearts." Cf. 36.1, 36.7. For the sentiment, compare Gellius 1.15.1 *qui sunt leves et futtiles et inportuni locutores . . . eorum orationem bene existimatum est in ore nasci, non in pectore.* Since Gellius shortly afterwards (1.15.8-10) quotes two fragments (111 and 112 Malcovati) of Cato's speech against M. Caelius (see on 39.6), we should ascribe this statement to that speech as well.

40.1 Thermopylae: Plutarch's source for the description of this battle of 191 BC is the work of Cato himself, whom he quotes in 41.2. Cato's description (in the *Origines*?) gave great prominence to his own role, in contrast to our other sources, which derive from a section of Polybius that is no longer extant. (Polybius' account may in turn derive from Antisthenes of Rhodes; cf. Phlegon, *FGrH* 257 F 36 III 1.) According to those sources (Livy 36.15-19, App. *Syr.* 17-18, Zonar. 9.19), it was Antiochus, not Cato, who recalled the **circling movement of the Persians** in 480 BC and, according to them, the Aetolians were asleep when Cato reached them. (Because of the brevity of their accounts, it is impossible to tell which source is being followed by Frontin. 2.4.4 and *DVI* 47.3 and 54.2.) For a reconstruction of the battle, see W. K. Pritchett, *Studies in Ancient Greek Topography* I (1965) 71-82.

40.1 despairing . . . frontal attack: Plutarch gives the impression (encouraged by Cato?) that the frontal attack that Glabrio did in fact mount was only made possible by Cato's circling manoeuvre, and that Cato was acting on his own initiative. The authors (see previous note) whose accounts derive from Polybius, however, either state or imply that Glabrio gave orders for an attack on the following morning and *then* dispatched Valerius Flaccus (not mentioned by Plutarch) and Cato to deal with the Aetolians guarding the mountain-passes.

40.2: Lucius Mallius cannot be identified with certainty. It is even possible that the man's name was Manlius, since the Greeks represent both names by the same spelling, the consonant-combination -nl- being alien to their language.

40.4 Firmian troops: Allies from the town of Firmum, modern Fermo, near the Adriatic coast.

40.5 capture alive one of the enemy: Cato had used this same device earlier during his consulship, unless Frontinus (1.2.5) has mistakenly transferred this incident to Spain.

40.5 διάκοσμος ἢ τάξις καὶ: For the text, see R. Till, *Hermes* 81 (1953) 438-39.

40.6 ὀρούσαντες: This verb, which Plutarch uses also at *Brut.* 8.7, 34.5 and *Cor.* 8.6, is almost exclusively poetic, occurring only very rarely in prose before Plutarch's day (Xen. *Eq.* 3.7, 8.5, Hipp. *Cord.* 2, *Mul. Affect.* 1.41). Here, the word is used to reinforce the impression of the soldiers as beasts of prey (cf. Hom. *Il.* 15.635, where it is used of the lion with which Hector is compared).

41.1 dashed out his teeth: The expression is perhaps taken from Homer (*Il.* 16.348). It is curious that we have just had a "Homeric" simile (see previous note) and that in Cicero (*de Sen.* 10.31; see 42.5 below) Cato justifies boasting of his accomplishments by referring to the Homeric figure of Nestor. Given Cato's familiarity with Homer (see 36.3, 54.6), we may wonder if his account of the Greek campaign was not tinged with epic color.

41.2 unstinting in his own praise: Cf. 46.7, 59.3, Cic. *de Sen.* 10.31, Livy 34.15.9 *haud sane detrectator laudum suarum.*

41.3 Immediately following the battle: The timing, as well as some details, of the journey to Rome are at variance with the account in Livy, according to whom (36.21.4-8) Glabrio first sent Lucius Scipio and then, a few days later, sent Cato, who arrived in Rome before Scipio. Phlegon (*FGrH* 257 F 36 III 1) mentions Cato, but not Scipio.

41.3 on the fifth day: Cf. Livy 36.21.6 *quinto die* (but according to Livy, Cato landed at Otranto, nearly a day's journey further to the south of **Brundisium**). This was an extraordinarily rapid journey, the distance between Brundisium (modern Brindisi) and Rome being 364 Roman miles. Even at the peak of the Roman empire, when the official post was at its most efficient and messages could be sent by relays of couriers, "a dispatch from Rome would reach Brindisi in about seven days" (L. Casson, *Travel in the Ancient World* [1974] 188).

41.4 thanksgiving and sacrifices: Cf. Livy 36.21.9 *supplicatio in triduum decreta est et ut quadraginta hostiis maioribus praetor, quibus diis ei videretur, sacrificaret.*

42.1 Now, as far as . . . As to: For the formal division, cf. 36.12.

42.1 τό τε περὶ τὰς: For the word-order, see J. D. Denniston, *The Greek*

Particles[2] (1954) 519 and add Plato *Phd.* 94d τά τε κατὰ τὴν γυμναστικὴν καὶ τὴν ἰατρικήν and Arist. *Hist. Anim.* 9.614b31 αἵ τ' οἰκήσεις μεμηχάνηνται πρὸς τοὺς βίους καὶ τὰς σωτηρίας.

42.1 he regarded that aspect: This was a view shared by Cicero: *Rosc. Am.* 20.55 *accusatores multos esse in civitate utile est, ut metu contineatur audacia* (cf. [Quintil.] *Min. Decl.* 313.10 *oportet esse in civitate et accusatores*). Quintilian (12.7.3-4) mentions both Cato and Cicero among those who undertook frequent prosecutions.

42.1 Petilius' prosecution of Scipio: There were in fact two tribunes named Petilius, who in 187 BC began to attack Scipio Africanus in the senate. It is suggested by Livy (38.54.2) that Cato was behind the action of the Petilii. For this incident, of which Livy (38.50.4-60.10) gives a long and confused account, see Kienast 57-67, Scullard 290-303.

42.2 his execution: Plutarch's text has fallen under suspicion because it cannot have been a question of a capital charge, but it is confirmed by Diodorus, who speaks (29.21) of Scipio as being threatened with death. Scullard (302 n. 2) attractively suggests that the error in Plutarch and Diodorus "might have arisen from a misunderstanding of a Latin text in which *caput* meant loss of *existimatio*."

42.2 large fine . . . appeal was made to the tribunes: Lucius Scipio was convicted of something like embezzlement and was fined. Eventually, he was spared imprisonment as a result of the intercession of the tribune Ti. Sempronius Gracchus (Livy 38.60.4-6, Val. Max. 4.1.8).

42.4 λαβὴν . . . παράσχοι: Cf. 25.10 λαβὴν παρέσχεν and note.

42.4 nearly fifty cases: Plutarch, as usual, uses round numbers. Cato was prosecuted 44 times (Pliny *NH* 7.100, Solin. 1.113, *DVI* 47.7) and never convicted (56.5).

42.4 the last of which: This was perhaps the case in which Cato defended himself with the speech On his own Behalf against Gaius Cassius (154 BC?), of which a single fragment (176 Malcovati) survives. See, however, below on 42.5 and Astin 108 note 15.

42.4 it was difficult: The same saying is reported at *mor.* 784d, where the date of the trial is given less precisely. (Plutarch merely says, "when Cato was over eighty.")

42.5 when he was ninety: In fact Cato, born in 234, died in his eighty-sixth year in 149. Again, Plutarch is using round numbers, although in this instance he has taken the number over from his source; Livy (39.40.12) also speaks of Cato being prosecuted in his eighty-sixth year (so also Val. Max. 8.7.1) and prosecuting Galba in his ninetieth. Cicero (*Brut.* 20.80) correctly says that Cato spoke against Galba in his eighty-sixth year, the year of his death.

42.5 action against Servius Galba: In 149 BC Cato delivered a speech, of which a few fragments (196-99 Malcovati) survive, against Ser. Sulpicius Galba, who had, during his praetorship in Spain in 151, treacherously murdered or enslaved a large number (7,000 according to Val. Max. 9.6.2; 30,000 according to Suet. *Galba* 3.2) of Lusitanians. Not only was Galba not convicted, but he was elected consul in 144. For the trial, see Scullard 235-36.

42.5 like Nestor: The comparison is already in Cicero (*de Sen.* 10.31), and may, indeed, go back to Cato himself. Homer describes Nestor as having lived among three generations of men (*Il.* 1.250-52, *Od.* 3.245). That Cato lived to be eighty-five should be enough to justify the comparison, but Plutarch has to spell it out: Cato was a contemporary of **the great Scipio** Africanus (born in 236 or 235 BC) and lived long enough to single out for praise (see 54.6) the ability of **the younger Scipio** Aemilianus (born in 185). The latter was **the son of** L. Aemilius **Paullus**, and was adopted by the elder son of Scipio Africanus.

42.6 as I have mentioned: See 30.5-7, 38.1-4.

43.1 Ten years after his consulship: Cato was consul for 195 BC. He held the censorship in 184, for which office he campaigned in the previous year.

43.1 καὶ τρόπον τινὰ τῆς πολιτείας ἐπιτελείωσις: Exactly the same expression at *Flam.* 18.1. For the importance of the censorship, cf. *Aem.* 38.7, *Cam.* 14.1, *mor.* 287c.

43.1 ἄλλην τε . . . βίους ἐξέτασιν: Cf. *Aem.* 38.7 ἥτις ἐστὶν ἀρχὴ πασῶν ἱερωτάτη καὶ δυναμένη μέγα πρός τε τἆλλα καὶ πρὸς ἐξέτασιν βίων and *Mar.* 30.6 τοὺς βίους αὐτῶν καὶ τὰ ἤθη πικρῶς ἐξετάζων· (similarly, D.H. 19.16.5, Suda s.v. τιμητής, Zonar. 7.19). The pair ἦθος καὶ βίος is common in Plutarch: *Cato min.* 12.2, *Per.* 39.2, *Sulla* 7.8, *Thes.* 9.2 and over a dozen times in the *mor.*

43.2 insight into a man's ethics: This opinion allegedly held by the ancient Romans (who are the subject of these sentences) would be congenial to Plutarch, who says, for example, at *Alex.* 1.2 that a man's virtue or vice is often better revealed in casual remarks and minor matters than in large-scale military actions.

43.2 guardians and correctors: Cf. 54.3, *mor.* 322e, 287c, D.H. 20.13.3.

43.2 patricians . . . plebeians: Plutarch is speaking of the practice in Cato's day. The censorship was originally a patrician office, but by Cato's time it was required that at least one of the censors be from a plebeian family.

43.3 demote . . . rank of knight: Literally, "deprive him of his horse" (= Latin *equum adimere*).

43.3 ἐκβαλεῖν . . . συγκλήτου: Normally in Plutarch, ἡ σύγκλητος (sc. βουλή) has the article. The article is, of course, regularly omitted when the noun is in the predicate (*Pomp.* 84.4, *Sert.* 22.5, 23.5, 25.3) and often when it is the object of a preposition. But Plutarch also omits the article when the word means "a meeting of the senate" (*Cam.* 25.4, *Mar.* 12.7, *mor.* 507e) and also to translate certain Latin expressions, such as *senatu movere* (here and *Aem.* 38.8; cf. below 44.7) and ***senatusconsultum*** (*Aem.* 29.1, *Pomp.* 11.1).

43.3 τὰ τιμήματα τῶν οὐσιῶν λαμβάνοντες: Cf. *Aem.* 38.8 τῶν οὐσιῶν . . . τὰ τιμήματα, *Sol.* 18.1 ἔλαβε τὰ τιμήματα.

43.3 political status: This appears to be the meaning of the Greek word (**πολιτείας**), although there is no parallel available. The census-list will have included an indication of the individual's class (Latin *ordo*), and this is perhaps what is intended.

43.3 ἔχει δυνάμεις: The office of the censor had lapsed by Plutarch's day and, in view of the imperfect tenses elsewhere in this passage, one is tempted to write εἶχε (= "involved the exercise"). While the variation in the tenses is a bit awkward, the present tense is perhaps justified by *Aem.* 38.7-8.

43.4-6: Plutarch's account has so much in common with Livy 39.41.1-3 that it is clear that either Livy is himself Plutarch's source or both authors are following a common source. Livy (39.40.2-3) gives the names of the seven other candidates for the censorship, and he says that they joined forces in order to keep Cato from winning election, both because they objected to seeing a "new man" (cf. 28.2 above) in the office and because they were afraid that Cato would enact harsh measures as censor. Livy also says, as Plutarch does in 43.6, that Cato went so far as to browbeat the electorate.

43.6 physicians: The comparison of the statesman with the physician is common in the Lives: *Agis* 31.7, *Brut.* 55.2, *Cam.* 9.3, *Dion* 37.7, *Lyc.* 4.4, *Marc.* 24.2, *Per.* 15.1, 34.5.

43.7 only with the aid of that man: Cf. Livy 39.41.4 *illo uno collega castigare se nova flagitia et priscos revocare mores posse.* But the following image of the **Hydra** is not in Livy and represents Plutarch's own elaboration. (The Hydra was a mythical, many-headed monster who sprouted two new heads for every one that was cut off; it was finally subdued by Heracles and Iolaus, to whom Cato and Valerius are implicitly compared, the former cutting off the heads while the latter cauterized the wounds to prevent further growth.) The comparison with the Hydra, which Plutarch employs also at *Gracch.* 42.2, *Pyr.* 19.7 and *mor.* 341f, presented itself to him as a result of the reference to **physicians** just above. At *mor.* 199b, which passage is virtually Plutarch's rough draft for this one, there is mention of the need for a "drastic physician," but no reference to the Hydra. The notion of amputating luxury along with the fact that Cato was seeking the censorship not only for himself but also for his associate Valerius made Plutarch think of Heracles and Iolaus. He was prompted in part by his knowledge of Plato's *Republic*, where metaphorical physicians are associated with the image of cutting off the Hydra's heads (426a-e). This association is found also at *Gracch.* 42.2 (where Plutarch refers to Plato explicitly).

43.8 they elected . . . Cato: For Cato's censorship (184 BC), see Astin 78-103, 324-28, Kienast 68-87, Scullard 153-165.

44.1 at the head of the list: Cato designated Valerius Flaccus as *princeps senatus*, a position of considerable influence, as it entitled him to be the first member of the senate to deliver his opinion on any matter. Valerius succeeded Scipio Africanus in this position.

44.1 banished a number of men: It was the prerogative of the censor to expel from the senate any member deemed unworthy for moral or other reasons. Livy (39.42.5) states that seven men were banished by Cato and his colleague. In contrast, "the censors of 199, 194, and 189 had expelled none, three, and four respectively" (Scullard 157 n. 4).

14.1 Lucius Quinctius: The following account of his expulsion from the senate is repeated by Plutarch at *Flam.* 18.4-19.8. See also Cicero *de Sen.* 12.42, Livy 39.42.5-43.5, Val. Max. 2.9.3, *DVI* 47.4. Plutarch's sources for the incident include Livy and Cicero, whom he cites, but are not confined to them, as he includes details not found elsewhere (Astin 80 n. 6). It is difficult to imagine what the origin of these details might have been. It cannot have been Cato himself, since Livy's account is explicitly derived from Cato's speeches.

14.3 serving as governor: The incident occurred in Gaul during Lucius' consulship in 192 BC.

14.3 at home: That is, in Rome. According to Livy (39.42.8-9), the boy, whom he identifies as a Carthaginian named Philip, was lured from Rome by the promise of lavish gifts just before a gladiatorial combat.

14.4 condemned to death . . . axe: In these details, Plutarch agrees with Cicero and Valerius Maximus (cf. also *DVI*). They are also to be found in an account attributed by Livy (39.43.1-3) to Valerius Antias, in which the object of Lucius' affections is not a boy but a woman. In Livy's own account, the victim is not a criminal and the weapon is a sword.

14.6 formal wager under the law: Latin *sponsio* (Livy 39.43.5), whereby one party to a litigation formally agrees to pay a certain amount of money should his assertion be proved false. Cf. *Flam.* 19.4, *Gracch.* 14.5.

14.6 When, however: This account of the (partial) rehabilitation of Lucius' reputation is found also at *Flam.* 19.8 and Val. Max. 4.5.1.

14.7 Manilius: This incident is referred to also at *mor.* 139e (where Plutarch suggests that the penalty may have been excessive) and Amm. Marc. 28.4.9, but the man's name is given only here. Since no one of this name is known to fit the description, it has been suggested that the name is an error, perhaps for Manlius; see Scullard 158-59, Astin 80-81.

14.7 kissed his own wife in broad daylight: Cf. *Per.* 24.9, where Plutarch reports that Pericles used to greet Aspasia (punning in Greek on the woman's name) with a kiss in broad daylight as he went to and from the agora. But the time of day (which is not mentioned at *mor.* 139e or Amm. Marc. 28.4.9) is apparently less damning than the presence of the daughter (which is). In any case, while this lapse may have been a contributing factor, it was presumably not the sole grounds for expulsion.

14.7 never embraced his wife: That is, in broad daylight.

14.7 except after a loud thunderclap: According to A. B. Cook (*Zeus: A Study in Ancient Religion* II [1925] 827), citing Ar. *Vesp.* 626 with scholiast and Pliny *NH* 28.25, it was customary among both the Greeks and Romans that, "when a lightning-flash was seen, folk at once made a loud smacking noise with their lips."

14.7 adding that he made: The wording here shows that Plutarch's source must have been Cato's *Origines*, in which he repeated the witticism that he had originally pronounced in his speech at the time o Manilius' expulsion.

45.1 demoted . . . from the rank of knight: See on 43.3. Luciu Scipio had celebrated a triumph on 6 November 189 for his victor over Antiochus at Magnesia. His right to celebrate a triumph, how ever, had been challenged, by a party presumably led by Cato, on th grounds that the decisive battle was rather the one at Thermopyla (Livy 37.58.7). Thus, personal motives are likely to lie behind Cato' expulsion of Lucius. See Livy 39.44.1, *DVI* 53.2, Scullard 159-60.

45.1 οἷον ἐφυβρίζων: A favorite phrase of Plutarch's: *Cam.* 28.6, *Lys.* 5.1 23.11, *Mar.* 8.6, *Per.* 29.1, *Phil.* 16.6, *mor.* 80c, 288f, 579c.

45.1 the dead Scipio: The date of Scipio's death is not known for cer tain, but it appears to have occurred before the end of Cato's censor ship: Kienast 148 n. 61, Scullard 152 n. 1. There is thus no good reaso for Flacelière to follow those manuscripts that omit reference to Scip io's death. (Anyway, even if the word "dead" were historically inaccu rate, the error would more likely have been that of Plutarch or hi source than that of a scribe.)

45.2 to cut back the proliferation of luxury: Just as this had bee a concern of Cato's in his personal life (see 29.3), so this became th theme of his censorship. Cf. Nepos *Cat.* 2.3 *multas res novas in edictun addidit, qua re luxuria reprimeretur, quae iam tum incipiebat pullula re*, Astin 91-97. For the concern about the evil influence of luxury i Cato's day, see 31.2.

45.2 imposed a reassessment . . . : This passage (down to **three as ses per thousand**) is a fairly close translation of Livy 39.44.2-3, ex cept that Plutarch has converted Livy's "15,000 asses" into **1,50 drachmas**.

45.2 articles of clothing . . . 1,500 drachmas: It will be remem bered that Cato claims (31.4) that he himself "never wore a garmen worth more than one hundred drachmas."

45.2 the amount of their payments: These were, strictly speaking fines rather than taxes, as the censors had no authority to impose tax es: C. Nicolet, *The World of the Citizen in Republican Rome* (1980) 73.

45.4 the philosopher Ariston: Either the Stoic philosopher fror Chios, who lived in the first half of the 3rd century BC, or the Peripa tetic philosopher from Ceos of the same name, who was cited in 2.3 (The moral tone and the attitude toward wealth are slightly mor appropriate to the Stoic.)

45.5: Scopas the Thessalian was one of the patrons of the poet Si monides of Ceos. (Could this anecdote, therefore, along with the pre vious one, have come from the pen of Ariston of Ceos?) For the wealt for which the family of Scopas was famous, see the couplet of Critia quoted at *Cim.* 10.5. Plutarch repeats this anecdote at *mor.* 527c.

46.1 ἐλάχιστα φροντίζων: An expression common in Plutarch (*Aem.* 34 2, *Alex.* 1.3, 15.9, *Caes.* 63.10, *Fab.* 8.2, 21.3, *Flam.* 9.5, *Pomp.* 25.8, *mor* 42c, 80d) but almost unknown elsewhere (once each in Lucian an Photius).

46.1 cutting off pipes: Cf. Livy 39.44.4 *aquam publicam omnem in privatum aedificium aut agrum fluentem ademerunt* (sc. *M. Porcius et L. Valerius*). Fragments (99-105 Malcovati) survive of a speech of Cato's entitled Against L. Furius on the Subject of Water, presumably to be connected with Cato's censorship. During the republic, supervision of the water-supply was in the charge of the censors and, when there were no censors in office, the aediles. See Frontin. *Aquaed.* 2.94-97 for measures taken to curb the unauthorized use of public water.

46.1 demolishing any buildings: Cf. Livy 39.44.4 *quae in loca publica inaedificata immolitave privati habebant, intra dies triginta demoliti sunt.*

46.1 minimizing . . . revenues were sold: Cf. Livy 39.44.7 *vectigalia summis pretiis, ultro tributa infimis locaverunt.* For Cato's relationship with the *publicani*, the private entrepreneurs with whom the Roman state contracted for the collection of public revenues and for the supervision of the expenditure of public funds, see E. Badian, *Publicans and Sinners* (1972) 35-37.

46.2 brought about a repeal: This incident is referred to by Livy (39.44.8) without mentioning Flamininus, and by Plutarch again at *Flam.* 19.6. According to Livy, the censors negotiated the contracts anew at slightly lower rates, thereby reaffirming the censors' power in the face of senatorial opposition; see Badian (previous note).

46.2 summoned before the people: That is, to be publicly brought to account. The failure of this manoeuvre is apparently reflected in the title of Cato's speech (frr. 111-20 Malcovati), If the Tribune of the People M. Caelius had Summoned Me. See R. Till, *Hermes* 81 (1953) 440-43.

46.3 known as the Basilica Porcia: Cf. Livy 39.44.7 *basilicamque ibi fecit, quae Porcia appellata est.* For the grammatical construction, see on 13.3 οἵ. The basilica (see also *Cato min.* 5.1, *DVI* 47.5) stood just to the west of the Curia, the building in which the senate met. It was destroyed along with the Curia in the fire that resulted from the riots at the funeral of Clodius in 52 BC. It was one of the earliest basilicas in Rome (see G. E. Duckworth, "Plautus and the Basilica Aemilia," in P. de Jonge et al. [edd.] *Ut Pictura Poesis* [1955] 58-65). For the development of the basilica, which is of eastern origin, see especially the article "Basilika," in *Reallexikon für Antike und Christentum* I (1950) 1225-59.

46.4 temple of Health: Plutarch means the temple of Salus, on the Quirinal hill, which was dedicated in 303 BC. (For the same identification, see Cassius Dio 37.24.1, 51.20.4, 54.35.2.) The statue, with its inscription (which Plutarch appears to know in its Latin form), is not otherwise attested. It can hardly have been erected by Cato's contemporaries, as Plutarch seems to think; see Astin 103 n. 89.

46.5 images . . . in their hearts: The contrast between the (questionable) products of the sculptor's art and the (true) images residing in the soul (e.g. Cic. *Orator* 2.8-9, Dio Chrys. 12.71, Philostr. *VA* 6.19) is ultimately of Platonic origin, as is Plutarch's phrase here (cf. *Phlb.*

39b). Plutarch perhaps also has in mind here the contrast (made explicit at *Per.* 2.1-4) between the beautiful products of the artist's skill, which do not inspire us to imitate the artist, and the glorious deeds of the virtuous man, which inevitably engender emulation.

46.6 I would rather: The same saying is recorded at *mor.* 198e, 820b and Amm. Marc. 14.6.8.

46.7 no one more ready to sing his own praises: See on 41.2.

46.7: For the statesman as **helmsman**, cf. *Arat.* 38.5, *Brut.* 46.4, *Cleom.* 15.1, *Per.* 33.6, *Phil.* 17.3, *mor.* 787d-e, 788d. The "ship of state" is a frequent metaphor in Plutarch (see F. Fuhrmann, *Les images de Plutarque* [1964] 234-37) and, indeed, in Greek and Latin literature in general (see Nisbet and Hubbard on Horace *Odes* 1.14).

47.2 He married: This is Licinia, Cato's first wife (for his second, see chapter 51). Everything we know about her we learn from Plutarch, except her name, which must be inferred from the name of her and Cato's son, M. Porcius Cato Licinianus. Cato's marriage must be placed earlier than 192 BC, the approximate date of their son's birth. According to Gellius (13.20.8), Licinia died when the son was a young man (*adulescens*).

47.3 Socrates: Cato's unfavorable opinion of Socrates is repeated at 50.1. His objection to the Athenian philosopher no doubt resulted from his own highly pragmatic outlook; as far as Cato was concerned, Socrates wasted his time in theoretical discussion when he ought to have served his fatherland with *actions*.

47.3 civility and restraint: For this combination, see *Caes.* 15.4, *Fab.* 30.2, *Gracch.* 2.5, *Per.* 39.1, *Pyr.* 8.8, 23.3, *Sert.* 25.6, *mor.* 80b, 456a, 488a, 537d, 729e, 1104b. For the latter, see on 23.1.

47.3 shrewish wife and retarded children: The nasty character of Socrates' wife Xanthippe was proverbial; see for example D.L. 2.36-37, where Socrates' refusal to beat his wife would have met with Cato's approval. Socrates' sons, like those of Cimon and Pericles (Arist. *Rhet.* 1390b30), were probably merely average individuals who had the misfortune of not duplicating their father's accomplishments.

47.5 She nursed it herself: That is, she dispensed with the services of a wet nurse. That a mother should nurse her own child is recommended by the author of a treatise included in Plutarch's *moralia* (3b-c) and by Plutarch's friend, Favorinus of Arelate (test. 38 Barigazzi = Gell. 12.1). In contrast, Plutarch's Roman contemporary Tacitus (*Germ.* 20) regards it as a sign of barbarism that German mothers suckle their own young; see K. R. Bradley, "Wet-Nursing at Rome: A Study in Social Relations," in B. Rawson (ed.), *The Family in Ancient Rome* (1986) 201-29. Cato perhaps favored the practice for reasons of economy, while Plutarch has retrojected his own more humane considerations.

47.5 Cato himself undertook to teach: A father's extensive personal involvement in his son's education was not unheard of in Cato's day; see S. F. Bonner, *Education in Ancient Rome* (1977) 10-12.

47.6 the river: Presumably the Tiber; cf. Hor. *Carm.* 3.7.27-28.

47.7 his historical books: Whatever work or works Plutarch is referring to must have been composed by Cato in the 180s, during his son's childhood. The *Origines*, according to Nepos (*Cato* 3.3), were the work of his old age. But, since Nepos refers to the *Origines* simply as "histories," perhaps they are a later revision of a work that Cato composed for his son and did not originally intend for publication.

47.7 himself with his own hand: That is, he did not have a slave copy down from his own dictation, as was the usual practice. (For the pleonastic expression, cf. 44.5, 47.5.)

47.8 general habit of the Romans: Compare *mor.* 274a, Cic. *de Off.* 1.129 *nostro quidem more cum parentibus puberes filii, cum soceris generi non lavantur.*

47.8 reinfected: For the expression, cf. 50.2.

47.8 even in the presence of women: Our earliest evidence for mixed bathing among the Romans comes from the first century after Christ. Even then it did not become a widespread practice, but was engaged in only by the very poor and the morally depraved; J. P. V. D. Balsdon, *Roman Women* (1962) 266-70.

47.9 σύντονον . . . κεκολασμένον τῆς διαίτης: For the language, compare *Brut.* 38.6, *Cato min.* 3.9, *Lyc.* 22.3, *Phil.* 7.3, *Sulla* 41.2, Arrian *Parth.* fr. 77 Roos, Luc. *Herm.* 86.

47.10 the battle against Perseus: This is the battle of Pydna (22 June 168), fought by Aemilius Paullus against the Macedonian king Perseus. Plutarch repeats this account of young Cato's bravery at *Aem.* 21.1-5; cf. also Val. Max. 3.2.16, Justin. 33.2.1-4.

47.11 σάγμασιν: There is no justification for the regular practice of translating this word as "heap" or "pile" here. The word refers to cases for arms (*JHS* 95 [1975] 129-30) or packs carried by pack-animals (*Arat.* 25.2, *Pomp.* 41.6). If we are dissatisfied with this detail (which does seem slightly odd), we might read ἐν πολλοῖς ἄγμασιν, "among many fragments."

47.11 there exists a letter: A letter from Cato to his son, which may be identical with the one mentioned here, is referred to also at *mor.* 273e and Cic. *de Off.* 1.37.

47.12 Paullus' daughter Tertia: She was the third (hence her name) daughter of L. Aemilius Paullus and **the sister of Scipio** Aemilianus (for whom, see 42.5, 54.6-7). She was still a young girl at the time of the battle of Pydna; *Aem.* 10.6-8, Cic. *de Div.* 1.103.

48.1 τροφὴν καὶ παίδευσιν: Cf. *Gracch.* 41.2, *Numa* 5.6, *mor.* 65e, 592a.

48.3 he made it a rule: The purpose of the rule was to ensure monogamy among the slaves. Similarly, at *de Agr.* 143, Cato recommends that the overseer of the farm remain faithful to the wife that his master has provided for him.

48.3 not at all fastidious: Cf. 28.9.

48.4 τῶν πραγμάτων ἐπιδιδόντων: Cf. *Arat.* 48.3, *Demetr.* 35.5.

48.4 dissension and dispute: Plutarch's assertion is in conflict with Cato's own statement in his *de Agricultura* (5.1), that the corps of slaves should refrain from quarrels. It has been argued that the contradiction arises out of a misunderstanding of Cato's Latin; see J. Nováková, "Litibus Familia Supersedeat," in *Studia Antiqua Antonio Salac Septuagenario Oblata* (1955) 90-95. But this explanation is unnecessary in view of the fact that there are several other clear discrepancies among the sources for Cato's views on farming, business and the like (see Astin 249-51, G. Colin, *Rome et la Grèce* [1905] 591-94). Inasmuch as Cato himself is chief among those sources, it is reasonable to assume, as Plutarch does, that his views were not consistent throughout the course of his long life.

48.5 more as an avocation: Cf. 52.1. This is in contrast to Philopoemen who, Plutarch tells us, did not treat farming as a mere pastime (*Phil.* 4.5).

48.5 fisheries: For these (= Latin *piscinae*) and for the profits that could be derived from them, see Varro *de Re Rustica* 3.17.2-9, Pliny *NH* 9.167-70. In 35.2 Cato decried the inflated price of fish; this is another of the inconsistencies noted on 48.4.

48.5 fullers' establishments: These required a large amount of space for the vats and particularly for the frames on which the cloth was stretched to dry after fulling; see R. J. Forbes, *Studies in Ancient Technology*^{2} IV (1964) 82-98.

48.5 ἔργα πίσσια: That this, the reading of manuscript S, is impossible, has been demonstrated convincingly by E. Müller-Graupa (*Philologische Wochenschrift* 61 [1941] 60-63), whose arguments also invalidate Flacelière's ἔργα πίσσι⟨ν⟩α. The reading of UA (ἐργατησίαν) is also impossible: the word is unattested; if it were a genuine word it would be an unaccountably recherché (and possibly poetic) variant for the expected ἐργάσιμον; its meaning ought to be "arable," which is an inappropriate epithet for pasture land and timberland. Blass' ἐργαστήρια (= "factories") gives acceptable sense, but does not account for the corruption.

48.5 damage by Jupiter: As the weather-god (see 44.7), Jupiter determined the success or failure of agricultural investment. Nevertheless, in the preface to *de Agr.*, Cato recommends farming as less risky than trade.

48.6 disreputable branch of moneylending: Cato's distaste for moneylending is attested both by his own statement in the preface to *de Agr.* and by a saying of his preserved by Cicero (*de Off.* 2.89; for the form of the saying, cf. *de Agr.* 61), in both of which moneylending is associated with some sort of crime. Bottomry loans, in which the interest rate could be as high as 33%, were even more usurious than ordinary loans, which were regularly made at 12%; see J. Rougé, *Ships and Fleets of the Ancient Mediterranean* (1981) 161-62, 185-86. Still, unlike Plutarch, Cato must not have regarded bottomry loans with the same distate that he felt toward moneylending in general. For an attempt to explain this apparent inconsistency, see Astin 320. Alternatively, it is again possible that Cato's views changed in his later years.

48.6 This was how he operated: Cato's practice has been much discussed, most fully by J. Rougé, who considers (*Recherches sur l'organisation du commerce maritime en Méditerranée sous l'Empire romain* [1966] 386 n. 4, 426-28) that Cato was engaged solely in moneylending. But, in the first place, loans in which the risk was spread out over a number of associates were not so unusual that Plutarch would have to explain the details to his readers (see Kienast 142 n. 30, with bibliography, and G. E. M. de Ste. Croix, "Ancient Greek and Roman Maritime Loans," in H. Edey and B. S. Yamey [edd.], *Debits, Credits, Finance and Profits* [1974] 41-59). In the second place, the detail that Cato **would himself retain one share in the name of his freedman** (see next note) makes sense only if Cato was himself participating as a business partner, for the loan itself would be in Cato's name and there can be no question or a fiftieth share in connection with the loan. Rather, if one ship sank, Cato lost only 2% of his investment whereas, if it completed its voyage, he recovered not only his principal with interest but 2% of the profits on the venture as well.

48.6 Quintio: Cato employed his freedman for this purpose because he was himself prevented by the Lex Claudia of 218 BC, which provided (Livy 21.63.3) that "no senator or son of a senator could own a seagoing vessel having a capacity of more than 300 amphoras." (The average freighter would have a capacity of approximately 2,000-3,000 amphoras; L. Casson, *Ships and Seamanship in the Ancient World* [1971] 183-84, 369.)

48.8 tried to persuade his son: This will have been Cato's elder son (47.2-12), as his younger son was a mere child at the time of Cato's death. The work referred to here, then, was composed in Cato's sixties or seventies (roughly between the time of his son's attaining his majority in about 172 BC and his death in 152). A number of fragments, on a variety of subjects, survive of a work or works addressed to his son (for which see Astin 332-40). One may surmise that a large portion of chapters 48 and 50 derives from that source.

49.1 old age: The embassy described in this chapter took place in 155 BC, that is, when Cato was 78 or 79 years old. For the embassy, which was famous as a milestone in the cultural history of Rome, see Astin 174-76 and Walbank on Polybius 33.2, who provide other ancient references to the event and recent bibliography. Plutarch's sources included Polybius, whose description of the embassy is no longer extant, and Cleitomachus, an Academic philosopher of the second century BC (see Cic. *Acad.* 2.137). For Plutarch's familiarity with Cleitomachus, see J. Glucker, *Antiochus and the Late Academy* (1978) 276-80.

49.1 οἱ περὶ . . . φιλόσοφον: Ziegler and Flacelière adopt Reiske's conjecture φιλόσοφοι, which gives satisfactory sense; M. Dubuisson, ΟΙ ΑΜΦΙ ΤΙΝΑ - ΟΙ ΠΕΡΙ ΤΙΝΑ: *L'évolution des sens et des emplois* I (1977) 109, S. L. Radt, *Zeitschrift für Papyrologie und Epigraphik* 38 (1980) 51 n. 5. But the manuscript reading gives essentially the same sense, and there is no compelling reason to change it; A. Garzya, *Boll. del Comitato per la Prep. della Ediz. Naz. dei Classici Gr. e Lat.* 9 (1961) 41.

49.1 Carneades the Academic and Diogenes the Stoic: These men were the heads of their respective schools. It is not clear why Plutarch omits to mention the fact that there was a third member of the embassy, namely Critolaus, the head of the Peripatetic school.

49.1 seeking the abrogation of a judgment: Some time previously, the Athenians had invaded the town of Oropus, whose citizens then made an appeal to Rome. The senate appointed the city of Sicyon to act as arbitrator. When the Athenians failed to send a representative to the hearing, the Sicyonians imposed a fine of 500 talents. See Paus. 7. 11.4-5 and Walbank on Polybius 32.11.5.

49.2 οἱ φιλολογώτατοι τῶν νεανίσκων: See H. Kuch, ΦΙΛΟΛΟΓΟΣ (1965) 86-87 (who interprets the word a bit too narrowly here) and L. Robert, *Hellenica* XIII (1965) 46-50. For Roman interest in Greek culture at this period, see E. S. Gruen, *The Hellenistic World and the Coming of Rome* (1984) 250-72.

49.2 ἀκροατηρίων: For the meaning (here = **audiences** rather than "lecture-halls"), cf. *mor.* 522e, 937d, D.H. *Dem.* 15, Themist. *Or.* 20.236c.

49.2 like a gale: In his Life of Carneades, Diogenes Laertius says (4.63, trsl. Hicks), "His voice was extremely powerful, so that the keeper of the gymnasium sent to him and requested him not to shout so loud." Other sources also speak of the forcefulness of his delivery and argumentation: Cic. *de Or.* 1.45, 2.161, 3.68, *Rep.* 3.9, Gellius 6.14.10.

49.5 ἐξ ἀρχῆς τε . . . ἐπεὶ δὲ: For the combination of particles, cf. *Per.* 2.5; J. D. Denniston, *The Greek Particles*[2] (1954) 513-14.

49.5 disturbed by this passion for words: According to Quintilian (12.1.35), Cato heard Carneades argue on one day in favor of justice and on the following day, with no less conviction, against justice (cf. also Pliny *NH* 7.112-13). One can imagine that Cato regarded the philosopher with the same distaste that many Greeks felt toward the sophists in the fifth century and many classicists feel toward deconstructionists today.

49.5 Gaius Acilius: Cf. Gellius 6.14.9 *et in senatum quidem introducti interprete usi sunt C. Acilio senatore.* This is surely the same as the Gaius Acilius (the only other man known of that name) who wrote in Greek a history of Rome, cited at *Rom.* 21.9; M. Schanz and C. Hosius, *Geschichte der römischen Literatur* I (1927) 177-78.

49.6 he reproached . . . so long: Compare the impatience that Cato exhibits a few years later when the senate again deliberates concerning Greek matters (36.2).

50.1 discredit Greek civilization and culture as a whole: This is clearly a considerable exaggeration. (That it is not confined to Plutarch is clear from similar statements in Pliny: *NH* 7.113, 29.14.) For a balanced view of Cato's ambivalent attitude toward the Greeks, see Astin 157-81.

50.1: Socrates, toward whom Plutarch has, and expects his readers to have, nothing but positive feelings, is an important element in the comparison between Aristeides and Cato. Aristeides was, like Socrates, poor (chapter 1) and a descendant of his may have been personally involved with the philosopher (27.3); Cato, on the other hand, can find almost nothing good (cf. 47.3) to say about him.

50.2 his disciples reached old age: Isocrates boasts (4.87-88) that his pupils studied with him for three and even four years, and that they enjoyed his tuition so much that their leavetakings were marked by regrets and tears.

50.2: Minos was, according to Greek legend, one of the judges in the underworld. One wonders if Cato has not somehow conflated Isocrates and Socrates. (One manuscript, in fact, mistakenly reads "Socrates" here.) According to Plato's *Apology* (41a), the latter actually looked forward to meeting Minos in the underworld.

50.2 playing the role of soothsayer: Pliny (*NH* 29.14) gives a direct quotation from Cato, which includes the following prophecy concerning the Greeks: *et hoc puta vatem dixisse: quandoque ista gens suas litteras dabit, omnia conrumpet.* Pliny's quotation is, like Plutarch's reference, explicitly attributed to a work addressed to Cato's son (see on 48.8), which is likely to be the source of most, if not all, of this chapter.

50.2 infected: For the expression, cf. 47.8.

50.4 the saying of Hippocrates: Plutarch is referring to the fifth "Epistle of Hippocrates" (vol. 9, pp. 316-18 Littré), which purports to be a letter from Hippocrates to Hystanes, a satrap of the Persian king Artaxerxes (who died in 425 or 424 BC). In it, "Hippocrates" rejects the king's generous offer, saying that it is not right for him to heal barbarians, who are the enemies of Greece. Cato did not himself cite this letter, as is clear from Plutarch's wording (**It seems that he had heard**) and from the absence of the reference from Pliny's direct quotation (*NH* 29.14).

50.4 enemies of the Greeks: For the sentiment, cf. 16.3.

50.4 common pact: Cf. Pliny *NH* 29.14, quoting Cato's comments on Greek physicians: *iurarunt inter se barbaros necare omnes medicina.*

50.5 treatise: Pliny also mentions this treatise (*commentarium*, *NH* 29. 15), "with which he cured his son, his servants and the members of his household," but does not say that Cato had written it himself. It was undoubtedly a compilation of recipes (for which see *de Agr.* 70-73, 102, 122-23, 125-27) that Cato had gathered from various sources.

50.5 vegetables . . . duck, pigeon: Cf. *mor.* 131e where, shortly after alluding to the saying of Cato's given in 35.1, Plutarch refers to vegetables and fowl as being light and easily digested. The vegetable that especially appealed to Cato was the cabbage; see *de Agr.* 156-57, where Cato gives a number of recipes which involve the use of cabbage as a cure, not only for digestive ailments, but for arthritis, cancer and various lesions as well.

50.6 light and suited to those in a weakened condition: Perhaps because hares are themselves light (in weight) and weak. This sort of magic is not inappropriate to the author of *de Agr.*; cf. J. Scarborough, *Roman Medicine* (1969) 19-21.

50.6 caused . . . frequent dreams: The fourth-century grammarian Diomedes preserves a brief quotation (p. 362.22 Keil; cf. also Pliny *NH*

28.260) from a work of Cato's addressed to his son: *lepus multum somni adfert qui illum edit.* Plutarch has evidently confused *somnus* (which = "sleep") with *somnium* ("dream").

51.1 the anger of the gods: Plutarch regards the loss of Cato's wife and son as divine retribution (in Greek, *nemesis*) for his presumption. This idea is not uncommon in the Lives: e.g. *Ages.* 22.3, *Cam.* 13.2, *Demosth.* 22.4, *Mar.* 10.2, 26.5, *Per.* 37.5.

51.1 sound bodily constitution: Cf. 28.5.

51.1 ἐκ τοιαύτης προφάσεως: For the expression, cf. *Demetr.* 38.12, *Numa* 13.1, *Pyr.* 6.2 and (with Holden's note) *Tim.* 20.2. Its meaning is no different from that of ἐξ αἰτίας τοιᾶσδε (53.1 and elsewhere).

51.2 the death of his wife: It is not known precisely when Cato's first wife Licinia (for whom see 47.2) died.

51.2 one of Paullus' daughters: See 47.12.

51.2 the house itself being a small one: This is Plutarch's own contribution, based upon his conviction that Cato was, like Aristeides, "poor."

51.3 as was his custom: One of the invariable rituals of Roman public life was the practice whereby clients escorted their patron to the forum (*deducere ad forum*). For the important development of this practice, particularly in the late republic, see C. Nicolet, *The World of the Citizen in Republican Rome* (1980) 356-61.

51.6 formalize the betrothal: Gellius (4.4) quotes the jurist Ser. Sulpicius Rufus for the procedure: The man intending to marry and the man giving away the prospective bride gave public pledges of their intentions. The contract into which they entered was binding on both parties, who were subject to fines should they fail to abide by the terms of the contract.

51.7 stepmother: For the common belief in the nastiness of stepmothers, see M. L. West, *Hesiod: Works and Days* (1978) 363, and add Eur. *Alc.* 305-10, *Ion* 1025, 1329.

51.7 It is my desire: Plutarch applauds Cato's sentiment, but considers it neither original (51.8) nor sincere (60.2-3).

51.8 earlier expressed by Peisistratus: At 35.4-5 Plutarch had pointed out another instance of Cato's apparent appropriation of earlier Greek material. See also on 29.6.

51.9 the agnomen Salonius: In fact, the son's name was M. Porcius Cato *Salonianus* (Gellius 13.20.8; cf. Pliny *NH* 7.62), for which reason Flacelière and N. C. Conomis (in ΦΙΛΤΡΑ: Τιμητικὸς τόμος Σ. Γ. Καψωμένου [1975] 79) prefer to change Plutarch's text here. But, since the same form occurs (twice) in 54.7 below, it is more likely that the error is Plutarch's than that the manuscripts have unanimously and consistently misrepresented what he wrote.

51.9 The elder son: M. Porcius Cato *Licinianus* (47.2; the agnomen distinguishes him from his half-brother) actually died before taking office, probably in 152 BC (Cic. *Tusc.* 3.70, Gell. 13.20.9). Cicero (*de Sen.* 6. 15, 19.68, 23.84) represents Cato as speaking with great affection for his son.

51.10 philosophical self-control: The same expression at *Alex.* 40.1, *mor.* 468a. Cf. on 23.1 (**forbearance and compassion**). Plutarch similarly praises the restraint of Fabius Maximus on the occasion of his son's death (*Fab.* 24.6; cf. *Per.* 36.8).

51.11 Lucius Lucullus and Metellus Pius: Plutarch wrote a Life of L. Licinius Lucullus, in chapter 38 of which he describes Lucullus' withdrawal from politics in favor of a life of leisure. Q. Caecilius Metellus Pius was consul in 80 and celebrated a triumph in 71 BC. Plutarch mentions his withdrawal from politics, on account of his age, also at *Luc.* 6.5.

51.11 λειτουργίαν τὴν πολιτείαν ἡγούμενος: Cf. *mor.* 823c τὴν πολιτείαν . . . οὐκ ἀσχολίαν ὥσπερ οἱ πολλοὶ καὶ λειτουργίαν ἡγούμενος.

51.11 Scipio Africanus: Shortly before his death, Scipio withdrew from Rome and retired to Liternum; H. H. Scullard, *Scipio Africanus: Soldier and Politician* (1970) 223.

51.11 Dionysius: This anecdote concerning Dionysius I of Syracuse is found also at *mor.* 783c, Isocr. 6.44-45, D.S. 14.8.5, 20.78.2, Ael. *VH* 4.8. When he was besieged by the Carthaginians and contemplated abandoning his rule, one of his friends convinced him to retain his position of power as long as he lived by saying that tyranny is the most beautiful of shrouds.

51.11 wrapping . . . trappings: This formulation is not Plutarch's, but appears to derive from Cato himself; cf. Cicero's allusions to it in three of his letters to Atticus (12.25.2, 29.2, 44.2). D. R. Shackleton Bailey (*Cicero's Letters to Atticus* V [1966] 405) comments, "I suspect that Cato's saying was originally to the effect that a free state, *res publica*, is the best place to grow old in, though in the Plutarchian context one has to understand 'public life is the best way of spending an old age'." Still, one wonders if it is possible that Cato made a comment that included a Greek word (ἐγγήραμα, apparently an ad hoc coinage) that is so rare that it is nowhere else attested. Perhaps the comment rather originates with the cultured philhellene Atticus, in his correspondence with Cicero, and has no connection with Cato. If so, Cornelius Nepos, the friend and biographer of Atticus, will have picked up the comment and applied it to Cato in his Life of Cato, of which only an abridgement now survives and from which Plutarch has taken it.

52.1 speeches . . . works of a historical nature: These are the pursuits that Cicero also (*de Sen.* 11.38) represents Cato as engaged in in his old age. For the former, see frr. 176-200 Malcovati, which are the remains of a number of speeches from the last five years of Cato's life. The latter is a reference to the *Origines*, which Nepos (*Cato* 3.3) assigns to Cato's old age. For the fragments, see M. Chassignet, *Caton: Les origines* (1986).

52.1 farming: Compare the lengthy praise of the joys of farming put into the mouth of the elderly Cato by Cicero (*de Sen.* 15.51-17.60). At 48.5 also Plutarch had described the elderly Cato's interest in farming as an **avocation**.

52.2 a book on farming: *De Agricultura*, the only work of Cato's that survives in its entirety. There is no evidence whatsoever, nor does Plutarch's language imply, that *de Agr.* is a work of Cato's old age. Still, scholars are disposed to regard it as a late work. So the rational argument of V. I. Kuziscin that would date it to before 187 BC is simply dismissed out of hand by R. Goujard (*Caton: De l'agriculture* [1975] xxxiii n. 1) and O. Schönberger (*Marcus Porcius Cato: Vom Landbau* [1980] 404). The latter's argument, according to which the work was composed after Cato was 70 years old, fails to distinguish between coarse stucco (*de Agr.* 92, 128) and fine plaster (31.5 above, Gell. 13.24. 1). For **how to prepare flat cakes**, see the recipe at *de Agr.* 76; for **how to preserve fruit**, *de Agr.* 7, 99, 143. Already in Varro (*de Re Rustica* 1.2.28) Cato had been gently criticized for including such items in a work on agriculture.

52.3 **feasts . . . on his farm:** Plutarch is here heavily indebted to Cic. *de Sen.* 13.45-14.46, where the elderly Cato is made to talk about his fondness for the company of the dinner-table.

52.3 **his contemporaries . . . the young:** Cf. Cic. *de Sen.* 14.46, *nec cum aequalibus solum . . . sed cum vestra etiam aetate.*

52.4 **neither censure nor commendation:** Why would anyone wish to commend **worthless and wicked** men? In fact, Plutarch, like the Greeks generally, was so used to employing expressions involving polar opposites or contrasting pairs that phrases like "praise or blame," "alive or dead," "word or deed" tend to occur even in circumstances in which one member is not strictly appropriate (cf. G. E. R. Lloyd, *Polarity and Analogy* [1966] 90-94). Compare, for instance, *Alex.* 47.12, where Plutarch says that neither Hephaestion nor Craterus ever said *or did* anything to the other even in jest.

53.1 **annihilation of Carthage:** Rome captured and destroyed Carthage, in 146 BC, to end the Third Punic War. This was after Cato's death but, as Plutarch suggests, Cato had been the inspiration behind the act, which was carried out by Scipio Aemilianus (**the younger Scipio**).

53.2 **Cato was dispatched:** This was in 152 BC, when Cato was over eighty years old. For this embassy, see also App. *Lib.* 310-15. Plutarch's chief source for this, and for the Third Punic War in general, is likely to have been Polybius, Books 33-36 of whose history exist in only a fragmentary state.

53.2: **Massinissa the Numidian** had been a Roman ally for half a century (he died in 148 BC at the age of ninety), having assisted **Scipio** Africanus in his **defeat** of Hannibal and **the Carthaginians** at the battle of Zama (202 BC). He transformed Numidia, originally a loose federation of nomadic (hence their name) tribes, into a substantial empire on the southern border of the territory of Carthage.

53.2 **from the very start:** This is not strictly true. Massinissa had been an ally of the Carthaginians and had fought under Hasdrubal against the Romans in Spain until, in 206 BC, Scipio Africanus won him over and he allied himself with the Romans.

53.2 **subject to a treaty:** The terms of the treaty that followed the battle of Zama (see H. H. Scullard, *Scipio Africanus: Soldier and Politician* [1970] 156-59) included an indemnity payable in annual installments over a fifty-year period and territorial restrictions. These last caused frequent disputes between Carthage and Numidia, occasioning periodic intervention and arbitration from Rome. For this last dispute, which led to the Third Punic War, and for Cato's role in it, see Astin 125-30 and 283-88, with further references.

53.3 ἀπίστως: It is perhaps just possible that the adverb, which occurs only here in Plutarch, means "treacherously" rather than **to an incredible extent**. Compare App. *Lib.* 313 πόλεως δυσμενοῦς τοσῆσδε καὶ γείτονος εὐχερῶς οὕτως (= "so unscrupulously"?; cf. e.g. Plut. *Lys.* 8.4) αὐξανομένης, Livy *Per.* 49 *contra foedus naves haberent*, Florus 1.31.3 *contra foederis legem.* The Romans used the expression *Punica fides* as a byword, meaning "perfidy" (see Walbank on Polybius 3.78.1), just as the inhabitants of Albion describe a person who refuses to pay his gambling debts as "welshing."

53.4 warming-up exercise: The word προανακινεῖσθαι is very rare, occurring only here, *mor.* 948c, Arist. *Rhet.* 1416a3 and Oribasius *Coll. Med.* 10.7.14. The basic notion seems to be that of engaging in preliminary activities designed to incite the spirit. For the military application, compare *Luc.* 5.1 and *Pomp.* 16.1, but the proper sphere of the word seems to be either that of musical performance (Pl. *Leg.* 722d) or athletic activity (Pl. *Leg.* 789c, Hippocr. *Vict.* 2.64, 3.76; also the passage from Oribasius).

54.1 rearranging the folds of his toga: Despite what Shakespeare's Brutus says, the Romans had no pockets. Instead, they carried small objects in the folds of their toga across their chest, which objects will have fallen out if the wearer incautiously (or, as here, intentionally) threw the end of the toga back over his left shoulder to rearrange the folds.

54.1 Libyan figs: Plutarch implies (as Cato may have done), though he does not state, that these fruits had been picked in Africa. When Pliny tells this same story (*NH* 15.74-75) he makes this implication explicit. But F. J. Meijer (*Mnemosyne* 37 [1984] 117-24) has argued, on the basis of the perishability of figs and the improbability of sailing from Carthage to Rome in three days during the season when figs are ripe, that these were more likely figs of the African variety (cf. Cato *de Agr.* 8.1) that had been transplanted and were growing on Cato's estate.

54.2 carried things too far: For a similar, and similarly phrased, criticism, cf. 48.8.

54.2 Carthage should not be allowed to exist: Cato's most famous saying is frequently alluded to: D.S. 34/35.33.3, Pliny *NH* 15.74, App. *Lib.* 315, Vell. 1.13.1, Livy *Per.* 49, Florus 1.31.4, *DVI* 47.8, Aug. *Civ. Dei* 1.30. Still, the form in which the Latin saying came to be known in the nineteenth century is as much a modern fabrication (*Gymnasium* 81 [1974] 465-75) as the salt with which the site of Carthage was sown (*Classical Philology* 81 [1986] 140-46 and 83 [1988] 39-42).

54.2: Publius Cornelius **Scipio Nasica** Corculum had been consul in 162 and 155 and censor in 159. He was the son-in-law of Scipio Africanus and was to become *princeps senatus* (see on 44.1) after Cato's death. For his opposition to Cato and his arguments against the destruction of Carthage (which are recorded in sources earlier than Plutarch), see A. E. Astin, *Scipio Aemilianus* (1967) 276-80. The background to the debate is illuminated by H. Bellen, *Metus Gallicus—Metus Punicus* (1985) 30-35.

54.2 ἐπικαλούμενος: Cf. *Aem.* 15.3 ὁ Νασικᾶς ἐπικαλούμενος Σκιπίων. The word does not mean "when called upon for his vote" (Perrin) or "appelé à donner son opinion" (Flacelière and Chambry).

54.3 like a bridle: A common image in Plutarch: e.g. *Aem.* 27.6, *Fab.* 28.4 (both passages dealing with the restraint of pride and impudence), *Arat.* 38.10, *Caes.* 57.1, *Cat. min.* 59.9, *Galba* 6.4.

54.3 corrective: Cf. 43. 2 (**correctors**). By using this word, which is quite rare in Greek, Plutarch is subtly continuing his criticism (see 54. 2) of Cato. One is given the impression that Cato's status as chastener of the Roman people, the status on which his reputation rests, has lapsed in his old age.

54.4 βακχεύοντι . . . δι' ἐξουσίαν: Cf. *mor.* 337f βακχευθεὶς ὑπ' ἐξουσίας καὶ δυνάμεως.

54.4 τῆς ἡγεμονίας φόβους: An unusual phrase (an objective genitive with φόβος normally designates that which one fears), but with a parallel at *Numa* 26. 5 φόβῳ τοῦ ἰδίου.

54.4 ἀναφορὰς αὐτοῖς . . . ἀπολιπόντας: Cf. Demosth. 18.219 ὑπέλειπε . . . ἑαυτῷ . . . ἀναφοράν, Aeschin. 2.104 αὐτοῖς μὲν κατέλιπον . . . ἀναφοράν.

54.5 following the outbreak of war: Cato died at the age of eighty-five in 149 BC (Pliny *NH* 29.15), during the consulship of L. Marcius Censorinus and M'. Manilius (Cic. *Brut.* 15.61, Vell. 1.13.1). This was the year in which the Third Punic War began.

54.5 the man who would bring the war to completion: Scipio Aemilianus (53.1), who was then in his mid-thirties and whose sister was the widow of Cato's son (47.12). Cicero (*de Sen.* 6.18-19) portrays Cato as expressing the wish that Scipio might some day destroy Carthage.

54.6 Only he . . . shades: A line from the *Odyssey* (10.495), in which Circe tells Odysseus that Teiresias alone among the spirits in the underworld possesses consciousness. (The line is similarly adapted for the praise of a hypothetical wise man at Pl. *Meno* 100a and of Chrysippus at D.L. 7.183.) Cato's quotation of the line (attested also at *mor.* 200a, 805a, Polyb. 36.8.7, D.S. 32.9a, Livy *Per.* 49, Suda s.v. Κάτων) is further evidence of his familiarity with Greek literature, particularly toward the end (29.5) of his life. He had also made reference to the *Odyssey* in an incident, datable to 150 BC, that is recounted at 36.3.

54.7 Salonius: See 51.9.

54.7 that son of Cato's who had died: M. Porcius Cato Licinianus (47.2).

54.7 his son Marcus attained the consulship: Plutarch is in error. "Salonius" had two sons, Marcus and Lucius, of whom only the latter attained the consulship (in 89 BC), while the former attained no higher office than that of tribune of the plebs. Either Plutarch has confused the two sons or he has confused M. Porcius Cato, son of Salonianus, with M. Porcius Cato, son of Licinianus, who was consul in 118 BC. This is an easy error to make, as both men have the same name and both were grandsons of Cato the censor. That confusion of this sort was rife in the second century after Christ is clear from Gellius' attempt (13.20) to set the record straight.

54.7 This man: Plutarch is referring not to Marcus, who was the father of **Cato the philosopher**, but to "Salonius." For Plutarch is well aware that Cato the censor was the great-grandfather of the other Cato of whom he wrote a Life (*Cato min.* 1.1; cf. also 57.5 below), here called "the philosopher" because of his devotion to Stoic philosophy.

54.7 a man . . . nobility: Plutarch thus forecasts the Life of the younger Cato, which he had not yet written. He opens that Life with a reference to this one and with a comment, similar in language to what we read here, on the character of the elder Cato: "a man of the utmost distinction and influence on account of his virtue."

55.1 καὶ περὶ τούτου: Cf. *Sulla* 39.1 καὶ τὸν τούτου . . . βίον. The reading of the manuscripts (τούτων) would have to mean "the memorable achievements of these men (i.e. Aristeides and Cato, in addition to the other men whose Lives I have written)." But reference to other Lives is irrelevant here, and the corruption is easily accounted for by the surrounding plurals.

55.1 memorable achievements: An expression found also in the opening of some of the other comparisons (*Alc.* 40.1, *Cic.* 50.1, *Eum.* 20. 1, *Marc.* 31.1, *Rom.* 30.1). We are reminded that Plutarch aims to be selective in what he records in each man's Life. He would certainly not approve of our fashion, which requires that the biographer record the name of the hotel in which Winston Churchill spent the night of 23 August 1931.

55.2 a poem or a painting: Plutarch gives the impression that it was not uncommon, perhaps in the schools, to compare works of art or literature **piecemeal**, but there seems to be little evidence that this was the case. Although we do know of comparisons of poets (e.g. Aristophanes' *Frogs* and Plutarch's own comparison of Aristophanes and Menander, *mor.* 853a-54d) and of artists (e.g. Quintilian 12.10.3-9), Dio Chrysostom's fifty-second discourse, in which he subjects three tragic treatments of the Philoctetes-myth to detatiled comparison, seems an isolated phenomenon. And the comparative examination of musculature or drapery, the foundation of modern connoisseurship, seems to have been unknown to the ancient critics.

55.2 ἐξ οὐχ ὑπαρχούσης . . . προελθεῖν: Cf. *mor.* 202a ἐκ γένους ἀδόξου προϊὼν εἰς πολιτείαν.

55.3 highest income bracket: See 1.2 and Plutarch's fuller account at *Sol.* 18.1.

55.3 φέρων: Cf. *Them.* 24.3 (where Holden notes that the word "marks a degree of determination or urgency emphasizing the action of the principal verb with which it is used"), *Arat.* 9.6, *Caes.* 69.13, *Demetr.* 52.2, *Fab.* 6.2, *Galba* 8.1, *Luc.* 6.5, 46.2, *Per.* 7.3, 12.5, *Phoc.* 23.1, *Pomp.* 27.6.

55.3 the yawning billows: A favorite expression of Plutarch's: *Aem.* 25.6, *Cic.* 6.4, *Mar.* 26.2, *mor.* 76b, 1107a.

55.3 Curius and Fabricius and Atilius: For Manius **Curius** Dentatus, see on 29.1. Curius and C. **Fabricius** Luscinus, consul in 282 and 278, censor in 275 BC, are named together again in 58.4 (see also on 29. 2). An **Atilius** Serranus is said to have been found sowing when an official delegation sought him out (Cic. *Rosc. Am.* 50, Pliny *NH* 18.20, Val. Max. 4.4.5). The example that would come to our mind first to illustrate the entry into political office **straight from the plough** is Cincinnatus, but he is perhaps too early to suit Plutarch's purpose here and, in any case, Plutarch seems to give no indication of knowing the story of Cincinnatus.

55.4 μήτ' ἀπὸ γένους λαμπρῷ καὶ: For οὔτε . . . καί (μήτε is used here to avoid hiatus), cf. *Aem.* 1.4, *Gracch.* 21.1, *Tim.* 1.5, 16.5, *mor.* 45a, 579b, 1115b.

55.4 three, or perhaps five, talents: Cf. *Them.* 25.3, Aelian *VH* 10.17 (three talents).

55.4 Africanus . . . Galba . . . Flamininus: For **Africanus**, see 30. 5-7, 38.1-4; for **Galba** 42.5; for **Flamininus** 44.1, 46.2.

56.1 one of ten generals: In the Life of Aristeides, however, Plutarch portrayed him as commander in chief at Plataea (11.1).

56.1 the seven most distinguished . . . opponents: Cf. 43.4-5.

56.2: Herodotus says (9.64.1) that at Plataea "Pausanias **won the most glorious victory** of all the victories with which we are acquainted."

56.2 Sophanes . . . Cynegeirus: According to Herodotus (9.74.1), **Sophanes** distinguished himself among the Athenians at the battle of Plataea. **Ameinias** of Pallene, whom later tradition made out to be the brother of the playwright Aeschylus, initiated combat with the Persian fleet at Salamis and was singled out for praise by Herodotus (8.84. 1, 93.1; cf. Plut. *Them.* 14.4). **Callimachus** was the Athenian polemarch who commanded the right wing at the battle of Marathon (Hdt. 6. 111.1). Herodotus singles him out for praise for his valor at Marathon, as he does **Cynegeirus** (6.114). For the latter, who was in fact Aeschylus' brother, see the references collected in *Tragicorum Graecorum Fragmenta* III (1985) 40-46.

56.3 the Spanish war . . . at Thermopylae: For the former, see chapters 37-38; for the latter, chapters 40-41.

56.3 μεγάλας ἐπ' Ἀντίοχον . . . κλισιάδας: Cf. *Alc.* 10.3 μεγάλας δ' αὐτῷ κλισιάδας ἐπὶ τὴν πολιτείαν ἀνοίγοντος, *mor.* 360a μεγάλας μὲν τῷ ἀθέῳ Λέοντι κλισιάδας ἀνοίγοντας, Hdt. 9.9.2 μεγάλαι κλισιάδες ἀναπεπτέαται ἐς τὴν Πελοπόννησον τῷ Πέρσῃ. (This passage from Herodotus was on Plutarch's mind, as it is one of the sources for 10.7-9.) For this metaphorical use of κλισιάδες, see also Liban. *Or.* 17.2, Clem. Alex. *Paed.* 3.8.44.2.

56.3 clearly the result of Cato's action: For the exaggeration of

Cato's role in this battle, see on 40.1.

56.3 drove Asia from Greece: The wording encourages us to recall that Aristeides too (9.5-6) had been responsible for expelling Asiatic invaders from Greece.

56.3 Scipio: This was Lucius Scipio, Africanus' brother, who defeated Antiochus at Magnesia in 189 BC. See on 45.1.

56.4 ἐξοστρακισθεὶς καὶ καταστασιασθεὶς ὑπὸ Θεμιστοκλέους: Cf. *Them.* 5.7 κατεστασίασε . . . ἐξοστρακισθέντα τὸν Ἀριστείδην, 11.1 ἐξωστράκιστο . . . καταστασιασθεὶς ὑπὸ Θεμιστοκλέους. On the former passage Holden notes, "The verb καταστασιάζειν . . . is a favorite one with Plutarch for 'to overpower by forming a counter party'." Add to the examples that he gives *Brut.* 22.3, *Cic.* 45.4, *Dion* 37.6, *Phil.* 13.8, 15.11, *Pomp.* 47.3, *Thes.* 35.5, *mor.* 605d.

56.4 like some athlete: For the comparison, see on 31.3. Much of the vocabulary here contributes to the image of Cato as wrestler: **adversaries** (ἀντιπάλοις), **enter the ring** (ἀγωνιζόμενος), **undefeated** (ἀπτῶτα). For the latter, compare *Eum.* 16.7 and see M. Poliakoff, *Studies in the Terminology of the Greek Combat Sports* (1982) index s.v.

56.5 actions at law: See 42.4-5.

56.5: Antipater the Macedonian was a general, first of Philip II, then of Alexander the Great. He was a student of **the philosopher Aristotle**, and he left behind a collection of letters, in two books, including some addressed to his son Cassander (Suda s.v., Cic. *de Off.* 2.48). It is from one of his letters that this quotation is taken, as is clear from Plutarch's reference to it again at *Alc.* 42.3.

57.1 more comprehensive: Plutarch is here influenced by Aristotle, according to whom (*Eth. Nic.* 1094b8-9, *Pol.* 1252a5) the good of the state is greater and more comprehensive than the good of individual citizens. (For the influence of Aristotle on the biographical tradition in general, see A. Dihle, *Studien zur griechischen Biographie* [1956] 57-87.) The **virtue** that is **exercised in civic life**, which Plutarch carefully refrains from naming, is justice (*Pol.* 1253a37), the virtue that comprehends the rest (see *Eth. Nic.* 1129b25, Plato *Rep.* 434c) and of which Aristeides is the conspicuous exemplar. Thus the criticism of Aristeides in this chapter is subtly undercut.

57.1 the state . . . households: Further Aristotelian influence; cf. *Pol.* 1252b16 and 28, 1253b3.

57.1 currency consisting of iron: Compare the more detailed account at *Lyc.* 9.2-3. There Plutarch informs us that Lycurgus forbade the use of gold and silver currency (which, it should be pointed out, was probably not introduced in Greece until after the supposed date of Lycurgus' "reforms") and prescribed instead the exclusive use of iron. This iron had been plunged when red-hot into vinegar and so made useless, according to Plutarch, for any practical application. See, however, H. Michell, *Sparta* (1964) 301: "To say that immersion in vinegar had any particular effect is nonsense. . . . tempering in this way only gives a thin surface hardness and the iron beneath is unaffected. The whole account is absurd and may be disregarded."

57.2 served as an instructor: See on 5.2. Here, Cato's role as instructor is represented by his authorship of the didactic *de Agricultura*.

57.2 those who denounce justice: Plutarch is thinking of Thrasymachus in Plato's *Republic*, who characterizes justice (343c) as "the other fellow's advantage" and who asserts (343e) that the just man, when he holds political office, neglects his own affairs and fails to profit from his position of authority. Compare Aristeides, who came away from his service as assessor of tribute poorer rather than richer (24.2).

57.3 Yet: Plutarch's argument is that, since Hesiod and Homer, who are taken to be the ultimate authorities, do not regard justice and successful management of the household as incompatible, they cannot be so. Therefore Aristeides' failure in this regard represents a flaw in his character, and cannot be explained away as an inevitable concomitant of his adherence to justice.

57.3 Hesiod: Plutarch does not have a particular passage in mind. He is thinking rather of the *Works and Days* as a whole, the twin concerns of which are justice and domestic economy. The poet does condemn **idleness** at line 311, but not in connection with **injustice**.

57.3 But I had no taste . . . : These lines are from the *Odyssey* (14. 222-25). They form part of the false tale that Odysseus tells to Eumaeus. Needless to say, they neither affirm nor imply that **those who neglect their households and those who live by injustice are one and the same**. This cavalier treatment of the evidence of poetic texts is not unusual among the ancients (and is in danger of returning to fashion).

57.4 the physicians tell us: In fact, the physicians tell us no such thing. Plutarch is relying on Plato *Prot.* 334b-c, where Protagoras says that olive oil is beneficial to the body when applied externally but harmful to the innards, for which reason all physicians (a considerable exaggeration) require those in a weakened condition to take little or no olive oil on their food.

57.4 his little daughters: Aristeides' daughters were not yet married at the time of his death, but that is not why Plutarch refers to them here with a diminutive (they are just "daughters" at 1.1 and 27.2). Rather, the diminutive serves to enhance our sympathy for them and lends subtle support to Plutarch's condemnation of Aristeides' neglect.

57.5 four generations: This means, in accordance with the normal Greek practice of inclusive reckoning, the four generations ending with that of Cato's great-grandsons (cf. 54.7), two of whom were praetors. Three of Cato's grandsons were consuls (in 118, 114 and 89 BC).

57.5 degraded some of them: Plutarch knows of only one such descendant (cf. 27.4). The practice of generalizing from a single example is frequent in Plutarch.

57.5 begging for public donations: Cf. 27.2 and 27.5, where we are told that the citizens of Athens gave grants to some of Aristeides' female descendants (but not that the latter *begged* for them). The comparisons tend to be more heavily incrusted with rhetorical color.

57.5 ἐράνῳ: For the interesting history of this word, see J. Vondeling, *Eranos* (1961), in Dutch with an English summary 258-67 and with a full discussion (160-68) of the meaning (= "alms") that it bears here.

58.1 cause for shame: Compare what Pericles says in his funeral oration (Thuc. 2.40.1): "To admit to poverty is not cause for shame; rather it is more shameful to fail to avoid poverty by means of hard work."

58.1 δημοσιεύοντι ταῖς ἀρεταῖς: Cf. *mor.* 823c δημοσιεύων ἀεὶ ταῖς φροντίσι.

58.1 magnanimity: At 32.7 Plutarch had left open the question of whether Cato possessed this virtue; here he clearly attributes it to Aristeides.

58.2 dispense with . . . public affairs: Plutarch had used very similar language to assert precisely that *Cato* dispensed with luxuries (31. 2) and neglected his private life so as to devote himself to public affairs (35.15).

58.2 most nearly god-like: Compare what Socrates says (Xen. *Mem.* 1. 6.10): "I consider it god-like to have no needs, and the closest thing to being god-like is to have as few needs as possible." Plutarch earlier (48.8) criticized Cato for calling "god-like" the man who increases the value of the estate that he inherits.

58.4 bread . . . wine: At 30.2 we were told that Cato ate the same bread and drank the same wine as his **servants**; at 31.4 (see note there) that he drank the same wine as the **rowers**.

58.4 purple garment . . . plastered walls: For the latter, see 31.5. But Plutarch has not told us that Cato dispensed with purple garments. (Indeed, Cato rails against women's desire to wear purple precisely because he regards it as men's prerogative to do so: *Origines* Book 7, frr. 8 and 10 Jordan, Livy 34.3.9, 34.4.10-14.) Perhaps Plutarch has conflated the account of Cato's disposal of a Babylonian rug (31.5) with his saying about purple fabric (35.6).

58.4 Manius Curius or Gaius Fabricius: For the former, see 29.1, 35. 14; for the latter, see on 29.2.

58.5 turnips: Plutarch is either very careless or is trying to engage in deception. It was not Cato but Curius (29.2) who was discovered boiling turnips himself, nor was anything said about him regarding them as **the finest delicacy**.

58.5 while his wife makes barley-cakes: This detail has not been mentioned before. If Plutarch is not deliberately embellishing, he may be confusing Cato's wife with the wife of Phocion (*Phoc.* 18.3).

58.5 chatter . . . about an as: Cf. 31.6 "if one paid even an as for something one did not need, it was too high a price" (a sentiment that is perfectly congruent with what Plutarch is saying in this chapter).

58.5 the kind of business: Cato opens his *de Agricultura* with a brief discussion of the relative merits of various means of earning a livelihood. But Plutarch is perhaps more likely thinking about Cato's work addressed to his son; see 48.5-8 with note on 48.8.

58.6 the statement: Cf. 25.8 "To be ashamed of poverty was a mark of those who could not help but be poor."

58.7 merely by plundering: That is, after the battle of Marathon; see 5.6.

59.2: For **Antiochus**, see on 39.1; for the **tearing down of the fortifications**, see 37.3.

59.2 second to none: And yet just above (56.2) Plutarch had said that, not only was Aristeides not the hero of any of these engagements, but his claim even on second place was challenged in each instance.

59.2 ὥσπερ ἀμέλει: In this expression, which is a favorite of Plutarch's (*Caes.* 28.1, *Lyc.* 17.8, *Marc.* 31.7, *Phoc.* 2.3, 6.2 and over twenty times in the *mor.*), the second word merely adds liveliness.

59.3 constantly glorifying himself: See 41.2, 46.7.

59.4 forbearance: For the importance of this quality in Plutarch's view, see on 23.1.

59.4 cooperated: See 8.1. For cooperation as one of the salient features of Plutarch's portrayal of Aristeides, see on 8.3, 12.3, 15.5 and 16.1.

59.4 opposition to Scipio: See 30.5-7.

59.4 hounded him out of the city: See on 51.11.

59.4 his brother: See 42.2.

60.1 self-control: For the importance of this virtue among the Greeks in general, see H. North, *Sophrosyne: Self-Knowledge and Self-Restraint in Greek Literature* (1966). By concluding his comparison with an assertion of Aristeides' possession, and Cato's lack, of this cardinal virtue, Plutarch leaves us in no doubt as to which of the two men he regards as morally superior.

60.1 ἄθικτον . . . καὶ καθαρὰν ἐτήρησεν: Cf. 37.6, *Cim.* 10.8, *Cleom.* 25.1, 26.6, *Numa* 26.2, *Per.* 13.5, *Pomp.* 23.4, *mor.* 38b, 438c, 793f.

60.1 marriage: Plutarch is referring to Cato's second marriage, which he described in chapter 51.

60.2 the explanation: See 51.7, "It is my desire to leave behind more sons like you." But Plutarch gave no indication there that it was given **condescendingly**.

60.3 ought to have contracted: One is perhaps intended to recall Medea's decisive refutation (Eur. *Med.* 585-87) of Jason's explanation for his desire to take a second wife. If so, the reminiscence is grotesquely tendentious, for there is no comparison between Jason's villainy (he is, after all, abandoning a wife who is very much alive) and Cato's peccadillo. In any case, Plutarch's tendentiousness is apparent from his decision to emphasize this incident at the very end of the comparison.

INDEX TO COMMENTARY

English

Greek

PLUTARCH

LIFE OF CICERO, edited by J.L.Moles *(Durham)*

Plutarch's *Lives* are required reading both as history and as literature. The *Life of Cicero* draws on important contemporary sources and preserves valuable information about Cicero's life and personality, and about events in 63 BC. This work shows Plutarch's many gifts as a writer; his varied tone and style, ability to create a unified narrative from diverse material, and sheer storytelling skill. The commentary, linked to a precise and accurate translation, assesses the *Life*'s historical value and the many different facets of Plutarch's art.

(1989) cloth 0 85668 360 4, limp 0 85668 361 2

Other Greek texts in this series include:

Aeschylus *Eumenides* ed. A.J. Podlecki *(1989)*
Aristophanes *Acharnians* ed. A.H.Sommerstein
Birds
Clouds
Knights
Peace
Wasps
Dio Cassius *Roman History Book 53.1-55.9*
ed. J.W.Rich *(1989)*
Euripides *Alcestis* ed D. Conacher
Electra ed. M.J. Cropp
Hecuba ed.C.Collard
Medea ed. B.Gredley
Orestes ed. M.L. West
Phoenician Women ed. Elizabeth Craik
Trojan Women ed. Shirley Barlow
Greek Orators I *Antiphon, Lycias*
ed, M.Edwards & S.J.Kern
Lucian *A Selection* ed. M.D.McLeod
Hellenica Oxyrhinchia ed. P.R.Mckechnie & S.J.Kern
Menander *Samia* ed. D.M. Bain
Plato *Meno* ed. R.W. Sharples
Phaedrus ed. C.J. Rowe
Republic 10 ed. S. Halliwell
Sophocles *Antigone* ed. A.L. Brown
Thucydides *History* 2 ed. P.J. Rhodes
Pylos 425 B.C. ed. J. Wilson

Other Latin texts in this series include:

Cicero	*Philippics II* ed. W.K.Lacey	
	Tusculan Disputations I ed.A.E.Douglas	
	Tusculan Disputations 2 & 5 ed. A.E.Douglas	
	Verrines II,1 ed.T.N.Mitchell	
Joseph of Exeter	*The Trojan War I-III* ed.A.K.Bate	
Lucan	*Civil War VIII* ed R.Mayer	
Lucretius	*De Rerum Natura IV* ed. J.Godwin	
Ovid	*Metamorphoses I-IV* ed. D.E.Hill	
Persius	*The Satires* ed. J.R.Jenkinson	
Plautus	*Bacchides* ed. J.A.Barsby	
Anon.	*The Ruodleib* ed. C.W.Grocock	
Seneca	*Letters: a selection* ed. C.D.N.Costa	
Tacitus	*Annals IV* ed.D.C.A.Shotter *(1989)*	
Terence	*The Brothers* ed.A.S.Gratwick	
	The Mother-in-Law ed.S.Ireland	
	The Self-Tormentor ed. A.J.Brothers	
Virgil	*Aeneid Book VI* ed. F.M.Ahl *(1989)*	
William of Newburgh	*The History of English Affairs* ed. P.G.Walsh & M.Kennedy	